# An
# Operating Systems
# Vade Mecum

## SECOND EDITION

RAPHAEL A. FINKEL

*University of Wisconsin-Madison*

Prentice-Hall International, Inc.

ISBN 0-13-637760-2

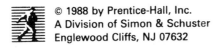 © 1988 by Prentice-Hall, Inc.
A Division of Simon & Schuster
Englewood Cliffs, NJ 07632

Printed in the United States of America

10   9   8   7   6   5   4   3   2   1

ISBN    0-13-637760-2

Prentice-Hall International (UK) Limited, *London*
Prentice-Hall of Australia Pty. Limited, *Sydney*
Prentice-Hall Canada Inc., *Toronto*
Prentice-Hall Hispanoamericana, S.A., *Mexico*
Prentice-Hall of India Private Limited, *New Delhi*
Prentice-Hall of Japan, Inc., *Tokyo*
Simon & Schuster Asia Pte. Ltd., *Singapore*
Editora Prentice-Hall do Brasil, Ltda., *Rio de Janeiro*
Prentice-Hall, Inc., *Englewood Cliffs, New Jersey*

# TRADEMARK INFORMATION

Balance is a registered trademark of Sequent Computer Systems, Inc.
CMS is a registered trademark of IBM.
CP/M is a registered trademark of Digital Research.
Cray-1 is a registered trademark of Cray Research.
Cray-2 is a registered trademark of Cray Research.
Cyber is a registered trademark of Control Data Corporation.
DEC is a registered trademark of Digital Equipment Corporation.
DECnet is a registered trademark of Digital Equipment Corporation.
Dynix is a registered trademark of Sequent Computer Systems, Inc.
Exec-8 is a registered trademark of Sperry Rand.
IBM is a registered trademark of International Business Machines Corporation.
Locus is a registered trademark of Locus Computing Corporation.
MS-DOS is a registered trademark of Microsoft Corporation.
MVS is a registered trademark of IBM.
NonStop is a registered trademark of Tandem Computers.
OS/360 is a registered trademark of IBM.
PDP-10 is a registered trademark of Digital Equipment Corporation.
PDP-11 is a registered trademark of Digital Equipment Corporation.
RT-11 is a registered trademark of Digital Equipment Corporation.
Tenex is a registered trademark of BBN.
Tops-10 is a registered trademark of Digital Equipment Corporation.
Tops-20 is a registered trademark of Digital Equipment Corporation.
Univac is a registered trademark of Sperry Rand.
Unix is a registered trademark of Bell Laboratories.
VAX is a registered trademark of Digital Equipment Corporation.
VM/370 is a registered trademark of IBM.
VMS is a registered trademark of Digital Equipment Corporation.

# Contents

# Preface

Traditionally, a vade mecum (pronounced "VAHdee MAYkem") is a laboratory manual that guides the student step by step through complex procedures. Operating systems are complex mixtures of policy and mechanism, of algorithm and heuristic, and of theoretical goals and practical experience. This vade mecum tries to unify these diverse points of view and guide the novice step by step through the complexities of the subject. As a text, this book is intended for a first course in operating systems at the undergraduate level. The subject has so many individual parts that its practitioners and teachers often concentrate on subareas and ignore the larger concepts that govern the entire subject. I have tried to rectify that situation in this book by structuring the presentation about the dual ideas of resource management and beautification.

To unify disparate threads of discussion, I have taken the liberty introducing names for recurrent themes and glorifying them with the title "principles." I hope that this organization and nomenclature will help the reader to understand the subject better and to integrate new ideas into the same framework.

Each technical term that is introduced in the text is printed in **boldface** the first time it appears. All boldface entries are collected and defined in the glossary. I have striven to use a consistent nomenclature throughout the book. At times this nomenclature is at odds with accepted American practice. For example, I prefer to call computer memory "store." This name allows me to unify the various levels of the storage hierarchy, including registers, main store, swap space, files on disk, and files on magnetic tape. I also prefer the single word "transput" to the clumsier but more common term "input/output." Although I found this term jarring at first, I have grown to like it.

Each chapter closes with a section on perspective, suggestions for further reading, and exercises. The perspective section steps back from the details of the subject and summarizes the choices that actual operating systems have made and rules of thumb for distinguishing alternatives. It also fits the subject of the chapter into the larger picture. The suggestions for further reading have two purposes.

First, they show the reader where more information on the subject discussed in the chapter may be found. Second, they point to research articles related to the subject that describe actual implementations and areas of current activity. The exercises also serve two purposes. First, they allow the student to test his or her understanding of the subject presented in the text by working exercises directly related to the material. More importantly, they push the student beyond the confines of the material presented to consider new situations and to evaluate new policies. Subjects that are only hinted at in the text are developed more thoroughly in this latter type of exercise.

A course in operating systems is not complete without computer projects. Unfortunately, such exercises require a substantial investment in software. The most successful projects for a first course in operating systems involve implementing parts of an operating system. A complete operating system can be presented to the class, with well-defined modules and interfaces, and the class can be assigned the task of replacing modules with ones of their own design. A less ambitious project has the students first build a simple scheduler for a simulated machine. After it is completed, it can be enhanced by adding virtual memory, transput, and other features. If the necessary software is not available for these assignments, students can be asked to simulate particular policies or algorithms in isolation from a complete operating system. Several exercises in the book give guidelines for this sort of project.

This second edition of the text differs from the first in several ways. Many figures have been added, both to clarify individual points and to unify the treatment of different subjects with similar diagrams. For example, the history of operating system styles is now adorned with consistent pictures. The nuts and bolts of process switching has been moved from Chapter 2 to Chapter 1, and a new section on virtual-machine operating systems has been added. The discussion of page-replacement policies in Chapter 2 has been enhanced with fault-rate graphs drawn from a simulation. Analysis and simulation are described near the end of Chapter 2. Chapter 9 on cc-operating processes has been enlarged with a major new section on the communication-kernel approach. The Hysteresis Principle has been introduced. Minor errors and inconsistencies have been fixed throughout the text.

I owe a debt of gratitude to the many people who helped me write this text. The students of Bart Miller's operating system class all wrote book reviews for an early draft. My parents Asher and Miriam and my brothers Joel and Barry devoted countless hours to a careful reading of the entire text, suggesting clarifications and rewording throughout. My colleagues Bart Miller, Mary Vernon, and Michael Carey read and criticized individual chapters. Michael Scott's careful reading of Chapter 8 and his keen insight into language issues in general were of great help. I am also grateful to Charles Shub, Felix Wu, Aaron Gordon, Mike Litskow, Ianne H. Koritzinsky, Shlomo Weiss, Bryan Rosenburg, and Hari Madduri for their helpful comments. This book was prepared using the Troff program on a Unix operating system. I would have been lost without it. Finally, I would like to thank my wife, Beth Goldstein, for her support and patience, and my daughter, Penina, for being wonderful.

*Raphael A. Finkel*
*University of Wisconsin — Madison*

# Introduction

The development of operating systems has progressed enormously in the last few decades. Open shop computing has given way to batch processing, which in turn has yielded to interactive multiprogramming as emphasis shifted first to efficient use of expensive machines and then to effective shared use. The recent trend to personal workstations has turned full circle back to the earliest beginnings: a single user associated with a single machine.

The long and complex journey has not been pointless. As computer use has expanded, so has the sophistication with which we deal with all of its aspects. Ad hoc mechanisms have become standardized, then formalized, then analyzed. Standing at the present and looking back, we have the advantage of seeing the larger picture and of knowing how originally unconnected ideas fit together and reinforce each other. We realize that the proper software for a personal workstation has more in common with large operating systems for interactive multiprogramming than it has with open shop computing.

The future holds the promise of increased use of networking to interconnect computers in various ways. Multiple-user machines will soon be built of communities of communicating computers. This new theme has already begun to be played. It is an exciting time to be studying operating systems.

## 1 PHILOSOPHY OF THE BOOK

In this book, I have carefully tried to distinguish mechanisms from policies. **Mechanisms** are techniques that perform activities. **Policies** are rules that decide which activities to perform. The mechanisms are the "nuts and bolts" of operating systems and often depend to some extent on the hardware on which the operating system runs.

We will give examples of nuts-and-bolts programming in a high-level language. Most modern operating systems are written in such languages, reserving assembler language for those few aspects that cannot be captured in a higher level language. For the sake of concreteness, we will present programs in a Modula-like syntax. Modula is closely related to Pascal. (See the Further Reading section at the end of the chapter.) The examples are all carefully annotated, so it should be possible to follow them even if you have only a nodding acquaintance with any language in the Algol family, such as Pascal. In most cases, written algorithms are supplemented with pictures.

You should be able to read this book comfortably if you have had an undergraduate course in data structures and in machine organization. Some sophistication in mathematics (for example, one semester of calculus) would also be helpful but is not required.

A glossary at the end of the book provides in one place simple definitions of words that are used repeatedly. When these words appear for the first time in the text, they are set in **boldface** type. I have taken some pains to use words consistently in order to make this book clear. Unfortunately, computer literature often employs the same term to mean different things in different contexts. (An excellent example is "heap," which means "free storage pool" in the Pascal context but "data structure for implementing a priority queue" in the operating systems context.) You will discover that I avoid certain words altogether. In particular, the word "system" has lost all its power because it has acquired a multitude of meanings, many of which are fuzzy at best. I treat "operating system" as a compound word with a well defined connotation that should become increasingly clear as you study this book. The terms "control program" or "monitor" would have been preferable, but those terms have already become associated with other specialized meanings.

This book sorts through a large body of knowledge, covering a continuum from elementary concepts through advanced ideas. Intended primarily as a text for an undergraduate course in operating systems, it also introduces topics of interest to graduate-level students and professionals. In addition, the book presents a continuum from terrible ideas through workable ideas to great ideas. Often the first way one tries to solve a problem is easy to understand and easy to implement but works poorly. With some cleverness, one finds a better method that is far superior to the first. Then a host of other solutions, mostly variations on the second method, come to mind. These refinements are often worth mentioning but usually not worth implementing. We call this observation the **Law of Diminishing Returns**.

The Latin phrase *vade mecum* means "walk with me." Books with this title are usually laboratory manuals explaining techniques step by step. This vade mecum is different in that it explains the problems and explores various solutions before giving advice. It can be useful both in the classroom and in the home or office library. Although each chapter is fairly self-contained, some subjects cannot be easily separated from others and must be explained, at least in part, before all the related issues have been covered. If you are a novice, your journey should start at the beginning of the book. If you are an expert looking for a particular subject, try the glossary first, then the index. If you are a teacher using this book as a text, feel free to choose which algorithms of the "sophisticated variation" type to cover.

Let's begin the journey: Vade mecum!

# 2 THE RESOURCE PRINCIPLE

In this book you will find both specific and general information about the structure and behavior of operating systems. We will start by presenting two very different "definitions" of an operating system. These definitions will serve to introduce the major concepts that are elucidated in the rest of the book. Our first definition is called the **Resource Principle**. The second is the **Beautification Principle**. We will also introduce the **Level Principle**, an important structuring concept for operating systems. Here is the Resource Principle:

> ## Resource Principle
> An operating system is a set of algorithms that allocate resources to processes.

A **resource** is a commodity necessary to get work done. The computer's hardware provides a number of fundamental resources. Working programs need to reside somewhere in main store (the computer's memory), must execute instructions, and need some way to accept data and present results. These needs are related to the fundamental resources of **space**, **time**, and **transput** (input/output). In addition to these fundamental resources, the operating system introduces new resources. For example, **files** are able to store data. Programs might be able to communicate with each other by means of **ports** that connect them. Even higher-level resources can be built on top of these, such as **mailboxes** used to pass messages between users.

The notion of a process is central to operating systems, but is notoriously hard to define. To a first approximation, a **process** is the execution of a program. It is a fundamental entity that requires resources in order to accomplish its task, which is to run the program to completion.

One can picture processes as actors simultaneously performing one-actor plays in a theater; stage props are their resources. As actors need props, they request them from the property manager (the operating system resource allocator). The manager's job is to satisfy two conflicting goals on behalf of the actors:

- to let each actor have whatever props are needed
- to be fair in giving props to each actor.

The manager also is responsible to the owners of the theater (that is, the owners of the computer), who have invested a considerable sum in its resources. This responsibility also has several goals:

- to make sure the props (resources) are used as much as possible
- to finish as many plays (processes) as possible.

Another way to look at processes is to consider them as agents representing the interests of users. When a user wants to compose a letter, a process runs the program that converts keystrokes into changes in the document. When the user wants to mail that letter electronically, a process (perhaps a new one) runs a different program that knows how to send documents to mailboxes. In general, processes run programs that help the user. In order to do their work, they may in turn need help from the operating system for such operations as receiving keystrokes and placing data in long-term storage. They require resources such as space in main store and machine cycles. The Resource Principle says that the operating system is in charge of allocating such resources.

# 3 HISTORICAL DEVELOPMENT

## 3.1 Open shop

Operating systems developed as technology and demand increased. The earliest computers were massive, extremely expensive, and difficult to use. Individuals (called **users**) would sign up for blocks of time during which they were allowed "hands-on" use of the computer. This situation is depicted in Figure 1.1, which shows a single program, submitted by the user through a device like a card reader, executing on the machine. The machine had two major components, its transput devices and its ability to execute a program. A typical session on the IBM 1620, a computer in use around 1964, involved several steps in order to compile and execute a program. First, the user would load the first pass of the Fortran compiler. This operation involved clearing main store by typing a cryptic instruction on the console typewriter; putting the compiler, a 10-inch stack of punched cards, in the card reader; placing the program to be compiled after the compiler in the card reader; and then pressing the "load" button on the reader. The output would be a set of punched cards called "intermediate output." If there were any compilation errors, a light would flash on the console, and error messages would appear on the console typewriter. Assuming everything had gone well so far, the next step would be to load the second pass of the Fortran compiler just like the first pass, putting the intermediate output in the card reader as well. If the second pass succeeded, the output was a second set of punched cards called the "executable deck." The third

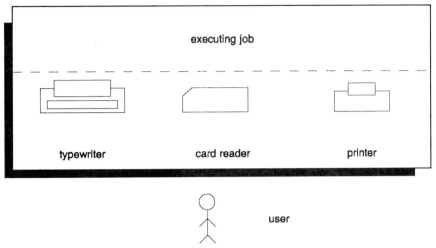

**Figure 1.1** Open shop

step was to shuffle the executable deck slightly, load it along with a massive subroutine library (another 10 inches of cards), and observe the program as it ran.

The output of a program might appear on cards or paper. Frequently, the output was wrong. To figure out why involved **debugging**, which often took the form of peeking directly into main store and even patching the program by using console switches. If there was not enough time to finish, a frustrated user might get a line-printer listing of main store (known as a **dump** of store) to puzzle over at leisure. If the user finished before the end of the allotted time, the machine might sit idle until the next reserved block of time.

## 3.2 Operator-driven shop

The economics of computers made such idle time very expensive. In an effort to avoid such idleness, installation managers instituted several modifications to the **open shop** mechanism just outlined. An **operator** was hired to perform the repetitive tasks of loading jobs, starting the computer, and collecting the output. This situation is shown in Figure 1.2. The operator was often much faster than ordinary users at chores such as mounting cards and magnetic tapes, so the setup time between job steps was reduced. If the program failed, the operator could have the computer produce a dump. It was no longer feasible for users to inspect main store or patch programs directly. Instead, users would submit their runs, and the operator would run them as soon as possible. Each user was charged only for the amount of time the job required.

The operator often reduced setup time by batching similar job steps. For example, the operator could run the first pass of the Fortran compiler for several

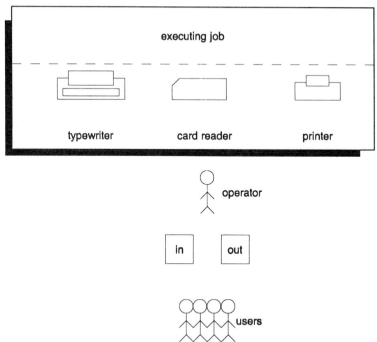

**Figure 1.2** Operator-driven shop

jobs, save all the intermediate output, then load the second pass and run it on all the intermediate output that had been collected. In addition, the operator could run jobs out of order, perhaps charging more for giving some jobs priority. Jobs that were known to require a long time could be delayed until night. The operator could always stop a job that was taking too long.

## 3.3 Offline transput

Much of the operator's job was mechanical. The next stage of development was to automate that job, as shown in Figure 1.3. First, input to jobs was collected **offline**, that is, by using a separate computer (sometimes called a "satellite") whose only task was the transfer from cards to tape. Once the tape was full, the operator mounted it on the main computer. Reading jobs from tape is much faster than reading cards, so less time was occupied with transput. When the computer finished the jobs on one tape, the operator would mount the next one. Similarly, output was generated onto tape, an activity that is much faster than punching cards. This output tape was converted to line-printer listing offline.

A small **resident monitor** program, which remained in main store while jobs were executing, reset the machine after each job was completed and loaded the

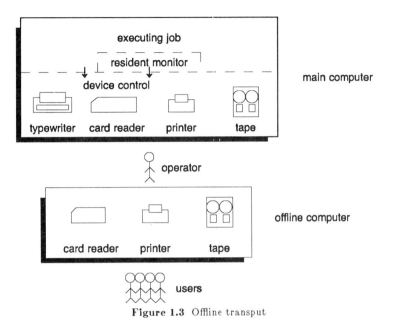

**Figure 1.3** Offline transput

next one. Conventions were established for cards (or "card images," as they are called once they are on tape) to separate jobs and specify their requirements. These conventions were the rudiments of **command languages**. For example, one convention was to place an asterisk in the first column of control cards, to distinguish them from data cards. The compilation job we just described could be specified in cards that looked like this:

| | |
|---|---|
| `*JOB SMITH` | The user's name is Smith. |
| `*    PASS CHESTNUT` | Password to prevent others from using Smith's account |
| `*    OPTION TIME=60` | Limit of 60 seconds |
| `*    OPTION DUMP=YES` | Produce a dump if any step fails. |
| `*STEP FORT1` | Run the first pass of the Fortran compiler. |
| `*    OUTPUT TAPE1` | Put the intermediate code on tape 1. |
| `*    INPUT FOLLOWS` | Input to the compiler comes on the next cards. |
| `   ...` | Fortran program |
| `*STEP FORT2` | Run the second pass of the Fortran compiler. |
| `*    OUTPUT TAPE2` | Put the executable deck on scratch tape 2. |
| `*    INPUT TAPE1` | Input comes from scratch tape 1. |
| `*STEP LINK` | Link the executable with the Fortran library. |
| `*    INPUT TAPE2` | First input is the executable. |
| `*    INPUT TAPELIB` | Second input is a tape with the library. |
| `*    OUTPUT TAPE1` | Put load image on scratch tape 1. |
| `*STEP TAPE1` | Run whatever is on scratch tape 1. |
| `*    OUTPUT TAPEOUT` | Put output on the standard output tape. |
| `*    INPUT FOLLOWS` | Input to the program comes on the next cards. |
| `   ...` | Data |

The resident monitor had several duties:

- to interpret the command language
- to perform rudimentary accounting
- To provide device-independent input and output by substituting tapes for cards.

The running program could deal with tapes directly, but as a convenience, the resident monitor provided a few subroutines for reading from the current input tape and writing to the current output tape.

## 3.4  Spooling systems

Next, transput units were designed to run at the same time the computer was computing. They generated an **interrupt** when they finished reading or writing a record instead of requiring the computer to monitor their progress. An interrupt causes the computer to save some critical information (such as its current program counter) and to branch to a location specific for the kind of interrupt. Device-service routines, known as a **device drivers**, were added to the resident monitor to deal with these interrupts.

Disks were introduced as a secondary storage medium. Now the computer could be computing one job while reading another onto the disk and printing the results of a third from the disk. Unlike a tape, the disk allowed programs to be stored anywhere, so there was no need for the computer to execute jobs in the same order in which they were entered. A primitive **scheduler** was added to the resident monitor to sort jobs based on priority and amount of time needed, both of which could be specified on control cards. The operator was often retained to perform several tasks.

- to mount data tapes needed by jobs (also specified on control cards)
- to make policy decisions, such as which priority jobs to run and which to hold
- to restart the resident monitor when it failed or was inadvertently destroyed by the running job.

This mode of running a computer was known as a **spooling system**, and its resident monitor was the start of modern operating systems. (The word "spool" originally stood for "simultaneous peripheral operations on line," but it is easier to picture a spool of thread, where new jobs are wound on the outside, and old ones are extracted from the inside.) One of the first spooling systems was HASP (the Houston Automatic Spooling Program), an add-on to OS/360 for the IBM 360 computer family. A spooling system is shown in Figure 1.4.

Spooling systems prevent users from fiddling with console switches to debug and patch their programs. The era of spooling systems introduced the long-lived tradition of the users' room. The users' room was characterized by long tables, often overflowing with oversized fan-fold paper, and a quietly desperate group of users, each politely ignoring the others, drinking copious amounts of coffee, buying junk food from the vending machines, and staring bleary-eyed at the paper.

## 3.5  Batch multiprogramming

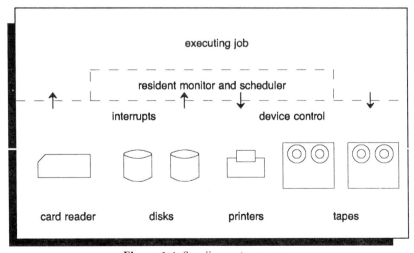

**Figure 1.4** Spooling system

Spooling systems did not make efficient use of all of their resources. The job that was currently running might not need the entire main store. A job that performed transput would idle the computer until the transput was finished. The next improvement was the introduction of **multiprogramming**, a scheme in which more than one job is active simultaneously. We show this situation in Figure 1.5. While one job is waiting for a transput operation to complete, another can compute. With luck, no time at all is wasted waiting for transput. The more jobs run at the same time, the better. However, a **compute-bound** job (one that performs little transput but much computation) could easily prevent **transput-bound** jobs (those that perform mostly transput) from making progress. Competition for the time resource and policies for allocating it are the main theme of Chapter 2.

Multiprogramming also introduces competition for space. The number of jobs that can be accommodated at one time depends on the size of main store and the hardware available for dividing up that space. In addition, jobs must be secured against inadvertent or malicious interference or inspection by other jobs. It is more critical now that the resident monitor not be destroyed by errant programs, because not one but many jobs will suffer if it breaks. In Chapter 3, we will examine policies for space allocation and how each of them provides security.

The form of multiprogramming we have been describing is often called **batch** multiprogramming because each job batches together a set of steps. The first might be compilations, the next a linking step to combine all the compiled pieces into one program, and finally the program would be run. Each of these steps requires the resident monitor to obtain a program (perhaps from disk) and run it. The steps are fairly independent of each other. If one compilation succeeds but another fails, it is not necessary to recompile the successful program. The user can

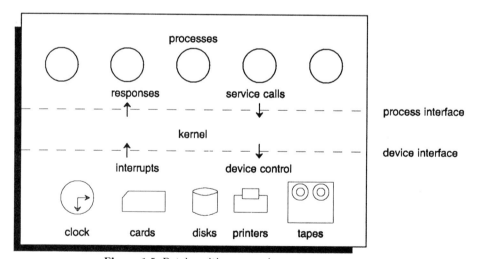

**Figure 1.5** Batch multiprogramming

resubmit the job with one of the compilations omitted.

Since job steps are independent, the resident monitor can separate them and apply policy decisions to each step independently. Each step might have its own time, space, and transput requirements. In fact, two separate steps of the same job can sometimes be performed at the same time! The term **process** was introduced to mean the entity that performs a single job step. The scheduler creates a new process for each job step. The process will terminate when its step is finished. The operating system (as the resident monitor may now be called) keeps track of each process and its needs. A process may request assistance from the kernel by submitting a **service call** across the **process interface**. Executing programs are no longer allowed to control devices directly; otherwise, they could make conflicting use of devices and prevent the kernel from doing its job. Instead, processes must use service calls to access devices, and the kernel has complete control of the **device interface**.

Granting resources to processes is not a trivial task. A process might require resources (like tape drives) at various stages in its execution. If a resource is not available, the scheduler might block the process from continuing until later. The scheduler must take care not to block any process forever. Chapter 4 deals with the issues raised by allocation of resources like tape drives that can be reused after one process finishes but should not be taken from a process while it is running.

Along with batch multiprogramming came new ideas for structuring the operating system. The **kernel** of the operating system is composed of routines that manage central store, time, and devices, and other resources. It responds both to requests from processes and to interrupts from devices. In fact, the kernel runs only when it is invoked either from above, by a process, or below, by a device. If no process is ready to run and no device needs attention, the computer sits idle.

Various activities within the kernel share data, but they must be not be interrupted when the data are in an inconsistent state. Mechanisms for **concurrency control** were developed to ensure that these activities do not interfere with each other. Chapter 8 introduces the mutual-exclusion and synchronization problems associated with concurrency control and surveys the solutions that have been found for these problems.

## 3.6 Interactive multiprogramming

The next step in the development of operating systems was the introduction of **interactive multiprogramming**, shown in Figure 1.6. The principal user-oriented transput device changed from cards or tape to the interactive terminal. Instead of packaging all the data that a program might need before it starts running, the interactive user is able to supply input as the program wants it. The data can depend on what the program has produced so far.

Interactive computing is sometimes added into an existing batch multiprogramming environment. For example, TSO ("timesharing option") was an add-on to the OS/360 operating system. In contrast, batch is sometimes added into an existing interactive environment. Unix installations, for example, often provide a

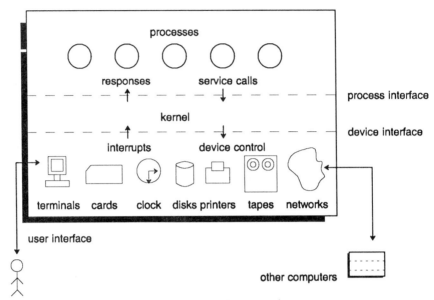

**Figure 1.6** Interactive multiprogramming

batch service.

Interactive computing caused a revolution in the way computers were used. Instead of being treated as number crunchers, they became information manipulators. Interactive **text editors** allowed users to construct data files online. These files could represent programs, documents, or data. Instead of speaking of a job composed of steps, **interactive multiprogramming** (also called "timesharing") deals with **sessions** that last from initial connection (**logon**) to the point at which that connection is broken (**logoff**). During logon, the user typically gives two forms of identification: a name and a password. (The password is not echoed back to the terminal, or is at least blackened by overstriking garbage, to avoid disclosing it to onlookers.) These data are converted into a **user identifier** that is associated with all the processes that run on behalf of this user and all the files they create. This identifier helps the kernel decide whom to bill for services and whether to permit various actions such as modifying files. (We discuss file protection in Chapter 6.)

During a session, the user imagines that the resources of the entire computer are devoted to this terminal, even though many sessions may be active simultaneously for many users. Typically, one process is created at logon time to serve the user. That first process may start others as needed to accomplish individual steps. This main process is called the **command interpreter**. The command interpreter and other interactive facilities are discussed in Chapter 7, which discusses the general subject of the user interface.

The development of computing strategies has not ended. Recent years have seen the introduction of personal computers. The operating systems of these machines often provide for interactive computing but not for multiprogramming. CP/M is a good example of this approach. Other operating systems provide multiprogramming as well as interaction and allow the user to start several activities and direct attention to whichever is currently most interesting.

## 3.7 Distributed computing

The newest development in operating systems is **distributed computation**. Computers can be connected together by a variety of devices. The spectrum ranges from tight coupling, where several computers share main storage, to very loose coupling, where a number of computers belong to the same international network and can send one another messages. Chapter 9 discusses inter-process communication and other issues that become especially important in the distributed-computing domain.

# 4 THE BEAUTIFICATION PRINCIPLE

We have seen the Resource Principle as a way to define operating systems. An equally important definition is the **Beautification Principle**:

| **Beautification Principle** |
| --- |
| An operating system is a set of algorithms that hide the details of the hardware and provide a more pleasant environment. |

Hiding the details of the hardware has two goals.

- **Security**. We have already seen that the operating system must secure itself and other processes against accidental or malicious interference. Certain instructions of the machine, notably those that halt the machine and those that perform transput, must be removed from the reach of processes. Modern hardware provides several **processor states** that restrict the use of instructions. For example, some architectures provide two states, called **privileged state** and **non-privileged state**. Processes run in non-privileged state. Instructions such as those that perform transput and those that change processor state cause traps when executed in non-privileged state. These traps force the processor to jump to the operating system and enter privileged state. The operating system runs in privileged state. All instructions have their standard meanings in this state. As we will see in Chapter 3, the operating system can restrict access to main store so that processes may not access all of it.

- **Abstraction**. Operating systems, like other software components, construct higher-level (**virtual**) resources out of lower-level (**physical**) ones. Details of the lower-level structures are hidden, and higher-level structures are introduced. From the point of view of a process, the physical machine is enhanced by the operating system into a virtual machine. Enhancement includes both simplicity (hiding details) and function (introducing new structures). Neither time (ability to execute) nor space (main store) appears to be shared with other processes. The virtual machine is thus simpler than the physical machine. The process interface provides extra instructions that improve on the basic hardware instruction set, particularly with respect to transput. The virtual machine is thus more functional than the physical machine.

  From the point of view of the user, the operating system provides services that are not present in the underlying machine. These services include loading and running programs, providing for interaction between the user and the running programs, allowing several programs to run at the same time, maintaining accounts to charge for services, storing data and programs, and participating in networks of computers.

An important example of the beautification role of the operating system is found in transput services. transput devices are extremely difficult to program efficiently and correctly. Most operating systems provide **device drivers** that perform transput operations on behalf of processes. These drivers also ensure that two processes do not accidentally try to use the same device at once. The operations that are provided are often at a much higher level than the device itself provides. For example, device-completion interrupts might be hidden; the operating system might block processes that perform transput until the transfer completes. Chapter 5 is devoted to a discussion of transput devices and how they are manipulated by the operating system. An abstract file structure is often imposed on the data stored on disk. This structure is higher-level than the raw disk. Chapter 6 describes files and how they are implemented.

## 5 THE KERNEL AND PROCESSES

Before we study how operating systems manage resources such as time and space, we must first lay some foundations. In particular, you must understand how an operating system represents processes and how it switches between them. The core of the operating system is the **kernel**, a control program that reacts to interrupts from external devices and to requests for service from processes. We have depicted the kernel in Figures 1.5 and 1.6. The kernel is a permanent resident of the computer. It creates and terminates processes and responds to their requests for service.

## 5.1 Context blocks

Each process is represented in the operating system by a collection of data known as the **context block**. The context block includes such information as the following.

- state and scheduling statistics (described in Chapter 2)
- use of main and backing store (described in Chapter 3)
- other resources held (described in Chapter 4)
- open transput devices (described in Chapter 5)
- open files (described in Chapter 6)
- accounting statistics
- privileges.

We will single out several important pieces of information. Here is a Modula declaration that will serve our purpose:

```
1 const
2     MaxNumProcesses = 10; { the number of processes we are
3         willing to let exist at any one time }
4     NumRegisters = 16; { the number of registers this computer has }
5 type
6     ContextBlockType = { per-process information }
7         record
8             { state vector information }
9             ProgramCounter : Address;  { execution address of the program }
10            ProcessorState : integer; { state of processor, including
11                such information as priority and mode.  Depends on the
12                computer hardware. }
13            Registers : array 1:NumRegisters of integer;
14            { other information here }
15        end; { ContextBlockType }
16 var
17     ContextBlocks : { all information about processes }
18         array 1:MaxNumProcesses of ContextBlockType;
```

We will concentrate for the time being on the **state vector** part of the context block (lines 8–13). This is the part of the context block that the operating system keeps available at all times. Other less frequently used parts of the context block might be stored on backing store (disk, for example). In the simple state vector shown here, the operating system records the **program counter** (line 9) and the **processor state** (line 10) of the process. The meaning of these fields depends on the type of computer for which the operating system is designed. The program counter tells where the next instruction to be executed by this process is stored, and the processor state indicates hardware priority and other details that we shall ignore for now. In addition, the state vector holds the values of the computer's registers as they were when the process last stopped running.

Assume that process **A** has been picked to run next. We are not interested at present in the policy that decided that **A** should run, only the mechanism by which the kernel causes **A** to start executing. The ground rules that we will follow for this exercise are the following:

(1)  There is only one processor, so only one process can run at a time. (**Multiprocessor** computers have several processors, so they can run several processes simultaneously. We will discuss multiprocessors in Chapter 9.)

(2)  The kernel has decided to start running **A** instead of the process that is currently using the computing resource.

(3)  The state vector for **A** accurately represents the state of the program counter, the processor state, and the registers the last time **A** was running. All these must be restored as part of turning the processor over to **A**.

(4)  **A**'s program is currently in main store, and we can ignore all aspects of space management. Space management is a large subject that we will take up in Chapter 3.

Switching the processor from executing the kernel to executing **A** is called **context switching**, since the hardware must switch from the context in which it runs the kernel to the one in which **A** runs. In Figure 1.7, the currently executing object is highlighted with a double border. Before the context switch, the kernel is running. Afterwards, process **A** is running. Switching back to the kernel from process **A** is also a context switch. This kind of context switch happens when **A** tries to execute a privileged instruction (including the service call instruction) or when a device generates an interrupt. Both these situations will be described in more detail. In either case, a context switch to the kernel gives it the opportunity to update accounting statistics for the process that was running and to select which process should be run after the service call or interrupt has been serviced.

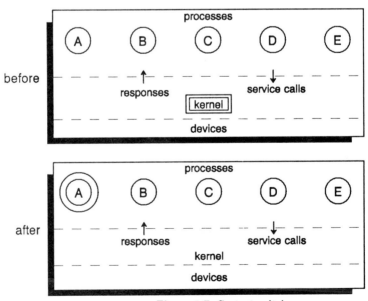

**Figure 1.7** Context switch

Not only does the kernel have its own register contents and its own program counter, but it also has special privileges that allow it to access transput devices. These privileges must be turned off whenever a process is running. Privilege is usually conferred by the processor state, so a process has a different processor state from the kernel. Some computers provide only separate privileged and non-privileged states, whereas others have several gradations between them. The ability to change from one state to another requires special privilege.

Since this is our first detailed example of the work that an operating system performs, we will say a word about how operating systems are constructed. In the early days of computers, operating systems were written as single large programs encompassing hundreds of thousands of lines of assembler instructions. Two trends have made the job of writing operating systems less difficult. First, high-level languages have made programming the operating system much easier. Second, the discipline of structured programming has suggested a modular approach to writing large programs; this approach allows large problems to be decomposed into smaller pieces. The program that switches context can be seen as one such small piece. It could be a procedure written in a high-level language like Modula. These pieces can often be arranged in layers, with each layer providing services to the ones above it. For example, one could build the layers as follows:

- Context- and process-switch services (lowest layer)
- Device drivers
- Resource managers for space and time
- Service call interpreter (highest layer)

For example, the CP/M operating system provides three levels: (1) device drivers (the BIOS section of the kernel), (2) a file manager (BDOS), and (3) an interactive command interpreter (CCP). It supports only one process and provides no security, so there is no need for special context-switch services.

Switching context from the kernel back to a process involves copying information between the context block and hardware registers of the machine. This information includes the program counter, the processor state, and the contents of addressible registers. Most high-level languages (including Modula) do not provide the necessary facility to deal with these hardware issues directly. Luckily, some newer computers (such as the DEC VAX) have single instructions that do all the context-switch work themselves. Still, high-level languages are unlikely to generate those instructions. Furthermore, the speed of context switching is critical because this operation takes place every time an interrupt is serviced by the kernel or a process makes a request to the kernel. The result is that context switching is usually performed by a procedure written in assembler language.

## 5.2 Process lists

The context blocks for processes are stored in lists. Each list is dedicated to some particular class of processes. These classes can be divided as follows.

- **Running.** The process that is currently executing. On most computers, only one process is running at any time. However, on multiprocessors, which we discuss in Chapter 9, several processes can run at once.
- **Ready.** Processes that are ready to run but are not currently running because of a policy decision. As we will see in Chapter 2, there may be several ready lists.
- **Waiting.** Processes that cannot run now because they have made requests that have not yet been fulfilled. The kernel might keep a different list for every type of service that may have been requested. For example, space management sometimes causes processes to wait in a "main-store wait" list until there is enough room to run them. A process reading data from a file might wait in a "file transput wait list" until the data are read in. Each device that a process may use for transput might have its own wait list. While a process is in a wait list, we say it is **blocked**.

These lists are commonly called "queues," but they need not be built as queues usually are, with entry only at one end and departure from the other. They may be represented implicitly, with each context block holding a field that indicates which list it is on. They may be stored in a heap data structure according to some priority so that the one with the most urgency can be accessed quickly.

## 5.3  Service calls

Various events can cause a process to be moved from one list to another. A process makes a request of the kernel by submitting a **service call**, which might ask for resources, return resources, or perform transput. As a result of this call, the scheduler might decide to place that process back on the ready list and start running another process from the ready list. This operation, which we call a **process switch**, usually takes more time than a simple context switch. After the process switch, a context switch starts executing the new process. Figure 1.8 shows the effect of the kernel switching process from **A** to **B**.

Most operating systems build service calls from instructions that cause processor traps. Processor traps always switch context to the kernel. On the DEC PDP-11, for example, the EMT and the TRAP instructions are both used by various operating systems to achieve communication between processes and the kernel. A similar effect is achieved on the IBM 360 and 370 computers with the SVC instruction and on the DEC PDP-10 with the UUO instruction. A trap causes the hardware to copy certain hardware registers, such as the program counter and the processor state, to a safe place (typically onto a stack). The hardware then loads those hardware registers with the appropriate new context (which includes the program counter for the location in the kernel where its trap-handler program is stored). It then sets the processor to privileged state. The operating system must

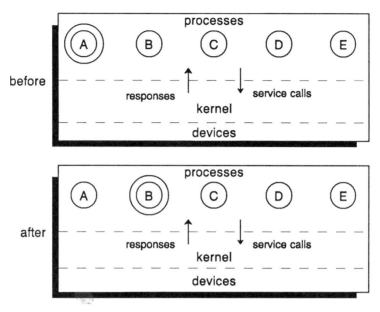

**Figure 1.8** Process switch

then move the context information saved by the hardware into the context block of the process that was running at the time of the trap.

Some operating systems use ordinary subroutine-call instructions for service calls. CP/M, for example, uses a jump to location 5 to invoke service calls. Again, the operating system may save context information in the context block while it is handling the service call.

Service calls are like subroutine calls from the point of view of the calling process. Arguments are first placed in a standard place (on a stack, in registers, right after the call, or in a communication area), and then the service-call instruction is executed. When control is returned by the kernel to the process, the process is ready to execute the next instruction. Results passed back from the kernel are stored in registers, on the stack, or in a communication area.

Sometimes service calls are simple matters that should not cause the process making the request to wait. For example, a process might request the current time of day. This information is readily available, so the kernel just switches context back to the calling process, giving it the information it wanted. If the process must wait before the service it requested can be provided, process switching is involved. We will see that store management introduces extra costs for process switching.

Interrupts caused by a transput device also cause context to switch from the current process to the kernel. The same sequence of actions (saving old context, loading new context, changing state) occurs for interrupts as for traps. The interrupt might indicate completion of an operation that some other process was waiting for, in which case the kernel might place that process on the ready list. A policy decision could switch to that process, at the expense of the former process. We will discuss devices in Chapter 5.

One very important interrupt is generated by a device called the **clock**. Clocks can be designed to interrupt periodically (every 60th of a second, for example) or to accept an interval from the computer and interrupt when that time has expired. If it were not for clock interrupts, a running process could sit in an accidental infinite loop that performs no service calls, and the kernel would never be able to wrest control from it. The kernel therefore depends on the clock to force a context switch back to the kernel so that it can make new policy decisions.

The fact that processes belong to lists points to an important insight into operating system structure:

> # Level Principle
> Active entities are data structures when viewed from a lower level.

The Level Principle applies to processes in this way: A process considers itself an active entity that executes instructions and makes service calls on the kernel. From the kernel's point of view, however, the process is just a data structure (largely contained in the context block, but also including all the store used by the process) that can be manipulated. Manipulations include moving the process from list to list and causing the process to execute.

Even an executing program like the kernel is subject to the Level Principle. Each instruction appears to be an active entity that moves information from one place to another. However, instructions are just data to the hardware, which interprets those instructions and causes the information to move.

The converse of the Level Principle sometimes sheds new light as well. Objects that appear as data can occasionally be seen as active objects in some sense. For example, adding two numbers can be seen either as an action taken by some external agent or as an action taken by the first of the numbers on the second. Such a novel approach does make sense (the Smalltalk language is implemented this way!) and can lead to a useful decomposition of work so that it can be distributed. We will discuss distributed work in Chapter 9.

## 6 VIRTUAL MACHINES

Although most operating systems interpret the Beautification Principle to mean that processes should have an enhanced or simplified view of the hardware, some take a different tack. They make the process interface look just like the hardware interface. In other words, a process is allowed to use all the instructions, even the privileged ones. The process interface is called a **virtual machine** because it looks just like the underlying machine. The kernel of such an operating system is called a **virtualizing kernel**. We will devote some attention to this style of operating system because it clearly shows the interplay of traps, context switches, processor states, and the Level Principle.

Virtual machine operating systems are both useful and complex. They are useful because they allow operating system designers to experiment with new ideas without interfering with the user community. Before virtual machine operating systems, all operating system testing had to be performed on separate machines dedicated to that purpose. Any error in the kernel, no matter how trivial, could bring the entire operating system down. Any user unfortunate to be running programs at that time could lose a significant amount of work. With a virtual machine operating system, the test version of the operating system can run as a process controlled by the virtualizing kernel. The other processes, which are running ordinary programs, are not affected by errors in the test version. The only effect is that they don't run quite as fast, because the test version competes with them for resources. This arrangement is shown in Figure 1.9.

A second use of virtual machine operating systems is to integrate batch and interactive modes by letting them occupy different virtual machines. This scheme, shown in Figure 1.10, can be a fast way to piece together two fundamentally different operating systems for the same machine.

The ability to run several operating systems at once on the same machine has other advantages as well.

- It can alleviate the trauma of new operating system releases, since the old release may be used on one of the virtual machines until users have switched over to the new release, which is running on a different virtual machine under the control of the same virtualizing kernel.

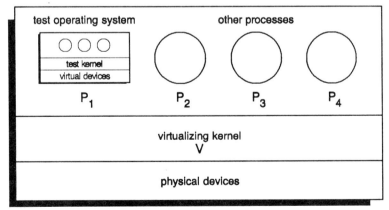

**Figure 1.9** Testing a new operating system

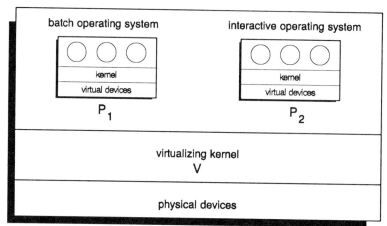

**Figure 1.10** Integrating two operating systems

- It can permit students to write real operating systems without interfering with the other users of the machine.
- It can enhance software reliability by isolating software components in different virtual machines.
- It can enhance security by isolating sensitive programs and data to their own virtual machine.
- It can test network facilities, such as those discussed in Chapter 9, by simulating machine-machine communication between several virtual machines on one physical machine.
- It can provide each user with a separate virtual machine in which a simple single-user operating system runs. Designing and implementing this simple operating system can be much easier than designing a multi-user operating system, since it can ignore protection and multiprogramming issues. The CMS (Conversational Monitor System) operating system for the IBM 370 computer, for example, is usually run in a virtual machine controlled by the VM/370 virtualizing kernel. CMS provides only one process and very little protection. It assumes that the entire machine is at the disposal of the user. Under VM/370, a new virtual machine is created for each user who logs on. Its control panel is mapped onto the user's terminal, and buttons are "pushed" by typing in appropriate commands. These commands allow for initial program load (to start up CMS, for instance) and for interrupting the virtual machine.

Virtual-machine operating systems are complex. To provide acceptable speed, the hardware executes most instructions directly. One might think that the virtualizing kernel **V** can run all its processes $\mathbf{P}_i$ in privileged state and let them use all the hardware instructions. However, privileged instructions are just too dangerous to let processes use directly. What if $\mathbf{P}_i$ executes the halt instruction? Instead, **V** must run all $P_i$ in non-privileged state to prevent them from accidentally or maliciously interfering with each other and with $V$ itself. In fact, virtual-machine operating systems cannot be implemented on computers where dangerous instructions are ignored or fail to trap in non-privileged state. For example, the PDP-11/45 in non-privileged state fails to trap on several dangerous instructions. In general, an instruction is dangerous if it performs transput, manipulates address-translation registers (discussed in Chapter 3), or manipulates the processor state (including interrupt-return instructions and priority setting instructions).

To let $P_i$ imagine it has control of processor states, even though it does not, $V$ keeps track of the virtual processor state of each $P_i$, that is, the processor state of the virtual machine that $V$ emulates on behalf of $P_i$. This information is stored in $P_i$'s context block inside of $V$. All privileged instructions executed by $P_i$ cause traps to $V$, which then emulates the behavior of the bare hardware on behalf of $P_i$.

- If $P_i$ was in virtual non-privileged state, $V$ emulates a trap for $P_i$. This emulation puts $P_i$ in virtual privileged state, although it is still run, as always, in physical non-privileged state. The program counter for $P_i$ is reset to the proper trap address within $P_i$'s virtual space. (We will see in Chapter 3 how virtual space is managed for virtual machine operating systems.) We say that $V$ has **reflected** the trap to $P_i$.
- If $P_i$ was in virtual privileged state, $V$ emulates the action of the instruction itself. For example, it terminates $P_i$ on a halt instruction, and it executes transput instructions interpretatively.

Some dangerous instructions are particularly difficult to emulate. Transput can be very tricky. Channel programs (discussed in Chapter 5), which control some sophisticated transput devices, must be translated and checked for legality. Self-modifying channel programs are especially hard to translate. The virtualizing kernel may wish to simulate one device by another, for example, simulating a printer on a disk or a small disk on a part of a larger one. A device-completion interrupt can indicate that a transput operation started on behalf of some $P_i$ has terminated. In this case, the interrupt must be reflected to the appropriate $P_i$. In contrast, emulating a single transput operation for $P_i$ may require several transput operations, so device-completion interrupts often indicate that $V$ may proceed to the next step of emulating an operation already in progress. Such interrupts are not reflected. If the computer communicates with devices through registers with addresses in main store, all access to that region of store must cause traps so that $V$ can emulate the transput. Address translation also becomes quite complex. We will defer discussing this subject until Chapter 3.

A good test of a virtualizing kernel is to let one of its processes be another virtualizing kernel. This arrangement can also be useful to test out a new version of $V$. However, dangerous operations can be quite slow when there are many levels. The number of reflections grows exponentially with the number of levels. For example, consider Figure 1.11, in which there are two levels of virtualizing kernel, $V_1$ and $V_2$, above which sits an ordinary operating system kernel, **OS**, above which a compiler is running. The compiler executes a single service call (marked *) at

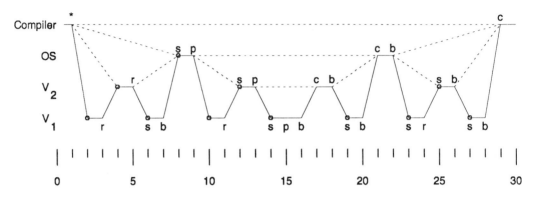

**Figure 1.11** Emulating a service call

time 1. As far as the compiler is concerned, **OS** performs the service and lets the compiler continue (marked c) at time 29. The dashed line at the level of the compiler indicates the compiler's perception that no activity below its level takes place during the interval.

From the point of view of **OS**, a trap occurs at time 8 (marked by a dot on the control-flow line). This trap appears to come directly from the compiler, as shown by the dashed line connecting the compiler at time 1 and the OS at time 8. **OS** services the trap (marked s). For simplicity, we assume that it needs to perform only one privileged instruction (marked p) to service the trap, which it executes at time 9. Lower levels of software (which **OS** cannot distinguish from hardware) emulate this instruction, allowing **OS** to continue at time 21. It then switches context back to the compiler (marked b) at time 22. The dashed line from **OS** at time 22 to the compiler at time 29 shows the effect of this context switch.

The situation is more complicated from the point of view of $V_2$. At time 4, it receives a trap that tells it that its client has executed a privileged instruction while in virtual non-privileged state. $V_2$ therefore reflects this trap at time 5 (marked r) back to **OS**. Later, at time 12, $V_2$ receives a second trap, this time because its client has executed a privileged instruction in virtual privileged state. $V_2$ services this trap by emulating the instruction itself at time 13. By time 17, the underlying levels allow it to continue, and at time 18 it switches context back to **OS**. The last trap occurs at time 25, when its client has attempted to perform a context switch (which is privileged) when in virtual privileged state. $V_2$ services this trap by changing is client to virtual non-privileged state and switching back to the client at time 26.

$V_1$ has the busiest schedule of all. It reflects traps that arrive at time 2, 10, and 23. (The trap at time 23 comes from the context-switch instruction executed by **OS**.) It emulates instructions for its client when traps occur at times 5, 14, 19, and 27.

This example demonstrates the Level Principle: Each software level is just a data structure as far as its supporting level is concerned. It also shows how a single privileged instruction in the compiler became two privileged instructions in **OS** (p and b), which became four in $V_2$ (r, p, b, and b) and eight in $V_1$. In general, the situation can be far worse. A single privileged instruction at one level might require many instructions at its supporting level to emulate it.

The virtualizing kernel can be complex, and the emulation of privileged instructions can be slow. These drawbacks can be mitigated to some extent.

- Don't try to emulate one device by another.
- Disallow some features, such as self-modifying channel programs. Of course, such a design will compromise the purity of the virtual machine and will make it harder to transfer programs from bare machines to run under the virtual-machine operating system.
- Provide some extra features so that processes won't have to use as many privileged instructions. A certain amount of file support (discussed in Chapter 6) could help. This design makes it harder to transfer programs from the virtual-machine operating system to a bare machine.
- Use special hardware to pass traps directly to the correct software level. The IBM 370 has some hardware support for VM/370, for example.

# 7 FURTHER READING

A number of other operating system textbooks are available. Brinch Hansen's early text (1973) is especially good in its treatment of concurrency issues. Another early classic was written by Madnick and Donovan (1972). The standard texts by Shaw (1974) and Habermann (1976) are full of useful details. Calingaert (1982) presents an overview of a large number of subjects, whereas Turner (1986) shows a few essential subjects in some depth. Excellent texts are by Deitel (1983) and by Peterson and Silberschatz (1985). Some advanced subjects can be found in a new book by Maekawa (1987). Beck's book on systems programming (1985) devotes an excellent chapter to operating systems. Recently, several books have appeared that cover both the theory of operating systems and an annotated listing of a Unix-like kernel. These texts, including two by Comer (1984; 1987) and one by Tanenbaum (1987), are an excellent source of information about operating systems and how to build them. Books describing the internals of particular operating systems, such as the book on VMS by Kenah and Bate (1984), are often full of fascinating detail.

The distinction between mechanism and policy was championed by the Hydra operating system (Levin *et al.*, 1977). The Modula programming language that we use in examples was defined by Wirth (1972). It is based on his earlier language Pascal (Jensen and Wirth, 1974). Virtual machines are discussed in a survey article by Goldberg (1974), and a case study for the PDP-11 is described by Popek (1975).

# 8  EXERCISES

1. Compute the utilization for open shop. We define the **utilization** $u$ as the fraction of time used for computation. Assume that a typical job requires $r = 10$ seconds to read in from cards, $c = 3$ seconds to compute and $p = 30$ seconds to print the results on paper. Programmers sign up for 15-minute slots and run their programs twice per slot.

2. Compute the utilization for the same situation, using operator-driven shop. Assume that an operator takes $s = 30$ seconds to remove the output from one job and set up the next job. There are enough jobs to ensure that the operator always has another job to start as soon as one finishes.

3. Compute the utilization for the same situation, using offline transput. Assume that it takes only 1/100 as long to read information from tape as from cards and only 1/100 as long to write information to tape as to paper. The resident monitor takes $s = 0.1$ seconds to reset the machine between jobs. The operator spends 60 seconds to unload and load tapes after every ten jobs. There are several offline computers, so there is no bottleneck reading jobs and printing results.

4. Compute the utilization for the same situation, using spooling. Assume that the computer has enough card readers and printers so that there are always jobs waiting to be run and printing is not a bottleneck. It takes only 1/1000 as long to read or write information from or to disk as from or to cards or paper. The computer spends 1 percent of its time servicing interrupts for transput; this time is not counted as computation time. It takes $s = 0.01$ seconds to reset the machine between jobs.

5. Construct formulas for exercises 1−4 that describe the utilization in terms of the parameters $r$, $c$, $p$, and $s$.

6. Find out what computers are available at your institution and discover whether they use spooling, batch, interactive, or some other kind of computing.

7. In an interactive multiprogramming situation, several people could be running the same program at once. Would there be one process or many to support this situation?

8. If two processes are using the very same main storage, what data do they *not* share?

9. Throughout the book, we will suggest various service calls that the kernel may provide. Suggest a few that you think every kernel should have.

10. How can a user submit a service call?

11. How can a device submit a service call?

12. Does a service call always require a context switch? Does it always require a process switch?

13. When a device interrupts, is there always a context switch?

14. Describe the user in two ways, using the Level Principle.

15. Is the Pascal compiler part of the kernel?

16. Is the code that causes the disk to send some data into main store part of the kernel?

17. Experiment to find out what restrictions your installation places on passwords. Does it disallow passwords that are too simple? Does it prevent you from making very long passwords?

18. Three conventions for communicating the arguments of a service call to the kernel are to place them on a stack, in registers, or right after the call. What are the advantages and disadvantages of these three strategies?

19. In the example of virtual machines, with a compiler above an operating system above two levels of virtualizing kernel, how many privileged instructions would be executed at each level if the instruction executed by the compiler can be emulated without use of privileged instructions by the operating system?

# Time Management

The first resource we will discuss is time. Time management is usually called **scheduling**. The goal of scheduling is to provide good service to all the processes that are currently competing for the computing resource, that is, the execution of instructions. We can distinguish several classes of scheduling based on how often decisions must be made.

**Long-term scheduling** decides which jobs or job steps to start next. In a spooling system, this decision is made when a job finishes and is based on the order in which other jobs have arrived and on their priorities. In batch multiprogramming, the decision may be based on the different requirements of the competing jobs and the resources currently available. Interactive multiprogramming often does not have this level of scheduling at all; it is up to the user to decide which job steps to run. We will not discuss long-term scheduling as such in this book, but Chapter 4 is devoted to some of the resource-contention issues that are central to that subject.

**Medium-term scheduling** decides which running processes to **block** (deny service) temporarily, because resources (such as main store) are overcommitted or because a resource request cannot be satisfied at the moment. Chapter 3 discusses the intricacies of space management and describes policies for medium-term scheduling.

**Short-term scheduling**, the subject of this chapter, decides how to share the computer among all the processes that currently want to compute. Such decisions may be made frequently (tens of times each second) to try to provide good service to all the processes. When the medium- or long-term scheduler readies a process or when a transput event that the process is waiting for finishes, the process arrives in the domain of the short-term scheduler. It stays there until it terminates, it waits for transput, or a higher-level scheduler decides to block it. Processes generally alternate between a computing burst, during which they are in the short-term scheduler, and a transput burst, during which they are in a wait list.

Figure 2.1 shows these three levels of scheduling. Within the domain of short-term scheduling, a process may be either running or ready to run. The short-term scheduler is in charge of deciding which ready process should be running at any time. Within the domain of medium-term scheduling, a process may be running (that is, it may have entered the domain of the short-term scheduler), may be ready to run, or may be waiting for some resource like transput. The medium-term scheduler is in charge of deciding when ready processes should be allowed to enter the domain of the short-term scheduler and when they should leave that domain. This decision is based on an attempt to prevent overcommitment of space, as we will see in Chapter 3, as well as a desire to balance compute-bound processes with transput-bound processes. The long-term scheduler distinguishes between ready and running processes.

We have already seen the distinction between compute-bound and transput-bound processes. From the point of view of the short-term scheduler, a compute-bound process remains in view for a long time, since it does not terminate soon and seldom waits for transput. For this reason, we will call compute-bound processes **long processes**.

In contrast, a transput-bound process comes and goes very quickly, since it disappears from the view of the short-term scheduler as soon as it waits for transput. A process that interacts heavily with the user tends to be transput-bound. The user gives it a command, which it interprets and acts on. Shortly thereafter,

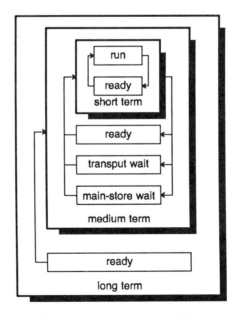

**Figure 2.1** Three levels of scheduling

the process is ready to receive the next command. The user, however, is still puzzling over the response to the previous command. The process spends most of its time waiting for the user to submit the next command and only a little time computing in response to the command. Text editor programs usually exhibit this sort of behavior. Other transput-bound processes are not interactive at all but spend a lot of time bringing data in from devices or sending data back out, performing very little computation in between. Programs written in Cobol often have this flavor. Both kinds of transput-bound process are similar in that small amounts of computation are sandwiched between longer periods of waiting. For this reason, we will call them **short processes**.

It is important to give special service to interactive processes, because otherwise the user might get very frustrated. A user interacting with a process would ideally like to see an immediate response to every command. Failing that, "consistent" response is better than good average response. Response that always takes about 2 seconds is better than response that averages about 1 second but occasionally takes 10 or only 0.5. Formally, a low variance of response time is better than a low mean.

Transput-bound processes must also be given special treatment. Here the mean is more important than the variance. Let's take as an example a process that needs to compute for 1 millisecond and then waits 20 milliseconds for transput. This sequence repeats 1000 times. In total, the process needs 1 second of computation and 20 seconds of transput, a total of 21 seconds. But if it is delayed half a second every time it becomes ready, it will take 521 seconds. Even if some delays are longer, a small average delay will pay off handsomely. A 1-millisecond average delay will allow the process to finish in 22 seconds.

# 1 GOALS, MEASURES, AND ASSUMPTIONS

As mentioned earlier, there are several competing goals that scheduling policies aim to fulfill. One is "good throughput" — getting lots of work done. For short-term scheduling, good throughput means minimizing the number of process switches, because each one costs some time during which no productive work is accomplished.

The other goal is "good service." We can be more precise by defining three related measures that tell how well we are treating a particular process. Say a process $p$ requires $t$ time in execution before it can leave the ready list because it will either finish or will need to wait for something. Then we define the following service measures for that process.

> **response time** $T$: time that $p$ is present; finish time $-$ arrival time
> **missed time** $M$: $T - t$
> **penalty ratio** $P$: $T / t$
> **response ratio** $R$: $t / T$

The **response time** $T$ counts not only how long $p$ needs, but also how long it sits in the ready list while other processes are run. It might wait its turn for a while. Once it starts, we might be nasty and stop it after some time, letting it continue later. The entire time that process $p$ is on the ready list (until it leaves our view to go to other lists) is charged to $T$. The process is not visible to the short-term scheduler while it is waiting for transput or other resources, and therefore such wait time is not included in $T$.

The **missed time** $M$ is the same thing, except we don't count the amount of time during which $p$ is actually running. $M$ measures the amount of time during which $p$ would like to run but is prevented.

The **response ratio** $R$ and the **penalty ratio** $P$ are inverses of each other. $R$ represents the fraction of the time that $p$ is receiving service. If the response ratio $R$ is 1, then $p$ never sits in the ready list while some other process runs. If the response ratio $R$ is 1/100, then $P = 100$ and the process seems to be taking 100 times as long as it should; the user may be annoyed. A response ratio greater than 1 doesn't make any sense. Similarly, the penalty ratio $P$ ranges from 1 (which is a perfect value) upward.

If we are discussing a class of processes with similar requirements, like short processes or long processes, we extend this notation as follows.

> $T(t)$: average response time for processes needing $t$ time
> $M(t)$: $T(t) - t$
> $P(t)$: $T(t) / t$
> $R(t)$: $t / T(t)$

If the average response measures turn out to be independent of $t$, we will just write $T()$, $M()$, $P()$, and $R()$.

We will also refer on occasion to kernel time and idle time. **Kernel time** is the time spent by the kernel in making policy decisions and carrying them out. This figure includes context-switch and process-switch time. A well-tuned operating system tries to keep kernel time between 10 and 30 percent. **Idle time** is spent when the ready list is empty and no fruitful work can be accomplished.

One surprising theoretical result sheds light on the tradeoff between providing good service to short and to long processes. It turns out that no matter what scheduling method you use, if you ignore context- and process-switching costs, you can't help one class of jobs without hurting the other class. In fact, a minor improvement for short processes causes a disproportionate degradation for long processes. We will therefore be especially interested in comparing various policies with respect to how well they treat processes with different time requirements.

The values we will get for the service measures under different policies will depend on how many processes there are, how fast they arrive, and how long they need to run. A fairly simple set of assumptions will suffice for our purposes. First, we will assume that processes arrive (into the view of the short-term scheduler) in a pattern described by the **exponential distribution**. One way to describe this pattern is to say that no matter how recently the previous process arrived, the next one will arrive within $t$ time with probability $1 - e^{-\alpha t}$. As $t$ goes to infinity, this probability goes to $1 - e^{-\infty} = 1$. The average time until the next arrival is $1/\alpha$. Another way to describe this pattern is to say that the probability that $k$ processes will arrive within one time unit is $e^{-\alpha}\alpha^k / k!$. The reason we pick this particular distribution is that even though it looks forbidding, it turns out that the exponential distribution is the easiest to deal with mathematically and still mirror the way processes actually do arrive in practice. The symbol $\alpha$ ("alpha") is a **parameter** of the distribution, which means that we adjust $\alpha$ to form a distribution with the particular behavior we want. We call $\alpha$ the **arrival rate**, since as $\alpha$ increases, arrivals happen more frequently. Figure 2.2 shows the exponential distribution for various values of $\alpha$. The exponential distribution is **memoryless**: The expected time to the next arrival is always $1/\alpha$, no matter how long it has been since the previous arrival. Observations on real operating systems have shown that the exponential arrival rate assumption is reasonable.

Our second assumption is that the service time required by processes also follows the exponential distribution, this time with parameter $\beta$ ("beta"):

Probability($k$ processes serviced in one time unit) $= e^{-\beta}\beta^k / k!$

The memoryless property here implies that the expected amount of time still needed by the current process is always $1/\beta$, no matter how long the process has been running so far.

We will often combine $\alpha$ and $\beta$ to form $\rho$ ("rho"), the **saturation** level, which represents how busy the computer is on the average. We define $\rho$ to be $\alpha / \beta$. If $\rho$ is 0, new processes never arrive, so the machine is completely idle. If $\rho$ is 1, processes arrive on the average just exactly at the same rate as they can be

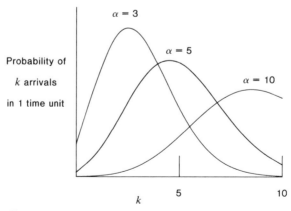

**Figure 2.2** Probability of $k$ arrivals under the exponential distribution

finished. If $\rho$ is greater than 1, processes are coming faster than they can be served. In this last case, we would expect the ready list to get longer and longer. In fact, even if $\rho$ is just 1, the expected length of the ready list is unbounded. The value of $\rho$ affects the response measures differently for different scheduling policies. We will therefore express these measures in terms of $\rho$.

As you can see, the formal study of time management involves a certain amount of mathematics. It is important to realize that any comparison of policies requires that there be a way of describing their behavior (such as $R$) and a way to characterize the situation in which the policies are measured (such as the distribution of service times). We will express the behavior of various policies using the notation just presented but will omit all the derivations. We will discuss formal analysis later in the Perspective section.

# 2 POLICIES

As we have seen, short-term scheduling refers to allocating time to processes that are in the ready list. Every time a process **arrives** at the ready list, we will treat it as a new process. It may truly be a new process, but more often it is an old one that has been brought back to the ready list from outside the short-term scheduler. It may have returned because the transput it was waiting for has completed, some resource it was requesting has been granted, or the medium-term scheduler has decided to favor it. Every time it leaves the ready list, either because it has terminated or because it must wait for something like transput, we will forget about the process. We will say that the process has **departed** when we do not need to state why it has left. This narrow view will allow us to concentrate on the fundamentals of short-term scheduling.

Unfortunately, no policy is truly fair. Any improvements in performance for one class of processes is at the expense of degraded performance for some other class. We will therefore examine how policies treat a wide range of classes. For each policy, we will first show its behavior for a simple set of processes:

| Process name | Arrival time | Service required |
|:---:|:---:|:---:|
| A | 0 | 3 |
| B | 1 | 5 |
| C | 3 | 2 |
| D | 9 | 5 |
| E | 12 | 5 |

This set depicted in Figure 2.3.

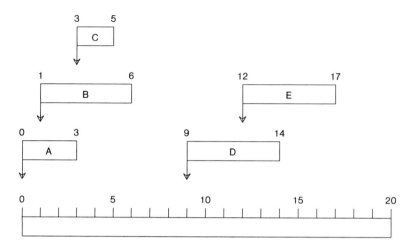

**Figure 2.3** Processes requiring service

The time units are not important; if we like, we can imagine they are seconds. We assume that the arrival time and service time required are whole numbers of whatever unit we have picked.

Second, we will compare scheduling policies by simulating them for a large number of arrivals. Figure 2.4 shows the penalty ratio for many of the policies we will study as a function of time required. This figure is based on a simulation of 50,000 processes. Service times were randomly drawn from an exponential distribution with $\beta = 1.0$, and arrival rates were similarly drawn from an exponential distribution with $\alpha = 0.8$. The saturation level was therefore $\rho = 0.8$. Statistics were gathered on each process except for the first 100 to finish in order to measure the **steady state**, which is the behavior of a system once initial fluctuations have disappeared. Processes were categorized into 100 service-time percentiles, each of which had about 500 processes. The average penalty ratio for each percentile is graphed in the figure. The lines in the graph have been smoothed slightly (simulation results are somewhat bumpy).

The average service time needed by processes in each percentile is shown in Figure 2.5. Figure 2.6 shows the missed time for each percentile under the various methods. Although these simulation results only display the situation for one value of $\rho$, they provide useful insight into the general behavior of the algorithms we will study.

## 2.1  First come, first served (FCFS)

In keeping with the Law of Diminishing Returns, we will start with a method that has horrid performance. Like many very poor methods, it is easy to dream up, easy to implement, and easy to disparage. Under FCFS, the short-term scheduler runs each process until it departs. Processes that arrive while another process is being served wait in line in the order that they arrive. This method is also called "first

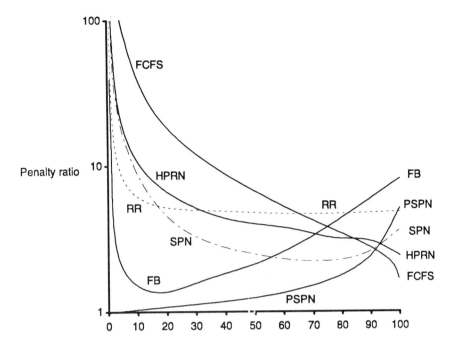

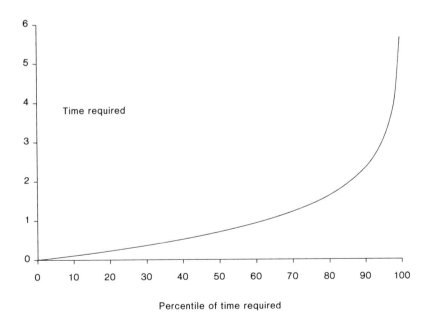

**Figure 2.5** Average service time for each percentile

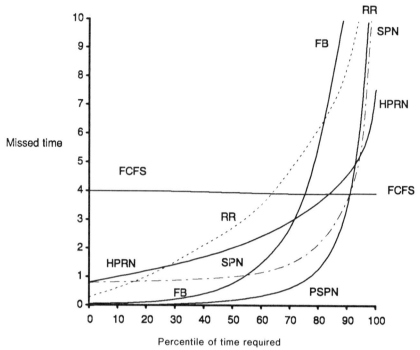

**Figure 2.6** Missed time for short-term scheduling policies

in, first out" (FIFO).

Figure 2.7 shows how FCFS schedules our standard set of processes. The dark regions indicate missed time for each process.

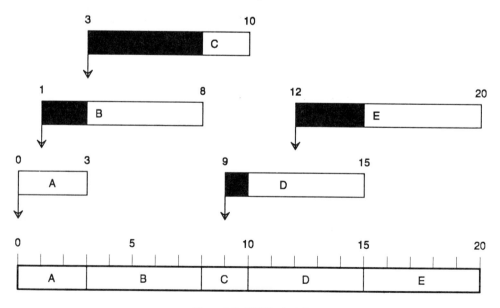

**Figure 2.7** FCFS schedule

The following table shows the same information.

| Process name | Arrival time | Service required | Start time | Finish time | T | M | P |
|---|---|---|---|---|---|---|---|
| A | 0 | 3 | 0 | 3 | 3 | 0 | 1.0 |
| B | 1 | 5 | 3 | 8 | 7 | 2 | 1.4 |
| C | 3 | 2 | 8 | 10 | 7 | 5 | 3.5 |
| D | 9 | 5 | 10 | 15 | 6 | 1 | 1.2 |
| E | 12 | 5 | 15 | 20 | 8 | 3 | 1.6 |
| Mean | | | | | 6.2 | 2.2 | 1.74 |

FCFS is an example of a **non-preemptive** policy, which means that we never block a process once it has started to run until it leaves the domain of the short-term scheduler. (We might terminate a process that has exceeded an initial time estimate, but such termination is different from preemption.) The decision of when to run a particular process is based solely on the relative order in which it arrives at the ready list.

Non-preemptive policies are an example of the **Hysteresis Principle**, which we will encounter repeatedly.

---

### Hysteresis Principle

Resist change.

---

All change has a cost. In our case, preemption involves switching to a new process, which requires updating software tables and often hardware tables as well. Non-preemptive scheduling policies avoid the cost of change by resisting process switching until it is inevitable.

How well does FCFS work? Long processes love it, and short ones hate it. To see why, assume that four processes enter the ready list at almost the same time. They require 1, 100, 1, and 100 seconds, respectively. Here is how the measures come out:

| Process name | Arrival time | Service required | Start time | Finish time | T | M | P |
|---|---|---|---|---|---|---|---|
| A | 0 | 1 | 0 | 1 | 1 | 0 | 1.00 |
| B | 0 | 100 | 1 | 101 | 101 | 1 | 1.01 |
| C | 0 | 1 | 101 | 102 | 102 | 101 | 102.00 |
| D | 0 | 100 | 102 | 202 | 202 | 102 | 2.02 |
| Mean | | | | | 101.5 | 51.0 | 28.1 |

The penalty ratio $P$ for process **C** is indefensible. Any short process caught behind a long one will suffer a wait time much longer than the time it really needs to execute. Long processes, in contrast, will generally receive reasonable values for $P$, even if they have to wait behind a few other processes. Process **D** had to wait but still got a pretty good penalty ratio.

The penalty ratio for FCFS, as seen in Figure 2.4, is very bad for short processes. One third of all processes have a penalty ratio worse than 10. The upper 10 percent of all processes, however, find FCFS has an excellent penalty ratio (less than 2.5).

The amount of missed time under FCFS is fairly equitable, as seen in Figure 2.6. All classes of processes had about the same missed time: 4 seconds. This result stands to reason. The amount of missed time for some process depends on the processes ahead of it in the ready list and is independent of the amount of service the process itself needs.

Given our assumptions that both arrival and service time fit an exponential distribution, we can express the behavior of the first come, first served scheduling policy analytically, without resorting to simulation.

$$M() = \frac{\rho}{\beta(1-\rho)} \qquad T(t) = t + \frac{\rho}{\beta(1-\rho)} \qquad P(t) = 1 + \frac{\rho}{t\beta(1-\rho)}$$

These formulas represent averages, and only hold for the steady state. The first formula predicts our simulated result that $M = 4$, independent of $t$. The third formula predicts our result that the penalty ratio is high for short processes and low for long processes.

What if $\rho > 1$? FCFS eventually services every process, although the missed time gets longer and longer as $\rho$ remains above 1. (Actually, $\rho$ cannot remain higher than 1 for very long, since the rate at which processes arrive at the short-term scheduler depends to some extent on the rate at which they leave. We do not actually have an infinite population of processes.) We will see that some other methods do not guarantee eventual service. The situation in which a process is ready to run but never gets any service is called **starvation**. Starvation while waiting for other resources besides time is discussed in Chapters 4 and 8.

## 2.2 Round robin (RR)

Our next example, **round robin**, is a vast improvement over FCFS. The intent of round robin is to provide good response ratios for short processes as well as long processes. In fact, it provides identical average response ratio for all processes, unlike FCFS, which provides identical average response time.

The round robin policy services a process only for a single **quantum** $q$ of time. Typical values of $q$ range between 1/60 and 1 second. If the process has not finished within its quantum, it is interrupted at the end of the quantum and placed at the rear of the ready queue. It will wait there for its turn to come around again and then run for another quantum. This periodic interruption continues until the process departs. Each process is therefore serviced in bursts until it finishes. New arrivals enter the ready queue at the rear.

Round robin can be tuned by adjusting the parameter $q$. If we set $q$ so high that it exceeds the service requirement for all processes, RR becomes just like FCFS. As $q$ approaches 0, RR becomes like **processor sharing** (PS), which means that every process thinks it is getting constant service from a processor that is slower proportionally to the number of competing processes. The Hysteresis Principle tells us that we should resist such frequent switching. In fact, PS is only theoretically interesting, because as $q$ approaches 0, process switching happens more frequently, and kernel time rises toward 100 percent. The trick is to set $q$ small enough so that RR is fair but high enough so that kernel time is reasonable.

Figure 2.8 shows how RR schedules our sample processes for both $q = 1$ and $q = 4$. If a process finishes during its quantum, another process is started immediately and is given a full quantum. Newly arrived processes are put at the end of the ready list. If a process arrives at the same time as a quantum finishes, we assume that the arrival occurs slightly before the quantum actually expires.

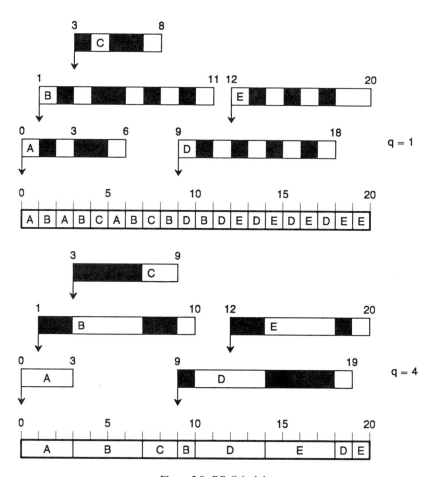

**Figure 2.8** RR Schedule

The statistics for RR are therefore as follows.

$$q = 1$$

| Process name | Arrival time | Service required | Finish time | $T$ | $M$ | $P$ |
|:---:|:---:|:---:|:---:|:---:|:---:|:---:|
| A | 0 | 3 | 6 | 6 | 3 | 2.0 |
| B | 1 | 5 | 11 | 10 | 5 | 2.0 |
| C | 3 | 2 | 8 | 5 | 3 | 2.5 |
| D | 9 | 5 | 18 | 9 | 4 | 1.8 |
| E | 12 | 5 | 20 | 8 | 3 | 1.6 |
| Mean | | | | 7.6 | 3.6 | 1.98 |

$$q = 4$$

| Process name | Arrival time | Service required | Finish time | $T$ | $M$ | $P$ |
|:---:|:---:|:---:|:---:|:---:|:---:|:---:|
| A | 0 | 3 | 3 | 3 | 0 | 1.0 |
| B | 1 | 5 | 10 | 9 | 4 | 1.8 |
| C | 3 | 2 | 9 | 6 | 4 | 3.0 |
| D | 9 | 5 | 19 | 10 | 5 | 2.0 |
| E | 12 | 5 | 20 | 8 | 3 | 1.6 |
| Mean | | | | 7.2 | 3.2 | 1.88 |

Figures 2.4 and 2.6 display RR with a quantum of 0.1. The shortest 10 percent of all processes can be serviced in one quantum. All other processes suffer a penalty ratio of approximately 5. RR therefore penalizes all processes about the same, unlike FCFS, which causes all processes to miss the same amount of time. Figure 2.6 shows that the missed time is very small (on the order of one quantum) for very short processes and that the missed time rises steadily as processes become longer.

Under PS, which is a limiting case of RR, we have the following service measures:

$$T(t) = \frac{t}{1 - \rho} \quad P() = \frac{1}{1 - \rho}$$

The second formula agrees with our observation that the penalty ratio has the value 5, independent of $t$.

## 2.3  Shortest process next (SPN)

We have seen that RR improves the response ratio for short processes but that it requires preemption to do so. The SPN method is an attempt to have the same effect without preemption. Instead, it requires a different ingredient: explicit information about the service-time requirements for each process. When a process must be selected from the ready list to execute next, the one with the shortest service-time requirement is chosen.

How are these service times discovered? It obviously won't do to execute the process, see how long it takes, and then schedule it according to this knowledge. One alternative is to have the user characterize the process before it starts. For example, a process could be characterized as **transput-bound** or **compute-bound**. A highly interactive process, such as a text editor, is transput-bound. A long simulation that uses internally generated random data is compute-bound. More precisely, the average service time needed (averaged over each entry into the short-term scheduler) could be specified. It seems an unreasonable burden to have the user characterize each process. Processes could describe themselves (in their load image, discussed in Chapter 3), but that description would be at best a guess. Besides, processes often go through phases, some of which require more computation between transput events and some of which require less.

Instead, the short-term scheduler can accumulate service statistics for each process every time it departs. Say a given process $p$ used $s$ seconds of time during its most recent stay in the short-term ready list. Then the **exponential average** $e_p$ can be updated this way:

$$e_p' := 0.9\, e_p \; + \; 0.1\, s$$

The number 0.9 is called a "smoothing factor," and may be set to a higher number (like 0.99) to make the estimate less responsive to change, or to a lower number (like 0.7) to make the estimate more responsive to change. The initial estimate, for the first time the process arrives, can be the average service time for all processes.

To demonstrate the SPN method, we will assume that the scheduler has complete and accurate knowledge of the service requirement of each process. Our sample set of processes is serviced as shown in Figure 2.9.

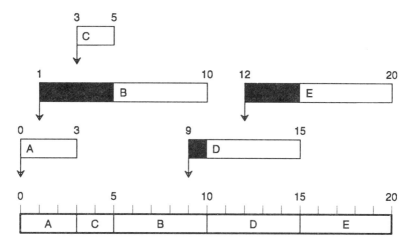

**Figure 2.9** SPN Schedule

Here are the statistics when these processes are scheduled under SPN:

| Process name | Arrival time | Service required | Start time | Finish time | T | M | P |
|---|---|---|---|---|---|---|---|
| A | 0 | 3 | 0 | 3 | 3 | 0 | 1.0 |
| B | 1 | 5 | 5 | 10 | 9 | 4 | 1.8 |
| C | 3 | 2 | 3 | 5 | 2 | 0 | 1.0 |
| D | 9 | 5 | 10 | 15 | 6 | 1 | 1.2 |
| E | 12 | 5 | 15 | 20 | 8 | 3 | 1.6 |
| Mean | | | | | 5.6 | 1.6 | 1.32 |

The response time under SPN is particularly good for short processes, as you might expect. In contrast, long processes may wait a long time indeed, especially if $\rho$ approaches 1. Overall, $T()$ and $M()$ are lower under SPN than any method that does not use a time estimate. Although analytic results are hard to derive, Figures 2.4 and 2.6, our simulation results, show that the penalty ratio and missed time for SPN are better than for RR, except for the shortest 15 percent of all processes, where the figures are still far better than for FCFS.

## 2.4 Preemptive shortest process next (PSPN)

We saw that RR achieves a good penalty ratio by using preemption, and that SPN does even better by using extra information about each process. We would expect to do still better by combining these techniques. The PSPN preempts the current process when another process arrives with a total service time requirement less than the remaining service time required by the current process. The value of $T(t)$

turns out to be lower than for SPN for all but the longest 10 percent of all processes in our simulation of Figure 2.4.

Our five-process example behaves the same under SPN and PSPN; there is never any preemption because short processes do not arrive near the start of execution of long processes. Figures 2.4 and 2.6 show that for all but the longest 7 percent of all processes, PSPN is better than SPN. It has an excellent penalty ratio, and the missed time stays very low for a large majority of processes. Even for very long processes, PSPN is not much worse than RR. In fact, PSPN gives the best achievable average penalty ratio because it keeps the ready list as short as possible. It manages this feat by directing resources toward the process that will finish soonest, and will therefore shorten the ready list soonest. A short ready list means reduced contention, which leads to a low penalty ratio.

## 2.5  Highest penalty ratio next (HPRN)

Non-preemptive scheduling policies seem to give unfair advantage either to very long processes (FCFS) or to very short ones (SPN). The HPRN method tries to be fairer and still not introduce preemption. As a new process waits in the ready list, its value of $P$, which starts at 1, begins to rise. After it has waited $w$ time on the ready list, $P = (w + t)/t$. When an old process departs, the ready process with the highest penalty ratio is selected for execution. As long as the saturation is not unreasonable ($\rho < 1$), the HPRN method will not starve even very long processes, since eventually their penalty ratio reaches a high value.

If $t$ is not known, it can be estimated by an exponential average of service times during previous compute bursts, as we discussed earlier. Alternatively, we can base the HPRN method on a medium-term penalty ratio, which is $(M + t)/t$, where M is the total time missed while the process has languished either on the short-term ready list or on a medium-term main-store wait list (but not on a transput-wait list) and $t$ is the total cpu time used during previous compute bursts.

HPRN strikes a nice balance between FCFS and SPN. If we use the actual value of $t$, our sample process set behaves the same under HPRN and FCFS. Our simulation, reported in Figures 2.4 and 2.6, also used the actual value of $t$. HPRN fits neatly between FCFS and SPN, for short processes, where HPRN is much like SPN; for middle-length processes, where HPRN has an intermediate penalty ratio; and for very long processes, where SPN becomes worse than FCFS but where HPRN is still in the middle.

However, HPRN has some disadvantages. First, it is not preemptive, so it cannot beat RR or PSPN for short processes. A short process that unluckily arrives just after a long process has started executing will still have to wait a very long time. Second, it is generally not as good as SPN (at least in our simulation), which uses the same techniques: knowledge of process length without preemption. Third, HPRN is more expensive to implement, since the penalty ratio must be calculated for every waiting process whenever a running process completes.

## 2.6 Multiple-level feedback (FB)

The multiple-level feedback method splits the ready list into a number of queues: queue 0, queue 1, queue 2, and so on. Lower-numbered queues have higher priority. When the current process is interrupted at the end of its quantum, a new process is selected from the front of the lowest-numbered queue that has any processes. After a process has used a certain number of quanta in its queue, it is placed at the end of the next-higher-numbered queue. (The word "feedback" in the name of this method refers to the fact that processes can move from one queue to another.) In Figure 2.10, a process is allowed only one quantum in its queue before being bumped to the next one. The statistics for our process set are as follows.

| Process name | Arrival time | Service required | Finish time | $T$ | $M$ | $P$ |
|---|---|---|---|---|---|---|
| A | 0 | 3 | 7 | 7 | 4 | 2.3 |
| B | 1 | 5 | 18 | 17 | 12 | 3.4 |
| C | 3 | 2 | 6 | 3 | 1 | 1.5 |
| D | 9 | 5 | 19 | 10 | 5 | 2.0 |
| E | 12 | 5 | 20 | 8 | 3 | 1.6 |
| Mean | | | | 9.0 | 5.0 | 2.16 |

Short processes have priority over long ones, since they finish while still in the first queue, whereas long processes eventually migrate to low priority queues. $T()$ is the same as for RR, so since short processes do better than under RR, long

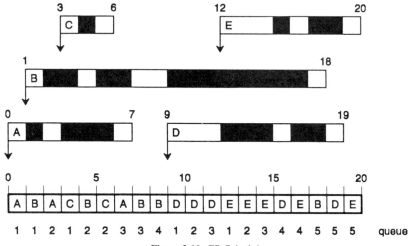

**Figure 2.10** FB Schedule

processes must do more poorly. This prediction is borne out by the results in Figures 2.4 and 2.6. FB is better than RR for about 80 percent of all processes but worse for the longest 20 percent.

The FB method has several variations.

(1)    Let the quantum size depend on the queue. A queue numbered $n$ could have a quantum of length $2^n q$, where $q$ is the "basic quantum" size. Therefore, the queues have quanta of sizes $q, 2q, 4q, 8q$, and so on. The quantum given to any process is based on the queue it is taken from. A process that needs a long time suffers process switches after times $q, 3q, 7q, 15q$, and so on. The total number of process switches is therefore $\log(t(p)/q)$ instead of $t(p)/q$, which is the number needed by RR. Therefore, this method reduces process switch overhead while still behaving much like RR.

The quantum length could be calculated by slower-growing functions, such as $n \cdot q$. Such functions keep the quantum size within reasonable bounds while still reducing the total number of process switches needed for long processes.

Figure 2.11 shows how our sample processes are treated with exponentially growing quanta.

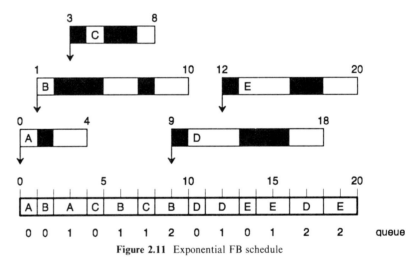

**Figure 2.11** Exponential FB schedule

The statistics for our process set are as follows.

| Process name | Arrival time | Service required | Finish time | $T$ | $M$ | $P$ |
|---|---|---|---|---|---|---|
| A | 0 | 3 | 4 | 4 | 1 | 1.3 |
| B | 1 | 5 | 10 | 9 | 4 | 1.8 |
| C | 3 | 2 | 8 | 5 | 3 | 2.5 |
| D | 9 | 5 | 18 | 9 | 4 | 1.8 |
| E | 12 | 5 | 20 | 8 | 3 | 1.6 |
| Mean | | | | 7.0 | 3.0 | 1.8 |

(2) Let a process in queue $n$ be scheduled by RR for $2^n$ (or perhaps just $n$) quanta before being demoted to the next queue.

(3) Promote a process to a higher-priority queue after it spends a certain amount of time waiting for service in its current queue.

(4) Instead of granting absolute priority to low-numbered queues, grant slices of time to each queue, with lower-numbered queues receiving larger slices.

These variants can be used by themselves or in any combination.

## 2.7  Selfish round robin (SRR)

The selfish round robin method adds a new dimension to round robin by giving better service to processes that have been executing for a while than to newcomers. Processes in the ready list are partitioned into two lists: **new** and **accepted**. New processes wait. Accepted processes are serviced by RR. The **priority** of a new process increases at rate $a$. The priority of an accepted process increases at rate $b$. Both $a$ and $b$ are **parameters**; that is, they can be adjusted to tune the method. When the priority of a new process reaches the priority of an accepted process, that new process becomes accepted. If all accepted processes finish, the highest priority new process is accepted.

Assume that there are no ready processes, when the first one, **A**, arrives. It has priority 0 to begin with. Since there are no other accepted processes, **A** is accepted immediately. After a while another process, **B**, arrives. As long as $b/a < 1$, **B**'s priority will eventually catch up to **A**'s, so it is accepted; now both **A** and **B** have the same priority. We can see that all accepted processes share a common priority (which rises at rate $b$); that makes this policy easy to implement. Even if $b/a > 1$, **A** will eventually finish, and then **B** can be accepted.

Adjusting the relative values of $a$ and $b$ has a great influence on the behavior of SRR. If $b/a \geqslant 1$, a new process is not accepted until all the accepted processes have finished, so SRR becomes FCFS. If $b/a = 0$, all processes are accepted immediately, so SRR becomes RR. If $0 < b/a < 1$, accepted processes are selfish, but not completely.

To demonstrate how SRR schedules our running example, let us set $a = 2$ and $b = 1$. If a new process achieves the priority of the accepted processes at the end of a quantum, we place it on the ready list first and then preempt the running process. Figure 2.12 shows the resulting schedule, including the priority of each process at the end of each quantum. The letter d indicates that the process is done.

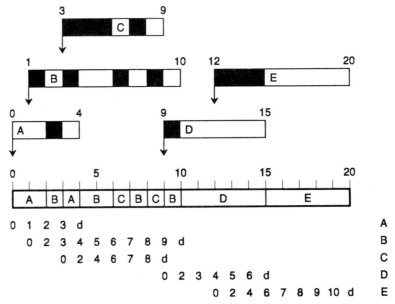

**Figure 2.12** SRR Schedule

The statistics for our process set are as follows.

| Process name | Arrival time | Service required | Finish time | T | M | P |
|---|---|---|---|---|---|---|
| A | 0 | 3 | 4 | 4 | 1 | 1.3 |
| B | 1 | 5 | 10 | 9 | 4 | 1.8 |
| C | 3 | 2 | 9 | 6 | 4 | 3.0 |
| D | 9 | 5 | 15 | 6 | 1 | 1.2 |
| E | 12 | 5 | 20 | 8 | 3 | 1.6 |
| Mean | | | | 6.6 | 2.6 | 1.79 |

## 2.8 Hybrid methods

All sorts of methods can be invented by combining ones that we have mentioned. Here are some examples.

(1)   Use FB up to a fixed number $z$ of quanta; then use FCFS for the last queue. This method reduces the number of process switches for very long processes.

(2)     Use RR up to some number of quanta. A process that needs more time is put in a second run queue that is treated with SRR scheduling. Very long processes are eventually placed in a third queue that uses FCFS. RR could have absolute predence over SRR, which has precedence over FCFS, or each could have a fixed percentage of total time.

## 2.9  State-dependent priority methods

These three methods adjust parameters based on the current state.

(1)     Use RR. However, instead of keeping the quantum constant, adjust it periodically, perhaps after every process switch, so that the quantum becomes $q / n$, where $n$ is the size of the ready list. If there are very few ready processes, each gets a long quantum, which avoids process switches. If there are very many, the algorithm becomes more fair for all, but at the expense of process switching. Processes that need only a small amount of time get a quantum, albeit a small one, fairly soon, so they may be able to finish soon. The quantum should not be allowed to drop below some given minimal value so that process switching does not start to consume undue amounts of time.

(2)     Give the current process an extra quantum whenever a new process arrives. The effect of this gift is to reduce process switching in proportion to the level of saturation.

(3)     Some versions of Unix use the following scheduling algorithm. Every second an internal priority is calculated for each process. This priority depends on the external priority (set by the user) and the amount of recent time consumed. This latter figure rises linearly as the process runs and decreases exponentially as the process waits (whether because of short-term scheduling or other reasons). The exponential decay depends on the current load (that is, the size of the ready list); if the load is higher, the central processing unit (cpu) usage figure decays more slowly. Processes with higher recent cpu usage get lower priorities than those with lower recent cpu usage. The scheduler runs the process with the highest priority in the ready list. If several processes have the same priority, they are scheduled in RR fashion.

## 2.10  External priority methods

These three methods adjust parameters on the basis of some external priority.

(1)     Use RR, but let the quantum depend on the external priority of the process. That is, allow larger quanta for processes run for a user willing to pay a premium for this service.

(2)     The **Worst Service Next** (WSN) method is a generalization of many others. After each quantum, compute for each process how much it has suffered so far. Suffering is an arbitrarily complex figure arrived at by crediting the

process for how much it has had to wait, how many times it has been preempted, how much its user is paying in premiums, and how urgent it is. The process is also debited for such items as the amount of time it has actually used and the other resources it has consumed (resources like space and access to secondary store). The process with the greatest suffering is given the next quantum.

(3)     The user buys a response ratio guarantee. A suffering function is used that takes into account only the difference between the guaranteed response ratio and the actual response ratio at the moment.

# 3 PERSPECTIVE

This chapter has looked in some detail at a few scheduling policies and has given brief descriptions of others. Operating systems seldom use any of the policies we have shown in a pure form. Short-term scheduling often merges with medium-term scheduling (in periodic calculations of internal priorities, for example), and many operating systems use ad hoc policies. These policies often have a number of tunable parameters that can be adjusted at each installation to fit its specific workload. Some sophisticated schedulers even adjust their own parameters occasionally as the current load changes. The proper setting during the middle of the night may well be different from the setting during the middle of the afternoon.

## 3.1  Classification of scheduling policies

To put the large number of scheduling policies in perspective, we can develop a language to characterize the most important scheduling policies. We first want to distinguish **preemptive** from **non-preemptive** methods. In the first, typified by RR, service can be interrupted by various external events. We have seen the clock interrupt as one example of such an event. Other reasons for preempting the current process include new arrivals in the ready queue and changes of priority within that queue. We will soon see methods that use such reasons. Under non-preemptive methods, typified by FCFS, service is interrupted only when the process enters a wait list or terminates.

Once it has been decided to start another process, the policy that selects the new process makes a priority decision: The most urgent process should run next. Policies differ in how they compute urgency. In both RR and FCFS, priority is based on the order of arrival in the ready queue. More generally, priority information may be based on the following properties.

- **Intrinsic properties**: characteristics that distinguish one process from another. Intrinsic characteristics include service-time requirements, storage needs, resources held, and the amount of transput required. This sort of information may be placed in the context block. For example, the MVS operating system for the IBM 370 gives a longer quantum to processes holding certain resources. Tops-10 gives a higher priority to processes using small amounts of main store, particularly if the main store is **tied down**, that is, prevented from being displaced by other processes. (We discuss tying down in Chapter 3.)

These characteristics might be determined either before the process starts or while it is running. They may even change while the process is running. For example, in spooling and batch systems, service-time requirements may be explicitly declared as part of the job description. For example, a user might indicate that this process needs 45 seconds to complete. If it takes more, the operating system is justified in terminating it. Even rough guesses can be useful to the operating system. Experience shows that less than 10 percent of processes actually exceed estimates. In interactive multiprogramming, service time is usually not known (or even estimated) before the process starts, but it may be estimated implicitly once the process has been running. Storage needs either can be declared explicitly ahead of time or can be deduced implicitly by the operating system. Storage needs may change during the lifetime of a process. Likewise, the user may declare explicitly which devices will be used, or the operating system can wait until the process starts performing transput to record this property.

- **Extrinsic properties**: characteristics that have to do with the user who owns the process. Extrinsic properties include the urgency of the process and how much the user is willing to pay to purchase special treatment.

- **Dynamic properties**: the load that other processes are placing on resources. Dynamic properties include the size of the ready list and the amount of main store available.

We can arrange the policies we have examined according to whether they use preemption and whether they use intrinsic information. This arrangement is shown in Figure 2.13.

## 3.2 Evaluating policies

Given a policy, how can we evaluate its performance? Three common approaches are analysis, simulation, and experimentation.

**Analysis** involves a mathematical formulation of the policy and a derivation of its behavior. Such a formulation is often described in the language of **queueing networks**, which are pictures like the one shown in Figure 2.14. This picture shows a simplified **model** of the transitions through which a process might pass. Lines indicate transitions, rectangular objects represent queues, and circles represent servers. The model in this figure shows a multiprocessor with two cpu's that share a single queue. A process (called a "customer" in the jargon of queueing theory) enters from the right and is queued for execution. It can be served by either cpu after waiting in the cpu queue. After the cpu burst, the process moves to one of the

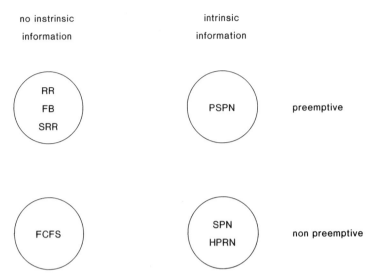

Figure 2.13 Classification of scheduling policies

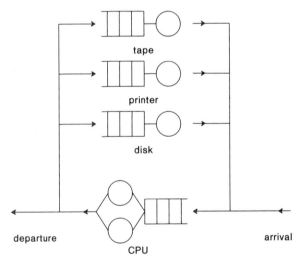

Figure 2.14 A typical queueing network

three transput-wait queues, depending on which one it needs.

To complete the model, one describes the probability of taking any branch (for example, how likely it is for an average process to need disk, as opposed to printer, service), and the queuing parameters for each service station. In particular, one needs to know the arrival distribution for all the arrival arcs in the network, the service distribution for all servers (how long does it take to service a disk request?), and the scheduling policy at each queue.

Of course, such a model is only an approximation of the reality. It always ignores some details (in our example, we ignore long-term scheduling) and is incapable of describing other details (the service distributions at different stations may depend on the class of the process). It is, however, a useful tool for performing analyses.

Mathematical methods can produce information about a queueing network, such as the expected length of each queue, the expected response time from entry to exit, and the percentage of time that each server is busy. These results can sometimes be found exactly by mathematical manipulations. Little's result, for example, says that the number of processes in a queue is equal to the arrival rate times the average wait time for the queue. Sometimes results can only be approximated by numerical methods. This is especially true for distributions other than the exponential distribution, scheduling policies other than FCFS, and complex queuing networks.

Once a model has been built and results have been derived, the next step is to validate the model by comparing its predictions against reality. This step is easy if the model describes an actual situation. It is harder if it describes a hypothetical situation. For example, before an installation decides to buy another tape drive, the managers might undertake an analysis of the expected improvement in throughput with that drive. First a model would be built of the current installation, and that model would be validated. Then the model would be modified to include the new tape drive. The managers would have to trust the validity of the new model in order to use its predictions.

There are cases where analysis is inadequate, such as when the models become so complex that analytic methods fail or when queuing networks do not adequately describe the situation. In these cases, **simulation** may be used. Simulation involves tracking a large number of processes through a model (such as a queueing network) and collecting statistics. Whenever a probabilistic choice must be made, such as when the next arrival should occur or which branch a process takes, a pseudo-random number is generated with the correct distribution. It is also possible to drive the simulation with traces of real systems to match reality better. We saw the results of simulations in Figures 2.4 and 2.6, which tracked thousands of processes through a simple network with only one queue and one server.

Simulations, just like analytic models, must be validated to ensure that they are adequate descriptions of the situation that is being modeled. They are often run several times in order to determine how much the particular pseudo-random numbers chosen affect the results. Simulations tend to produce enormous amounts of data that must be carefully distilled before they are useful. Simulations often use extremely detailed models and therefore consume enormous amounts of computer time. For these reasons, simulations are usually appropriate only if analysis fails.

If simulation doesn't work, usually due to the complexity of the model, experimentation is the last resort. Experimentation often requires a significant investment in equipment, both to build the system to be tested and to instrument it to acquire the required statistics. It can be far cheaper to simulate the SPN scheduling method, for example, than to implement it properly, debug it, impose it on a user community for a while, and measure the results. Likewise, it is cheaper to simulate the effect of installing a new disk than to rent it, connect it, see how well it works, and then disconnect it after the managers decide that the improvement is not cost-effective. However, experimentation is sure to give accurate results, since by definition it uses an accurate model.

## 3.3 Scheduling levels

We have been concentrating on short-term scheduling. Some of our short-term methods, however, contain aspects of medium-term scheduling. Any method that calculates priorities at a slower rate than it schedules processes (SRR is one example) is applying a form of medium-term scheduling. These priorities may influence short-term decisions without causing processes to depart from the short-term scheduler's view. Tuning the parameters of a short-term method is another form of medium-term scheduling. For example, we may adjust the $b/a$ ratio in SRR in order to keep the size of the accepted group right, or we may modify the quantum of RR as the load changes.

Similarly, the realm of medium-term scheduling is not sharply demarcated. Different reasons for waiting may lead to very different blocking times. Processes in the new list under SRR do not stay there very long. Processes waiting for transput usually wait less than a second. Processes waiting for main store generally wait between 1 and 10 seconds. Processes waiting for other processes (as discussed in Chapter 9) or for serially reusable resources (as discussed in Chapter 4) may wait for minutes or hours.

Long-term scheduling also blends into medium-term scheduling somewhat. The decision not to allow a process to start may be based on explicitly declared resource needs that are not currently available, in which case we might say that the process has really started (as far as the long-term scheduler is concerned) but is still waiting for resources (as far as the medium-term scheduler is concerned). The decision may be based on the process class and the time of day; evening-class processes (as declared by their users) are not started during the afternoon.

## 3.4 Countermeasures

A user who knows what policies a particular operating system uses can sometimes use that knowledge to achieve an unfairly high level of service. For example, some operating systems allow a user to have many processes at the same time. A user can circumvent the scheduler's attempts at fairness by building many processes, each of which is treated as an independent and equal contender for the computation resource. One common form of this trick in the Unix operating system is to create a "background" process that executes some time-consuming operation, like a compilation, while the user interacts with a text editor to prepare some other program. (We discuss this idea in more detail in Chapter 9.)

A scheduler can institute a policy that lumps together all processes that belong to the same user, giving each one less time in proportion to how many belonging to that user are in the ready list at the same time. The processes in wait lists do not contribute to the load, so they may be ignored for this purpose. The Utah Tenex scheduler makes use of a fancy version of this algorithm that includes a suffering function.

If the scheduler follows a policy that favors short processes, the user can program processes to do only a small bit of computation before artificially pausing for a very short time. For example, the process can periodically write a single character to the terminal. When the process returns from the wait list, it is treated by the short-term scheduler as a new arrival. New arrivals are assumed to be short. On some interactive operating systems, the user can benefit by repeatedly interrupting the process by using a keyboard "interrupt" key, then allowing the process to continue. To prevent such abuse requires that the scheduler treat processes returning from interrupt wait or transput wait in the same way as it would if they had continued computing. Such special treatment can be cumbersome to implement.

A similar situation arises under PSPN. Instead of submitting a long process, one can break its work into many small pieces. Each piece will have a very high priority, since it takes almost no time. The total missed time will then be very short, although the startup and termination expense for all the processes may be large.

Some schedulers, such as the one for CTSS (the Compatible Time Sharing System, an early interactive operating system at MIT), give poorer service to processes that require a large amount of main store. When such schedulers are used, programmers tend to concentrate their data and instructions, leading to less easily maintained and more bug-prone programs.

## 3.5 Guiding principles

How is one supposed to sift through our list of policies to pick the one that is best in a particular case? Here is a rule of thumb: Preemption is worth the extra switching cost. Since context must switch at every interrupt from the running process back to the kernel, it does not usually cost much extra for the kernel to make a decision and allow a different process to run. Clock devices are almost universal these days, from mainframe computers down to board-level microcomputers.

The quantum size should be large enough so that kernel time does not become excessive. A process switch might cost about 100 microseconds, and other scheduling bookkeeping might occupy another 400 microseconds. If the quantum is 10 milliseconds, scheduling occupies about 5 percent of the time, which is a reasonable figure.

Some policies are more expensive than others to implement. FCFS only requires a queue for the ready list. FB requires a number of queues. WSN can require arbitrarily complex computation at every decision point. The implementer should try to balance the cost of making the decisions against the advantage that a particular strategy might yield. The complexity of the program itself is also worth minimizing. Simple programs are more likely to be correct and are certainly easier to maintain.

Many operating systems use a hybrid policy, with RR for short processes and some other method, possibly RR with a longer quantum and a lower priority, for longer ones. Space management, which we will discuss in the next chapter, affects scheduling. Processes that need a substantial amount of store are often given larger quanta so that they can get more work done while they are occupying main store.

The recent introduction of personal computing casts a different light on time management. It is not essential to keep the computer busy 100 percent of the time, even if there is work available. It is more important to provide interactive processes with good service. For example, when an interactive process waits for transput, it might not be appropriate to switch to another process immediately. Instead, the scheduler might wait for a while, letting the computer sit idle, in the hope that the interactive process will soon become runnable again and will not need to suffer a process switch before it can start. Similarly, an interactive process that enters a computationally intensive phase might still be considered interactive, and the scheduler might favor it instead of treating it as the equal of a background computational process. If all processes belong to the same user, the operating system does not have to live up to quite the same goal of fairness among processes.

# 4 FURTHER READING

The material covered in this chapter can be treated in a much more formal fashion. If you are interested in scheduling methods or in the extended area of performance modeling, analysis, and measurement, you may want to look at texts by Sauer and Chandy (1981), Lazowska and colleagues (1984), and Kleinrock (1976). Little's result can be found in a journal article (1961). A set of articles by Denning and Stone (1980) discusses how personal computers influence the way we look at scheduling and other aspects of operating systems. Shneiderman's review article on human-computer interaction (1984) comes to the conclusion that users prefer a response time of shorter than a second for most tasks and that error rates increase as the response time becomes too long. The article by Coffman and Kleinrock (1968) describes countermeasures to scheduling methods. CTSS, an early operating system that penalized large jobs and used a variant of FB, is described by Corbato and colleagues (1962). The Utah Tenex scheduler is described in the article by Ellison (1975).

# 5 EXERCISES

1.  What does the scheduler do under RR when there is only one process that can run?

2.  What does the scheduler do under RR when there are no processes that can run?

3.  Of all the policies discussed in the chapter, which requires the least amount of **overhead time**, that is, time needed to compute the policy?

4.  Which of the policies would you prefer if $\rho = 2$?

5.  The expected amount of time needed by a process is always $1/\beta$ under the exponential distribution. Is a process therefore expected never to terminate?

6.  Consider the following process arrival list:

| Name | Arrival time | Service time |
|:----:|:------------:|:------------:|
| A | 0 | 3 |
| B | 2 | 6 |
| C | 3 | 10 |
| D | 7 | 1 |
| E | 8 | 5 |
| F | 15 | 2 |
| G | 25 | 7 |

Figure 2.15 depicts this situation graphically.

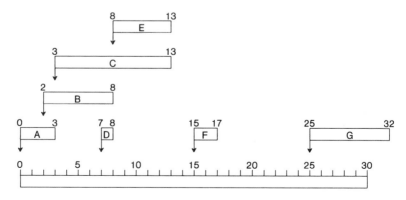

**Figure 2.15** Process arrival list

Complete the figure, showing which process is executing over time, and calculate *T*, *M*, and *P* for each process, under the following policies: FCFS, SPN, PSPN, HPRN, RR with $q = 1$, RR with $q = 5$, and SRR with $b / a = 0.5$ and $q = 1$. Assume that if events are scheduled to happen at exactly the same time, new arrivals precede terminations, which precede quantum expirations.

7. Here are some procedures that give you exponentially distributed random numbers:

```
function Random(var Seed : integer) : real;
{ Linear-congruential random number generator,
for 32-bit computers.   Start the Seed anywhere
you like, but then don't touch it.   Returns a
pseudo-random number between 0 and 1.   }
const
   Multiplier = 1103515245;
   Adder = 12345;
   Modulus = 2147483648; { 2 ** 31 }
begin
   Seed := (Seed * Multiplier + Adder) mod Modulus;
   Random := Seed / Modulus;
end Random;

function Expo(Lambda: real; var Seed : integer) : real;
{ Returns a random number distributed according
to the exponential distribution with parameter
Lambda.   Seed should be set once and then not
touched. }
begin
   Expo:= -ln(Random(Seed)) / Lambda;
end Expo;
```

Write a program to generate 1000 samples from Expo(3) and draw a histogram (a bar graph) showing how many samples fall in each interval of length 0.1 from 1 to 10. For example, how many samples were in the half-open interval (2.3, 2.4]?

8. Write a program that generates *n* processes, with arrival intervals drawn from an exponential distribution with parameter $\alpha$ and service requirements drawn from an exponential distribution with parameter $\beta$. The program then schedules these processes according to either FCFS or SPN and computes *T*, *M*, *P*, and *R* for each process. Run your program with $n = 100$ and $\rho = 0.5, 0.9, 1.5$.

9. Using a similar program, show the length of the ready list for FCFS and how it changes over time when $\rho = 0.5$, 0.9, and 1.5. Can you predict the average length just knowing $\rho$?

10. Devise a data structure that allows SRR to be implemented efficiently. In particular, how do we organize the new list, and how do we store the current priorities?

11. Predict the behavior of the LCFS (last come, first served) non-preemptive policy. Simulate this policy with a program, and compare the results to your prediction.

12. Repeat the previous exercise with a preemptive LCFS policy.

13. Consider a preemptive HPRN policy. Can it be implemented exactly? If not, how would you approximate it?

14. What countermeasures can an inherently short process take to get better service if the scheduling method favors long processes?

15. Which of the methods discussed in this chapter have a scheduling cost that is independent of the number of processes in the ready list?

16. Some operating systems are used in environments where processes must get guaranteed service. **Deadline scheduling** means that each process specifies how much service time it needs and by what real time it must be finished. Design a preemptive algorithm that services such processes. There will be occasions when deadlines cannot be met; try to discover these situations as early as possible (before starting a process at all if it cannot be finished in time).

# Space Management

The management of both time and main store is motivated by the fact that processes generally are designed to pretend that other processes don't exist. It shouldn't make any difference to **A** whether or not **B** is also in the ready list. **B**'s actions should not have visible repercussions on **A**'s store. Processes also ignore details about the machine, such as how much main store there really is and where the kernel is in main store. Both of these features are consonant with the Beautification Principle, which makes the operating system responsible for keeping ugly details out of view.

However, multiprogramming works best when several processes are kept in main store at the same time, because process switching among them requires less work if data need not be transferred between main and backing store. The fact that several processes share main store requires that the operating system allocate the main store resource effectively, in accord with the Resource Principle. In particular, the operating system must protect processes from each other, keep track of the current allocation state of main store. and arrange with the hardware for efficient execution.

# 1 PRELIMINARIES

## 1.1 Swapping

The operating system must arrange main store in such a way that processes can remain ignorant of each other (following the Beautification Principle) and still share main store. Processes that are blocked for a long time in wait lists should be removed from main store temporarily to make room for ready processes. We say these processes have been **swapped out** and later will be **swapped in** again. While a process is swapped out, it resides in **backing store**, which is usually a disk or a drum. We sometimes refer to the location in backing store used for swapping as **swapping space**. The context block of a swapped-out process should indicate where it has been placed in backing store. The context block itself is usually not swapped out.

Swapping should follow the **Cache Principle** of operating systems, a principle that we will encounter several times in this book.

| **Cache Principle** |
|---|
| The more frequently data are accessed, the faster the access should be. |

A **cache** is a repository for data from which they can be accessed quickly. We will use the term **archive** to refer to the slower storage in which the data may also be stored. Copying the data from the cache to the archive is called **archiving**, and copying data from the archive to the cache is called **caching**. If data are both in the cache and in an archive, the cache holds the more accurate version. The Cache Principle says that the most frequently accessed data should be kept in the cache.

In our case, main store is a cache, and backing store is its archive. Swapping a process out is equivalent to archiving it; swapping it back in is like caching it. The space occupied by ready processes is accessed more often than that occupied by blocked processes. Therefore, blocked processes may be swapped out to make room for active processes.

Violating the Cache Principle can lead to unfortunate results. In most situations involving caches, data must be cached from the archive before they can be used. If the frequency at which data are accessed is misjudged, the data may be repeatedly cached and archived. If this situation persists, a situation called **thrashing** results. When the operating system is thrashing, moving data between two levels of storage becomes the dominant activity of the machine. Thrashing due to continual swapping was a severe problem with early attempts at storage management.

## 1.2 Storage hierarchies

Storage organizations often use more than two levels. Each level can be considered an archive for the cache that sits above it. For example, Figure 3.1 shows a four-level storage organization. Imagine a program that is saved on a long-term magnetic tape. It may take about 50 seconds to read that tape onto the disk. (This operation of caching from tape to disk is sometimes called "staging".) It may then take about 50 milliseconds to read a particular block of the disk into main store. Before any given instruction is executed, the hardware loads it into a cache for fast access.

Data stored on the disk are generally stored on tape as well, except for recently modified data, which will eventually be archived to tape. Similarly, data in main store are generally also on disk, and data in the hardware cache are in main store. Each level therefore acts as an archive for the level above it.

Data that are currently accessed most frequently should be in the higher levels of the storage hierarchy. If we need to cache an item from an archive, access is significantly slower. We call such a situation a **cache miss**. In contrast, a **cache hit** is when we find the data we need in a cache and need not turn to the associated archive.

The effective size of store is the size of our tape library, shown in the figure as $10^{12}$ bytes. The effective access time depends on the percentage of accesses that

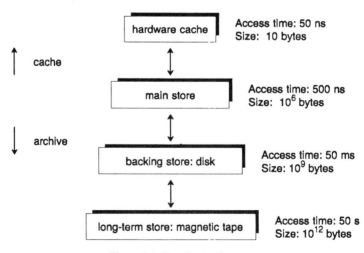

**Figure 3.1** Four levels of storage

result in cache hits at each level. For the sake of calculation, let's assume that the **hit ratio** is 95 percent for all the levels in our picture. The effective access time is then

$$0.95 \cdot (50 \text{ ns}) + 0.05 \cdot 0.95 \cdot (500 \text{ ns}) + 0.05 \cdot [0.95 \cdot (50 \text{ ms}) + 0.05 \cdot (50 \text{ s})] = 6.4 \text{ ms}$$

As the hit ratio increases, the effective access time decreases. With a hit ratio of 99 percent at all levels, the effective access time becomes 55 microseconds.

The Hysteresis Principle applies to caching in the following way. Once data have been brought into a cache, which incurs some transfer expense, they should be left there at least long enough to pay back that expense. We will encounter several examples of this application of the Hysteresis Principle in this chapter.

## 1.3 Physical and virtual store

We will repeatedly distinguish between physical and virtual store. **Physical store** is the hardware memory on the machine. Physical store usually starts at physical address zero and continues to some large physical address. Microcomputers might have as few as 4K or 8K bytes of main store; large mainframe computers often have 16M bytes. (A **byte** is 8 bits. We use K for *kilo* to mean $2^{10} = 1024$, M for *mega* to mean $2^{20} = 1,048,576$, and G for *giga* to mean $2^{30} = 1,073,741,824$.) The Cray-2 computer has 2G bytes of main store. Addresses can be described as binary numbers but are often represented by either base-8 (octal), base-10 (decimal), or base-16 (hexadecimal) numbers for convenience.

Certain locations in physical store may be reserved by the hardware for special purposes. For example, the DEC PDP-11 reserves the first 1K bytes for tables that direct the hardware when a device interrupts. The kernel often resides in "low core," which means physical store at low addresses. ("Core" is an old word for main store that derives from magnetic-core technology.) The rest of physical store may be partitioned into pieces for the processes in the ready list.

Each process has its own **virtual store**, which is the memory perceived by the process. We will often refer to all the virtual store of a process as its **virtual space**. As far as the process is concerned, there is no physical store. All address references refer to virtual space. In the simplest case, virtual store looks like a contiguous chunk, starting at virtual address zero and continuing to some maximum address. The largest virtual store possible is usually limited by the architecture of the machine, in particular, by the number of bits that make up an address. If there are $n$ bits in an address, the largest address is $2^n$. For example, the DEC PDP-10 has 18 bits of address, so the largest address is 256K. The DEC PDP-11 has only 16 bits of address; the largest address is thus only 64K. Therefore, the virtual space on the PDP-11 has one-fourth the addresses of the PDP-10. An address on the PDP-11 refers to an 8-bit byte, whereas an address on the PDP-10 refers to a 36-bit word; therefore, the PDP-11 actually allows only one eighteenth as large a virtual space as the PDP-10.

Although the virtual space is limited by the number of bits in an address, it is usually *not* limited by the amount of physical store on the machine. Virtual-space size and physical-space size are independent.

- Virtual space can be larger than physical space, especially if paging is used. We will discuss paging later in this chapter.
- Some machines can have far more physical store than can be addressed. Some models of DEC PDP-11, for example, can take 1,044,480 bytes of main store, but individual virtual spaces are still limited to 65,536 bytes.

Ordinarily a process may access any portion of its virtual store. When the process starts, instructions will fill part of virtual store. Besides the instructions area, the process may keep a data area and a stack area. (Stacks are used for implementing procedure calls; their details need not concern us here.) In more complicated cases, the operating system may divide virtual store into regions called **segments**, each of which has its own set of addresses called **offsets**, starting with zero and reaching some maximum for each segment. When a process wishes to access a location in main store, it must name both the segment and the offset within the segment.

## 1.4 Address translation

Processes deal with virtual addresses and ignore physical ones. However, every access a process makes must then undergo **address translation** to convert the virtual address to the associated physical address. Address translation is shown in Figure 3.2, which depicts the kernel and two processes each residing in the same physical main store. Process **A** is 13K in size, **B** is 10K, and the kernel is 19K. (Kernels

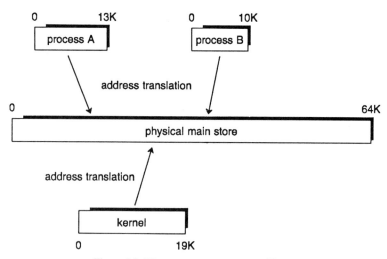

**Figure 3.2** The space management problem

range in size from about 5K to over 300K.) The size of a process is not usually an integer number of K, but we will use such sizes for **A** and **B** for simplicity. We will fill in details of this picture for the different storage management strategies that we will encounter.

Every time a program (whether a process or the kernel) executes an instruction, it generates one or more references to addresses in virtual store: one to access the instruction, a second to access the first operand, a third to access the second operand, and a fourth to deposit the result of the operation. (On some machines, like the Control Data Cyber 205, one instruction can manipulate a large array of data, generating hundreds of thousands of data accesses.) Since every reference must be translated, translation must be fast. This requirement means that we cannot afford to perform address translation in software. Instead, we require the hardware to perform most address translation for us. This result comes from a variation on the Cache Principle:

> ## Cache Principle (restated)
> Operations that must be performed often should be performed rapidly.

The operating system designer must work within the constraints imposed by the hardware. If the hardware uses **translation tables** to guide address translation, the operating system must construct those tables and make sure they hold correct information. The most active parts of these tables are often copied by the hardware into a cache called a **translation look-aside buffer**.

Some operating systems are designed so that the kernel uses physical store directly by turning off address translation. Most, however, give the kernel its own virtual store, called **kernel space**, which contains the instructions and data of the kernel. Kernel space might overlap the virtual store of a process to allow the kernel to transfer data easily between itself and the process. Since the kernel uses virtual, not physical, store, an address-translation table must exist for the kernel, too. Many machines allow several address-translation tables to be set up at the same time. The hardware picks the one to use on the basis of the current processor state (privileged, non-privileged, or perhaps some intermediate). Switching contexts between process and kernel is then fairly fast. The hardware just starts using another address-translation table.

However, placing a new process in the running state can be slow, since the kernel must change the process address-translation table to correspond to the virtual space of the new process. The translation table for each process is stored in the context block for that process. It is usually not part of the state vector, which means that the kernel may even swap it out. On some machines, the operating system need not copy the translation table from the context block into a fixed physical location reserved for process state tables; instead, only a pointer to the table in the context block needs to be placed in a reserved location.

Hardware **registers** make up a region of particularly fast store that acts as a cache for main store. Registers are also part of the virtual space of a process.

When context switches from a process to the kernel, the kernel must save the contents of all registers in the context block of the process so that they can be restored when context switches back. Many machines provide a separate set of registers for each processor state, a feature that reduces the context-switch cost but not the process-switch cost.

## 1.5 Sharing

It is sometimes useful for two processes to share parts of their virtual space. For example, all the processes simultaneously running the same program (a compiler, for example) might profitably share instructions to reduce their overall space requirements. In the early days of sharing, instructions had to be specially constructed in order to be "re-entrant" or shareable. The most important rule is never to modify instructions. In addition, return addresses must not be saved in the instructions area. Now that most programs are written in higher-level languages that use a central stack for return addresses and local variables, no extra effort is required to guarantee re-entrancy. Writeable data areas, however, must be distinct for different processes running the same program simultaneously. In particular, the register contents, including the program counter, must be maintained separately for each process sharing the same instructions.

   Occasionally, very large programs might be split into several processes that communicate by sharing a part of their virtual store. Special synchronization techniques are needed to maintain consistency in such situations. We will discuss these techniques in Chapter 8. In general, only space management techniques that divide virtual space into several segments lend themselves to sharing.

## 1.6 Initial loading and execution

When a process starts, its virtual space is initialized by the storage manager. The storage manager can figure out what to put in the virtual space of a process in two ways: by copying the virtual space of another process, which we will call **splitting**, or by reading a file that describes the initial virtual space, which we will call **loading**. We describe these methods in more detail in Chapter 9. Splitting might copy the entire virtual space or, if sharing is possible, might allow parts of the virtual space to be shared. The exact meaning is part of the design of the particular operating system. The Dynix operating system for the Sequent Balance multicomputer, for example, distinguishes between private and shared data regions in virtual store. A new copy is created for the private region, but not for the shared region.

   The file used for loading is called a **load image**. It contains the instructions and initialized data of the program and may also indicate how much space is needed for uninitialized data. It also tells where the program starts, that is, the initial value for the program counter. This information must be packaged in a form understood by the storage manager. A load image is prepared by a program called a **linker**, which combines the output of one or more compilation steps and searches libraries if necessary to find missing routines the compiled program needs. Bringing the load image from a file into main store to start execution is performed by the **loader**, which is either a separate program or part of the storage manager.

The format of a link module is designed at the same time as the operating system. It generally includes the following information.

- A header that indicates that the file is a link module. Different kinds of link modules can have different headers. For example, the header can indicate that some debugging sections are missing.
- A list of sizes for the various parts of the module. This entry lets the storage manager decide how much room to allocate.
- The starting address. The load-image format for Tops-10 also includes both a restart address and a debugger start address.
- The machine instructions that constitute the program.
- Data areas initialized with their first values.
- Size indications for uninitialized data regions. The loader can clear these regions to prevent the new process from discovering secrets in the space vacated by the previous user of main store.
- Relocation information that allows the loader to adjust instructions and data to work at the locations where they will be placed. Some operating systems avoid this section by using appropriate virtual store techniques, described later in this chapter.
- A symbol table to be used during interactive debugging. It associates locations in the data and instruction regions with labels.
- A cross-reference table to be used during interactive debugging. This table associates locations in the instruction region with lines in source files.

Whether the new process is split or loaded, it usually comes into being as a result of a service call submitted by another process. We will often call that instigator the **parent** and the new process the **child**. Service calls, as seen earlier, are like procedure invocations as far as the calling process is concerned. We will describe service calls by procedure headings and will set them off from the rest of the text with a square symbol (□). The kernel might provide two calls of interest here:

□ Load(file name). This call tells the operating system to take the load image stored in the named file and make it a new process.
□ Split. This call creates a new process whose virtual space is identical to the virtual space of the caller. The program counter of the child is set to the same value as the program counter of the parent.

The storage manager must allocate backing store for either Split or Load. The load image itself can act as backing store for the parts of the virtual space that are not modifiable, such as instructions and read-only data. In this way, processes that are formed by the Split call can share some backing store with their parents. Fresh backing store must be allocated for all the non-shared, writable parts of the new virtual space, although this allocation may be delayed until the process actually modifies the contents of its virtual store. (We discuss this technique, called **copy on write**, when we deal with segmentation.)

At the minimum, each service call must report back to the caller whether the request was honored. If not, it is sometimes useful to the caller to have some idea of what did not work. The error "NoRoom," which might apply to either Load or Split, might be caused by one of a host of problems.

- Swap space is full on backing store.
- There are no available context blocks for the new process.
- The caller has the maximum number of children already.
- The caller's user has the maximum number of processes already.

Once a process is running, it may need to acquire more virtual store. New store has several uses.

- To hold data structures whose size could not be determined until the program started to run
- To hold messages that will be sent to other processes (we discuss messages in Chapter 9)
- To serve as buffers for transput (we discuss transput buffers in Chapter 5)
- To hold local variables and return addresses for procedure calls

Later, a process may release this new space.

Different storage-allocation schemes support such dynamic changes to differing extents. A simple set of service calls might look like this:

☐ GetStore(descriptor). This call returns the virtual address of the start of the additional space. The space is specified by the descriptor, which indicates the how much space the process needs. This call may require the storage manager to allocate new backing store. The error "NoRoom" could apply to GetStore just as it does to Load.

☐ ReleaseStore(descriptor). This call deallocates space. The descriptor must indicate both where the space starts and how long it is. It may be impossible to release space that is not at the end of virtual store. After this call, accesses to the released space are treated as errors.

☐ Terminate(exit code). This call causes the process to terminate, releasing all its virtual space. The storage manager may reclaim backing store for all parts of the space that are not being shared. Other resource managers may also reclaim resources from the terminating process. The exit code is used to communicate status back to the parent of the process, which might be waiting for this child to complete.

The rest of this chapter is organized according to the type of address translation the hardware supports. This organization will provide some feeling for the history of space management because the simpler methods that we will start with were developed first. These early methods are important not only from a historical perspective but also because they serve to develop some of the ideas that will appear in even the most sophisticated hardware. The part of the kernel this chapter discusses is called the **storage manager** because it makes policy decisions with regard to space.

## 2  FIXED PARTITIONS

All forms of space management require hardware support. The **fixed-partition** method was standard in OS/360, where it is called MFT (for "multiprogramming with a fixed number of tasks" or MVT for "multiprogramming with a variable number of tasks." This operating system was designed for early IBM 360 models, which provided the necessary hardware. All physical store is divided by the operating system into a set of contiguous regions called **partitions**. Only one process can be executed at a time in each partition, and the virtual space of each process is just the single partition in which it executes.

Figure 3.3 shows processes **A** and **B** placed in partitions. The first partition, of length 20K, is reserved for the kernel. The next partition starts at location 20K and is 16K long. Process **A** fits there with 3K wasted at the end. Process **B** is in the next partition, which starts at 36K and is also 16K long. It wastes 6K of this partition. The last partition starts at 52K and is 12K long; it is currently unoccupied.

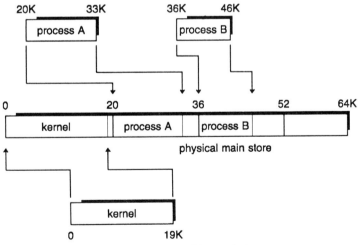

Figure 3.3  Partition method

Under the partition method, virtual addresses are identical to the physical addresses. Address translation is therefore easy; there is no need for a translation table. However, the process must know where in physical store it has been placed because it must know how to address its own data and instructions. We say that it must be **bound** to its virtual addresses, that is, its virtual references must be turned into physical references. Binding is performed in two ways. At **loading** time, when the process is brought into main store for the first time, all virtual addresses are bound to physical addresses by the position where the process is placed in physical store. At **execution** time, when the program is running, it can execute an instruction that places the current value of the program counter in a register, from which it can derive the virtual position of the rest of the program. This technique is known as "establishing addressability." It is usually performed once at the start of execution. After that time, all address binding is fixed.

Under MFT, partition boundaries are established independently of individual processes. They may be changed through manual intervention by the operator. For example, some installations provide many partitions of various sizes during the day but provide only a few very large ones at night. Processes that need a very large partition are blocked (by the long-term scheduler) until an adequately large partition is created. Under MVT, the operating system automatically changes the number and size of partitions in response to the requirements of new jobs.

As our example shows, some spare room often appears at the end of a partition. We call such spare room **internal waste** because it is space inside the virtual store that is not used. However, the process might use some of the spare room for dynamically growing data structures. For example, compilers build tables that may grow very large. Some programs can be compiled in smaller partitions, whereas others will need larger partitions. Once it has begun to run within a partition, a program can never expand beyond the limits of that single partition.

A process is either entirely in main store or entirely in backing store. There is no point swapping out part of a process, because the entire partition must be freed before it is safe to place another process in it. Many implementations do not swap a process out at all but allow it to execute until completion. If a process is swapped out, it must later be swapped back into the same partition that it was in before, because it has already been bound there. The process is unable to re-establish addressability because it does not realize it has been swapped out. In addition, it may have stored virtual addresses of important objects like data items or procedures within registers or data structures. It would be cumbersome to find all the places in which addresses have been stored in order to rebind them.

## 2.1 Security

The partition method cannot build virtual spaces that are larger than physical store; it can only provide smaller virtual spaces. However, a process can easily generate an address that is outside the virtual space. This ability could lead to chaos if it were allowed to go unchecked. Malicious users could write programs that modify any partition, including the areas where the kernel resides. Programs could steal sensitive information from the virtual store of other programs. Program errors could result in the execution of instructions (and data!) in another partition and cause wild modifications of data anywhere in physical store.

To prevent such chaos, the storage manager of the operating system must invoke a **security** mechanism, preferably with the assistance of the hardware. One classical partition method provides security through a scheme of **storage keys**. Physical store is divided into chunks of identical length, typically about 4K bytes. Partitions are always organized as an integral number of chunks. We say that partitions are **aligned** on chunk boundaries; that is, they always start at the beginning of a chunk.

The storage manager assigns a **lock** (perhaps 16 bits long) to each chunk. Each chunk in a partition has the same lock, and each partition has a different lock. If a process does not need all the physical space of a partition, unused chunks can be given a different lock.

The storage manager assigns a **key** to each process. The key is stored in the context block. When the kernel switches context to a process, it makes sure that the key is placed in the hardware processor-state register, along with an indication that the process is not privileged.

Every access performed by any process is checked by the hardware to make sure that the current key fits the lock in the chunk in which the reference falls. If the key does not fit, the hardware generates a **trap**, which switches context back to the kernel. The kernel then invokes some policy, usually to terminate the offending process. It may also produce diagnostic information to help the programmer recognize and correct the error.

The hardware might keep information about the locks in a **physical-store descriptor table**. Modifying this table is a privileged operation. The physical-store descriptor table has one entry for each chunk. Let's assume that an address has $b$ bits and that each address references an 8-bit byte. If we make a chunk $2^c$ bytes long, the most significant $b - c$ bits of each address specify the chunk in which the address falls. The following declarations describe the physical-store descriptor table. The mathematical constants $b$ and $c$ have been expanded into the mnemonic identifiers "BitsPerAddress" and "BitsPerChunkAddress."

```
1 const
2    BitsPerAddress = 16; { for example }
3    BitsPerChunkAddress = 6; { for example }
4    NumberOfChunks = 2^(BitsPerAddress-BitsPerChunkAddress);
5 type
6    Lock = integer;
7    ChunkData = Lock;
8 var
9    PhysicalStoreDescriptorTable =
10       array 0 : NumberOfChunks - 1 of ChunkData;
```

If we use the suggested constants, an address has 16 bits, meaning there are $2^{16}$ or 64K bytes in physical store. The largest virtual store is also 64K bytes. If 6 bits specify the chunk, each set of 1024 bytes has its own lock, and the length of each partition must be a multiple of 1024 bytes. There are 64 chunks in all. Figure 3.4 shows how the hardware checks addresses.

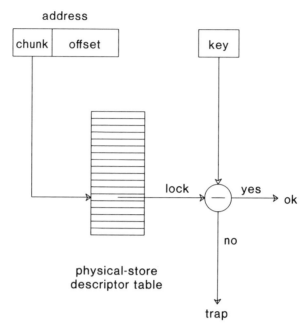

**Figure 3.4** Hardware address checking

Each access must be checked, whether it is for an instruction fetch or a data fetch or store. Security introduces a slight amount of extra work on each access, but not as much as address translation requires. This work can often be overlapped with the main store access, which can be cancelled if it turns out that the security check fails. Such overlap is crucial to making fast computers.

The kernel also has a key, and the hardware checks all its accesses, too. However, the kernel usually uses a special "master key," which opens all the locks. Most attempts to subvert the security on operating systems for the IBM 360 (many of them successful) have had the master key as their goal. Once a process is running with the master key, it can do anything.

The simple partition method described here does not provide the ability to share parts of virtual store among processes. Either the processes have the same key, in which case they share entirely, or they have different keys and cannot share at all. However, each process can be given a number of keys, and finer-grained sharing is therefore possible. The logical extension of this idea is called **capabilities**, an important concept discussed in Chapter 6.

## 2.2 Overlays

If a process is restricted to a partition that is too small, the **overlay** software technique can help it, although the operating system won't provide much assistance.

Figure 3.5 shows process **A** trying to cram into a small partition that starts at 20K and runs for 8K. The first 8K of **A** are placed at locations 20K to 28K; the last 5K are placed at 23K to 28K, overlapping some of the first part.

This cramming is a private affair of process **A**, which has created a new level of address translation by using the same region of virtual store for different purposes at different times. We will call this new level of virtualization the "pseudo-store." **A**'s virtual store has length of only 8K, but its pseudo-store has length 13K.

The process divides its pseudo-store into regions called **overlays**. Each overlay can fit into virtual space by itself. In fact, several overlays may be able to fit at the same time into virtual space. The process assigns each overlay a fixed place in virtual store. This region may overlap with the region given to some other overlay. At any given time during execution, some overlays are present and others are in backing store. The ones that are present do not overlap.

Whenever an access is made to an area in pseudo-store, either the overlay it needs is currently in virtual store, in which case the access is performed easily, or it is not. In the latter case, the process undertakes the necessary transput to remove the overlay or overlays that occupy the place where the desired one needs to reside and then to bring the required overlay into that position.

The hardware does not support overlays. Checking every reference would be unacceptably slow in software. Therefore, only procedure calls are allowed to require new overlays. Procedure invocation and return are therefore more expensive than they would be otherwise, because not only must the status of the destination overlay be examined, but it may also have to be brought into virtual store.

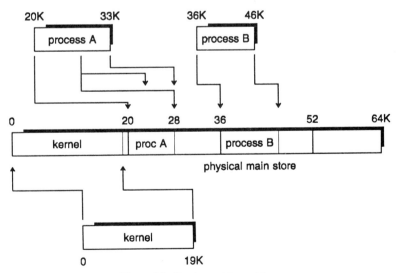

**Figure 3.5** Overlays with partitions

One could place every procedure in its own overlay. Instead, the programmer might specify the overlay structure in order to keep the number of cross-overlay calls to a minimum and to make sure that overlays that do call each other can be placed simultaneously in virtual store.

Compilers can be of great assistance, too. Algol-like languages are especially suited to overlays because the hierarchical nature of name scopes means that during execution of any one procedure, only variables local to that procedure or to enclosing procedures can be accessed. Therefore, each procedure can be given an overlay that starts in virtual store right after all the overlays for its enclosing procedures. They will all be in store at the same time, but other procedures at the same level will be absent.

Unfortunately, overlays will often be swapped out when room is still available in virtual store, because some other overlay that must reside at the same location has been accessed. Overlays work well only in applications where the execution of the program goes through well-defined phases, each of which requires different program units. Thrashing can result from the inappropriate use of overlays.

# 3  SINGLE SEGMENT

The DEC PDP-10 and CDC 6600 computers generalize fixed partitions by allowing their boundaries to move dynamically. We will call each region a **segment**. Figure 3.6 shows processes **A** and **B** each using a segment of main store. **A**'s segment starts at 20K and runs exactly 13K, the length of **A**'s virtual space. **B**'s segment starts at 42K and runs exactly 10K, which is what **B** needs.

As with the partition method, each process has a virtual space of exactly one segment. Unlike the partition method, virtual addresses within the segment begin at zero and continue to some maximum. The hardware must therefore translate each access. The size of the segment is determined by the storage manager of the operating system; programs that require more space are given longer segments.

## 3.1  Mechanism

Instead of forcing boundaries to lie on chunk boundaries, a region can start anywhere. This flexibility means that storage keys are no longer a reasonable protection mechanism because each word in physical store would need its own lock. The fact that virtual addresses are different from physical addresses provides a more reasonable implementation for protection. Instead of examining each physical (that is, translated) address to see if it is legal by consulting a physical-store descriptor table, the hardware can examine each virtual address by consulting a **virtual-store descriptor table**. Legal virtual addresses must lie between zero and the largest address in virtual space.

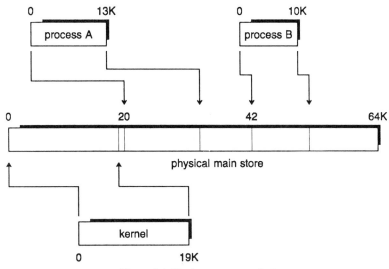

**Figure 3.6** Single-segment method

The hardware requires two pieces of information about the segment for the current process: where it starts in main store (so that it can translate addresses) and how long the segment is (so that it can check each access and forbid those that exceed the segment). These quantities are sometimes called the *base* and the *bounds* of the segment. Instead of building two tables, an address-translation table and a virtual-store descriptor table, the two functions are combined in the address-translation table, declared in line 6 below.

```
1 const
2     BitsPerPhysicalAddress = 24; { for example }
3 type
4     PhysicalAddress = integer; { BitsPerPhysicalAddress bits }
5 var
6     AddressTranslationTable =
7         record
8             Start : PhysicalAddress;
9             Size : integer; { length of virtual space }
10        end;
```

A physical address might not fit in one integer because the machine may have more physical store than can be addressed at one time, and integers may have only enough bits to address the largest virtual store. This detail can be resolved by using extra words for physical addresses. Another common approach is to truncate a $p$-bit physical address by retaining only the upper $v$ bits, where $v$ is the length of the largest virtual address. The lower $p - v$ bits are then assumed to be zero. This approach only allows physical addresses to be represented correctly if the lowest $p - v$ bits are in fact zero.

This method requires segments to be aligned on $(p - v)$-bit boundaries. For example, if virtual addresses are 18 bits long, but physical addresses are 24 bits, segments must start at physical addresses that end with six zeros, that is, addresses divisible by 64. As we saw with partitions, alignment wastes the physical store between the end of one segment and the beginning of the next because the latter must be aligned. In any case, the operating system designer has no choice in this matter; the design of the address-translation table is part of the hardware.

Each process needs its own address-translation table. Since the table is only about two words long, it is quite inexpensive to store it in the context block for the process. When the kernel switches context to this process, it copies the table to the hardware's base and bound registers. The hardware may have separate versions of these registers for privileged and non-privileged state to make context switching more efficient. The algorithm used by the hardware on every access is simple:

```
 1 procedure Translate (VA : VirtualAddress) : PhysicalAddress;
 2 begin
 3    with AddressTranslationTable do
 4       if (VA < 0) or (VA ⩾ Size) then
 5          trap("out of range");
 6       else
 7          Translate := Start + VA;
 8       end; { if }
 9    end; { with }
10 end Translate;
```

Figure 3.7 shows this algorithm. Figure 3.8 shows a concrete example that uses decimal notation and assumes that a virtual address is three digits long and that physical storage is 20,000 bytes.

## 3.2  Benefits

The single-segment approach is much more elegant than the partition approach. Processes benefit in two ways: All programs may assume that they start at location zero, and they never need to establish addressability. In fact, the binding to physical addresses is performed at access time, that is, on every access to virtual store. In addition, a program that runs out of room can request more from the operating system. Such a request may block the process for a while (in medium-term scheduling) as the storage manager rearranges physical store, but as long as the process does not require a larger space than physical store permits, the request can be granted.

The operating system also benefits from the single-segment approach. A process residing in a wait list may be swapped to backing store, freeing a contiguous piece of physical store for some other process. When the previously swapped process is ready again, it may be brought into main store anywhere that it fits. The storage manager need not place it in exactly the same position as before, as long as its context block reflects its current location.

Likewise, in order to make room for new processes, the storage manager may **shuffle** processes around within physical store. Shuffling collects all the free space into one large piece. A process that would not be able to fit in any of the previous smaller pieces might fit there. Shuffling is sometimes called "compaction" because

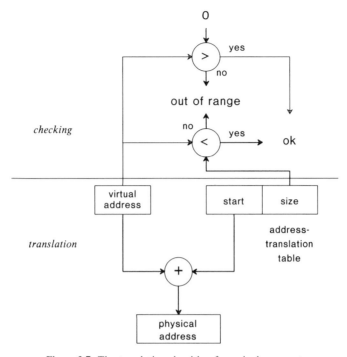

**Figure 3.7** The translation algorithm for a single segment

Start     13426
Size      726

| Virtual address | Physical address |
|:---:|:---:|
| 0 | 13426 |
| 232 | 13658 |
| 233 | 13659 |
| 725 | 14151 |
| 726 | trap: out of range |
| 999 | trap: out of range |
| 1436 | trap: out of range |

**Figure 3.8** Example of address translation

it squeezes all the free space out of the region in use. Figure 3.9 shows the results of shuffling the processes we showed in Figure 3.6. Now there are no tiny, useless holes between segments. The processes **A** and **B** need not know that shuffling has

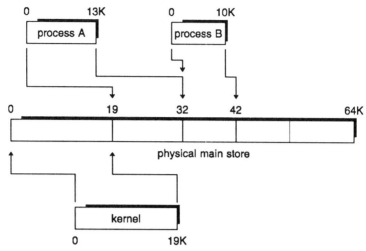

**Figure 3.9**   Result of shuffling

occurred; their virtual space is untouched.

Unfortunately, the single-segment approach has its drawbacks, too. Sharing between processes is not possible except for complete sharing, which is not very useful. Swapping and shuffling can be quite expensive. It has been estimated that as much as 30 percent of the time spent by Tops-10, an operating system for the DEC PDP-10, is spent in a single instruction, the Block Transfer instruction, which is used for shuffling. SCOPE, the operating system for the CDC 6600, reduces this cost by shuffling only when a process terminates. At that time, all free space is collected into one region.

## 3.3 Placement and replacement policies

When a segment is to be swapped in or created, where should it be placed? When not enough room is free to hold the segment, which segment should be swapped out? These policy questions are not particularly easy to answer. We can, however, present some guiding principles.

Several pieces of physical store may be currently available for a new segment. The **best-fit** method picks the free piece that will leave the minimal (but non-negative!) amount of waste if the new segment uses it. This method is generally very bad, since it leads to a proliferation of tiny and therefore useless free pieces and thereby forces large shuffle operations. The **first-fit** method picks the first free piece that is large enough, no matter how much waste there may be. This method is better, but if the algorithm always starts searching from the start of physical store, small pieces tend to cluster near the front. The average search therefore requires probing about half of all free chunks. Figure 3.10 shows how first fit and best fit differ in choosing a region of free space. The recommended allocation

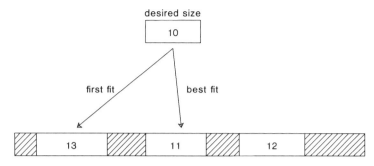

**Figure 3.10** First-fit and best-fit policies

method is **circular first fit**, which is like first fit but starts the search at the point that the previous search left off instead of always starting from the beginning of physical store. Now only a few probes are needed.

Two cautions are in order. First, free space allocation *within* processes shows very different behavior. Most applications require only a few different sizes of space. It is far more efficient to allocate each different space size from a different pool. Adaptive mechanisms that discover the appropriate sizes as they are called for can be used effectively. Second, circular first fit runs into unexpected problems when the total available space is much larger than the average request but some requests are large. The steady-state situation distributes moderate-sized free chunks throughout the total space, leaving none large enough for the occasional large request. In this case, noncircular first fit, even though expensive, leads to higher overall utilization.

To implement any of these methods, the storage manager needs to keep track of which pieces of physical store are in use and which are free. Two data structures are available for this purpose. In the first, called the **boundary-tag** method, each free piece has pointers (physical pointers, of course, which may require more than one word, as discussed earlier) that link all free pieces in a doubly linked list. They don't have to appear in order in that list. Also, each piece, whether free or in use, has the first and last words reserved to indicate its status, free or busy, and its length. When a free block is needed, the doubly linked list is searched from the last stopping point until an adequate piece is found. If necessary, it is split into a new busy piece and a new free piece. If the fit is exact, the entire piece is removed from the doubly linked free list. When a piece is returned to free space, it is joined to the piece before it and after it (if they are free) and then put on the free list.

The other data structure is a **bit map** with one bit for each chunk of physical store. If chunks are as small as one word, the bit map will be unreasonably large. Therefore, chunks are perhaps 16 or 32 words. If the hardware requires segments to begin at $(p-v)$-bit boundaries, then a reasonable chunk size is $2^{p-v}$. The bits in the bit map are packed into contiguous words. Each free chunk may be represented by a zero, and each busy chunk by a one. Finding a free piece of size $c$ chunks is equivalent to finding at least $c$ consecutive zero bits in the bit map.

When a piece is freed, the corresponding bits are reset to zero; it is not necessary to join the piece to its neighbors explicitly.

When adequate room is not available for a new segment, a choice must be made either to swap out some segment or to shuffle. Generally, shuffling takes less time than swapping, but no other activity can proceed meanwhile. Occasionally, swapping out a single small segment will allow two medium-sized free pieces to coalesce into a free piece large enough to satisfy the new segment. A policy to decide whether to shuffle or swap could be based on the percentage of time the storage manager spends shuffling. If that time is less than some fixed percentage, which is a tunable parameter of the policy, then the decision would be to shuffle. Otherwise, some segment would be swapped out.

When it has been decided to swap out a segment, either because shuffling is considered too expensive or because it wouldn't help anyway, which segment is the best victim? First, processes that are in wait lists are good victims. However, in some situations a waiting process must not be swapped out. If the process is waiting for completion of some transput and the operating system has told the relevant device to perform the transfer directly to main store (by a technique known as **direct memory access** or DMA, which is described in Chapter 5), the segments involved must not be swapped out or even shuffled until the transfer is complete. Most DMA devices do not translate addresses but rather deal directly with physical addresses. Even those that do translate addresses might get confused if the translation table changes in the middle of a transfer. We therefore **tie down** any segment that is undergoing DMA transput, rendering it unfit for swapping or shuffling.

For segments that belong to waiting processes and are not tied down, one policy would be to pick the one that belongs to the process that has been waiting the longest. Instead of discussing the ramifications of this policy here, let us defer that discussion to our treatment of paging, which has a similar problem.

If the foregoing methods have still not resulted in adequate space, some ready process must be swapped out. We will place such a process in a main-store wait list (in the medium-term scheduler). Once a process has entered that list, it should remain there for a while, or the cost of swapping it out is not justified by the amount of use we make of the space it makes available. Once a process is released from the main-store wait list, we should try not to penalize it again in the near future. The medium-term scheduler is in charge of the policy that honors some processes with ready status and victimizes others by swapping them out.

## 4 TWO SEGMENTS

The method just discussed, which gives every process a single segment, can be generalized. The first extension is to give each process two segments. In fact, the DEC PDP-10 does just that.

Virtual space is divided into two non-contiguous regions. They can be distinguished by the convention that addresses with a 1 in the most significant bit belong to the "upper" segment. The hardware uses two base-bound registers, one for each segment. With two segments, sharing is finally possible. The convention is to put the instructions of shared programs, like compilers and editors, in the upper segment and to put local data in the lower segment.

It is important that the shared segment not be accidentally or maliciously modified. For this purpose, a "permissions" field is placed in the base-bound register, that is, the address-translation table, which now looks as follows.

```
 1 const
 2    BitsPerPhysicalAddress = 24; { for example }
 3 type
 4    PhysicalAddress = integer; { BitsPerPhysicalAddress bits }
 5    AddressTranslationEntry =
 6       record
 7          Start : PhysicalAddress;
 8          Size : integer; { length of virtual space }
 9          Permissions : set of (Read, Write, Execute);
10       end;
11 var
12    AddressTranslationTable =
13       array 0 : 1 of AddressTranslationEntry;
```

The three permissions in line 9 require some explanation. "Read" means that the process may access the segment to find operands for operations. "Write" means that the results of operations may be stored in the segment. "Execute" means that the process may access the segment to find instructions. A common arrangement would be to have Read and Write permission on the lower segment and only Execute permission on the upper one.

The upper segment is sometimes shared for a different purpose, however. Very large programs cannot fit in one address space. They are split into several processes that communicate through shared data. Those shared data are placed in a shared upper segment. Now the upper segment has Read and Write privilege, whereas the lower has only Execute. Other combinations are possible as well.

Data structures to keep track of shared segments are more complicated. If a segment should be swapped out, it must be marked that way in the context block of each process sharing it. To find those processes, an auxiliary **shared-segment table** is preferable to a complete search of all the context blocks. This table lists all shared segments and the processes that are using them.

Policy decisions for swapping shared segments are also more complicated. A shared segment should be less likely to be swapped proportionally to the number of non-blocked processes that are using it. Tying shared segments down, however, is not a good idea because the processes that share the segment might all be in wait lists for a long time.

Instead of discussing the two-segment case in any greater detail here, let us postpone our curiosity and turn immediately to the more general case.

# 5 SEGMENTATION

We will now allow each process to have a number of segments, numbered 0 through $n-1$, where the process has $n$ segments. There will be some limit on the number of segments permitted, determined, of course, by the hardware. On the DEC PDP-11, there can be eight segments, each 8K bytes long. This limitation, both in the number of segments and in their maximum length, has led operating systems for the PDP-11 either to ignore segmentation entirely and give each process just one contiguous space or to restrict the use of segments. Unix, for example, gives each process three segments. The first is for instructions and may be shared. The second is for data, and the third is for the stack. Each of these segments of virtual space may be composed of several adjacent hardware segments. For example, one segment of virtual space could be 23K bytes long by occupying three hardware segments on the PDP-11.

Having lots of variable-sized segments can be an advantage. Segmentation allows the programmer or the compiler to partition the **name space** of a program — that is, the space of identifiers such as variables and procedures — into discrete segments. Hardware segmentation supports program modularity. For example, a program written in Pascal usually has to check the subscripts of each array reference to make sure they are within bounds. If a separate segment is devoted to that array, the hardware can automatically check the subscripts and relieve the software of that burden. It is also natural to put library routines in segments by themselves and then share those routines among all the processes that might need them.

## 5.1 Implementation

It is no longer sufficient to use the most significant bit of a virtual address to distinguish which segment is being used. Instead, the top $m$ bits of each virtual address are used to select one of $2^m$ segments. Of course, the maximum number of segments is therefore $2^m$. The remaining bits are used to select the **offset** within the segment. The translation table now has an entry for each segment, so we call it a **segment table**. That entry contains the start, size, and permissions of that segment:

```
1 const
2     BitsPerPhysicalAddress = 24; { for example }
3     BitsPerVirtualAddress = 16; { for example }
4     BitsPerSegmentAddress = 6; { for example }
5     BitsPerOffsetAddress  = BitsPerVirtualAddress − BitsPerSegmentAddress
6     SegmentLimit = 2^BitsPerSegmentAddress;
7     OffsetLimit  = 2^BitsPerOffsetAddress;
```

```
 8 type
 9    PhysicalAddress = integer; { containing BitsPerPhysicalAddress bits }
10    AccessType = (Read, Write, Execute);
11    SegmentTableEntry =
12       record
13          Start : PhysicalAddress;
14          Size : integer; { length of virtual space }
15          Permissions : set of AccessType;
16          Present : Boolean;
17       end;
18 var
19    SegmentTable : array 0 : SegmentLimit-1 of SegmentTableEntry;
20    NumberOfSegments : 0 .. SegmentLimit;
```

If we use the numbers suggested in the declarations (lines 2–4), virtual addresses are 16 bits long. Virtual space is therefore limited to 64K bytes. A process may have a virtual space ranging anywhere between 0 bytes and this limit, divided into segments. Of the 16 bits, 6 are used to name the segment. A process may therefore have at most 64 segments, each with a maximum size of 1K bytes. The only way for a process to have a full 64K-byte virtual space is to have all 64 segments and for each segment to be the full 1K bytes in length. In our example, a physical address is described by 24 bits. The largest amount of physical store that may be placed on the machine is therefore 16M bytes. A particular machine may have less store, of course. Main store for computers of this size is usually purchased in increments of 256K, 512K, or 1M bytes.

The algorithm used by the hardware on every access can be represented as follows:

```
21 procedure Translate (VA : VirtualAddress; AT : AccessType) : PhysicalAddress;
22 var
23    Segment : 0 .. SegmentLimit - 1;
24    Offset : 0 .. OffsetLimit - 1;
25 begin
26    Segment := VA div OffsetLimit;
27    Offset := VA mod OffsetLimit;
28    if Segment ≥ NumberOfSegments then
29       trap("invalid segment number");
30    else
31       with SegmentTable[Segment] do
32          if not Present then
33             trap("missing segment");
34             { segment fault; not an error }
35          elsif Offset ≥ Size then
36             trap("offset out of range";
37          elsif not AT in Permissions then
38             trap("security violation");
39          else
40             Translate := Start + Offset;
41          end; { if }
42       end; { with }
43    end; { if }
44 end Translate;
```

Figure 3.11 shows the algorithm followed by the hardware on every access to translate and check addresses. As a concrete example, consider the following

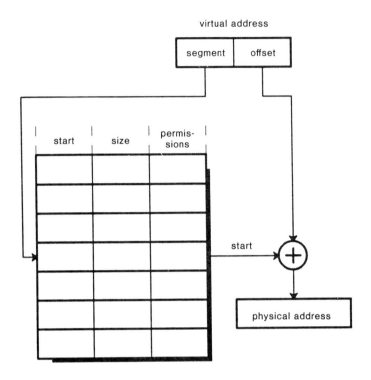

address-translation table

**Figure 3.11** Hardware translation for segmentation

situation. Again, let us use decimal notation. Assume that a virtual address is three digits long and physical store has 20,000 bytes, as before. Assume that the first digit determines the segment number and the other two digits determine the offset.

Segment Table

| Segment number | Start | Size | Permissions | Present |
|:---:|:---:|:---:|:---:|:---:|
| 0 | 13426 | 26 | R W X | yes |
| 1 | 2309 | 00 | R | yes |
| 2 | 1000 | 23 | W X | yes |
| 3 | — | 95 | W | no |
| 4 | 10000 | 100 | R W X | yes |

Number of segments = 5
R = Read, W = Write, X = Execute

| Virtual address | Access type | Physical address |
|:---:|:---:|:---|
| 0 | R | 13426 |
| 217 | W | 1017 |
| 217 | R | trap: security violation |
| 232 | R | trap: offset out of range |
| 394 | R | trap: missing segment, security violation |
| 499 | X | 10099 |
| 725 | X | trap: invalid segment number |

Several traps can apply to the same reference. For example, the Read reference to location 394 traps both because the segment is missing and because of security violation. If the machine can only report one trap for a reference, it is better to report traps that indicate program error (like security violation) than those that indicate that help from the storage manager is needed (like missing segment).

## 5.2 Storing the necessary information

Missing segments are, of course, swapped out. The segment table must indicate that accesses to such segments should generate traps. We have shown a Boolean (one-bit) field called "Present" in the segment table (line 16 of the declarations) to indicate this fact. Instead, we could have set the segment length to zero or removed all access privileges. Then the hardware would still trap to the kernel, but now the kernel would have to refer to the context block for the process to find out whether the trap signals that the process is attempting an invalid access or a valid access to a missing segment.

Such treatment of the segment-length or permissions field is an example of the **mirror tables** technique. Under this technique, the hardware table is intentionally misleading in order to have the hardware take some special action that would be too expensive in software. The actual state of affairs is honestly represented in a second set of tables stored by the kernel. Mirror tables are used either when the hardware lacks some needed field (for example, the hardware segment table lacks a Present field) or for reasons of efficiency (for example, composite page tables for processes that are themselves operating systems).

Before a missing segment may be accessed, the storage manager must swap that segment back into main store. To find it on backing store, the storage manager must remember its location. Some hardware provides another field in the segment table for this purpose. This field is ignored by the hardware. If the hardware provides only a Present field, the storage manager can use the Start and Permissions fields to store the backing-store address, if there is room. The use of the same field to mean different things at different times is called **overloading**. If overloading is not possible, the storage manager can save a mirror copy of the translation table in the context block, and this copy can have a "backing-store location" field.

## 5.3 Swapping

Once the missing segment has been swapped back in, the kernel switches back to the context in which the process was running. Its program counter is reset to the instruction that failed previously. The hardware then tries to execute that instruction again. If all is well, no new trap will occur. However, the instruction might still fail for several reasons. It might require another operand from another segment that is also missing. In fact, a single instruction on a three-address machine can cause five segment faults: one for each of the two operands, one for the result, and two for the instruction itself if it lies on a boundary between two segments. (We are not even considering the case where operands can cross segment boundaries!) The storage manager keeps bringing in segments until the process can continue. With luck, some other process is ready and can make use of the processor while the segments are being swapped in.

The decision to swap out a segment does not completely inactivate the process that was using it. As long as the process avoids accessing virtual addresses within that segment, it can continue to run. When it does require that segment, the hardware will trap to the kernel. We call this event a **segment fault**. The storage manager will swap that segment back in. While the segment is being swapped in, which takes on the order of 20 to 50 milliseconds (depending on what sort of backing store is used and how long the segment is), the kernel switches to some other process. Once the segment is in, the first process will be allowed to continue. It has no inkling that a segment fault occurred. (Otherwise, the operating system would violate the Beautification Principle.)

When the storage manager needs to swap some segment out in order to make room for some other segment, it is best to choose a segment that is not currently in use by any process. Otherwise, a segment fault in one process may impede progress in other processes as well. We will devote a great deal of attention to mechanisms to accomplish this feat when we discuss paging.

One danger should be mentioned. Since a single instruction might require five or more different segments in order to be executed, segments that have just been brought in should not be subject to swapping out before they have even been used the first time, or else the operating system might thrash by victimizing segments that are needed for the current instruction.

Swapping out a segment is not always expensive. A segment that does not have write permission (by any process that uses it) need not be written to backing store because it has not changed since it was last on backing store. It is only necessary to reset its Present field to false in the segment table and to reclaim its space. Similarly, writable segments that have not been changed since they were last swapped in are cheap to swap out. Some machines set a Boolean field called "Dirty" in the segment table entry to true whenever a write access occurs to the corresponding segment. The storage manager initializes Dirty to false whenever it swaps the segment in. When a segment is about to be swapped out, it only needs to be written to backing store if Dirty is true. Of course, this mechanism requires that a copy be kept on the backing store of all segments that are brought into main store.

## 5.4 Large segment spaces

On some machines, the number of bits devoted to the segment number is very large. For example, the Honeywell 645, which supports the Multics operating system, has 18 bits of segment number. Instead of using segments in a range from zero to some reasonably small number, programs in such machines may use a few segment numbers scattered within the enormous space of possibilities. The reason Multics uses so many segments is that every subprogram that exists has its own segment number that is reserved for as long as the subprogram is saved on secondary store; this time could be years.

The implementation just described does not work very well for large, sparse segment spaces because the segment table has one entry for each potential segment. The hardware is certainly not going to refer directly to a table with $2^{18} = 256K$ entries; such a table would require more physical store than most computers have! Instead, a hashing technique can be used, a technique that first converts the segment number into an index in a hash table where the desired entry can be found. Another alternative is to apply paging to the segment table. To understand that solution, we must first understand paging, which will be presented shortly.

The hardware either stores the entire segment table in registers if it is short or uses a cache to store the most frequently used entries, in conformance with the Cache Principle. If the hardware had to refer to main store each time it needed to translate an address, the effective speed of the machine would be halved. The storage manager does not need to know anything at all about the cache, except that whenever the kernel modifies the segment table itself, for example when switching processes, the hardware must find out which entries in the cache are invalid. Machines that have such **translation look-aside buffers**, as we will call these caches, have an instruction called "flush the cache," which informs the hardware that all the entries in its cache, if any, are no longer valid. The kernel should execute this instruction as part of process switching.

## 5.5 Shared segments

Two processes that share a segment don't have to use the same segment number, nor need they have identical privileges over that segment. One process could call it segment 5 and have RX privileges, and the other could call it segment 1 and have WR privileges. This segment has two separate entries, one in the segment table for each process. The same physical segment may even appear twice in the virtual space of one process. However, sharing an instruction segment with different segment numbers can be difficult. Such segments tend to refer to themselves (in jumps, for example). These references cannot have the segment number as part of the instruction. Instead, they must refer to a register that holds the segment number.

Shared segments cause problems with Dirty fields because a shared segment may be written by process **A**, and then swapped out when process **B** is running. The hardware only knows about process **B**'s segment table at this point, and the table will not indicate that the segment is dirty unless **B** has written into it. The storage manager must consult a shared-segment table in order to track down all the Dirty fields that correspond to this shared segment in all the context blocks for the processes that share it.

## 5.6  Unusable space

Segmentation creates three kinds of unusable space that cannot be applied to any process.

- Free pieces of physical store that are not in use at the moment are wasted. Some of these pieces may be too small to be of any use until the storage manager shuffles the current segments. We will call such unusable space **external waste**, since it is outside the space of any process. We also saw external waste under the partition method.
- Context blocks must hold copies of the segment table during the time that a process is not running. Space devoted to the segment table cannot be put to other uses when the process is running; it is a fixed cost of segmentation. If the segment tables are large, they may be swapped out to reduce this cost. Space that is unusable because it is needed for these tables we will call **overhead space**.
- A process might not be using all the space in a segment; it may have asked for a segment that is bigger than is really needed. This type of unused area is called **internal waste**.

Segmentation tends to have very little internal waste because processes generally request exactly the amount of space they need. Any internal waste that exists is not the storage manager's fault; it is due to restrictions imposed by the hardware that require segment lengths to be divisible by some power of 2.

External waste can be reduced by shuffling, but that solution is expensive. If segments are aligned to chunk boundaries, at the end of each segment there will be a small amount of unavoidable external waste ranging from 0 bytes to 1 byte less than the chunk size. On the average, this external waste will be one-half a chunk size for each segment in main store. The amount of overhead space depends on how many segments are allowed, a number that itself depends on the number of bits in a virtual address allocated to the segment number. The more segments that are allowed, the more space is devoted to overhead, and the smaller the segments may be. The amount of overhead space is not under the control of the operating system designer except for the decision to swap unused segment tables.

## 5.7 Initial loading and execution

A program needs separate segments to store different data items or subroutines. Cooperation between the storage manager and the loader establishes the initial assignment of segments in virtual store, and cooperation between the storage manager and the running process can change that assignment dynamically. The load image must specify in which segment each instruction or data section belongs. Instruction segments typically get Execute permission only; data sections can be specified to be either Read/Write or only Read. When the loader initializes virtual space, it can bring all the segments into main store or can leave them on backing store. In the latter case, the program will slowly acquire the segments it needs by faulting.

The Split service call might indicate the disposition of each segment in the parent's virtual space:

- **Unique**. The segment becomes the sole property of either the parent or the child. The segment table for the other process indicates that the segment is absent.
- **Shared**. The segment is listed in the segment tables of both parent and child.
- **Copied**. The child gets a private version, initialized as a copy of the segment still owned by the parent. The storage manager copies the data and builds a new segment, allocating backing store at the same time. Alternatively, the storage manager can employ a form of **lazy evaluation**: Let child and parent share the segment, but deny both of them Write permission. Perhaps neither will ever try to modify the data. As soon as either one does, the hardware will trap to the storage manager, which can make a new copy for the child and give both processes Write permission over their (now private) copies. This technique is called **copy on write**.

A process that wants to change the structure of its virtual store dynamically can use a variety of service calls:

- ☐ GetSegment(descriptor) / ReleaseSegment(segment). The first call returns the segment number of a newly allocated segment. The descriptor indicates the desired size and permissions. The second call removes the given segment from the caller's segment table.
- ☐ GetStore(segment, size) / ReleaseStore(segment, size). These calls lengthen or shorten a segment.
- ☐ ChangeSegment(segment, permissions). This call lets the process add or remove Read, Write, and Execute permissions to or from its segment. The operating system may disallow changing permissions on shared segments.

# 6 PAGING

We now turn to the most common storage management method in use. Paging has the same hardware flavor as segmentation except that the problem of allocating physical store among different-sized segments is removed by insisting that each segment-like chunk be exactly the same length. We will call each such chunk a **page**. The virtual space of a process is subdivided into as many pages as are needed, depending on its length.

We saw that segmentation supported software modularity by allowing a program's name space to be partitioned. Paging, in constrast, partitions virtual space without regard to logical entities residing in that space. Paging is therefore **transparent** to the process. The fact that virtual space is subdivided into pages does not affect the way the process is programmed or the way it treats virtual space. Later, we will examine combinations that incorporate the semantics of segmentation as well as the regularity of paging.

Paging is a pleasant contrast to segmentation from the point of view of the storage-manager implementer. Shuffling is eliminated because all free areas in physical store are one page-length long. A page may be placed in any such free area; there is no need to treat adjacent free areas together as part of a larger free area. We will treat physical store as an array of bins into which pages may be placed; these bins are called **page frames**:

```
1 const
2    BitsPerVirtualAddress = 18; { for example }
3    BitsPerPhysicalAddress = 24; { for example }
4    BitsPerVirtualPageAddress = 8; { for example }
5    BitsPerOffsetAddress =
6       BitsPerVirtualAddress − BitsPerVirtualPageAddress;
7    PageSize = 2^BitsPerOffsetAddress;
8    NumberOfPageFrames = 2^BitsPerPhysicalAddress / PageSize;
9       { maximum allowed by the hardware; we may have fewer }
10   PageLimit = 2^BitsPerVirtualAddress / PageSize;
11      { number of pages per virtual space }
12 type
13   PageFrame = array 0 : PageSize − 1 of byte;
14   PageFrameNumber = 0 .. NumberOfPageFrames − 1;
15   PhysicalStore = array PageFrameNumber of PageFrame;
```

If we use the constants suggested in lines 2−4, virtual addresses are 18 bits long. Virtual space is therefore limited to 256K bytes. A process may have a virtual space ranging anywhere between 0 bytes and this limit in increments of one page size. A virtual page address is 8 bits. The 256K bytes of virtual store are therefore divided into 256 pages, each having 1K bytes. The number of bits in an offset is $18 − 8 = 10$, which fits this page size. The largest virtual space has $256K/1K = 256$ pages. A physical address is described by 24 bits. As a result, the largest amount of physical store that may be placed on the machine is 16M bytes. A particular machine may have less store. Physical store can have as many as 16M/1K = 16K page frames. On this particular machine, physical space is much larger than any virtual space. This situation is found, for example, on some 16-bit computers like the DEC PDP-11. More typically, virtual spaces are allowed to be larger than the amount of physical store present.

Pages fit exactly into page frames in physical store, so there is no external waste. However, internal waste is likely because a program might not need a virtual store whose length is exactly divisible by the page size. On the average, each process will waste one half of the last page. The choice of page size, which is a policy bound at the time the operating system is designed, involves a tradeoff among various considerations:

(1)     overhead space — least with large pages, since page tables have fewer entries.

(2)     internal waste — smallest with small pages, since one-half of a small page is small. Figure 3.12 shows the contrast between small and large pages for the same virtual space. When pages are small, there is less internal waste, but the page table is longer.

(3)     cold-start faults — lower with large pages. These are the faults needed to bring the program into main store the first time. With larger pages, there are fewer total pages, hence fewer cold-start faults.

(4)     page-fault rate — generally lower with small pages, assuming that a fixed amount of main store is available. Regions of heavy use within a virtual space tend to be relatively small, and the computer can fit more such regions into a fixed-size main store if page size is small.

(5)     efficiency of transfer between main and backing store — best with large pages, since they take about the same amount of time as small pages to transfer. The total transfer time is dominated by disk rotational and seek latency, not transfer latency. (We discuss disk transfers in Chapter 5.)

Larger pages are generally better, unless they become so large that too few processes in the ready list can have pages in main store at the same time. As main store has become less expensive, page sizes have increased, until now they are sometimes as large as 8K bytes, although sizes from 512 bytes to 4K bytes are more common.

## 6.1 Implementation

The address-translation table used by the hardware is called a **page table**. Its structure is determined by the architecture of the computer. Entries in the page table do not contain a Size field, since they are all the same length. As with segmentation, address translation first splits the virtual address into two parts: the **page number** and the **offset**. Here is how a typical translation table might look:

small pages

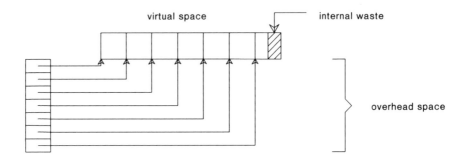

large pages

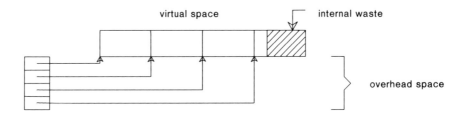

**Figure 3.12** Wasted space and page size

```
1 type
2    AccessType = (Read, Write, Execute);
3    PageTableEntry =
4       record
5          Location : PageFrameNumber;
6          Permissions : set of AccessType;
7          Present : Boolean;
8       end;
9 var
10    PageTable: array 0 : PageLimit-1 of PageTableEntry;
11    NumberOfPages : 0 .. PageLimit;
```

Because pages are aligned to page frames in physical store, the table need not keep physical addresses for the Location field; the page frame number suffices. Here is the algorithm followed by the hardware to translate each access:

```
12 procedure Translate (VA : VirtualAddress; AT : AccessType) : PhysicalAddress;
13 var
14    VirtualPage : 0 .. PageLimit — 1;
15    Offset : 0 .. PageSize — 1;
16 begin
17    VirtualPage := VA div PageSize; { performed by extracting bits }
18    Offset := VA mod PageSize; { performed by extracting bits }
19    if VirtualPage ⩾ NumberOfPages then
20       trap("invalid page number");
21    else
22       with PageTable[VirtualPage] do
23          if not Present then
24             trap("missing page"); { page fault; not an error }
25          elsif not AT in Permissions then
26             trap("security violation");
27          else
28             Translate := Location*PageSize + Offset;
29          end; { if }
30       end; { with }
31    end; { if }
32 end Translate;
```

Figure 3.13 shows the algorithm followed by the hardware on every access to
translate and check addresses. This algorithm involves checking the page table,
which is typically in main store, for every translation. (Some early machines, such

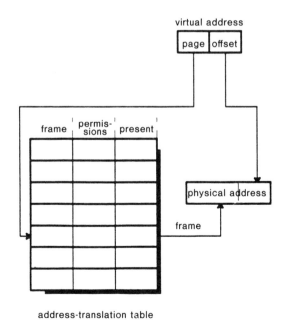

**Figure 3.13** Hardware algorithm for translating page-oriented access

as the Nova 3/D, stored page tables in high-speed registers, but this design has
become less popular with potentially large page tables.) To reduce the time
required for translation, many machines provide a **translation look-aside buffer**
(TLB) to hold the most frequently used parts of the current page table. The
hardware simultaneously tries to find the desired entry in the TLB and in main
store. If the entry is in the TLB (there is a cache hit), the hardware finds it very
quickly (on the order of 100 nanoseconds) and aborts its attempt to get the entry
from main store, an operation that would have taken about one microsecond to
complete. If the entry is not in the TLB (there is a cache miss), the main-store
reference is allowed to complete, and its value is not only used for address translation but also placed in the TLB for future use. We will postpone discussing which
entry in the TLB is discarded in this case; the policies are very similar to policies
we will introduce for page replacement. Typical translation look-aside buffers can
achieve a 95 percent hit ratio.

Here is an example of a paging situation with two processes, **A** and **B**. We
will assume that both are simultaneously using parts of physical store. For simplicity, we will make virtual addresses two decimal digits, of which the first is the
page number and the second is the offset. We will also show the contents of a
translation look-aside buffer that holds two entries of the current page table. For
this example, we will not let the TLB entries change, even if a cache miss occurs.
**A** is currently running, so entries in the translation look-aside buffer refer to it.

Page table for process A

| Virtual page number | Page frame |
|---------------------|------------|
| 0                   | 7          |
| 1                   | 8          |
| 2                   | absent     |
| 3                   | 4          |
| Number of pages = 4 |            |

Page table for process B

| Virtual page number | Page frame |
|---------------------|------------|
| 0                   | 2          |
| 1                   | absent     |
| 2                   | 8          |
| Number of pages = 3 |            |

Translation look-aside buffer (**A** is active)

| virtual page number | page frame |
|:---:|:---:|
| 1 | 8 |
| 3 | 4 |

Main Store

| 0 | 1 | 2 | 3 | 4 | 5 | 6 | 7 | 8 | 9 |
|---|---|---|---|---|---|---|---|---|---|
|   |   | **B**(0) |   | **A**(3) |   |   | **A**(0) | **A**(1) |   |
|   |   |   |   |   |   |   |   | **B**(2) |   |

Translations

| Virtual address | Physical address |
|:---:|:---|
| 71 | cache miss, invalid page trap |
| 14 | 84 |
| 23 | cache miss, page fault |
| 06 | 76 (cache miss) |

## 6.2 Security and sharing

The same security scheme that we saw for segmentation can be applied to paging. Page table entries may specify permissible access independently for each virtual page. Because each page has separate permissions, different items that require different access restrictions, such as instructions and data, should not reside on the same page. Sharing instructions between processes also requires that data be separated, or else some data may be inadvertently shared, a situation that could confuse both processes. However, because the process does not involve itself in the concept of pages, separating instructions from data on separate pages is not natural to the process. Still, compilers and assemblers can distinguish instructions from data and can pass this information on to the linker. The linker, in turn, can segregate regions that require separate access restrictions and can make sure that each starts on a new page. (This practice increases the amount of internal waste.) The load image is then marked so that the loader can identify and properly restrict access to each region.

One clever idea, found in VMS and Dynix, is for the linker to put nothing in the first page of virtual store. This page is then marked invalid by the storage manager. If the process accidentally tries to follow a null or uninitialized pointer, there is a good chance that it will generate an access into that first page. which will cause a trap.

## 6.3  Case study:  Multics

Multics is an operating system designed for the Honeywell 645 computer.  It was developed at M.I.T. in cooperation with Bell Labs and the computer department of General Electric.  Since its design around 1965, it has been in use at M.I.T. and elsewhere, and a version of it is now marketed by the Honeywell Corporation.

Multics combines paging and segmentation.  This structure is a natural consequence of two design goals.  First, the designers wanted to allow processes to refer to enormous numbers of segments.  They allocated 18 bits of each address to the segment name.  The segment table can therefore be much too long to maintain in main store, so it must be paged.  Second, they wanted to allow individual segments to be quite large.  They allocated the other 18 bits of each address to the offset within the segment.  Main store could hold only a few segments of full size. Therefore, segments are themselves paged.  Of the 18 bits showing offset in a segment, 8 indicate the page and the other 10 the offset within the page.  A virtual space therefore has up to $2^{18} = 256$K segments, each segment has up to $2^8 = 256$ pages, and each page has $2^{10} = 1$K words.  (Actually, pages of 64 words are available, but we will ignore them.)  The total virtual space is described by 36 bits, representing 64G words.  The top 18 bits, [0..17], represent the segment number. The next 8 bits, [18..25], represent the page number, and the lowest 10 bits, [26..35], represent the offset within the segment.

Each process has its own segment table.  This table is placed in a segment of its own (the "descriptor segment") that is usually not in the virtual space of the process.  Each entry in the segment table has the following information.

- a pointer to the page table for this segment
- the length of the segment (in pages)
- permissions for the segment (read, write, execute, use as stack)
- a Boolean Present field (if false, the entire segment, and possibly its page table, is swapped out)

The segment table is found by the hardware through a register that looks just like one of the segment table entries.  This register, called the DBR for "descriptor base register," holds a segment table entry for the segment table.  The 36-bit program counter is stored in another register.

Each segment, including the descriptor segment, is described by a page table. The page table holds one entry for each page in the segment, storing the following information.

- the page frame that holds this page
- a Boolean Present field (if false, this page is swapped out)

We are ignoring fields used for page-replacement algorithms, such as a Dirty and a Used field for each page-table entry.

Each such entry fits within one word, and a page table has at most 256 entries, so four complete page tables can be stored within a single page frame. We will assume that only one page table is stored in a page frame, so a page-frame number is enough to describe the location of a page table. Here is a formal description of the data structures and the address translation algorithm:

```
 1 const
 2     BitsPerVirtualAddress = 36;
 3     BitsPerPhysicalAddress = 24;
 4     BitsPerSegmentAddress = 18;
 5     BitsPerVirtualPageAddress = 8;
 6     BitsPerOffsetAddress  = 10;
 7     PageSize = 1024 = 2^10; { words per page }
 8     PageLimit = 256 = 2^8; { pages per segment }
 9     NumberOfPageFrames = 2^14; { page frames per physical store }
10     SegmentLimit = 2^18; { segments per virtual space }
11 type
12     PageFrameNumber = 0 .. NumberOfPageFrames − 1;
13     AccessType = (Read, Write, Execute, Stack);
14     SegmentTableEntry =
15        record { fits in one word }
16            PageTablePointer : PageFrameNumber;
17            Size : 1 .. 256; { number of pages }
18            Permissions : set of AccessType;
19            Present : Boolean;
20        end;
21     PageTableEntry =
22        record { fits in one word }
23            Location : PageFrameNumber;
24            Present : Boolean;
25        end;
26 var
27     DescriptorBaseRegister : SegmentTableEntry; { in hardware }
```

```
28 procedure Translate (VA : VirtualAddress) : PhysicalAddress;
29 var
30    Segment : 0 .. SegmentLimit - 1;
31    Page : 0 .. PageLimit - 1;
32    Offset : 0 .. PageSize - 1;
33    DescriptorPageTable : PhysicalAddress;
34    PageInSegmentTable : PhysicalAddress;
35    PageTable : PhysicalAddress;
36    PageFrame : PhysicalAddress;
37 begin
38    Segment := VA [0..17];
39    Page := VA [18..25];
40    Offset := VA [26..35];
41    DescriptorPageTable := DescriptorBaseRegister.PageTablePointer
42       * PageSize;
43    PageInSegmentTable :=
44       (DescriptorPageTable + Segment [0..7])^.Location * PageSize;
45    PageTable :=
46       (PageInSegmentTable + Segment [8..17]) ^.PageTablePointer
47       * PageSize;
48    PageFrame := (PageTable + Page)^.Location * PageSize;
49    Translate := PageFrame + Offset;
50 end Translate;
```

For clarity, all the security checks have been omitted. Even so, the algorithm is quite complicated. Figure 3.14 shows the essential steps for translating the virtual address (S,P,F). The circled numbers represent values that are computed at corresponding lines in the program. This figure omits the fact that the segment table is itself paged. Lines 41—44 of the program perform the translation shown in dotted lines in the figure. This part of the algorithm is shown in more detail in Figure 3.15. The machine uses a translation look-aside buffer to avoid address translation while finding the descriptor page table, the page of the segment table, and the segment page table.

In both figures, the letters a through f refer to the checks that might fail during translation:

a   The segment number is beyond the limit for this process.
b   The process does not have the necessary access permission over any part of its virtual store.
c   The segment table is missing.
d   The appropriate page of the segment table is missing.
e   The page number is beyond the limit for this segment.
f   The process does not have the necessary access permission over this segment.
g   The page table for this segment is missing.
h   The particular page accessed is missing.

Traps c, d, g, and h are failures due to swapped-out information that must be brought into main store before the access can complete. Traps a, b, e, and f signal errors in the process.

Shared segments are allowed in Multics. The storage manager maintains an "active-segment table" to record which segments are currently in use by any

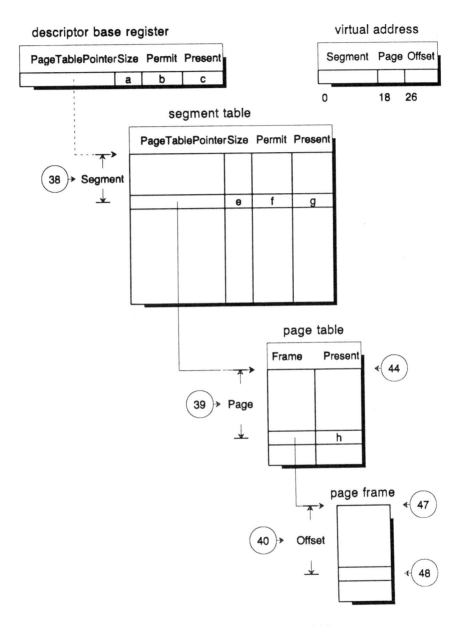

**Figure 3.14** Address translation under Multics

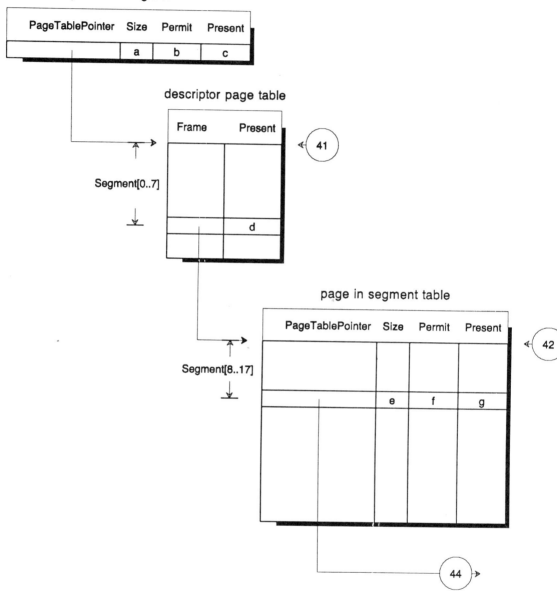

**Figure 3.15**  Paging the segment table

process.  Each entry in this table has the following information.

- the external name of the segment
- a Boolean Present field (if false, the entire segment is swapped out)

- a list of each process using this segment and the local segment number used by that process for this segment

This table is useful in deciding whether to swap out a segment, and it also points the storage manager to all the segment tables that are affected when a segment is swapped in or out. Each process that shares a given segment has its own entry for that segment in its segment table under its own local number for that segment. Each entry for the same segment points to the same page table. The page table for a shared segment is stored only once.

## 6.4 Case study: VAX

The DEC VAX is a family of computers, all of which share the same address translation techniques. Whereas Multics has two layers, the first segmentation and the second paging, the VAX has two paging layers; the user's page table is itself paged. The reason for this design is similar to the reasons for Multics: Processes are given so much virtual space that the page tables can be absurdly long.

In the VAX, a virtual address is 32 bits long. Bits [0..1] indicate which of three page tables to use. Each process has two page tables. The first is intended for program and fixed-size data, and the second for data structures that grow, like a stack. The third page table is shared by all processes and by the kernel, and is intended for shared subroutines and for kernel program. Processes are not allowed to access kernel program. In a sense, these three page tables are three predefined segments, so one could say that the VAX supports one level of segmentation and two levels of paging. Bits [2..22] of a virtual address is the page number. There are $2^{21} = 2M$ pages in a full address space, so it is unreasonable to store the entire page table in main store, which often contains only 2M bytes. It is unreasonable even on the largest VAX holding 32M bytes of main store. Therefore, the page tables are themselves paged. Bits [23..31] of a virtual address give the offset within a page. There are $2^9 = 512$ bytes in a page.

Access permissions are determined for each page based on a combination of the processor state and the type of access required. There are four processor states, ranging from the most privileged (kernel state) to the least (user state). There are two kinds of access, read and write. Read permission grants execute rights, and write permission grants read rights as well. One might expect $3^4 = 81$ different permission combinations for each page, requiring 7 bits (or 8 for the most straightforward encoding). Instead, only 3 bits are used to encode the 15 combinations in which any right granted to one processor state is also granted to more privileged states. In the data structures below, we represent these combinations with strings like NNRW, which means that the lower two processor states have no access, the next one has read access, and the most privileged state has write access.

```
 1 type
 2    PageFrameNumber = 0 .. 2²¹ - 1;
 3    Protection = (NNNN, NNNR, NNNW, NNRR, NNRW, NNWW, NRRR,
 4       NRRW, NRWW, NWWW, RRRR, RRRW, RRWW, RWWW, WWWW);
 5    PageTableEntry =
 6       record { 32 bits long }
 7          Present : Boolean; { bit [0] }
 8          Protection : Protection; { bits [1..3] }
 9          Dirty : Boolean; { bit [4] }
10          PageFrame : PageFrameNumber; { bits [15..35] }
11       end;
12 var
13    KernelBaseRegister : PageFrameNumber; { in a register}
14       { base of the kernel page table, which is contiguous in physical store
15    KernelLength : integer;
16       { Maximum kernel page accessible }
17    ProcessBaseRegister0, ProcessBaseRegister1 : integer; { 30 bits}
18       { interpreted in kernel virtual space }
19    ProcessLength0, ProcessLength1 : integer;
20       { Maximum process page accessible }
```

Figure 3.16 shows the tables and the translation algorithm for a reference made by a process. This figure does not specify whether access is through page table 0 or page table 1. As in the previous figures, Figure 3.16 shows the checks that are made. These are the traps that can occur:

a    The page table entry for this page is located beyond the end of kernel space.

b    The kernel does not have the read permission for the appropriate page of the process page table.

c    The appropriate page of the page table is missing.

d    The page is beyond the end of process space. (This check is made by comparing all the bits of Page against ProcessLength.)

e    The process does not have access permission for the type of access it is trying to make on this page.

f    The desired page is missing.

Of these, trap b is a kernel error, traps a, d, and e are process errors, and traps c and f are ordinary page faults that are treated by swapping in the necessary pages. The VAX architecture makes these tests in the order d, a, b, c, e, f.

## 6.5 Paging in virtual machines

In Chapter 1, we saw how a virtual machine operating system provides a process interface that appears identical to the hardware interface. We turn now to a subject we deferred then, how storage management fits into virtual machine operating systems.

The most significant issue is how to emulate address-translation tables. For the sake of concreteness, we will discuss paging, although the same issues arise for any of the other storage management mechanisms we have seen. Each virtual

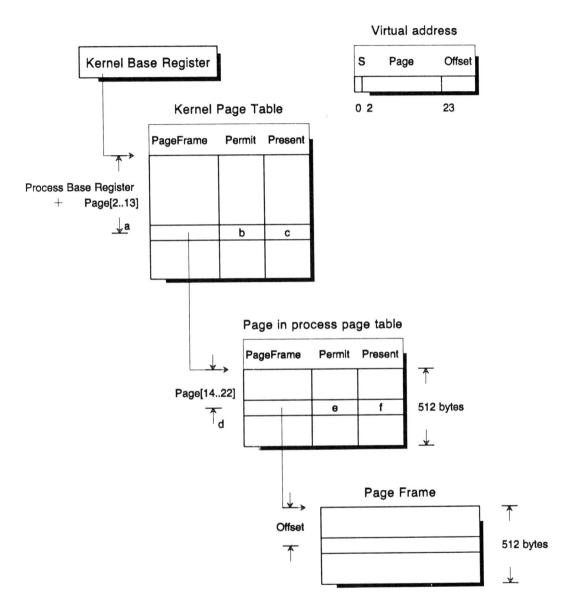

**Figure 3.16**  Address translation in the VAX

machine $P_i$ running under the control of a single virtualizing kernel **V** needs to access what it considers to be the true address-translation tables, since virtual machines are meant to look just like the bare machine. However, **V** needs to use those tables itself to manage space for the various $P_i$. Therefore, each $P_i$ has its own private copy of the address-translation tables, which it uses to convert what it considers physical space into a set of virtual spaces for its own clients. Those second-order clients have second-order virtual space.

This situation is sketched in Figure 3.17. **V**, the virtualizing kernel, has two clients, processes **P**$_1$ and **P**$_2$. Each of these inhabits its own virtual machine. To keep the example simple, these virtual machines are tiny: Each has a virtual main store of three pages. The figure shows the page tables maintained by **V** to manage the two virtual spaces, as well as a picture of main store as seen from **V**'s point of view. The only fields shown in the page tables are Page Frame and Present. Residing in **P**$_1$ is an ordinary operating system, which currently supports two processes, **D**$_1$ and **D**$_2$. Together, they occupy all the main store available to **P**$_1$. (In a more realistic example, we would have to leave some room in that store for **P**$_1$'s kernel as well.) Another operating system resides in **P**$_2$, and it has only one client, process **E**$_1$.

Let us imagine that **D**$_1$ is currently executing. None of the five page tables shown is appropriate for the hardware to use. When **D**$_1$ refers to page 0, that should map to page 2 of **P**$_1$, which is in page frame 6 of the main store. Similarly,

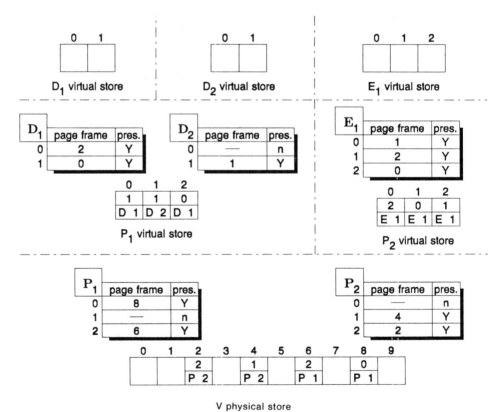

V physical store

**Figure 3.17** Two levels of address translation

$D_1$'s page 1 should map to page 0 of $P_1$, which is page 8 of main store. In other words, the proper page table for $D_1$ is a **composite** of the tables for $D_1$ and $P_1$. In mathematical terms, this page table composes the mappings specified by tables $D_1$ and $P_1$. If $P_1$ were also a virtualizing kernel, more adjacent levels of the virtual-machine hierarchy would need to be composed.

The composite page tables to use for $D_1$, $D_2$, and $E_1$ are shown in Figure 3.18. To run $D_1$ efficiently, its composite page table must be made available to the hardware. The ordinary page tables become a mirror that contains the "truth" about main-store allocation, and the hardware uses a table fabricated from these mirror tables. The hardware table is sometimes called a "shadow table" because it is just a fiction needed for efficient execution.

$P_1$ cannot be expected to prepare this composite table because it does not know anything about the $P_1$ table; it believes that it is executing on the bare machine. Therefore, it is $V$'s job to prepare these composite tables. Composite tables must be updated whenever any of their component tables changes. For example, the composite for $D_1$ depends on two tables. If $P_1$ should decide to swap out one of $D_1$'s pages, $P_1$ will modify $D_1$'s page table. $V$ must notice this change and update $D_1$'s composite page table. $V$ can follow either of two strategies to make sure the composites are accurate.

- **Eager evaluation**: $V$ can map $P_i$'s virtual space so that when $P_i$ modifies what it thinks is a page table, it actually writes into read-only store. The resulting trap informs $V$ of the attempt. As $V$ emulates the change, it also updates its composite table.
- **Lazy evaluation**: $V$ can map $P_i$'s virtual space so that $P_i$ may read and write what it thinks is the page table. Whenever $P_i$ tries to switch context to one of its processes, $V$ must emulate the context switch, at which time it builds a composite table for the process to which $P_i$ is switching.

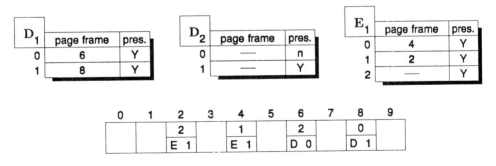

V physical store

**Figure 3.18**  Composite page tables

The eager-evaluation method must be used for the page tables that $P_i$ uses to control its own (privileged-state) access to main store. It is the only method possible if modifications to address-translation tables can only be made by privileged instructions. The lazy approach can be much less work in the long run, especially if there are many levels to the virtual-machine hierarchy. (Every virtualizing level builds its own composite tables.) Just as we saw in Chapter 1, enhanced hardware can make composition easier. The IBM 370 hardware can compose address-translation maps "on the fly," relieving the virtualizing kernel of this responsibility.

# 7  PAGE-REPLACEMENT POLICIES

The sum of all the virtual spaces in use by all processes may vastly exceed physical store size. This situation certainly holds under multiprogramming, whether batch or interactive. It can even hold under a one-process regimen if the process is very large. Whenever all of virtual space cannot fit in physical store, the storage manager must decide which pages should be in main store and which on backing store. Although these decisions may be made at any time, the storage manager is certainly forced to make a decision whenever a page fault occurs.

The process that suffers a page fault cannot continue until the missing page is swapped in. Meanwhile, the kernel can switch to another ready process so that time is not wasted. Typical times to swap in a page range from 20 to 50 milliseconds, during which a lot of computing can take place.

If free page frames are available, a newly swapped-in page may reside in any one of them; no replacement policy is necessary. However, if all page frames are in use, a **page-replacement policy** must then decide which page frame to vacate by swapping out its page. The following candidates for a page to swap out come to mind:

- Pages that belong to processes that have terminated. These pages don't even have to be swapped out; their frames can be overwritten immediately.
- Pages that belong to processes that have been blocked a long time. They are not likely to be needed soon.
- Pages that belong to ready processes but have not been accessed in a long time. We would hope that they are not needed soon.
- Pages that have not been modified since they were swapped in and therefore can be overwritten without being copied back out.

We would like to preserve pages that are currently enjoying heavy use.

One goal of the page-replacement policy is to minimize the number of page faults. This goal follows the Cache Principle. The accesses that processes make to virtual store should be fast. Every page fault limits the speed of those accesses because a process that suffers a fault must wait until a swap is completed. Swapping can reach a level at which all processes present need to swap, with the result that no progress can be made. If this situation persists, the operating system thrashes, spending all its time transferring pages in and out of main store.

Page-replacement policies take the following approaches.

- Choose pages to swap in and out cleverly so that processes usually find the pages they need already in main store.
- If clever choice is insufficient to keep the number of page faults low, reduce the level of multiprogramming — that is, lower the number of processes simultaneously competing for the computing resource. More main store can then be dedicated to each process, reducing the frequency of page faults. Processes that are entirely swapped out to keep the multiprogramming level low are kept on a main-store wait list in the medium-term scheduler. After a while, these processes are allowed to execute again, perhaps at the expense of other processes that are then swapped out. The Hysteresis Principle tells us that once a process is swapped in or out, it should be left in or out for a significant length of time, in order to recoup the cost of swapping it.

No amount of cleverness in choosing swaps can prevent thrashing by itself; reducing the level of multiprogramming is a necessary tool. However, reducing the multiprogramming level alone is not wise, since higher levels of multiprogramming tend to treat long and short jobs more fairly and allow more overlap of computing and transput.

We will begin our study of page replacement by simplifying the problem. Later, we will return and introduce more complexities. To start with, let's assume that one process is ready but that its virtual space is larger than physical store. When it needs a page brought in, one of its own pages must be discarded. We say the process is "paging against itself." Further, we will not try to be clever and bring in pages before they are actually referenced, nor will we swap out a page before we need its page frame. We will stick to pure **demand paging**, where all page traffic between main and backing store is based on the demand generated by the process.

To evaluate different policies, we will use a **page-reference string**, which is a list of all the pages referenced by the process in the order in which they are referenced. For example, a process with a virtual space of five pages, numbered 0 through 4, might have a page-reference string that starts as follows:

$$0\ 0\ 3\ 2\ 3\ 1\ 2\ 4\ 1\ 2\ 2\ 1\ 2\ 2\ 2\ 1\ 1\ 0\ 0\ \dots$$

The same page may be referenced two or more times in a row, and some pages might be referenced very seldom or never. We will define each page-replacement policy by describing which page, if any, is swapped out for each reference in the page-reference string. This decision will depend, of course, on how many page frames are available and what the reference string looks like.

Actual reference strings have been deduced by attaching hardware probes to computers while processes execute. These reference strings do not have the behavior you might expect, each page being equally likely to be referenced at any time. Instead, a phenomenon called **locality** is observed. At each instant in a program's execution, a few pages are in active use, and others are not in use at all.

Locality is especially pronounced in programs that use stacks and ones that scan arrays sequentially with small strides.

As the pages in the active set change, we say that the program has gone through a **phase change**. Such a phase change is observed, for example, when a compiler finishes its first pass and begins the second.

We will examine how various policies behave with respect to a synthesized page-reference string with 10,000 references selected from a virtual space of 100 pages. Details of how this string was generated can be found in the exercises at the end of the chapter. It is built to display locality of reference but not phase changes. In this page-reference string, only 71 of the 100 pages were actually referenced. This figure is not surprising, since 10,000 references is actually quite short for a program of 100 pages.

One way to present the behavior of a page-replacement policy is to show how many faults it suffers with our synthesized page-reference string for different sizes of physical space, ranging from 1 to 100 page frames. These results are often shown in a **fault-rate graph**, as shown in Figure 3.19.

When physical store only has one page frame, the fault rate is very high. When physical store has 100 page frames, the fault rate is very low. This graph omits faults that occur before all the page frames have been filled. That is, it ignores the first $f$ faults when there are $f$ page frames. When we ignore those initial faults, we are measuring the **warm-start** behavior of the replacement policy instead of the **cold-start** behavior. A cold-start curve would not trail off to 0 but

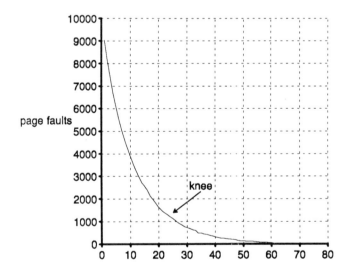

**Figure 3.19** A typical fault-rate graph

rather to the number of pages actually referenced (in this case, 71).

The point where the curve reaches a fairly low plateau, known as the "knee" of the curve, indicates the number of pages that are needed for good behavior.

The fault-rate graph summarizes the entire life of the program. The program might have several phases. If we were to draw the graph for each phase, we might find that some phases have a smaller page requirement and others have a larger one.

The fault-rate graph can itself be summarized by the area under the curve, that is, the total number of warm-start page faults for all main-store sizes. We will call this area the **characteristic number** of the method when applied to a particular page-reference string. The characteristic number is not a perfect measure of the value of a page-replacement policy. In practice, one also needs to evaluate the amount of computation necessary to achieve each method and the sophistication of the hardware needed to support it.

## 7.1  Random replacement

To illustrate the Law of Diminishing Returns, we will start with a poor method that is easy to describe. When a page frame must be freed, use the following rule:

| **Random replacement** |
| :--- |
| Select any page frame at random. |

Figure 3.20 shows the warm-start fault-rate graph on our synthesized page-reference string for random replacement as well as some of the other methods we will study. The curves are in the same order as the table in the corner of the graph.

The curve for random replacement shows the highest fault rate, with a characteristic number almost 115,000. It displays **anomalies**, in which increasing the size of main store occasionally makes the fault rate increase. The reason Random does so poorly is that the page frame we evacuate often contains a page in the current region of locality.

## 7.2  Min

Min, our next method, suffers fewer page faults than any other method. Unfortunately, it cannot be implemented. We use it as a yardstick for comparison with other methods. No implementable method will have as few page faults, but we can see how close they come to the unobtainable optimum.

The Min method follows a simple rule:

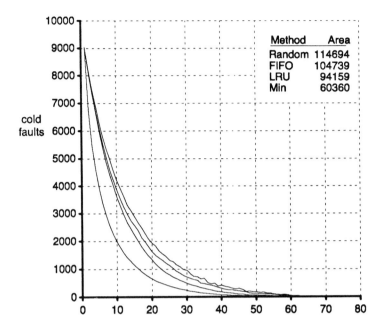

**Figure 3.20** Faults for four page-replacement strategies

| Min |
| --- |
| Select the page frame containing the page whose next access will be farthest in the future. |

This choice delays the next page fault as long as possible. Of course, no storage manager knows when each page will be accessed next, so the method cannot be implemented. The curve for Min, the lowest in Figure 3.20, shows that it is better than the other methods.

Looking at the curves for Random and Min, one might be led to the conclusion that there is little benefit to be gained by complex page-replacement strategies. After all, no matter how effective a strategy might be, it cannot beat Min, and any method ought to do at least as well as Random. The region for improvement is not particularly large. The characteristic numbers range only over a factor of 2 (from about 60,000 to about 115,000). At a main-store size of 20 page frames, the number of page faults ranges over a factor of 3 (from about 650 to

about 1950). The number of page frames needed to keep the number of page faults to 1000 — a 10% rate — ranges over less than a factor of 2 (from 17 to 29).

However, factors of 2 and 3 can make a large difference to the behavior of
the operating system. Improving the fault rate increases the sustainable level of
multiprogramming by the same factor. Programs that cannot execute without
thrashing can only be served by increasing the size of physical store or by improving the fault rate. A program exhibiting the page-reference string pictured in the
graph would manage acceptably (1 percent fault rate) with 39 page frames under
Min but would need 56 page frames under Random. In addition, this single graph
is not representative of all page-reference strings that occur in practice. The gap
between Min and Random could be much greater for some programs.

Figure 3.21 shows the same information as Figure 3.20, except that the curve
for Min has been subtracted from the other three curves. We see from this figure
that the page-fault rate of Random is particularly poor in comparison to Min when
main store is limited. When storage is extremely limited (fewer than 5 page
frames, in our example), all our methods do equally poorly in comparison with
Min. When storage is plentiful (more than 50 page frames, in our example), even
Random does fairly well. In the intermediate range, we can hope for significant
improvements over Random. The FIFO and LRU methods, which we will now
discuss, justify that hope.

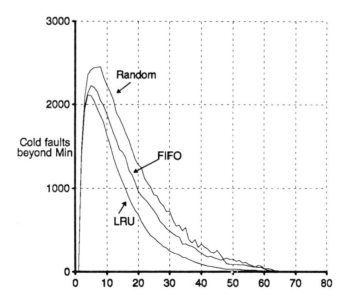

page frames available

**Figure 3.21** Number of page-faults beyond the number for Min

## 7.3 First in, first out (FIFO)

Our first realistic attempt to perform better than Random is to discard pages that are not expected to be needed for a long time. The first-in, first-out method keeps track of the order in which pages are brought in. When a page frame is needed, this rule is used:

---

### FIFO

Select the page frame containing the page that has been in main store for the longest period of time.

---

This method is usually better than the Random policy because it tends to save recently used pages, which have a higher probability of being used again soon because of program locality. It also follows the Hysteresis Principle, in that it resists swapping pages out for a long time after they are first brought in. Unfortunately, a frequently used page still gets swapped out when it gets to be old enough, even though it may need to be swapped back in immediately.

FIFO displays an unexpected behavior: For certain page-reference strings, the fault-rate graph temporarily increases! An example of such an **anomaly** (first discovered by L. Belady) is the following page-reference string, where the virtual space has 5 pages:

$$0\ 1\ 2\ 3\ 0\ 1\ 4\ 0\ 1\ 2\ 3\ 4$$

You can check that if physical store has three page frames, there are 9 faults: 3 for the cold start and 6 warm faults. There are 3 accesses without fault. If physical store has four page frames, however, there are 10 faults: 4 for the cold start and 6 warm faults. There are only 2 accesses without fault.

Anomalies are possible only in page-replacement algorithms that lack the **stack property**. An algorithm has this property if at each point in any page-reference string, the set of pages that would be in an $n$-page-frame main store is a subset of those that would be in an $(n+1)$-page-frame main store. FIFO and Random lack this property. In our example, after the first reference to page 4, FIFO would have pages 0, 1, and 4 in main store with three page frames but would not have 0 with four page frames. The next methods we will see have the stack property, and they also perform better than FIFO.

## 7.4 Least recently used (LRU)

The most common technique in use is the LRU method, or some variation on it. The idea behind this method is that the past is a mirror, albeit an imperfect one, of the future. The Min algorithm cannot be implemented because it requires looking into the future. LRU applies the same algorithm in the past:

| **LRU** |
| :---: |
| Select the page frame containing the page that has not been accessed for the longest period of time. |

This method is based on the assumption that the page-reference pattern in the recent past is a mirror of the pattern in the near future. Pages that have been accessed recently are likely to continue to be accessed and ought to be kept in main store.

This assumption works fairly well. As Figure 3.21 shows, LRU is significantly better than FIFO. Its characteristic number, 94159, is about 10 percent lower than the characteristic number for FIFO.

In a humorous vein, we might attempt to find the pessimal page-replacement strategy. MRU, Most Recently Used, ought to behave pretty poorly. It discards the page that has been accessed most recently. The theoretical pessimum is Max, which replaces the very page that will be needed soonest in the future. Just like Min, the Max method requires knowledge of the future, so it is not a feasible method. Figure 3.22 shows Max, MRU, and Min, along with their characteristic numbers, for our synthetic page-reference string. It is not surprising that Max is terrible. Although MRU is bad, it behaves better than one might expect.

Unfortunately, LRU is expensive to implement exactly. To find the page least recently used, either a list of pages must be maintained in use order or each page must be marked with the time it was last accessed. Hardware could certainly be designed and built to accomplish either, but it would be quite expensive. Luckily, an exact implementation is not needed because a simple variant works almost as well.

## 7.5 Not used recently (NUR)

The expensive hardware we contemplated for LRU can be reduced to a Boolean (1-bit) clock. True means "now," and false means "significantly earlier." A clock designed like this does not even have to tick. Every time a page is referenced, the hardware marks it (for example, in the page table) with the current time, that is, by setting a Used field to true. The storage manager may reset the field to false at any time. The Used field is like the Dirty field discussed earlier. The difference is that the Dirty field is only set to true when an access *writes* in the page or segment, whereas the Used field is set for references of any kind.

When a page frame is needed, pages with true Used field have been used more recently than those with false Used field. The replacement algorithm

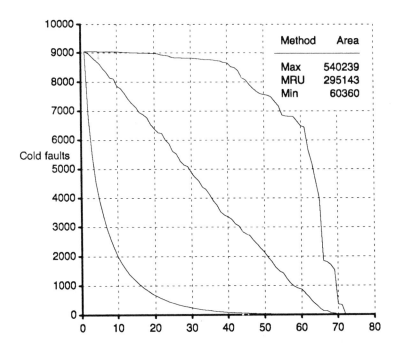

page frames available

**Figure 3.22** Faults for Max, MRU, and Min

therefore tries to find a page with false Used field to discard:

| **NUR** |
|---|
| Select any page frame whose Used field is false. |

To be fair and not victimize the same page excessively, the search for such a page should circulate through the pages in the page table, each search starting where the previous search ended. (You should be reminded of the circular first-fit technique of storage allocation for segments.) As each page is passed, its Used field is set to false, so it is certain that some page will eventually be chosen. Every time the storage manager rotates through all the pages in the page table, it discards all pages that have not been used recently. NUR is occasionally called the "clock algorithm," since it sweeps past each page frame much as a hand on a clock sweeps past each point on the circumference. The NUR method yields a characteristic number of 95949 for our synthesized page-reference string, only 2 percent higher than true LRU.

There are many variations on this theme. We can reset the Used field to false by different strategies.

- Don't change Used fields to false as they are scanned when the storage manager is looking for one to swap out. Instead, reset them all to false if a scan through all the pages fails to find any that has not been used. This variant gives a characteristic number 97741 on the synthesized page-reference string, about 4 percent higher than true LRU.
- Reset all Used fields after each page fault, after the next victim has been selected. This variant gives a characteristic number of 100604 on the synthesized page-reference string, about 7 percent higher than true LRU.
- Reset all Used fields to false on a regular schedule, say, 60 times a second.

The storage manager can also increase the memory capacity of the Used field by periodically right-shifting it into the most significant bit of a **timestamp** word kept for each page. In this case, Used holds an integer, not a Boolean. We assume that true is represented by a one and false by a zero. After four such shift events, for example, we might have the following values for four pages:

| Page | Timestamp |
|------|-----------|
| 0    | 0101      |
| 1    | 0011      |
| 2    | 1001      |
| 3    | 1110      |

The first time the storage manager shifted the Used field into the initially zero timestamps, pages 0, 1, and 2 had been referenced, but 3 had not. The next time a shift event occurred, pages 1 and 3 had been referenced. Pages 0 and 3 were referenced in the next interval, and pages 2 and 3 in the most recent interval. Based only on the highest-order (that is, most recently modified) bit of the Used field, we would select either page 0 or 1 to discard next, since neither was referenced recently. The additional history that we have retained tells us that page 1 is a better victim, since it was not used for two time intervals. In general, the page with the smallest timestamp in the Used field is the preferred victim.

## 7.6  Second-chance cyclic

The methods mentioned so far do not take into account the extra effort involved in swapping out a dirty page. The second-chance cyclic method tries to avoid such swaps. Once more, we cycle through the page table looking for a victim. The best victim is a clean page that has not been used in a long time — that is, one for which both Dirty and Used are false. To keep the algorithm simple, we will ignore the Used field. As we search for a victim, we keep passing dirty pages. As we do so, we reset Dirty to false. We will eventually reach a page with Dirty set false even if we have to come full circle to the place where the search began. The first such page is the victim.

Once the victim is chosen, it still might have to be written out even though it is marked as clean. The Dirty field is no longer a true indication of whether the page is dirty because our algorithm has reset that field without cleaning the page. Instead, we save a mirror copy of the Dirty field in the context block. This copy is set to true whenever we reset a Dirty field to false. When we decide to swap out a page, we check the mirror copy to see if it must be written out.

This algorithm not only gives a second chance to dirty pages, but it also continues to give a reprieve to pages that are being written to frequently. The chances are good that between the time we reset a Dirty field and the time we look at such a page again, the process has written in that page, and the Dirty field protects the page from being swapped out.

## 7.7  Global policies

We are now ready to examine some page-replacement policies that do not force processes to page only against themselves. After all, some processes need more physical store than others because their regions of locality are larger. If every process could page only against itself, we would have to make initial guesses as to the number of pages a process needs, and these guesses would sometimes be too low and at other times too high.

Any of the foregoing policies can be used in a global fashion. To implement the global NUR or second-chance cyclic method, the storage manager must be able to scan through all the page frames of main store, examining and modifying the Used and Dirty fields. Unfortunately, few machines are designed with these fields in a hardware **page-frame table**. Instead, they appear in the page tables for each process, because the hardware must refer to those tables during address translation, and they are therefore the obvious place to store this information. In this case, the storage manager builds a software page-frame table that records the correspondence between physical page frames and virtual pages. During a scan of the page-frame table, the storage manager can find the Used and Dirty fields in the per-process page tables. Here are declarations for a software page-frame table:

```
1 type
2    PageFrameTableEntry =
3       record
4          { All fields set by the storage manager }
5          Free : Boolean;  { true if unoccupied }
6          Process : ProcessNumber; { which process owns this frame }
7          VirtualPage : integer; { where in virtual store of that process }
8       end;
9 var
10    PageFrameTable = array PageFrameNumber of PageFrameTableEntry;
```

Processes that are in wait lists will lose all their pages after a while. Processes in the ready list will compete for page frames. The number of pages any process manages to acquire will depend on how many it needs and how often the scheduler gives it a chance to run. When a process is placed in the ready list after a long absence, it will encounter a page fault almost immediately. It will be slowed by page faults during the startup period but will finally have its most heavily used pages in physical store and will be able to make progress. However, the number of processes in the ready list may be so high that not one of them succeeds in swapping in an adequate number of pages. In that case, each ready process will make very little headway before the next page fault, and thrashing will set in.

The next few policies try to prevent this catastrophe. They do so by restricting the level of multiprogramming.

## 7.8  Working set

The storage manager can estimate which pages are currently needed by each process. This set is called the **working set** of that process. The **working set policy** restricts the number of processes on the ready queue so that physical store can accommodate all the working sets of ready processes. Any other ready processes are placed in the main-store wait list, where they remain until the medium-term scheduler decides to exchange some of them for ready processes. (Refer to Figure 2.6 to see how the scheduling levels are arranged.) When such a process is brought back to the ready list, the pages in its working set may be swapped back in before it starts running. These swaps are examples of **prefetching**, which is the opposite of demand paging.

When the medium-term scheduler makes an exchange, the process that is moving to the main-store wait list loses all its pages; they are all marked as available for swap out. When a page must be swapped out, the best victim is a page that does not belong to any of the currently ready processes. If there is no such page, any of the previous methods, preferably some form of NUR, may be applied in a global fashion.

The **working set** for each process is defined as the pages that have been accessed by the process during the most recent $w$ units of virtual time. **Virtual time** is a clock that is maintained separately for each process. (Whenever a process is switched out, the amount of physical time it was given when it was running is added to the virtual time that was recorded in its context block. The virtual time of a process that is running is the virtual time recorded in its context block plus the amount of physical time it has been running.) If the **working-size** parameter $w$ is too small, the working set will not contain all the pages that are really in use by the process. If $w$ is too large, then as the program changes phases, the working set will contain pages that are no longer needed by the process. Luckily, $w$ is not particularly critical; values of 0.5 second are common.

To calculate the working set of a process properly would require an accurate virtual clock. Whenever a page is accessed, the current time according to that clock is recorded in the page table. The working set contains all pages whose access time is within $w$ of the present. This implementation is reminiscent of LRU, which we rejected because it was too expensive.

## 7.9 Page-fault frequency (PFF)

The page-fault frequency policy employs an approximation of the working set. It requires only the Used fields for each page and a real-time clock. Instead of recording the time of each access, we make decisions about the working set only when a page fault occurs. At that time we compare how long it has been since the previous page fault. We will say that the (virtual) time lag is small if it is less than $p$ units of time, where $p$ is a tunable parameter. If the time lag is small, we will just add the new page to the working set. If the time lag is large, we first discard all pages from the working set that have not been referenced since the last page fault. The new page is, of course, added to the working set.

This policy can be implemented by resetting the hardware Used field to false every time a page fault occurs. When the next fault occurs after a long lag, all pages that still have a false Used field are discarded from the working set. A discarded page has its Present field reset to false, but it is not swapped out. Instead, the storage manager adds that page to a pool of reasonable victims for the next time a victim must be found. If the process accesses that page again before it is chosen as a victim, the kernel receives a missing-page fault, removes the page from the victim pool, and brings it back into the working set.

To facilitate finding a victim, this pool of potential victims should be kept non-empty. The length of the victim list is a barometer of multiprogramming effectiveness. If the list is practically empty, too many processes are competing for physical storage, and the level of multiprogramming should be reduced. If the list is very long, it may be possible to bring in some process that has been stranded on the main-store wait list.

## 7.10 Working size

The working-size technique is another way to approximate the working set. Instead of keeping track of all the pages in the working set, the storage manager maintains only the size of that set. When a process is placed in the main-store wait list, its working-set size is estimated by counting the number of pages it has recently accessed. This count can be performed by examining Used fields. The process is not put back on the ready list until that many page frames are available for it to use.

## 7.11 WSCLOCK

The WSCLOCK method was recently proposed as a hybrid between NUR and Working Set. As with NUR, it searches for pages to discard, starting with the page where the previous search left off. These searches are conducted in the page-frame table, not in any particular process page table. When a page fault occurs in any process, a scan starts through the table. Pages with true Used field are passed over, but the field is reset to false. In addition, the kernel stores the virtual time of the owning process in a "Referenced-time" field in that table. Referenced time is an estimate of the last time the page was used.

If the scan encounters a page with a false Used field, the page might still be in the working set of its owner. The current virtual time of its owner is compared with the referenced time. If the difference is less than $w$, the scan continues. Otherwise, the page has left the working set and may be swapped out.

An entire scan through all page frames may fail to find a replaceable page. This situation signals overcommitment of main store, a problem that can be relieved by reducing the multiprogramming level.

## 7.12  Missing Used field

The DEC VAX lacks a Used field. This flaw has led to a clever software simulation of that field. The storage manager resets the Present field to false in the page table whenever it wants to reset the non-existent Used field. A mirror table indicates to the storage manager that the page is still present. If the program accesses a page with false Present field, the hardware causes a page fault. However, the storage manager is not fooled and just sets Present back to true. At the same time, the storage manager has learned that the page has been accessed, so it records that fact in its mirror table, which does have a Used field.

This technique is fairly expensive because the trap takes some time to service (about 250 microseconds), so it must be used carefully. The Present field must be reset to false only occasionally, or the cost of handling phantom page faults will be unreasonable.

## 7.13  Classification of replacement methods

Now that we have looked at a few page-replacement methods, we should step back and examine the larger issues.

### When is a page swapped in?    The first issue, surprisingly, concerns when a swapped-out page should be swapped in. We have concentrated on **demand paging** so far, in which a page is brought in only when it is accessed by a process. Demand paging has the advantage that it never brings in a page that is not needed. Other techniques can reduce page faults by anticipating them before they happen.

The first method is **prefetching**, which we touched on earlier. When a process is placed on the ready list after a long residence in a transput or main-store wait list, the kernel restores the pages that the process had before it became blocked. Prefetching works on the reasonable assumption that until the process is given back its working set, it will not be able to make much progress. Instead of encountering a number of page faults immediately, the kernel can save effort by scheduling all the working set to be brought in before the process is placed back on the ready list.

Prefetching also applies the first time a process is started; instead of letting page faults bring in the necessary pages, a selection of pages can be brought in initially. Unfortunately, any guess about the correct number and identity of prefetched pages is likely to be inaccurate to some degree. Sometimes, useless pages will be prefetched and will waste main store until they are thrown out during normal replacement.

Another method is **advised paging**, in which the process may inform the storage manager through a service call that a particular page is about to be accessed and thus should be swapped in or that a particular page will not be used again for a long time and might as well be swapped out. Such a call would have this form:

☐ PageAdvice(starting address, ending address,direction). This call tells the storage manager that the process is about to use the region in virtual space between the two addresses, so it might swap the relevant pages in (if direction is "in") or that this region will not be accessed for a considerable period (if direction is "out").

Advised paging takes advantage of the programmer's or compiler's knowledge of how the program works, knowledge that can be more accurate than the storage manager's. However, the programmer has no knowledge at all of the other processes that are competing in the ready list, but the storage manager does know. It would be foolhardy for the storage manager to put too much credence in advice. At most, the storage manager might turn off the Used field for a page that the process claims will not be used for a while, making it a candidate for swap-out. For swapping in, the advice should most likely be ignored.

The method called **clustering** swaps in additional pages beyond the ones brought in by demand paging. Not only the required page but the next few pages as well are brought in at the same time. If adjacent pages in virtual store are placed in adjacent locations on backing store, the cost of bringing in a group of pages might be only slightly higher than bringing in just one. We will see the source of this efficiency when we discuss file storage in Chapter 6. Once a particular page is accessed, the pages nearby have a higher probability of being accessed soon. If they are not needed, they will soon be swapped out. Since they have not been touched, swapping out requires no work at all.

## Which page should be swapped out?

We have already seen several specific techniques for choosing a victim page to swap out. These methods can be classified as **local** or **global** methods, depending on whether they pick pages from only the process whose page fault requires finding a victim or from any process. Global methods may take into account scheduling information, such as the process priority, in order to avoid removing all the pages from an important process.

Methods that maintain a pool of free page frames are called **pool** methods. A page can be added to the pool when it leaves the working set of its process. Alternatively, the storage manager could continually place page frames in the pool, at a rate such that the backing store is kept relatively busy. If this "background discard" algorithm is the sole source of free pages, thrashing is avoided because pages cannot be brought in faster than they are being swapped out.

No matter how the pool is created, dirty pages in the pool can be "cleaned" by writing them out to backing store whenever the backing store device is idle. Later, swapping out the page will be free. If a process accesses a page that is in the pool, it is not expensive to place the page back into the virtual space of that process. The pool thus lets us resist swapping pages out, in keeping with the Hysteresis Principle. If a cleaned page is removed from the pool and returned to a process, the cleaning has cost some effort, but we hope not much.

We noticed that shared segments warrant special treatment. Since sharing on the basis of individual pages usually doesn't make sense, segmentation is joined to paging to provide sharing. Shared pages are then elements of segments that are entirely shared. Local methods don't really make sense for a shared page because swapping it out has a non-local effect. Instead, the entire segment can be considered a swappable entity. If it is decided to swap it out, all its page frames are placed in the free pool, and cleaning is scheduled for the dirty ones.

Pages that are tied down must not be swapped out. We have seen that pages involved in transput must sometimes be tied down. If the pages of the kernel are subject to swapping out, it must tie down those pages that hold the storage-manager programs for both the policy and the mechanism of paging. Otherwise the kernel will suffer a page fault from which it cannot recover. Also, some forms of real-time scheduling require that paging cost be avoided; an entire process may be tied down if it needs guaranteed service every tenth of a second. Some operating systems provide a service call by which a process requests that a segment be tied down. The scheduler might favor such a process, under the assumption that the more time that process receives, the sooner it will be willing to unlock the segment. This call should be used with discretion because it gives the caller both a space and a time advantage over other processes in the ready list.

### Startup-phase conflicts.
All the policies that control the level of multiprogramming are subject to a phenomenon called **startup-phase conflict**. The startup phase of a process is the period right after the scheduler has taken it from the main-store wait list until the process has acquired its working set of pages. During this phase, the virtual clock of the process moves very slowly because page faults are so frequent. If many processes are in startup phase simultaneously, they compete for access to the backing store. Their virtual clocks therefore advance still more slowly. In extreme situations, the processor becomes underused, and every process in the ready list is in startup phase.

Startup-phase conflict can be controlled by restricting the number of processes allowed to be in startup phase at one time. If there are too many such processes, new additions to the ready list are delayed. The kernel can decide that a process is in the startup phase by consulting its virtual clock. Any process whose virtual clock is less than the tunable parameter "startup-phase virtual duration" is considered in startup phase. Another tunable parameter, "startup-phase process limit," determines how many processes are allowed to be in startup phase simultaneously.

It makes sense, by the way, to allow more than one process to be starting up at the same time. We will see in Chapter 5 that the average time spent by the backing store in retrieving a page can be reduced by increasing the number of outstanding requests to the backing store. The time required to start two processes simultaneously can be less than the time required to start them one after the other. The purpose of controlling startup-phase conflict is to balance processor and backing store utilization.

# 8  PERSPECTIVE

Most modern operating systems use some form of space management, even operating systems for personal computers and workstations. We have devoted quite a lot of effort to paging because it is both complicated and very widely used. Paging works fairly well. In a well-tuned operating system, a process will access about 50 percent of the pages in its working set during any quantum. As long as main store is large enough to hold the working sets of all the ready processes, very little time is wasted by swapping. Reducing the level of multiprogramming cures thrashing when it occurs.

Unfortunately, many smaller computers, including the DEC PDP-11 and the Motorola MC68000, do not store enough information when page faults occur to allow the faulting instruction to be restarted. Segmentation is the primary facility implemented on these machines.

More often, the operating system designer is constrained by the hardware of the machine. The absence of a Used field has a major impact on the methods that are used. Whether the hardware saves the Used and Dirty fields in the page table or in the page-frame table also makes a difference. Newer machines have increasingly complex translation hardware. Two-layer page tables are not uncommon because processes that need very large virtual stores need very long page tables. Only the active part of the page tables needs to reside in main store.

We have seen that the storage manager has scheduling responsibilities as well as storage responsibilities. This blurring of function is unfortunately common within operating systems. In addition, the storage manager must deal with device drivers (discussed in Chapter 5) to swap pages in and out. Organizing the kernel to keep functions separate and modular is not always easy. Figure 3.23 shows one way to structure the kernel to contain the parts we have discussed so far. The kernel is not a monolithic program but is composed of individual managers for different resources. The managers may communicate in a variety of ways, some of which we will see in Chapters 8 and 9. For now we can assume that they share certain data structures such as process lists. The situations that can arise are represented by interrupts from devices and by service calls and traps from running processes. These interrupts, service calls, and traps switch context to the kernel, which then executes the appropriate manager.

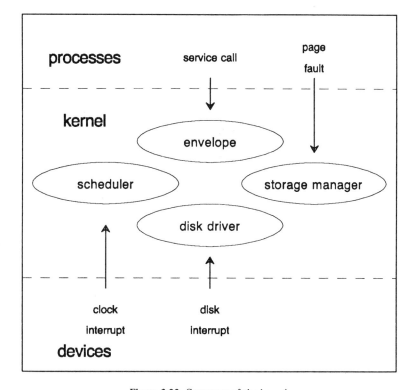

**Figure 3.23**  Structure of the kernel

A clock interrupt causes the scheduler to be called. The scheduler might take this opportunity to switch to a different process. A page (or segment) fault causes the storage manager to be called. The storage manager might decide that a particular page frame must be swapped out to make room for the page that this process needs. It asks the disk driver to perform this work by placing a request in the disk queue. Meanwhile, it places the process that suffered the page fault in a mainstore wait list and lets the scheduler switch to another process.

The disk driver accepts interrupts that tell it that work has been completed. (We discuss device drivers in Chapter 5.) Once the disk driver has swapped out the page, it can tell the storage manager, which might then request that a new page be swapped in. After that page has been swapped in, the storage manager can place the long-suffering process back in the ready list.

The envelope module shown in Figure 3.23 runs when no other manager has work to do. It performs the actual switch back to the process. If the process generates a service call, the envelope is the first part of the kernel to notice. The envelope can either satisfy the call itself (for simple requests, like returning the current time of day) or pass the request on to other parts of the kernel.

We began our discussion of virtual store by invoking the Beautification Principle. Each level of hardware and software hides lower levels and introduces new structures. At the bottom, physical store is arranged as a large array of words, each with a fixed number of bits. Address-translation hardware groups these words into pages and introduces address-translation tables. The paging storage manager erases page boundaries and hides the tables, providing a linear array of words whose length is independent of the length of physical store. If there is a layer of segmentation above paging, several linear arrays of words are grouped together to make up an address space. The result is far removed, both in form and in function, from the original material from which all these abstractions are built.

# 9 FURTHER READING

A good summary of virtual store techniques is given by Denning (1970). A substantial amount of research has been directed to design, modeling, simulation, and measurement of various space-management schemes. By far the greatest effort has been devoted to paging. Smith (1978) has compiled a large bibliography of the relevant literature. Belady, who showed that the Min algorithm is optimal (1966), also discovered the anomalies that FIFO can produce in the fault-rate graph (1969). An article by Masuda (1977) notices that a working set policy becomes less responsive as phase changes increase in frequency. The value of the window size $w$ becomes critical in these situations. Babaoglu and Joy (1981) describe how they modified a version of Unix that used segmentation to use swapping on the DEC VAX, which does not have a Used field. The WSCLOCK page-replacement policy was developed by Carr and Hennessy (1981). Database management systems have atypical page-reference behavior, which can lead to poor results with standard page-replacement algorithms. This issue is introduced in exercise 25. More details can be found in Stonebraker's article (1981).

Knuth (1973) gives a good review of the boundary-tag, first-fit, and best-fit storage allocation. The warning about circular first fit in large spaces was given by Shore (1975). Maintaining subpools for blocks of popular sizes has been suggested by Margolin (1971).

# 10 EXERCISES

1. In a single-segment scheme, the storage manager wants to shuffle. How should it find which process corresponds to which busy piece of physical store?

2. Design a data structure for the shared-segment table in the two-segment organization. How is the table addressed?

3. You are the president of Cheapo Computronics, and your star hardware designer has suggested a brilliant idea: Implement segmentation, but let the *least significant m* bits of a virtual address be used to select the segment, and let the other bits determine the offset. Should the designer retire or get a raise? Why?

4. A process generally has no inkling when a segment fault occurs. Describe how a process could use a TimeOfDay service call to guess that such a fault has occurred.

5. If we allow a process to have anywhere from zero segments to the maximum number of segments allowed by the hardware, it takes one more bit to represent the number of segments in use than to represent any particular segment. Why? What implementation difficulty does that create? What can be done about it?

6. There is a similar problem for segment sizes. What is the problem?

7. What is the relation between the size of physical store and virtual store under segmentation?

8. Suppose we wish to implement paging and want to use the load-image file as backing store for instructions and read-only data as a way to save space on the backing drum. What information must be stored in the load-image file? What constraints should we place on that file?

9. How long is a process page table on the VAX?

10. On the VAX, a process may access kernel space. What prevents a process from generating nuisance missing-page faults by trying to read regions in the kernel?

11. If a process releases the instructions segment in which it is currently executing, describe in detail the actions taken by the kernel that lead inexorably to catastrophe. How should the kernel treat the disaster?

12. Should the address translation table be in the virtual space of the associated process? Consider the ramifications of making the opposite decision.

13. Write a program to generate page-reference strings by using the following approach, which was used to generate Figure 3.21. All $n$ pages of virtual store are listed in order. Use the exponential distribution with mean $\sqrt{n}$ to pick a number between 1 and $n$. The page at that point in the list is the next page in the reference string. Move that page to the start of the list, and repeat the algorithm. (Elements near the front of the list were referenced recently; those near the end have not been referenced for a long time.)

14. What properties of true page-reference strings are not exhibited by the ones generated by the program of exercise 13?

15. Use the program from exercise 13 to generate a graph like the one in Figure 3.21.

16. Design a combination of the NUR and second-chance cyclic page-replacement policies.

17. Given the reference string 4 5 2 1 4 3 5 4 3 2 1 5, draw the cold-start fault-rate graphs for main store ranging between 1 and 7 pages, using Min, FIFO, LRU, and two forms of NUR, the ordinary one (resetting Used to false in each page table entry that the scan passes) and a variant (resetting Used to false everywhere in the page table when all the Used fields are true).

18. If a machine offers several states, each with its own register set, why not use different states for different processes to reduce the process switch cost?

19. Several processes sharing the same instructions are given separate register sets. (a) Why not let them all use the same registers? (b) Why not divide up the registers and let each process use a different subset in order to avoid duplication?

20. We claimed that segmentation hardware can check the subscripts of all array references to make sure they are in bounds. When is this claim false?

21. Evaluate the suggestion that segments that are brought into main store can be discarded from backing store. Under what circumstances would this mechanism be useful? How could it prove costly?

22. Suggest an architecture that would allow Dirty fields for shared segments to be set directly by the hardware.

23. The translation look-aside buffer on a particular machine has a 95 percent hit rate and takes 100 nanoseconds to yield a value. Main store takes 1 microsecond to read a value. The hardware for address translation needs to make one access to the translation table per access and an additional 30 nanoseconds to complete the translation. What is the average time per address translation?

24. When a process terminates, it may own a number of pages in physical store that have the Dirty field true. What should be done with these pages?

25. A particular database program repeatedly scans an array of 1,000 pages. Each scan starts with page 0 and continues to page 999. There is only enough main store to hold 100 pages. None of the page-replacement policies given in this chapter does very well. Suggest a different policy that will do as well as Min for this program.

26. How can the child distinguish itself from the parent after a Split service call?

27. Consider a computer that supports two different page sizes, 512 bytes and 4K bytes. All the pages in a virtual space must be of one size or the other. What advantages can the operating system derive from this ability? How hard is it to achieve these benefits?

28. Why is it necessary to use the eager method for updating composite address-translation tables when a client updates a privileged-state table?

# Resource Deadlock

We have dealt so far with two fundamental resources, time and space. Allocating these resources is a matter of scheduling — that is, deciding which process should receive which resources at a given time. The time resource is granted by placing the process in the ready list and then letting it execute. The space resource is granted by allowing part or all of the virtual space of the process to reside in main store.

Both time and space are special. Time — the ability to execute — is held by only one process at a time (unless the computer is a multiprocessor). After the resource has been held, it can be preempted and given for a while to another process. Space can be held by many processes at once and may be preempted after a while. All regions of physical space are alike to the process. Every process requires both time and space.

We will devote this chapter to allocation of resources that represent non-sharable, non-preemptable resources. Such resources represent extra facilities beyond space and time, such as devices: files, printers, and tape drives. For example, a file might be restricted so that only one process may use it at a time. Similarly, a printer or a tape drive may be acquired by a process for a while and then given back. Finally, a process may need five tape drives during the course of its computation, but not all at once.

Data structures within the kernel are often non-sharable, non-preemptable resources. For example, the kernel might have an array of context blocks. When a new process is started, a free context block must be allocated. As long as the process exists, that context block is neither shared nor preempted. Similarly, the file manager (which we discuss in Chapter 5) might have an array of descriptors for open files. When a file is opened, a free descriptor is allocated, and must not be shared or preempted as long as the file is in use. In a related vein, page frames that contain tied-down pages cannot be shared (unless processes are sharing pages) and are not preempted.

Once a process has been granted such a resource, it is not possible to preempt the resource without injuring the process or the resource. For example, if the use of a file is preempted, the process cannot assume that when it gets to use the file again, it will be in the same state as before. The process has been injured and most likely should just quit. Even worse, the process may have left the file in an inconsistent state. For example, the file may represent a load image that the preempted process was in the middle of linking. Some links are complete and others are not. In this case, preemption injures the resource, and it might never again be usable. The incompletely linked image cannot be loaded, nor can the linking be finished.

Even though they are not preemptable, the resources we will discuss are all **serially reusable**. After one process has finished using a tape drive, some other process may certainly use it without harm.

Another property of the resources we will discuss here is that they are both **discrete** and **bounded**. This means that they come in individual chunks and that the amount of the resource is limited, usually physically. For example, if an installation has only seven tape drives, it makes no sense to acquire 3.4 of them or 8 of them. Time, in contrast, is neither discrete nor bounded. The scheduler can divide it into pieces of any size, and there is always enough to satisfy any finite process.

We will speak of **resource classes**, which are sets of identical resources. If a process does not care which tape drive it gets, then all tape drives are identical as far as it is concerned, and they are therefore in the same class. Likewise, in an installation with several line printers, it is often immaterial which line printer is acquired; all line printers are in the same class.

## 1  NUTS AND BOLTS

We will assume that when a process needs a resource, it will ask the kernel for it by making a service call. The part of the kernel responsible for these requests is the **resource manager**. The same service call might ask for several resources at a time. If the resources desired are available and the resource manager decides to grant them, the process is allowed to continue. The fact that the process now possesses the resources is marked in its context block, and the resources are marked as belonging to that process.

The resource manager might decide not to grant the resources. In this case, the process is placed in a resource-wait list, where it remains until the resource manager decides to honor it with the resources. (Instead, the resource manager could report failure immediately or after a delay.)

When the process has finished using one or more resources, it returns them by issuing another service call. This call does not block the process, although the scheduler may take this opportunity to switch to a different process for a while. If a process tries to use a resource it has not acquired, the resource manager treats this action as an error.

Here is a sample of the declarations needed for these service calls:

```
1 type
2    ResourceClass = (Tape, Printer, ... ); { generic name of resource }
3    ResourceIdentifier = integer; { specific name of resource }
4    ResourceDescriptor =
5       record
6          Kind : ResourceClass; { set by process }
7          Which : ResourceIdentifier; { set by resource manager }
8       end;
9    Resources = list of ResourceDescriptor;
```

The service calls we provide might have the following form.

☐   GetResource(request). The request is of type Resources, with only the Kind field set. If a process wants, for example, three tapes and a printer, it makes a request with a Resources list containing four resource descriptors. When this call returns to the calling process (perhaps after a delay), the Request list has been updated by the resource manager to indicate which resources have been granted.

☐   ReleaseResource(request). Again, request is of type Resources. The resource manager reclaims the resources listed.

The standard scenario for a process that wishes to use some resources is as follows:

```
GetResource(Request);   { may block }
Use(resource);      { must terminate eventually }
ReleaseResource(Request);
```

If process **A** requests three tapes and a printer and the installation has five tapes and five printers, the resource manager will choose from these to give to **A**. When **A** later decides to write information to the tape, it might submit a service call that looks like this:

```
Write(tape,info);
```

where "info" is the data to be written, and "tape" is of type ResourceDescriptor and describes which tape drive to use. The Write call will fail if the tape has not been allocated to process **A**. (We will discuss transput service calls in Chapter 5.) Likewise, ReleaseResource will fail if **A** tries to release a resource that has not been allocated.

If a process terminates before it has released all its resources, the resource manager pretends that it has released them properly. This pretense is not as bad as preemption, because the terminating process cannot be hurt by taking away its resources. However, the resources may not be in a consistent state. The resource manager could just trust processes to leave resources in the right condition. For example, a tape drive should be rewound. It is better for the resource manager to handle this **finalization** part of the release operation itself, whether release was performed explicitly by the process or implicitly by the termination of the process. But the internal consistency of some resources, like files, cannot be enforced by the resource manager because it does not know how the file is interpreted by the processes that use it. The concept of **atomic transactions**, discussed in Chapter 6, can be applied to achieve proper finalization even in the case of files.

# 2 DEADLOCK AND STARVATION

At first glance, resource allocation seems trivial. It seems that we don't need any policy at all. If the resource is available, grant it; if not, block the process until the resource is released by whoever has it. This approach is the most **liberal** method imaginable.

The problem with this approach is that it can get stuck. The simplest scenario that fails has two processes, **A** and **B**. Both **A** and **B** will eventually want two tape drives, and the operating system has exactly two drives. However, since neither **A** nor **B** needs both tape drives to start out with, they ask for the drives one at a time, even though they could have asked for both at once. Here is the scenario that runs into trouble:

```
A requests one tape drive.
The resource manager grants tape drive 1 to A.
B requests one tape drive.
The resource manager grants tape drive 2 to B.
A requests another tape drive.
The resource manager blocks A, since no drives are available.
B requests another tape drive.
The resource manager blocks B, since no drives are available.
```

Both **A** and **B** are stuck: Each is waiting for a resource that is held by the other. This sort of circular waiting is called **deadlock**. In Europe, it is known by the more striking name "deadly embrace."

Figure 4.1 is a **resource graph** that shows processes and resources. We draw an arrow from a process (like **A**) to a resource it is waiting for (like tape 2). Similarly, we draw an arrow from a resource (like tape 2) to a process that currently is

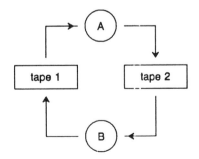

**Figure 4.1** A deadlocked resource graph

using it, if any (like **B**). We see that this resource graph has a cycle. In general, deadlock is a situation in which the resource graph has a cycle. (We will return to resource graphs later and generalize this principle.)

The only way to break a deadlock is by preempting a resource, which, as we have seen, can injure both the process and the resource. It is far better to avoid deadlock in the first place, as a less liberal policy might:

```
 1 A requests one tape drive.
 2 The resource manager grants tape drive 1 to A.
 3 B requests one tape drive.
 4 The resource manager blocks B, applying some clever policy.
 5 A requests another tape drive.
 6 The resource manager grants tape drive 2 to A.
 7 A returns tape drive 1.
 8 The resource manager grants tape drive 1 to B.
 9 B requests one tape drive.
10 The resource manager blocks B, since no drives are available.
11 A returns tape drive 2.
12 The resource manager grants tape drive 2 to B.
13 B returns tape drive 2.
14 B returns tape drive 1.
```

Figure 4.2 shows the resource graph at three points in this scenario. After line 6, **B** is waiting for either tape drive, so we have shown two arrows from **B**. However, there is no cycle in the graph. At the end, both **A** and **B** can successfully terminate.

Deadlock can exist among more than two processes. For example, we could accidentally get into the following state:

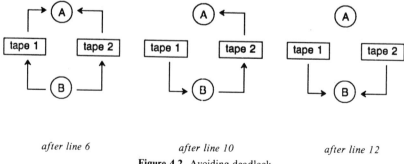

*after line 6*            *after line 10*            *after line 12*

**Figure 4.2**  Avoiding deadlock

| Process | Has     | Wants   |
|---------|---------|---------|
| **A**   | tape    | printer |
| **B**   | printer | plotter |
| **C**   | plotter | tape    |

This situation is shown in the resource graph of Figure 4.3. The essence of a deadlock is the existence of a cycle of processes, each of which is waiting for something held by the next process in the cycle. Our first example had a cycle of two processes. This second example has three.

Deadlock is an obvious problem when it happens; all the processes in the deadlock stop making any progress, even though other processes might continue unaffected. The way to prevent deadlock is for the resource manager sometimes to deny a resource when a process requests it and to block the process instead, even though the resource is available. Policies that deny resources even when they are available are **conservative**, as opposed to the liberal policy shown earlier.

Another way to picture deadlock is to draw a **progress diagram** such as the one shown in Figure 4.4. In this diagram, the two dimensions refer to virtual time in processes **A** and **B**. Process **A** requires a tape drive during part of its execution and a printer during another part. Likewise, process **B** requires both tape drive and printer. Let us assume that there is only one tape drive and one printer. The dashed path through the diagram shows how the processes might be scheduled. When process **A** is running, the path heads to the right. When **B** is running, the path heads upwards. If we have only one processor, there are no other possible directions for the path. The shaded regions are forbidden because of resource

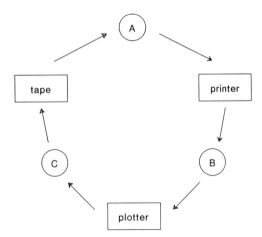

**Figure 4.3** Three-way deadlock

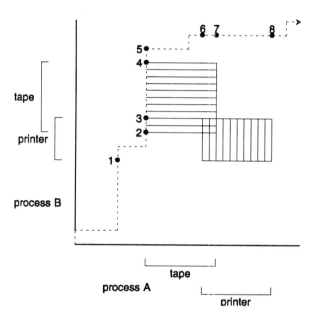

**Figure 4.4**  Progress diagram

conflicts. The region on the left must be skirted, because there is only one tape, and both processes need it in that region. The region on the right may not be entered because of conflict for the only printer.

The dots in the diagram are placed at important times in the execution of these processes. At point 1, process **B** acquires the printer. At point 2, it also gets the tape. It releases the printer at point 3 and the tape at point 4. Process **A** gets the tape at point 5 and the printer at point 6. It releases them at points 7 and 8.

This picture shows a safe path through the obstacle course. There is a dangerous turn, however, between points 1 and 2. If the path had continued to the right instead of heading upward, it would not immediately enter a forbidden region. However, since the path may never head down or left, it would have inevitably reached an obstacle that could not be surmounted. Virtual time would have to stop for both processes. They would be deadlocked. To avoid deadlock, the path must avoid the unsafe (but otherwise permissible) region in which **A** has a tape and **B** has a printer. We will see how various methods achieve this goal.

The most conservative approach of all is called **serialization**, in which processes are not allowed to have resources concurrently at all. Serialization in our two-tape example would result in the following scenario:

```
 1 A requests one tape drive.
 2 The resource manager grants tape drive 1 to A.
 3 B requests one tape drive.
 4 The resource manager blocks B, since A has a resource.
 5 A requests another tape drive.
 6 The resource manager grants tape drive 2 to A.
 7 A returns tape drive 1.
 8 A returns tape drive 2.
 9 The resource manager grants tape drive 1 to B.
10 B requests one tape drive.
11 The resource manager grants tape drive 2 to B.
12 B returns tape drive 2.
13 B returns tape drive 1.
```

Serialization works because all waiting processes are waiting for the same running process to release resources. The running process never waits for resources, so there can be no cycle. We would like to avoid serialization when we can because reduced concurrency means reduced throughput. The process that has resources and is running might be blocked for a while in a transput-wait list. During that time no other processes would run, because they are all in a resource-wait list.

Even if deadlock is avoided, a more subtle problem remains. If a process is blocked even when resources are available, it might never be allowed to run again. We call this danger **starvation**. Starvation arises from consistently awarding resources to the competitors of a blocked process. As long as one competitor has the resources, the blocked process cannot continue. Increased conservatism is needed to prevent this problem.

The spectrum from liberal to conservative is shown in Figure 4.5. Policies that are too liberal are subject to deadlock. Those that are too conservative reduce concurrency. Our goal is to achieve the most liberal resource-allocation policy we can without encountering deadlock. Serialization avoids deadlock but is very conservative. Figure 4.5 also shows the resource-allocation policies we will examine. The one-shot, hierarchical, and advance-claim algorithms put increasingly less onerous restrictions on the processes that wish to request resources. The advance-claim algorithm also requires a certain amount of prior knowledge about the

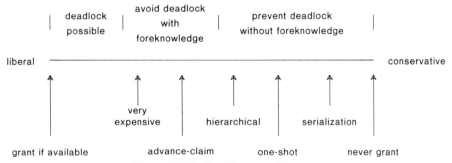

**Figure 4.5** The liberal-conservative spectrum

resources required by each process. The more information of this nature we know, the closer we can approach our goal. However, the algorithms that make use of such knowledge are increasingly expensive to execute.

Before we turn to these other algorithms, we will introduce a particularly instructive example of resource allocation.

# 3  DINING PHILOSOPHERS

The classical "Dining philosophers" problem demonstrates both deadlock and starvation issues.

### Dining philosophers problem

Five philosophers are seated around a circular table. Between each pair of adjacent philosophers is a chopstick, so there are five chopsticks all together. In front of each philosopher is a bowl of rice. It takes two chopsticks to eat rice, so a philosopher needs to grab both the chopstick to the left and the one to the right in order to start eating. While philosopher $n$ is eating, neither neighbor, that is, neither philosopher $n+1$ nor $n-1$, can be eating, because both need a chopstick that is in use by philosopher $n$. Each philosopher thinks for a while, then decides to eat, gets the chopsticks needed, eats, and puts the chopsticks down again, in an endless cycle. The challenge is to grant requests for chopsticks while avoiding deadlock and starvation.

Figure 4.6 shows each philosopher as a process and each chopstick as a resource. Each philosopher executes the following program.

```
 1 procedure Philosopher(Which : 0..4),
 2 var
 3     LeftChopstick, RightChopstick : ResourceDescriptor;
 4 begin
 5     { initialize Chopstick resource variables }
 6     LeftChopstick.Kind := Chopstick(Which);
 7     RightChopstick.Kind := Chopstick((Which+1) mod 5);
 8     loop { think — eat loop }
 9         Think; { occupy some finite amount of time in thought. }
10         GetResource(LeftChopstick);
11         GetResource(RightChopstick);
12         Eat;    { for a finite amount of time }
13         ReleaseResource(LeftChopstick);
14         ReleaseResource(RightChopstick);
15     end; { think — eat loop }
16 end Philosopher;
```

Deadlock can occur if every philosopher tries to get chopsticks at once and each gets as far as line 11. Each has asked for a left chopstick, and the allocator might grant all these requests. Now every philosopher is stuck at line 11, because each

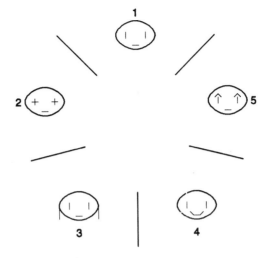

Figure 4.6  Dining philosophers

right chopstick is someone else's left chopstick; thus each is in use.  Figure 4.7 shows the resource graph in this situation.  A clever allocation policy might have prevented this disaster by keeping one chopstick free, which would have been more conservative.

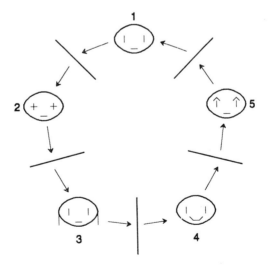

Figure 4.7  Deadlocked philosophers

The dining philosophers are also subject to starvation. Let's say that philosophers 2 and 4 are currently eating. Philosophers 1 and 5 are engaged in thinking great thoughts and will not be eating for a long time. Now philosopher 3 requests both chopsticks (one at a time or both together). Philosopher 3 is blocked, since the chopsticks are held by philosopher 2 and philosopher 4. Figure 4.8 shows the resource graph. Later, philosopher 2 finishes eating. Instead of granting 2's right chopstick as 3's left chopstick, which we have seen can lead to deadlock, let's let the resource manager be more conservative and leave that chopstick free. Later, philosopher 2 wants to eat again. Since philosopher 1 is engrossed in thought and oblivious to the real world, the resource manager gives philosopher 2 two chopsticks, leading again to the situation in Figure 4.8. Then philosopher 4 finishes eating. Again the resource manager decides not to grant philosopher 4's left chopstick to philosopher 3, because deadlock could result. Philosophers 2 and 4 keep eating whenever they want, but poor philosopher 3, although no doubt quite clever, starves to death.

The problem, then, is to follow a strategy that is not so liberal that it leads to deadlock or starvation, but not so conservative that it serializes, because serialization is a waste of resources.

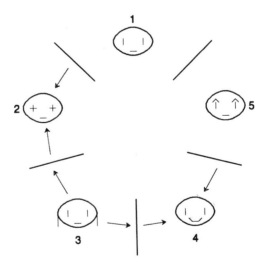

**Figure 4.8**  Philosopher 3 starves

# 4 ONE-SHOT ALLOCATION

To prevent deadlock, we only need to ensure that a cycle of waiting can never build up. One way to avoid a cycle is to partition all processes into two kinds: those that have all the resources they will ever need and those that have none at all. Processes in the first group are not blocked. Processes in the second group are blocked waiting for resources held by the first group. Therefore, no cycle of waiters can exist. This line of reasoning leads to **one-shot allocation**, which requires each process to acquire all its resources at once. The process is blocked until the request can be satisfied. Any attempt to request resources after the first time is an error.

In its pure form, the one-shot method requires each process to acquire all its needed resources at one time and never request resources again. Under this rule, each philosopher would request both chopsticks at the outset and never return them. Only two philosophers would ever eat; the other three would starve.

A more liberal form of one-shot allocation follows this rule:

| **One-shot allocation** |
| --- |
| A process may request resources only when it has none at all. |

A process may repeatedly acquire a number of resources, use them, return them all, and then later acquire a new set. To follow this policy, the philosophers should ask for both chopsticks at once. A resource manager that employs the one-shot policy should be careful to block any philosopher that cannot get both chopsticks at once. It must never grant requests partially (like allocating one of the two chopsticks requested by a philosopher), because such an allocation is equivalent to letting the philosopher make two requests.

Now if all the philosophers ask for chopsticks at the same time, the resource manager will grant one philosopher, say number 1, two chopsticks. Philosophers 2 and 5 cannot be satisfied at the moment, so they are given no chopsticks at all. Philosophers 3 and 4 are still candidates for resources; say the resource manager gives 3 two chopsticks. Now 4 must also be blocked. There is no deadlock, since there is no cycle in the graph, as shown in Figure 4.9. This allocation strategy has prevented deadlock, but it does not address starvation.

Our earlier situation in which processes **A** and **B** each need two tapes is also solved, since the one-shot method will enforce serialization.

However, one-shot allocation is too conservative to be practical. A process that will eventually need many resources will have to acquire them all at once and thus prevent other processes from using the resources, even though the process that holds them is not yet using them. Furthermore, a process may not know all the resources it will eventually need.

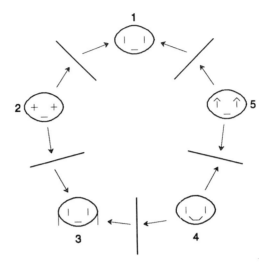

**Figure 4.9** One-shot allocation

# 5 HIERARCHICAL ALLOCATION

Another way to prevent a cycle is to associate some number with each process and somehow make sure that numbers only increase as we follow any chain of waiting processes. There clearly can't be a cycle of processes, each of which has a higher number than the previous one.

That is the theory, but how can it be made practical? First, give each resource class a "level" number. For example, tape drives can have level 1, plotters 2, and printers 3. The numbers need not all be different. We will associate each process with the number of the highest level resource it currently holds. To make sure the numbers increase on any chain of waiting processes, we impose the following rule.

---

### Hierarchical allocation

A process may request resources only at a higher level
than any resource it currently holds.

---

For example, if process **A** has a tape drive and a plotter, it can ask for two printers, but it may not request another tape drive or another three plotters. A process that only has a tape drive may ask for both plotters and printers but not for another tape drive. This rule is not so severe as the one-shot rule.

The hierarchical allocation rule solves the deadlock problem. To see why, let's say that there is a deadlock. We can show that some process must have broken the rules. Pick any member of the deadlock and call it process **A**. It must be blocked while waiting for some resource. That resource is at some level, say *a*. Some process **B** has that resource and is waiting for another resource. Since **B** already has a resource at level *a*, the one it is waiting for must be at a higher level, say *b*. This argument continues around the cycle until we find that process **A** must be holding a resource at level *z* , where $z > a$. But then **A** has broken the rules, because it is asking for a resource at level *a*. If **A** hasn't broken the rules, then somewhere else along the cycle a mistake was made. To enforce a hierarchical allocation, the resource manager should return an error indication instead of granting a resource when a process breaks the rule.

In our scenario of Figure 4.1, neither process has followed the hierarchical rule, since both have requested a tape drive after they already have one. Each should request both drives simultaneously. If they had followed the rule, they would not have encountered a deadlock. If we wish, we can distinguish the two tape drives and put them at different levels. Then both **A** and **B** must ask for the lower-level tape drive before the higher-level one. The second process to ask for its lower-level tape drive will be blocked. Again, deadlock is avoided.

The hierarchical strategy also protects the dining philosophers from deadlock. If all chopsticks are at the same level, the philosophers must ask for both chopsticks at once, which we have already seen prevents deadlocks. If each chopstick is at a different level, each philosopher must always ask for the chopsticks in the proper order. It cannot happen that the proper order for every philosopher is to ask first for the left chopstick and then for the right chopstick.

Unfortunately, the hierarchical strategy is still fairly conservative. Processes must ask for low-level resources long before they are really needed because after higher-level resources have been acquired, it is no longer possible to get low-level resources without giving the high-level ones back. Since resources are acquired in this artificial order, some processes are blocked for resources they don't need yet but must acquire now. Other processes are blocked for resources they need but are being held by another process that does not need them yet. In the extreme case in which all resources are at the same level, hierarchical allocation reduces to the one-shot technique.

When hierarchical allocation is used, the scarcest resources are usually given the highest levels. Requests for them will therefore be made only when they are actually needed by a process.

# 6 ADVANCE-CLAIM ALGORITHM

The advance-claim algorithm moves us closer to our goal of liberalism without deadlock by requiring extra information in advance. Consider a banker with an initial amount of cash with which to grant loans and customers who wish to take loans and later repay them. Customers often request additional loans before they can pay back anything. The banker must be conservative enough to avoid deadlocks among the customers but wishes to be liberal enough to make as many loans as possible.

We will require that each process make a **claim** before it acquires any resources. This claim indicates the greatest number of each resource class it will need at any one time. This claim allows the resource manager to foresee and prevent dangerous situations. The claim can be presented as a service call:

☐    Claim(resources). This call returns an error if the process already holds resources. It sets an upper limit on the number of resources the process may later use at one time. The resources argument may list several classes of resources.

A process is constrained by its claim; if it ever makes a request that, if satisfied, would cause the process to hold more of some resource class than its initial claim, the request is rejected. The sum of all the claims made by all the processes can be much larger than the total amount of resources available. However, no one process may claim more than the total number of physical resources because there would be a danger that this process could then legally request more than can be granted, and the process would not be able to continue.

The resource manager records the current **allocation state** for each resource class. For simplicity, we will assume that there is only one resource class, like tape drives. The current allocation state can be declared as follows:

```
1 type
2    ProcessResourceState =
3       record
4          Claim : integer;
5          Held : integer;
6          Request : integer; { if not zero, the process
7             is blocked waiting for this many more }
8       end;
9    AllocationState =
10      record
11         array 1:NumberOfProcesses of ProcessResourceState;
12         Free : integer; { unallocated resources }
13      end;
```

An allocation state is called **realizable** if it makes sense — that is, if the following conditions prevail:
(1)    No one claim is for more than the total resources available.
(2)    No process is holding more than its claim.
(3)    The sum of all the Held fields is not more than the total resources available.

Otherwise, the state is called **unrealizable**. The resource manager ensures that unrealizable states are never entered. Each claim is checked against the total resources, and each request is checked against the associated claim.

A realizable state is safe if it cannot possibly lead to a deadlock. Formally, a state is **safe** if there is a sequence of processes, called a **safe sequence**, such that these three conditions are met:

(1) The first process in the sequence can certainly finish, because even if it should request all the resources its claim allows, there are enough free resources to satisfy this request.

(2) The second process in the sequence can finish if the first finishes and releases everything it now has, because adding what the first has to the free resources can satisfy the entire claim of the second process.

(3) The $i$th process can finish if all the previous processes do, because the sum of all their resources and the currently free resources can satisfy the entire claim of the $i$th process.

Informally, the state is safe because at the worst, we can avoid deadlock by blocking all new requests except those made by the first process. When it finishes we will allow only the second to continue, and so forth. One hopes, of course, that such serialization will not be necessary.

Here is an example.

| Process | Holding | Claims |
|---------|---------|--------|
| A | 4 | 6 |
| B | 2 | 7 |
| C | 4 | 11 |
| **Unallocated** | 2 | |

**A** can certainly finish, because the 2 unallocated resources can be granted to it if necessary to bring its holdings to the 6 that it claims. When it finishes, it will release all 6 resources. We could then certainly finish **B** by applying 5 of those resources to bring its holdings up to its claim of 7. When it terminates, it will release all 7, giving us 8 unallocated resources. Those resources suffice to finish **C**. We have shown that {**A**, **B**, **C**} is a safe sequence, so the current state is safe. However, a very similar allocation state is unsafe:

| Process | Holding | Claims |
|---------|---------|--------|
| A | 4 | 6 |
| B | 2 | 9 |
| C | 4 | 11 |
| **Unallocated** | 2 | |

**A** could finish as before, but we cannot guarantee that either **B** or **C** would finish because after **A**'s termination, there are only 6 unallocated resources. We might be lucky, though, and **B** might finish without requesting its full claim. So an unsafe state does not necessarily have a deadlock.

Having established these concepts, we can define the advance-claim algorithm:

---

## Advance-claim algorithm

Never allocate a request if it causes the current
allocation state to become unsafe.

---

This algorithm is often called the **banker's algorithm**.

At first, this criterion appears expensive to evaluate. Whenever a process makes a new request, the resource manager must find a safe sequence under the assumption that the request has been granted. There are $n!$ ($n$ factorial, or $n \times (n - 1) \times (n - 2) \times \cdots \times 2 \times 1$) sequences of $n$ processes, all of which would be tried before the state is pronounced unsafe. However, this cost can be reduced to work proportional to $n^2$. If the state is safe and if some process **A** can finish given the currently available resources, there is a safe sequence that starts with **A**. We do not miss the only solutions by starting with a reasonable-looking first element. The $O(n^2)$ algorithm (the "O" means "order of") looks roughly like this:

```
1 S := [all the processes];
2 while S <> [] do
3    find A, an element of S that can finish
4    if impossible, fail:  the state is unsafe
5    remove A from S, add A's resources to the unallocated pool
6 end;
7 succeed: the state is safe.
```

The resource manager need not allocate resources to requesting processes according to the order of the safe sequence. It may allocate resources in the order of requests as long as there exists some safe sequence after each request is satisfied.

The advance-claim algorithm can be applied with a still cheaper algorithm developed by Habermann. The resource manager maintains an array $S[0..r - 1]$ of integers, where $r$ is the number of copies of the resource. For simplicity, we assume that there is only one resource class. Initially, $S[i] = r - i$ for all $0 \leqslant i < r$. If a process with a claim of $c$ holds $h$ units and requests 1 more, decrement $S[i]$ for all $0 \leqslant i < c - h$. If any $S[i]$ becomes negative, the new state is unsafe.

As an example, we return to the safe state shown above. To find the current values of S, we will assume that **A**, **B**, and **C** each started with no resources, then asked for their current holdings one by one. We will mark each decrement by $\times$.

| Index | 0 | 1 | 2 | 3 | 4 | 5 | 6 | 7 | 8 | 9 | 10 | 11 |
|---|---|---|---|---|---|---|---|---|---|---|---|---|
| **Original S** | 12 | 11 | 10 | 9 | 8 | 7 | 6 | 5 | 4 | 3 | 2 | 1 |
| **A** | × | × | × | × | × | × | | | | | | |
| **A** | × | × | × | × | × | | | | | | | |
| **A** | × | × | × | × | | | | | | | | |
| **A** | × | × | × | | | | | | | | | |
| **B** | × | × | × | × | × | × | × | | | | | |
| **B** | × | × | × | × | × | × | | | | | | |
| **C** | × | × | × | × | × | × | × | × | × | × | × | |
| **C** | × | × | × | × | × | × | × | × | × | × | | |
| **C** | × | × | × | × | × | × | × | × | × | | | |
| **C** | × | × | × | × | × | × | × | × | | | | |
| **Final S** | 2 | 1 | 0 | 0 | 0 | 0 | 1 | 1 | 1 | 1 | 1 | 1 |

The current state is safe. If we grant **A** one more resource, we would decrement $S[0]$ and $S[1]$, which does not make those entries negative. Therefore it would be safe to grant **A** another resource. But granting **B** one more resource would decrement $S[0]$ through $S[4]$, three of which would become negative. That state would be unsafe.

To see why this strange method works, let us see what the first column, $S[0]$, represents. Before any resources are granted, $S[0]$ is equal to $r$, the number of resources. Every time a resource is granted, the process that requested it must have had a claim higher than the number of resources granted so far, so × will be placed in at least the $S[0]$ column, if not in others. Therefore, the current value of $S[0]$ is the number of available resources, since we subtract one for each × in the column. If $S[0] < 0$, the state is not only unsafe, it is also unrealizable, since more resources have been granted than exist.

Next, let us see what happens if a process, say **D**, claims the entire set of resources and then acquires them all. We can see how S is calculated for $r = 4$:

| Index | 0 | 1 | 2 | 3 |
|---|---|---|---|---|
| **Original S** | 4 | 3 | 2 | 1 |
| **D** | × | × | × | × |
| **D** | × | × | × | |
| **D** | × | × | | |
| **D** | × | | | |
| **Final S** | 0 | 0 | 0 | 0 |

A process that acquires its entire claim makes a triangular "footprint" of × marks in our picture. In the case in which the initial claim is the entire set of resources, the footprint is large enough to reduce every entry in S to 0. When a process has received its entire claim, the footprint is complete and makes a triangle.

Now let us say that one or more entries of S have become −1. For concreteness, let us say that S[3] is the leftmost column with an entry of −1. What is the largest possible value for S[0], S[1], and S[2]? S[2] cannot be greater than 0 — that is, one larger than S[3] — since every × in column 3 is in a line that also puts × in column 2, and column 2 starts only 1 larger than column 3. S[2] cannot be negative, since column 3 was the first with a negative value. So S[2] must be 0. Similar reasoning shows that S[1] is either 0 or 1, and S[0] is 0, 1, or 2.

Since S[2] = 0 and S[3] = −1, there cannot be any line of exactly three × marks. Such a line would have × in column 2 but not in column 3 and therefore would have decreased S[2] more than S[3], so S[2] would have to be less than 0. Therefore, no footprint has a line with exactly three × marks. All footprints are either large and incomplete, with their last row having at least four × marks, or they are small, with their first row having at most two × marks. All the small footprints can finish. They belong to processes that form the start of a safe sequence. (There are at most two such processes, one with a claim of 2 and only one line of footprint and one with a claim of 1 and one line of footprint.) After these processes have terminated, S[0] will be 2 and S[1] will be 1. Only processes with large incomplete footprints are left. Not a single one of them can finish, because each has at least three lines of footprint to complete, so S[0] must be at least 3. But S[0] is only 2. Therefore, there is no safe sequence. This argument does not depend on the fact that we chose column 3 as the first with a negative value.

We have been assuming throughout that there is only one resource class. The situation becomes more complicated if there are several resource classes. It is not enough to find a safe sequence for each resource class independently; a sequence must be found that is safe with respect to each resource class.

The advance-claim algorithm is conservative insofar as it cautiously avoids entering an unsafe state even if this unsafe state has no deadlock. However, it achieves the most liberal policy that is guaranteed not to deadlock. One cost of this achievement is the requirement that processes enter claims, which may be unnatural. For example, a process that needs to modify a number of files needs to exclude other processes, but it might not know which files must be modified until it has read a significant amount of data from many files. A second cost of the advance-claim algorithm is the time and space needed for finding a safe sequence.

More complex methods exist that lead still closer to our goal. They require still more prior information about what the processes will need. For example, if we know the exact order in which each process will request and release resources, we can organize a more liberal schedule. The necessary calculation, however, is quite time-consuming.

# 7 DEADLOCK DETECTION

The methods described so far can be characterized as policies for **deadlock prevention**. If, however, we are willing to allow deadlocks, we must be able to discover
them when they occur. We call this strategy **deadlock detection**. A method similar
to the advance-claim algorithm can be used to check for a deadlock-free sequence
when the current allocation state is unsafe. We say that a state is **deadlock-free** if
there is a sequence of processes, called a **deadlock-free sequence**, such that the following three conditions are met.

(1)     The first process in the sequence might finish because there are enough free
        resources to fulfill its current outstanding request (what it has actually
        asked for) even if there are not enough to satisfy its entire claim (what it
        may potentially ask for).

(2)     The second process in the sequence might finish if the first finishes and
        releases everything it now has, because adding what the first has to the free
        resources can satisfy the entire outstanding request of the second process.

(3)     The $i$th process might finish if all the previous processes do because the
        sum of all their resources and the currently free resources can satisfy the
        entire outstanding request of the $i$th process.

A deadlock-free state has no current deadlock because the chain of waiting
processes is not cyclic. However, if it is unsafe, an unlucky set of requests can turn
it into a deadlocked state. Let us continue the previous unsafe example, adding a
column for the outstanding request, that is, the request that has been made that we
have not yet decided to honor. (We are either at the point of deciding whether to
honor it or we have placed the requesting process in a resource-wait list.) We no
longer need the Claims column, since we are not using the advance-claim algorithm.

| Process | Holding | Outstanding request |
|---------|---------|---------------------|
| **A** | 4 | 2 |
| **B** | 2 | 6 |
| **C** | 4 | 7 |
| **Unallocated** | 2 | |

As we saw before, this state could be unsafe (given the claims). However, {**A**, **B**, **C**}
is a deadlock-free sequence, so there is no deadlock yet. Again, a slight change can
make a big difference. If **B** should ask for one more resource, this is what we have:

| Process | Holding | Outstanding request |
|---------|---------|---------------------|
| A | 4 | 2 |
| B | 2 | 7 |
| C | 4 | 7 |
| **Unallocated** | 2 | |

Now **A** might finish, yielding 6 free resources, but there is no way to satisfy either **B** or **C**, both of which need 7. Processes **B** and **C** are deadlocked, but **A** is not.

Deadlock can be detected in such cases by building the resource graph and looking for cycles. If one resource class has several equivalent members (like tape drives, which might be functionally identical), the simple resource graphs must be improved slightly. We cluster all resources from one class into the same node of the graph. An arrow goes from any process waiting for a resource to the class node for that resource. If a process is waiting for several resources, we draw an arrow from the process to each of the appropriate class nodes. An arrow goes from a class node to any process using one of its resources.

A deadlock is no longer signaled by a simple cycle. For example, the generalized resource graph of Figure 4.10 is an extension of Figure 4.1. There are three tape drives and three processes. Each of **A**, **B**, and **C** has one tape drive. **A** and **B** are waiting for a second tape drive. The same cycle we saw in Figure 4.1 is present (passing through **A**, the tapes, **B**, and the tapes), but there is no deadlock. **C** may well finish its work and release its tape drive. Then either **A** or **B** can get it, finish, and let the other finish as well.

In generalized resource graphs, we look for knots, which generalize cycles in ordinary resource graphs. A **knot** is a set of vertices (including processes and resources) such that starting at any vertex of the knot, paths lead to *all* the vertices in the knot and to no vertices outside the knot. In our example, paths leading from **A**, **B**, or the tapes lead to **C**, but no path at all leads from **C**. Therefore, this graph

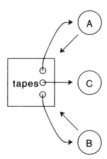

**Figure 4.10**  A deadlock-free generalized resource graph

has no knots and no deadlock.

If we enlarge the example we can build a deadlock, as shown in Figure 4.11. Now **C** is waiting for a printer, but both printers are allocated. This graph contains a knot, namely, all the vertices except for **D**. All the processes in the knot are deadlocked. Terminating any one of them will break the deadlock. For example, if we terminate **C**, one tape is released. Either **A** or **B** can then proceed. (Until we allocate that tape to either **A** or **B**, we ignore the knot, because it involves a resource that is not fully allocated.)

One way the resource manager can detect a knot, and therefore a deadlock, is to try to **reduce** the generalized resource graph. If it can't reduce the graph completely, there is a knot. To reduce the graph, we remove any process that is not waiting for any resources and any process that is waiting only for resource classes that are not fully allocated. These processes are not contributing to any deadlock; there is some chance they will finish and return their resources. As we remove these processes from the graph, we also remove any arrows pointing to them from resources in order to indicate that those resources are given back. This action may turn resources that were fully allocated before into partially allocated resources, thereby allowing us to remove more processes. If we can remove all the processes, there is no knot and no deadlock.

In Figure 4.10, we would first remove **C**, since it is not waiting. Then the tapes resource is no longer fully allocated, so both **A** and **B** can be removed. In Figure 4.11, however, no processes can be removed, so there is a deadlock.

The onset of deadlock is always at the time a process makes a request and is blocked waiting for a resource. A resource manager that depends on deadlock detection needs to check for deadlock only at this time. A reasonable alternative, taken by VMS, is to start a timer for 10 seconds (or however long is specified by the deadlock-wait parameter) whenever a request blocks. If the request is still blocked when the timer expires, an attempt is made to detect deadlock. The goal of the attempt is to remove the blocked process that triggered the detection episode from the resource graph. If that process can be removed, it is not necessary to continue and remove the others; there is no deadlock involving that process.

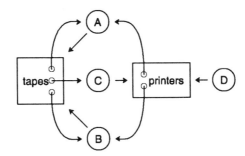

**Figure 4.11** A deadlocked resource graph

# 8  DEADLOCK RECOVERY

When a deadlock occurs, one of the processes participating in the deadlock must be terminated for the good of the community. A policy that chooses a victim process is called a method of **deadlock recovery**. Terminating a process might injure data, as we have seen. A process currently modifying shared data should be able to warn the resource manager not to terminate it to recover from deadlock. If data consistency presents no problems, the terminated victim might be restarted later. The designers of database management packages have developed very sophisticated mechanisms to allow database transactions to be aborted in such a way that restart is always possible. We will discuss some of those mechanisms in Chapter 6.

To select a victim process, the resource manager could take into account the external priority of the process and how expensive it will be to restart it. One good measure is the amount of computation the process has already performed. The larger this amount, the more expensive it is to restart the process and get it to its present state. Also, one would hope that processes that have consumed large amounts of computation are almost finished.

# 9  STARVATION

Our discussion has concentrated on deadlock, which is due to overly liberal policies for allocation of resources. Starvation, in contrast, is the result of overly liberal policies for reassigning resources once they are returned. When resources are freed, they can be applied to any process waiting for them in the resource-wait list. (The short-term scheduler should most likely not switch to the waiting process but should continue with the releasing process, in accord with the Hysteresis Principle.) Not all policies for applying those resources prevent starvation.

For example, consider a situation with one resource class. A straightforward policy is to apply all released resources to the first-blocked process. However, the blocked process may be the last in all possible safe sequences for the current allocation state. We can't unblock it, or the state becomes unsafe. We can't apply the resources to other jobs because they were not blocked first. Hence this policy does not work at all.

We might allow other small requests to be satisfied meanwhile, in the hope that the processes we favor in this way will eventually release enough resources to satisfy the first-blocked process. More precisely, we might sort the resource-wait list by the order in which processes block. When resources are freed, we scan this list and grant resources only to processes whose current request can be fully satisfied. Unfortunately, this **first-fit** policy will starve the first-blocked process if there is a continuous stream of new jobs with smaller requirements.

One way to modify this strategy is to allow partial allocation. As many units of the resource are granted to the first process in the list as may be done safely; the rest may be applied (if safe) to later processes in the list. Even this policy fails, because there are situations in which no resources may safely be granted to the first blocked process, even though others may continue.

Another modification is to order the resource-wait list according to some safe sequence. (If there are several safe sequences, any one will do.) Resources are granted, either partially or fully, starting at the head of this list. However, there is no way to guarantee that any particular process will ever reach the start of this list. A process may remain near the end of the safe sequence and never be allocated resources.

The **starvation detection** approach is modeled after deadlock detection. By the time deadlock is detected, it is too late, but it is never too late to fix starvation. Starvation might be signaled by a process remaining on the resource-wait list for too long, measured in either time units or units of process completions.

Once starvation has been detected, new processes may be denied resources until starving processes have completed. Of course, processes that already have resources must be allowed to get more, since they may appear earlier on the safe sequence. This approach is certain to work, but it must be tuned carefully. If starvation detection is too sensitive, new processes are banned too often, with the result that there is an overall decrease in throughput. In other words, the policy is too conservative. If detection is not sensitive enough, however, processes can starve for a long time before they are finally allowed to run.

Luckily, starvation is seldom a problem in actual operating systems, because non-preemptable, serially reusable resources such as printers and tape drives tend to be underused, and the existence of idle periods tends to prevent starvation.

# 10 PERSPECTIVE

Deadlock arises from dynamic resource sharing. If resources are not shared, there can never be a deadlock. Deadlocks are especially dangerous in time-critical work. If the operating system is used to run programs that control factory processes or pilot aircraft, deadlock is unacceptable.

The danger of deadlocks is mitigated by several considerations. First, deadlocks can often be avoided by proper design of the algorithms that share resources. For example, different parts of the kernel may share information, like process context blocks. Those parts will want exclusive access during the time they modify that information; such access is like holding a resource. A hierarchical design inside the kernel is often used to make sure that no deadlocks arise from using these resources. We will return to this point in Chapter 8, where we discuss mechanisms for achieving exclusive access.

Second, deadlock is an unacceptable situation only if everyone is infinitely patient. In interactive environments, the resource manager need not recover from or even detect deadlocks because the user will eventually get bored waiting for an answer and will manually terminate the process.

The service call we described for requesting resources could be enhanced by including a **timeout** parameter. If the resource manager cannot or will not honor the request within the time specified by this parameter, it unblocks the calling process and gives it a failure indication. The process could try again, try a different request, back out of whatever action it is trying to perform, or terminate.

Some authors distinguish deadlock prevention from avoidance. Prevention includes any method that negates one of the following three conditions that lead to deadlock.

- Resources may not be shared. One can sometimes get the effect of sharing an otherwise non-sharable device by buffering all output to that device (in parallel) and then serializing the output of those buffers. Buffering can therefore be used as a prevention method, but deadlock can still arise over the use of the buffers themselves.

- Resources may be requested while others are already being held. As we have seen, the one-shot method prohibits such action, and is therefore a prevention method. The hierarchical method prevents such requests within a level; by induction, it prevents circular wait across levels as well.

- Resources may not be preempted. Under batch multiprogramming, some jobs may allow cancellation and restarting. However, jobs that have made changes to files are unlikely to be restartable.

Avoidance, on the other hand, includes methods like the banker's algorithm that take advantage of advance knowledge (such as maximum claims). That advance knowledge allows them more freedom to navigate the progress diagram and still avoid dangerous regions.

The conservative-liberal metaphor helps in rating various policies that we have seen. Liberal policies have a greater potential for parallelism and throughput because they allow more flexible navigation of the progress diagram, but they have an equal potential for deadlock and starvation. The advance-claim algorithm provides a reasonably liberal method that is still conservative enough to prevent deadlock. To prevent starvation as well, other conservative steps must be taken, such as banning new arrivals or concentrating resources on particular processes. Overly conservative methods like one-shot allocation remove all worries about deadlock and starvation, but the cost is severe reduction of concurrency.

Although we have devoted a significant amount of attention to the advance-claim algorithm, it is mostly interesting in the theoretical, not the practical, sense. As we pointed out, many applications are unable to compute reasonable claims before they start working; they only discover what they will need once they have made some progress. Furthermore, resources can disappear suddenly if the hardware malfunctions. Therefore, most operating systems don't implement the advance-claim algorithm. It is much more common to grant resources to processes following the most liberal policy imaginable. If this policy leads to deadlock, the deadlock is detected (either by the resource manager or by disgruntled users) and broken by injuring some process. Hierarchical allocation has also been used successfully, especially within the kernel to make sure that its modules never become deadlocked.

# 11  FURTHER READING

A good mathematical treatment of deadlocks is given in Shaw's textbook on operating systems (1974). The problem of deadlock avoidance was formalized and analyzed several years ago (Holt, 1972; Coffman *et al.*, 1971; Hebalkar, 1970; Shoshani and Coffman, 1970; Minoura, 1982). The advance-claim algorithm was first proposed by E. Dijkstra (1968). A generalization of the binary safe-unsafe criterion to a measure of the minimum number of resources needed for safety has been suggested by Madduri and Finkel (1984). Starvation has also been called "effective deadlock" by Holt (1971), who, along with others, has pointed out that partial allocation does not guarantee freedom from starvation (Parnas and Habermann, 1972; Rossi and Fontao, 1981).

Starvation control has not been dealt with extensively. Holt suggested maintaining periodically incremented counters for each blocked process (Holt, 1972). When a counter exceeds a critical value the scheduler has to find a safe sequence and finish jobs in that order. He also suggested partial allocations but required that resources not be granted to jobs with zero holdings. The approach of banning new jobs was introduced by Madduri and Finkel (1984). Another approach to starvation, which allocates resources according to a safe-sequence order, is found in the Boss 2 operating system for the RC4000 computer (Lauesen, 1973).

# 12  EXERCISES

1. The service calls for allocating and releasing resources look suspiciously like the calls for allocating and releasing segments. Is there any fundamental difference between the two situations?

2. The service call for allocation of resources cannot specify "either one resource of class 1 or one of class 2." However, our dining philosophers might want to ask for whichever chopstick is available first, then ask for the other one specifically.
   (a) Why aren't all the chopsticks in the same resource class?
   (b) What could happen if we allow this sort of "selective resource allocation" and use a liberal allocation policy?

(c)  How well would selective allocation mesh with the hierarchical allocation policy?

(d)  How well would selective allocation mesh with the advance-claim algorithm?

3.  What is a one-process deadlock?  Why does this situation not cause any problems to the resource manager?

4.  Under the hierarchical resource allocation policy, suppose that a process is holding a resource of level 3 and finds it needs to acquire a resource of level 2.  Is there any way it can do this?

5.  Let's number all the chopsticks in the dining philosophers problem and require that each philosopher request an even-numbered chopstick before an odd-numbered chopstick.  Will this allocation strategy work?  Is it a form of a well-known strategy?

6.  Assume that there are two classes of resources.  For the following resource-allocation state, tell which, if any, of the processes are deadlocked.

| Process | 1 | | 2 | |
|---|---|---|---|---|
| | Holding | Request | Holding | Request |
| A | 3 | 1 | 4 | 5 |
| B | 2 | 3 | 3 | 6 |
| C | 4 | 2 | 2 | 0 |
| Unallocated | 2 | | 3 | |

7.  Assume that there are two classes of resources.  For the following resource-allocation state, tell which, if any, of the processes are deadlocked.

| process | 1 | | 2 | |
|---|---|---|---|---|
| | Holding | Request | Holding | Request |
| A | 3 | 7 | 4 | 5 |
| B | 2 | 3 | 3 | 6 |
| C | 4 | 2 | 2 | 0 |
| Unallocated | 2 | | 3 | |

8.  Draw the resource graphs for the situations in exercises 6 and 7.

9.  Construct an unsafe resource-allocation state in which there are three processes, there is one class of resource with four resources, and each process has a claim of three resources.

10. Construct an unsafe resource-allocation state in which there are three processes, there is one class of resource with four resources, and each process has a claim of two resources.

11. Which of the following events can lead from a safe state to an unsafe state? Which can lead from a deadlock-free state to a deadlocked state?
    (a) A process makes a request within its claim.
    (b) A process makes a request beyond its claim.
    (c) A request within the claim is satisfied.
    (d) A process is blocked on a resource-wait list.
    (e) A process releases a resource it had previously acquired.
    (f) A process increases its claim.
    (g) A process decreases its claim.
    (h) A process terminates.
    (i) A process is created and it makes its claim.

12. We have shown for Habermann's method that if $S[i] = -1$ for some $i$, there is no safe sequence. Show that if all $S[i] \geq 0$ for all $i$, there is a safe sequence.

13. Show a situation in which there are several resource classes and for each class there is a safe sequence but the situation is still unsafe.

14. Find a situation in which the first-fit starvation control policy fails.

15. Find a situation in which the first-fit starvation-control policy fails even when we make partial allocations.

16. Why is testing the length of the resource-wait list an inadequate measure of starvation?

17. Why don't we measure the length of time on the resource-wait list in virtual time?

# Transput

Thus far we have treated operating systems as resource-allocation schemes, as suggested by the Resource Principle. We will now turn to the view of operating systems suggested by the **Beautification Principle** introduced in Chapter 1.

> ## Beautification Principle
> An operating system is a set of algorithms that
> hide the details of the hardware
> and provide a more pleasant environment.

From this point of view, storage management is not an attempt to allocate the main-store resource but rather is meant to hide address translation and its implementation so that processes can live in a more pleasant, virtual world. All a process needs to know for segmentation is how to get and release segments.

Controlling transput is another way the kernel beautifies the process interface. Computer devices (sometimes called "peripherals") are often quite unpleasant to use directly. Processes are interested in moving data between their virtual space and the device. They are not interested in the peculiarities of line printers, for example. Nor do they care to know that different brands and models of tape drive require completely different controlling programs. In fact, they may not care to know whether output is being directed to a tape drive, to a printer, or even to another process. All such details can be hidden, in which case we say that transput is **transparent** with respect to brand, model, or device type.

Just as processes enjoy the benefits of virtual store, they also enjoy the benefits of **virtual devices**. These devices are simulated by the kernel, with data actually kept either in main store or on other devices, typically large disks. For example, the VM operating system has the concept of "minidisks," which are meant to simulate small disks. They are actually implemented by allocating cylinders on much larger disks. Another example comes from spooling systems, in which printer output is actually sent to a disk to wait for the printer to become available.

For the kernel to provide transparency and virtual devices, it must deal with physical devices without interference from processes. Therefore, all machine instructions that might affect devices, such as a "Start transput" instruction, are disabled when the computer is in non-privileged state. A process that uses such an instruction causes a trap to the kernel, which treats this event either as an error in the process (invalid instruction) or as a request for the kernel to provide transput services itself (service call).

In return for this monopoly over physical devices, the kernel provides service calls for transput (such as reading a block from a tape) and device control (such as rewinding the tape drive). The kernel usually attempts to schedule transput so that it overlaps with computation, possibly blocking the requesting process until the transput completes. It can also schedule competing transput requests from different processes so that they are executed in an efficient order.

An amazingly large proportion of the instructions in the kernel, often 50 percent, is devoted to device handling. Even though the subject has not been formalized very well, the sheer bulk of transput program in kernels makes this subject vital to a study of operating systems. Our discussion will begin at the lowest level, the hardware, and will end at the highest level of software. We will start by describing transput devices. Then we will see the **device interface**, that is, the way devices are connected to the computer. We then turn to **device drivers**, which are kernel modules that interact with these devices. Finally, we will discuss the **process interface** through which processes gain access to transput services from the kernel.

# 1 DEVICE HARDWARE

A great number of devices have been designed for computers. Some, like disks and drums, are used for backing and secondary store. (We use **backing store** to hold swapped-out parts of virtual store. We use **secondary store** to hold files that are to be kept after a process terminates.) Tapes are intended for **archival store** — that is, to hold large amounts of data that will not be needed for a long time. Tapes are also used for temporary store when algorithms require enormous amounts of data and for transferring large amounts of information between computer installations. Keyboards and video displays, together called "terminals," allow users to interact with their processes. Special devices, like robot arms and television cameras, are used for real-time control. Communication lines connect computers and peripherals.

We cannot hope to give a complete description in this book of all these devices. Instead, we will present general principles and concentrate on just a few devices.

## 1.1 Disks

Disks are the most common devices for backing and secondary store. They come in a wide variety of capacities, speeds, and prices, but all disks share some common characteristics. Disks accept and provide data at a high rate (approximately 2 megabits per second). Data are transferred to and from the disk in increments of one **block**, which is typically between 256 and 1024 bytes. It is generally impossible to read or write less than one block from or to a disk. If the operating system wishes to write out only a few bytes without destroying the rest of the block, it must first read in the block, modify those few bytes, and then write out the entire block.

The disk unit contains a **disk pack**, which is sometimes designed to be removable. The disk pack physically resembles a stack of phonograph records, called **platters**. Information is recorded magnetically, usually on both sides. All the platters rotate as one unit, usually at 60 rotations per second. Each platter is divided into bands called **tracks**. There are typically on the order of 200 tracks per side on a disk pack, but some disks, like the IBM 3380, have almost 900, and some newer Winchester disks, which have a sealed head-disk assembly, have more than 1500. Unlike phonograph record grooves, the tracks do not spiral toward the center but are concentric. Each track is divided into **sectors**, each of which holds one block of information. There are about 30 sectors in a track on a large disk pack. Figure 5.1 shows the layout of a disk.

Floppy disk drives are similar, but they accommodate only one platter, which can be removed. Some only use one side of the platter. Floppies come in two standard sizes (8 inches and 5¼ inches) and various densities. They rotate more slowly than conventional disks. If their motors are allowed to run continually, both the motors and the floppies wear out very quickly, so the motors are only turned on when a transfer needs to be made. By the Hysteresis Principle, the motor is not turned off again immediately, but is left on for a few seconds in the expectation that another transfer will be needed soon.

In addition to a block of data, a sector may also hold addressing information (which sector it is), a bit that indicates whether the sector is usable (if one sector is damaged, the rest of the disk pack may still be usable), and some error-checking information such as a checksum. (We will discuss checksums shortly.)

The operating system usually does not need to be aware of this extra sector information, but it must know how the disk is **formatted** — that is, how many sectors there are in a track and how many bytes may be stored in a sector. On many disk units, the formatting is performed under software control when the disk pack is brought into service. Formatting also discovers bad sectors and marks them. Extra tracks may be available to make up for bad parts of the disk. Some sophisticated disk controllers automatically remap good sectors from these extra tracks onto sectors that were discovered to be bad during formatting so that the operating system does not need to remember which sectors to avoid.

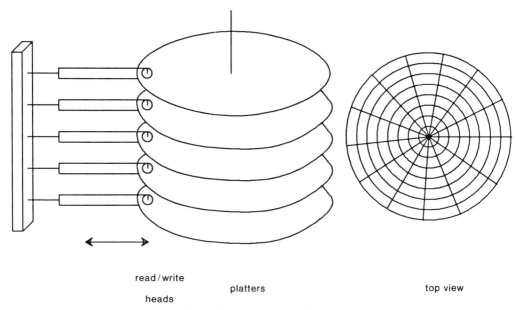

read / write
                                    platters                                      top view
heads

**Figure 5.1** Structure of a disk pack

The disk is only able to read or write from the track where the read/write head currently sits. This head can move in and out when necessary to access other tracks; this motion is called **seeking**. It takes on the order of 20 to 40 milliseconds to complete a seek. Of course, it takes longer to seek across many tracks than to seek across just a few. After a disk has been in use for a while, a seek operation may fail to move to exactly the right track. In this case, the software must ask the disk head to recalibrate itself by moving all the way out to a well-known position.

The read/write heads for all the disk surfaces are usually physically tied together so they all access the same track number at the same time. This combination of similarly located tracks on different surfaces is called a **cylinder**.

Three types of delay, or **latency**, affect how long it takes to read data from or write data to the disk. **Seek latency** is the amount of time needed to seek to the desired cylinder. **Rotational latency** is the amount of time needed for the desired sector to arrive under the read/write head. **Transfer latency** is the amount of time needed for those sectors with data to be completely scanned. (A single transput operation can involve more than one contiguous sector.)

## 1.2  Magnetic tape

Magnetic tape has three major uses: archival store, data transfer between computers, and intermediate storage of large amounts of data. Magnetic tape is the medium of choice for archival storage of large amounts of data. Periodic backups of disk are typically made onto tape, which can then be stored for long periods of time. Even though computer networks link many installations, massive amounts of data are still most economically transmitted by magnetic tape. A tape written at one installation with one brand of tape drive can usually be read at a different installation with a different brand of tape drive. In fact, the two installations may have different operating systems and different brands of computer. Such standardization makes it possible to transfer data practically anywhere by tape. Many programs of importance in the business world take a large number of input records, extract some data from each one, and then generate an output record. Magnetic tape is often used for the input because it is relatively inexpensive and can be read sequentially very quickly. Algorithms to sort massive sets of data generate large intermediate results, which can also be stored on tape. Tapes created during one pass over the data are read back in during the next pass.

Like disks, tapes store data by maintaining magnetic regions. There are typically nine such regions across the width of the tape (hence the name "nine-track tape"). A set of nine bits is called a **frame**. Eight bits of the frame are used to store one byte of data, and the ninth is a **parity bit** set to make the number of one bits in the frame an even number. This redundancy is used to help detect errors on the tape. We will discuss parity and other techniques for reliability shortly. Tapes are typically packed at densities of 1600 or 6250 frames per inch. The entire tape is written at the same density even though some tape drives are capable of writing at either density. Frames are grouped into **record**s separated by **inter-record gaps**. The gap indicates the end of a record and gives the tape drive room to speed up as it starts to read or write a record and to slow down after it finishes. Magnetic tape is always read and written in entire records. A collection of records constitutes a **file**. An **inter-file gap**, which is larger than an inter-record gap, marks the end of a file. Figure 5.2 shows the layout of a magnetic tape.

Unlike disks, magnetic tapes are not formatted to have a particular record size. Records may be of any convenient length, and successive records on the tape may have different lengths. When the tape is read, adequate main store must be available to hold an entire record at a time, regardless of its size. The use of larger records packs more data on the tape, because there aren't as many inter-record gaps. However, it requires larger main-store buffers for transput. A typical record size is on the order of 2000 bytes. Smaller virtual records can be packed together to gain the efficiency of larger physical records.

Many operating systems place an initial record on the tape that describes the tape, including a serial number, owner, and other information. This record is called a **label**. Such tapes also have header and trailer records surrounding files to aid in identifying and separating them.

Tapes can be read either forward or backward. When they read backward, the buffer in main store is filled from the end to the start. The operating system (or applications programmer) must remember one essential rule about magnetic tape: Never write in the middle of the tape. If the tape is positioned somewhere in the middle — that is, if there are records ahead of the current position — then any write operation destroys those records, because the new record written out will be followed by an inter-record gap. Since the gaps are not of reproducible sizes, that

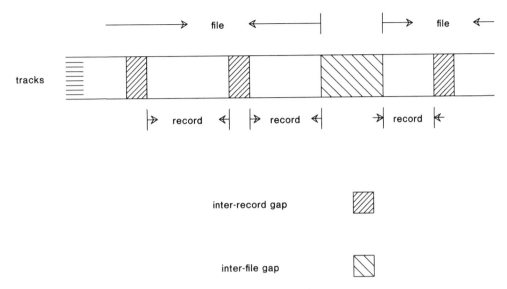

**Figure 5.2** Structure of magnetic tape

gap may overwrite some data from the next record on the tape. When the tape is then read, there may or may not be an extra record. Since it is not possible to assure reproducibility, writing in the middle of the tape is assumed to destroy any further contents.

**Winding latency**, the time needed to wind the tape to the desired place, is much longer than rotational or seek latency on a disk, although once the tape is spinning, data arrive in main store at about the same rate (about 2 megabits per second). Typical applications use tape in a strictly sequential sense, writing an entire tape before trying to read any of it and reading the entire tape from start to finish.

## 1.3 Drums

In the 1950s, drums were used for main store. (The IBM 650 computer worked this way.) Later they were used for secondary store (that is, files). They are principally used now for backing store (that is, swapping). A drum is shaped like a cylinder and is divided into circular tracks, each with its own read/write head. Like a disk, the drum is constantly in motion. There is no seek latency, but there is still rotational latency. Even rotational latency can be avoided for writing by always writing an entire track and starting at any point in the rotation. More often, each track is divided into sectors, and the operating system must wait for an available sector to come around. For swapping pages, one sector is as good as another; the first free sector to appear (on any track) may be chosen. Figure 5.3 shows how drums are arranged. Drums are not used very much any more. Disks

tracks

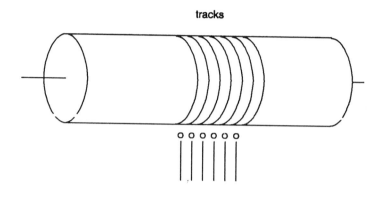

read/write heads

**Figure 5.3** Structure of a drum

and "solid-state drums," which are banks of memory chips behaving like drums, have replaced them.

## 1.4 Communication lines

**Communication lines** are devices used to connect computers to terminals and to each other. Since the operating system must deal with these lines, it is important to understand some of their hardware details. In **simplex** lines, data travel in only one direction. **Half-duplex** lines allow data in both directions, but not at the same time. **Duplex** lines are like two simplex lines tied together; they allow simultaneous communication in both directions.

**Hardware characteristics.** Whether the communication line is connected to a terminal or to another computer, certain characteristics are important. The first is the speed at which information can be transferred. Speed is usually measured in **baud**, which, strictly speaking, is the number of electrical transitions per second. These may be transitions between voltage levels or waveforms. Usually the baud rate is equivalent to bits per second. Commonly available baud rates for terminals are 110 (10 cps), 300 (30 cps), 1200 (120 cps), 9600 (960 cps), and 19200 (1920 cps). The abbreviation "cps" stands for "characters per second." In the standard ASCII character code, a character requires 7 bits for data. Additional bits are used to make sure that the sender and the receiver agree which bits are the first in a character. Inter-computer communication lines can be much faster. High-quality telephone lines can transmit data at 56K baud. The Ethernet, a multiple-access communication line, runs at 3M to 10M baud, and some experimental lines run at 100M baud. We will discuss computers linked by such lines into networks in Chapter 9.

No matter what form of transmission is used, all parties to the conversation must agree on conventions for formatting information, acquiring the rights to use the transmission medium, and interpreting messages. These conventions are called a **protocol**. There are thousands of protocols serving hundreds of purposes. We will glance at only a few.

### Synchronous transmission.

"Synchronous" comes from Greek roots meaning "at the same time." The essential feature of synchronous transmission is that both the sender and the receiver share a common clock. Bits are converted by the sender into voltages, which are sent across the communication line and are sampled at the appropriate rate by the receiver. If they both use the same clock, the receiver knows when to sample the voltage — namely, at the center of the time during which each bit is transmitted. (If it samples too near the end, it may be confused by the transition between one bit and the next.)

This simple picture is complicated by the fact that the sender and the receiver usually do not have the same clock. They must use their own clocks to achieve the same result. Therefore, each transmission is prefixed by a **header** containing a prearranged pattern of bits that allows the receiver to adjust its clock to match the sender for the rest of the transmission. As long as the adjustment is close, the transmission will be properly understood. The clocks can be expected to drift slowly with respect to each other, so after a while it is necessary to resynchronize. Therefore, the transmission is divided into **frames**, each of which starts with the header.

Since the header is treated specially by the receiving hardware, it is necessary to avoid using the header's bit pattern inside the message itself. Therefore, the sending hardware might insert an extra bit in the message every time it would otherwise accidentally send a bit combination that looks like the header. Likewise, the receiving hardware automatically strips those extra bits when they are discovered. This technique is called **bit stuffing**.

If transmissions are restricted to multiples of full bytes, we say the protocol is **character-oriented** instead of **bit-oriented**. In this case the header is an entire byte with special contents. An entire byte is stuffed instead of a single bit when necessary to prevent an accidental header. The byte that is introduced is an example of an **escape convention**, where a special character means the following character is an ordinary piece of data, not a special character. We will see escape conventions again when we look at terminal control.

BISYNC is an example of a character-oriented synchronous protocol. To send some text, a packet is formed with the following contents:

```
<SYN><SYN><SOH>control<STX>text<ETX>checksum
```

By <SYN> we mean the single character that means "synchronize." It is used as a header. The <SOH> character means "start of header," and it introduces the control section. This section contains the source, the destination, sequence numbers, and other data of interest to the transmission protocol. The <STX> and <ETX> characters (for "start of text" and "end of text") delimit the data part of the message. The whole frame is closed by a checksum, which is used by the receiver to check that the message arrived undamaged. A <DLE> character is used as an escape convention to allow any of the special characters, including <SYN>, <SOH>, <STX>, <ETX>, and <DLE>, to be present in the message.

**Asynchronous transmission.**     In comparison with synchronous transmission, **asynchronous transmission** is much simpler but requires a higher proportion of extra bits. Instead of allowing a frame to be very long and contain many characters, we put header and trailer bits on each character. If only a few characters need to be sent, the asynchronous method actually uses fewer bits. For example, 110-baud asynchronous transmission starts each character with a zero bit, then sends eight data bits, then two one bits. Fewer ending bits are used at higher baud rates.

## 1.5 Summary of device characteristics

We have concentrated on magnetic media (disk and tape) and transmission lines because they are often more complex than paper and card equipment. However, it is often useful to know the characteristics of various devices in order to compare prices, capacities, and speeds. The following table displays the current situation for typical devices.

| Medium | Device | Bytes per record | Bytes per second | Bytes per medium | Cost per medium ($) | Cost per device ($) |
|--------|--------|------------------|------------------|------------------|---------------------|---------------------|
| Cards | Reader | 120 | 1–2K | 120 | < .01 | 8–40K |
|       | Punch | 120 | 1K | 120 | < .01 | 20–30K |
| Paper | Dot matrix | — | 30 | 5K | .03 | 200 |
|       | Daisy | — | 100 | 5K | .03 | 300 |
|       | Train printer | 132 | 1–7K | 9K | .03 | 12–75K |
|       | Laser printer | — | 1–25K | 5–10K | .03 | 2–300K |
| Tape | 9-track | — | 120–390K | 50M | 10 | 12–50K |
|      | Streaming | — | 100K | 80M | 5 | 1–3K |
| Disk | Floppy | 256 | 100K | 100–500K | 1 | 500 |
|      | Hard | 512 | 1–3M | 10–1000M | 1–10K | 1–50K |
| Drum | Fixed head | 512 | 1M | 2M | — | 20K |
| Display | Glass tty | — | 1K | 2K | — | 500 |
|         | Bit-mapped | — | 1M | 100K | — | 1–5K |

Notes:

(1)   One can typically stack up to 3000 cards in the bin on large card readers and punches.

(2)   Laser printers are limited in speed both by their connection to the computer (often a 9600-baud line) and by the speed at which they can emit paper (ranging from 10 to 200 pages a minute). They have resolutions ranging from 300 to 600 dots per inch, so they can effectively print about 2M bytes per page.

(3)   The figures for magnetic tape are for 2400-foot reels at 1600 frames per inch. One can also get 600- or 1200-foot reels, and they can be written at densities of 800, 1600, or 6250 frames per inch. The latency for starting the tape or stopping it is about 5 milliseconds. Tape drives usually need controllers, which cost about $20K.

(4)   The seek latency for a small floppy is about 0.2 seconds.

(5)   The seek latency for a drum about 4 milliseconds. Drums are no longer common.

(6)   Displays can usually run at a number of speeds, ranging from 10 to 1920 characters per second. They hold about 24 lines of 80 characters.

## 2  THE DEVICE INTERFACE

The speed and complexity of a device determine how it is connected to the central processing unit (**cpu**). Slow devices, like terminals, usually have a simple, computation-intensive connection, whereas faster devices, like magnetic tape drives, could not transfer effectively if computation must be involved. Simple devices can be given commands and return results in just a few bytes. Complex devices may need more information before they are ready to execute a command. We will examine three styles of connection, ranging from the simplest to the most complex.

### 2.1  Device registers

Devices may be connected to the computer's cpu by **device registers**, which are accessible either directly as part of physical store or indirectly via transput instructions provided by the hardware. Figure 5.4 shows a simple view of a device connected by registers to the computer. Device registers are used for four purposes.

- To transfer status information from the device to the cpu
- To transfer instructions from the cpu to a device
- To transfer data from the cpu to a device
- To transfer data from a device to the cpu.

Sometimes the same register is overloaded to combine various meanings. For example, let's examine the keyboard on a DEC PDP-11. This device can be used only for input. Two device registers are associated with each keyboard. They appear to be in main store as far as the kernel is concerned, although the architecture of the PDP-11 actually implements the registers in an area distinct from main store. Here are declarations that define these registers:

```
1 const
2    InterruptEnable = [bit 6];
3    InputReady = [bit 15];
4 type
5    KeyboardRegisters =
6       record
7          Status : bits; { 16 bits long }
8          Unused : char; { 8 bits }
9          Data : char; { 8 bits }
10      end;
```

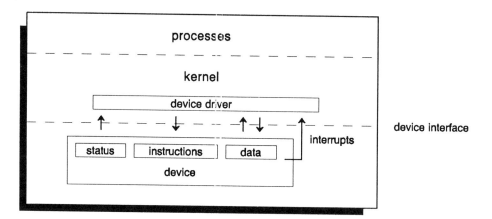

**Figure 5.4** Device connected by registers

The only instruction given by the cpu to the keyboard is "cause an interrupt when the next character is typed." This instruction is given by setting the InterruptEnable bit in the Status register (line 7). The keyboard sets the InputReady bit in the same register to indicate that there is a character that has been typed but has not yet been read by the cpu. The cpu never sends any data to the keyboard. The keyboard transmits data to the cpu by placing a character in the Data field.

The cpu can tell if an operation has completed in two ways. **Polling** involves checking periodically all the device registers of busy devices to see if the Ready bit has been set by the device in the Status register. (We called this bit "InputReady" for the keyboard.) An extreme form of polling is **busy waiting**, in which the cpu executes a loop continually examining a Ready bit and waiting for it to be set by the device.

Because polling is time consuming, it is more common to request the device to cause an **interrupt** instead when the device next becomes ready. As shown in Figure 5.4, device drivers in the kernel are typically arranged to respond to such an interrupt, switching to the kernel from any process. The kernel can then perform whatever actions are appropriate — for example, starting the next transput order to that device. We call this activity **servicing** the interrupt. If the interrupt signals the completion of an operation for which a process has been blocked, the kernel might move that process from its transput-wait or main-store wait list back to the ready list before switching context back to the interrupted process.

More complex devices, like tapes and disks, are not connected directly to the cpu. Instead, they are first connected to a **controller**, which monitors the device status, applies control to motors, performs data checking, and knows the format of the medium. Figure 5.5 shows this situation. The controller accepts *orders* from the cpu and either accepts or returns data. The controller communicates with the cpu through its device registers. A single controller may manage several devices of the same type. For example, a disk controller can simultaneously perform a seek on one disk and a transfer on another. (Simultaneous transfers are not possible.) However, a tape controller cannot manage a disk unit, nor can a disk controller manage a tape unit. Occasionally, controllers, which are computers in their own right, encounter program errors due to an unanticipated sequence of events. Most controllers accept a "reset" order that restores them to a default state.

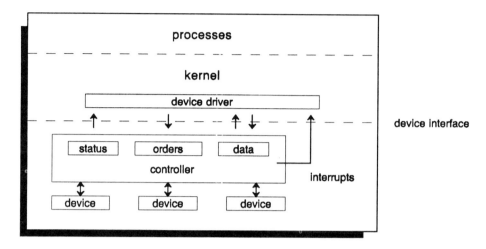

**Figure 5.5** Devices connected by a controller

## 2.2  Direct memory access (DMA)

Using device registers to transfer data places a heavy burden on the cpu, which must service an interrupt after every word has been transferred to or from the device. This burden is especially severe for devices that transfer information so rapidly that the cpu could not keep the device busy because it could not service interrupts fast enough. However, some of these devices cannot wait very long for the next word of data. A writing tape drive or a disk drive that is not sent data quickly enough is likely to write garbage on the tape or disk. Polling, especially busy waiting, would keep up with the device at the cost of preventing any other computation from taking place.

**Direct memory access (DMA)** is a hardware technique designed to relieve the cpu of this burden for fast devices. DMA is demonstrated in Figure 5.6. Data are not transferred through device registers but are placed in or retrieved from main store directly by the device. The cpu can transmit instructions or orders to the device or controller through registers, as before, but the instructions include information describing where the data should be placed or found in main store. Physical store is usually used because the DMA hardware is not attached to address-translation hardware. Interrupts are used to signal the end of an entire transfer, which could transmit thousands of words between the cpu and the device. During the course of the transfer, the status of the device is available to the cpu if it should want to find out how it is going.

For fast devices like disks, there is a chance that main store cannot keep up with the device, especially if there are several DMA transfers taking place at once. If main store cannot supply the next byte to write to the disk when it is needed, the transfer terminates with an **overrun** error. Likewise, overrun can occur if main store cannot save data being read from the disk before the next data are available.

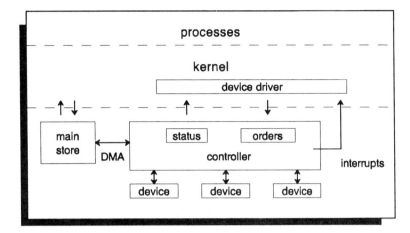

**Figure 5.6** DMA

Overruns are prevented by disk controllers that perform some internal data buffering. Some disk controllers have a cache that can hold a track of data. These controllers can read entire tracks from the disk at one time and store the data in the cache until the computer asks for them.

## 2.3 Channels

Sometimes controllers are themselves connected not to device registers but rather to a **channel**, also known as an **IOP**, for "input/output processor." Figure 5.7 shows how a channel is connected. The purpose of the channel is to provide some amount of device transparency to the cpu. Channels are subsidiary cpu's that use a different machine language. Their instructions are called **commands**. Sequences of commands are called **channel programs** and are stored in the same main store used by the cpu. Typical channels can take channel programs containing more than one command; this facility is called **command chaining**. In addition, they can often gather output data from various places or scatter input data to various places in main store. This facility is called **data chaining** or **scatter-gather**. DMA is universally available with channels.

The cpu sets up the program and then tells the channel to start running it. When the channel program is finished, the channel indicates that fact by setting a bit in a status register or by interrupting the cpu. While the channel program is running, the cpu can investigate its status and halt it if something has gone wrong.

Channels come in various levels of sophistication. A *selector* channel can manage many devices, but only one may be transferring data at one time. A *multiplexor* channel can manage many devices, all simultaneously active.

Processes use virtual addresses, while the channel deals with physical addresses. Therefore, if the operating system wishes to let processes submit their

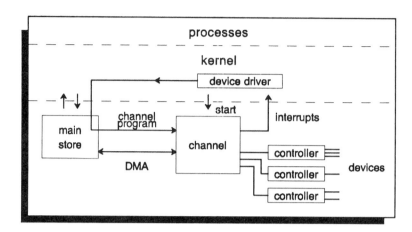

**Figure 5.7** Devices connected through a channel

own channel programs, the kernel must translate the addresses in each such program before it is given to the channel.

# 3  DEVICE DRIVERS

The bewildering variety and number of devices for computers is one of the severest challenges of the operating system writer. Each brand of disk, channel, tape, or communication device has its own control protocol, and new devices come on the market with great frequency. It is essential to reduce this variety to some sort of order; otherwise, every time a new device is attached to the computer, the operating system will have to be completely reworked. Forcing a regular structure, at least at some level inside the kernel, works across a wide range of devices. The device-specific parts of device control can then be sequestered into well-defined modules.

The Unix operating system sets a good example of forcing order on the chaos of device types. Each device can be described by two numbers: the type (each different brand of tape drive is usually a different type) and the instance (each separate drive of the same type has its own instance number). Each type is associated with a **device driver** that accommodates the peculiarities of that device type. The device driver for a given type maintains separate data structures for each instance.

Device drivers provide a standard interface to the rest of the kernel. They provide routines for **opening** and **closing** the device (used by the kernel when a process wants to start or stop using the device) as well as routines for transmitting data to or from the device. Only a few data formats are used, so that the device driver knows what to expect. For example, data may be transmitted in fixed-size blocks, with a standard header. This header might include the following information.

- device type
- device number
- address of the data on the device
- address of the data in main store
- amount of data to transfer
- whether the data are to be read or written
- what kernel module is waiting for the completion of this operation

## 3.1  Two levels of device driver

Device drivers must serve two masters: the rest of the kernel and the device itself. The kernel indicates its desires by calling the routines just mentioned, asking for data to be read or written. When these transfers are complete, the device driver is expected to inform the appropriate kernel module. (We will discuss how the individual kernel modules can signal each other in Chapters 8 and 9. For now, imagine that there are little processes, which we will call **tasks**, in the kernel, and that one is waiting for the completion of this transput operation. It is the job of the device driver to unblock that task once its request has been satisfied.) The device itself is given commands by the device driver. When these commands have been accomplished, the device causes an interrupt. This interrupt is set to transfer control to the appropriate device driver.

One useful organization for device drivers to help them deal with these very different sorts of requests is to divide them into two pieces. Each driver has an "upper" and a "lower" part. The two parts communicate by sharing data structures. This organization is shown in Figure 5.8.

The upper part accepts requests from the rest of the kernel. For example, the upper part of the disk driver might accept a request from the storage manager to write out a page onto backing store. Similarly, a process that wants to write to a printer might pass data by a system call, which some kernel task might then pass on to the printer driver. The upper part of the device driver transforms these requests into entries in a list of pending work for the lower part. It may even sort the entries in the pending-work list so that some transput operations precede others.

The lower part only wakes up when there is an interrupt or when new work is placed on its pending-work list. It usually sets the processor status in such a way that other interrupts from the same device are prevented until it is finished with its current work. If the interrupt that awakens the lower part indicates completion of some transput, the appropriate data structure is so marked, and the kernel task that was waiting is unblocked. The upper driver need not be informed. The lower driver then checks to see if there is any more work queued up for it, and if so, it initiates the next operation.

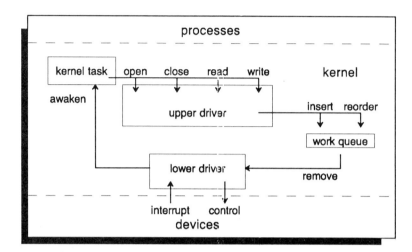

**Figure 5.8**  Two-level structure of a device driver

To give some feeling for the sources of complexities in device drivers, we will consider three devices: the clock, terminals and disks.

## 3.2  Clock device driver

Clocks come in several styles.  The simplest, a **line clock**, generates an interrupt every "tick," that is, every 60th (or 50th) of a second.  It might also have a register that indicates how many ticks have occurred since the register was reset.  The clock may be protected against power failure by a battery, which allows it to continue ticking even when the computer is down or without power.  Slightly more complex clocks have a register that indicates how many interrupts were missed due to the cpu running at a priority too high to let the clock interrupt.  **Programmable clocks** also have a count register that may be set by the software.  The clock decrements that register at a standard rate (often every microsecond) until it reaches 0, at which time it generates an interrupt.  Some computers have both line clocks, which are used for recording the time of day, and programmable clocks, which are used for marking scheduling events.  If there is no programmable clock, the line clock alone can be used for scheduling.

When a line clock interrupts, the clock driver typically performs the following functions:

• Increment the software time data structure.
• If this clock is used for scheduling, decrement the remaining-time field of the currently running process, if any.  If that value has become zero, invoke the scheduler.

● Perform simple accounting. For example, the currently running process might be charged for one tick worth of time and for its current main-store use.

● If there is no programmable clock, decrement the counter for the next alarm, and if it is now zero, invoke whatever kernel task was waiting for an alarm. Alarms are used for timeouts, which are used in communication protocols and elsewhere. If there is a programmable clock, it will be used to schedule alarms.

● If the current process wishes to be profiled, use its program counter to determine in which region of the program it is executing and increment the associated counter. (For example, each page of the virtual space of the process could have a separate counter.) These counters can be used by the programmer to determine where the program is spending its time.

The necessary actions can often be accomplished very quickly, and context can then switch back to the interrupted process.

## 3.3 Terminal device drivers

The Beautification Principle applies to both the process interface and the user interface. The user interface is heavily influenced by the device driver for the terminal. When the user types a key on the keyboard, the lower part of the driver might **echo** the character on the associated display device. (A terminal on a half-duplex line does not need this service.)

Often a user will type ahead before any program has asked to read the information. The device driver might store a certain amount of type-ahead in a buffer so that it is not lost. Most operating systems echo typed-ahead characters as soon as they are typed, but some, like Tenex, wait until the characters are read by some process before echoing. This latter approach has the advantage that the display is never cluttered with typed-ahead characters. In addition, the process that wants to read the characters might not want them echoed at all; deferring the echo lets the driver accommodate such wishes. But it is hard to type accurately if you can't see what you are typing.

Many operating systems provide **editing** facilities that the user can invoke before a program reads data that have been typed in. Mistakes can be removed by deleting or overwriting the offending characters. Most operating systems define at least two editing characters, one to erase the entire line that has been typed in so far and another to erase the last character on the line. These facilities are available until the user **activates** the line by pressing the carriage-return key. Special characters are reserved for editing purposes. The backspace key, which is the same as <control>H in the ASCII character set, is quite common for erasing a single character. The <control>U key is often used for erasing an entire line. These keys echo in such a way that the user can tell how much has been erased. One convention is to repeat the character that is being erased. Another, which works only on video displays, is to erase the character from the screen. Erasure is usually performed by moving the cursor back, printing a space, and then moving the cursor back again. Erasing a tab character from the screen requires special effort, since the number of repetitions of this erasure sequence depends on the exact position of the character before the tab.

More sophisticated operating systems provide additional features, including the following.

- Erasing one word
- Moving backward or forward in the input line
- Deleting or adding text at the current location in the input line
- Searching for characters in the line
- Recalling previous lines that have already been activated. This facility is particularly useful if the user types in a command to a program, but the command has an error. After the program has rejected it, the user can recall the erroneous line, correct it by using the editing features, and then resubmit it.

There are many different terminals on the market, and each seems to have its own conventions for such actions as clearing the screen and moving to a particular place on the screen. In addition, terminals are capable of transferring data at different rates. Some operating systems provide some amount of **customization** in how they deal with terminals. For example, once the terminal driver knows what kind of terminal is being used, it can decide how to echo editing characters. Users have personal preferences, as well. Some prefer to use <control>X to erase lines. Customization can be provided by service calls that establish these special characters. The user who wants a particular set of conventions can run a program that submits these calls. Even the activation character, which is usually just the carriage return, can be reset in many operating systems.

## 3.4  Disk device drivers

One trivial function of a disk device driver is to smooth out the chunky structure of the physical disk, with its sectors, tracks, and cylinders, and provide the abstraction of a virtual disk that is a linear array of sectors. Sector $s$ on track $t$ in cylinder $c$ has this identifying number:

$$SectorId = (c \cdot TracksPerCylinder + t) \cdot SectorsPerTrack + s$$

Higher levels of software in the kernel can use sector identifiers instead of triples to describe locations on a disk.

A less trivial function of the disk driver is to reduce the effect of latencies in accessing the disk. Several techniques are available.

- Processes that require disk access may be blocked in a disk-wait list until the request can be satisfied. Meanwhile, other processes can run. We call this technique **synchronous transput**. Alternatively, a process that can perform useful computation before the transput completes may be allowed to continue.

We call this technique **asynchronous transput**. We discuss this difference later. In either case, it is important to overlap transput and computation.

- Large data objects can be stored in contiguous regions on the disk so that once the first seek has finished, the rest of the data can be accessed without additional delays. For this reason, allocation of disk space is often made in increments of entire tracks or even entire cylinders.

- Similarly, the blocks that constitute a file might be constrained to reside close to each other. (We will discuss physical allocation of files in Chapter 6.)

- When the same disk pack is used both for secondary store (files) and backing store (swap space), the swap space should occupy the tracks halfway between the center and the edge, because items in this location can be accessed with the lowest average seek latency.

- Disk requests are continually generated by main-store management (swapping of pages or segments) and file usage; often several requests are pending. We can impose an order on the outstanding disk requests so that they can be served efficiently.

We will direct our attention to this last strategy, which is known as **disk-head scheduling**.

In general, disk-head scheduling makes the following assumptions:

- There is only one disk drive. If there are several, each is scheduled independently.
- All requests are for single, equal-sized blocks.
- Requested blocks are randomly distributed on the disk pack.
- The disk drive has only one movable arm, and all read/write heads are attached to that one arm.
- Seek latency is linear in the number of tracks crossed. (This assumption fails if the disk controller has mapped tracks at the end of the disk to replace ones that have bad sectors.)
- The disk controller does not introduce any appreciable delays.
- Read and write requests take identical time to service.

We will evaluate various policies by describing how long requests have to wait as a function of the load. Both the average wait time and the variance of the wait time are important. A low average with a high variance means that some requests are taking a very long time even though most are served quickly. The load is measured in requests per second. We could also use the length of the outstanding-request list.

The simplest policy is to order disk requests on a first-come, first-served (FCFS) basis. FCFS makes sure that every request is eventually served; there is no starvation. However, every request is likely to suffer a seek operation. This method works fine for very low loads, but it saturates quickly — that is, the load doesn't have to grow very large before the disk can no longer keep up with the work. The variance of the mean wait time is fairly low.

FCFS disk-head scheduling and its refinements once again illustrate the Law of Diminishing Returns, which we first saw in Chapter 1. There are many alternatives to FCFS, and they are all much better. For example, the Pickup method keeps the requests in FCFS order to prevent starvation, but on its way to the track where the next request lies, it "picks up" any requests that can be serviced along the way.

Another alternative policy is Shortest Seek-latency First (SSF), which next serves the request whose track is closest to the current one. This policy does allow starvation, but if a request is consistently bypassed, the disk must be incapable of keeping up with the disk requests in any case. This kind of starvation is not as bad as the underlying problem, which is very likely that the main-store allocation policy is causing thrashing. SSF has the advantage of minimizing the total seek latency and saturating at the highest load of any policy. On the negative side, it tends to have a larger wait-time variance.

One very popular policy is called Look. The disk head is either in an inward-seeking phase or an outward-seeking phase at any time. As it seeks inward, it picks up any requests it passes. It changes direction only when there are no more requests ahead; it then switches to seeking outwards and fills all requests in that direction as it gets to them. When requests come so frequently that the disk can barely keep up, a circular variant, C-Look, can lead to better variance among the request latencies. This variant always seeks inward. When the last request has been serviced in that direction, a single seek is performed to the outermost track with a pending request without picking up any requests on the way out.

To illustrate these disk-scheduling algorithms, let us consider a disk with 200 cylinders (a typical number). Let's assume that at a given instant, the read/write head is sitting at cylinder 100. Transfers to or from the following cylinders have been requested. The requests are listed in the order in which they arrived. It is irrelevant whether they are read or write requests.

23 89 132 42 187 165 21 34 101 102 34 2 167 3 34 199 20

We will assume that no new requests arrive while we service this set. (By the way, it is quite unusual for more than three or four requests to be outstanding in a well-tuned operating system.) The algorithms we have seen have the following behavior.

| Requests | 23 | 89 | 132 | 42 | 187 | 165 | 21 | 34 | 101 | 102 | 34 | 2 | 167 | 3 | 34 | 199 | 20 | motion |
|---|---|---|---|---|---|---|---|---|---|---|---|---|---|---|---|---|---|---|
| FCFS | 23 | 89 | 132 | 42 | 187 | 165 | 21 | 34 | 101 | 102 | 34 | 2 | 167 | 3 | 34 | 199 | 20 | **1472** |
| Pickup | 89 | 42 | 34 | 34 | 34 | 23 | 101 | 102 | 132 | 165 | 167 | 187 | 21 | 20 | 3 | 2 | 199 | **623** |
| SSF | 101 | 102 | 89 | 132 | 165 | 167 | 187 | 199 | 42 | 34 | 34 | 34 | 23 | 21 | 20 | 3 | 2 | **322** |
| Look | 101 | 102 | 132 | 165 | 167 | 187 | 199 | 89 | 42 | 34 | 34 | 34 | 23 | 21 | 20 | 3 | 2 | **296** |
| C-Look | 101 | 102 | 132 | 165 | 167 | 187 | 199 | 2 | 3 | 20 | 21 | 23 | 34 | 34 | 34 | 42 | 89 | **383** |

The SSF and Look methods have similar results, but if requests had continued to arrive during the time others were serviced, it is likely that SSF would have turned back to pick up some new requests close to its current position. Look turns back only when there is no further work in the current direction. As expected, FCFS has the worst behavior.

To compare these methods further, we turn to simulation results. The simulated disk has 200 tracks. Seek latency is $(0.5 + 0.4 \cdot Distance)$ milliseconds if the

distance is at least one track and zero otherwise. (The 0.5 term represents time
needed just to start and stop the head.) There are 20 sectors per track. The disk
spins at 3600 revolutions per minute. Rotational latency depends on when the head
arrives at the track and the sector that is needed. The simulation compares the
behavior of the five policies on a workload of 1000 requests, with interarrival time
selected from an exponential distribution. The average arrival rate is allowed to
vary between 5 and 100 arrivals per second. Both the track and the sector needed
by each request are selected from a uniform distribution. (Very similar results
were obtained from using a normal distribution for tracks, with average value 100
and standard deviation 100.)

Figure 5.9 shows the average time for a disk request to be serviced for the
different methods across the given workloads. The FCFS method is clearly terrible.
The other methods are not particularly easy to distinguish. Surprisingly, C-Look
did not perform as well as Look, even with high arrival rate. (It did perform
slightly better than Look with requested tracks selected from a normal distribution.) Figure 5.10 shows the throughput — that is, the number of requests served
per second — for the five methods. This figure shows even more clearly that FCFS
is by far the worst but that all the other methods are essentially indistinguishable.
If the arrival rate is less than 22 requests per second, FCFS manages just as well as
the others with respect to throughput, although its response time starts falling
behind the others at about 10 requests per second.

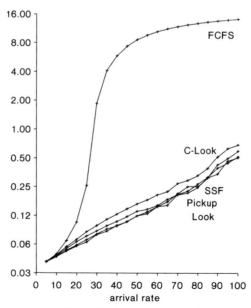

**Figure 5.9** Average response time

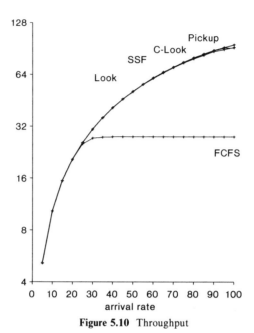

**Figure 5.10** Throughput

# 4 DATA MODIFICATION

Data sent to a device need not be an identical copy of the data found in main store. Three distinct kinds of modification may be performed, each for a different reason.

## 4.1 Data compaction

When a great deal of information is to be sent across an expensive transmission line, modifying the data to occupy fewer bits is worthwhile. Similarly, if data must be saved for a long time on an expensive medium, it will be cheaper if the data can be crammed into fewer bits.

There are often obvious ways to save space. For example, a file that represents a computer program may have many space characters. Instead of sending all the spaces, each blank region can be encoded by a count of how many spaces there are. This method is an example of **run-length encoding**. Television pictures are large arrays of intensity values. Instead of sending a 6-bit intensity value for each element of the array, a 3-bit difference between that element and the previous one often suffices. Some escape mechanism can be used when the difference cannot be represented in 3 bits. This method is an example of **difference encoding**. More sophisticated coding methods exist, such as Huffman codes, which assign often-used characters a short code, and less used ones a longer code.

## 4.2  Data encryption

Another sort of transformation can be applied to data to hide their contents. Actually, **secrecy** (can anyone else read the data?) is only one part of a larger set of security considerations that includes **authentication** (who generated the data?) and **protection** (can anybody modify the data?). The transformation used for these purposes is called **encryption**. Data before the transformation is applied are in **cleartext** form. The encrypted data are in **ciphertext** form. A particular encryption algorithm may have an associated **decryption** algorithm that is used to transform ciphertext back into the original cleartext.

You might think that an encryption algorithm that has no decryption would be useless. Actually, such **trap-door** encryption algorithms have an important use in authentication. Many operating systems identify each user by a user name and a password, which the user is expected to keep secret. Any person who knows that name and password has all the privileges of that user. Most operating systems store the passwords in a file; anyone with access to that file can therefore learn everyone's password. This situation is very vulnerable because any loss of security endangers everyone's security, and security depends on powers entrusted to humans.

A far better approach (taken by Unix) is to encrypt each password with a trap-door function and to store the encrypted passwords in a publicly accessible file. The encryption method is publicly available. Now any program that wishes to authenticate a user may ask for a password, encrypt it, and compare the result to the value in the file. If the values match, the password is correct. In particular, the logon program, which greets the user at the beginning of the interactive computer session, can tell if the user knows the correct password. However, the huge number of possible passwords and the fact that no decryption method exists make it infeasible for an intruder to guess the password, because every conceivable password would have to be encrypted and compared with the file. This scheme assumes, of course, that people choose fairly long and fairly irregular passwords. Some installations of Unix refuse to allow a password that is too short or too closely related to an English word. VMS can be set to insist that specific users change their password every so often.

Most applications of encryption, however, require that the ciphertext be convertible back into cleartext. Unfortunately, all current encryption methods have problems. The "one-time pad" is the only provably secure method known at this time. It derives the ciphertext by a byte-wise exclusive-or operation between the cleartext and a "key" whose length must be at least as long as the message. The decryption method uses the same key and the same algorithm. The key must never be used again, or it becomes easier and easier to guess. Since both the originator and the recipient of the ciphertext must agree on the key, it must be transmitted as well, a procedure that is just as difficult as the original problem of secure transmission. Computer-generated pseudo-random numbers create keys that are too easy to guess, by the way.

A currently popular encryption method is the Data Encryption Standard (DES). The DES method was developed by the National Bureau of Standards with several goals in mind. Many commercial applications are currently using DES. The algorithm (either encryption or decryption) can be performed efficiently with a special-purpose chip, but far less efficiently with a program. Since the key is 56 bits long, there is plenty of room for picking unique keys. Unfortunately, some keys turn out to be weak; if a weak key is used to encrypt, the ciphertext can be analyzed quite easily to discover the cleartext. It is not certain how many keys are weak or "semi-weak." There is some suspicion that 56 bits is insufficient to prevent a successful attack that uses massive amounts of computer time. It is possible that a longer key (perhaps 100 bits) would be sufficient.

The one-time pad and DES are considered "conventional;" they share the property that the same key is used for encryption and decryption. A non-conventional approach called "public-key cryptography" uses different keys for the two transformations. One public-key method, called RSA after its inventors (Rivest, Shamir, and Adelman), has resisted attacks so far, although it has not been proved to be computationally secure.

The RSA method itself is too complex to discuss here. The general properties of public-key methods are elegant, however, so we will outline them. Every user U has a pair of keys, one for encryption, $E_U$, and one for decryption, $D_U$. It is impossible to guess $E_U$ from $D_U$ or vice versa. Ciphertext encrypted with $E_U$ is decrypted by $D_U$. Everyone's E key is considered public; it is saved in a public place where anyone may access it. Let's say **A** and **B** are two parties (programs, computers, or people) that want to send secure messages to each other. **A** encrypts messages for **B** using **B**'s public key $E_B$. **B** can decrypt them using its private key $D_B$, but no one else can decrypt them because no one else knows $D_B$. Similarly, **B** encrypts messages for **A** using **A**'s public key $E_A$. These messages are secret. However, **B** cannot be sure that **A** has sent the messages because anyone could have used $E_B$, **B**'s public key.

If we want **B** to be able to authenticate **A**'s messages, to be sure that **A** sent them, we also need to assume that if we take cleartext and apply $D_U$, we get a sort of reverse ciphertext, which is also secure and can be decrypted by applying $E_U$. Now let **A** encrypt its messages to **B** by using **A**'s secret key $D_A$. **B** can decrypt the messages by using **A**'s public key $E_A$. **B** is sure that **A** sent the message because only **A** knows $D_A$. However, anyone else who gets this message can also apply **A**'s public key $E_A$ and decrypt it, so the message is not secure.

These two ideas can be combined to create messages that are both secure and authenticated: Let **A** first encrypt the message with its private key $D_A$, then encrypt the result with **B**'s public key $E_B$. Only **B** can read this message because only **B** knows $D_B$. Once **B** has applied $D_B$, it then applies **A**'s public key $E_A$ to derive the cleartext and be sure that **A** composed the message. Figure 5.11 shows the three cases we have just discussed.

We see that the RSA method is able to send secure, authenticated messages. The transformations, however, are very time-consuming. It is currently used

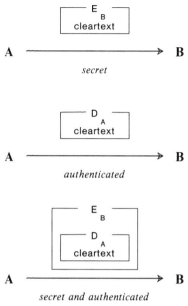

**Figure 5.11** Secure and authenticated messages with public-key encryption

principally as a way of securely transmitting keys that can then be used by other, cheaper methods such as DES.

## 4.3 Reliability

We have seen that data transformations are useful to compress data and to introduce security. A third type of transformation is used for reliability. Communication lines suffer from damaged messages for many reasons, depending on the physical nature of the line. Electrical disturbances, such as lightning and nearby power sources, can introduce spurious signals. Contention for a shared line can cause competing messages to destroy each other. The signal may be attenuated over distance to the point that it cannot be reliably detected. Similarly, bits stored on a disk or a tape might be recorded too faintly, or the medium might have a small flaw. When they are read back, they may appear different from how they were written. Even bits stored in main store are subject to a low level of error.

There is only one mechanism for providing reliability — **redundancy**, which means using extra bits. This single mechanism takes many forms, depending on the types of errors that are expected and their expected frequency. For example, an extra bit, known as the **parity** bit, can be added to each word in main store. It is set to ensure that the total number of one bits in the word is even. (Sometimes odd parity is used instead. They are equivalent in purpose.) Any word with a one-bit error will have the wrong parity, which can be detected. Most computers have at

least one bit of redundancy in their main store for this purpose. If two errors strike
the same word, the error will not be detected. The probability of this event is fairly
low. If the probability of double errors is not low enough, more than one redundant
bit can be placed on each word. Now not only can one-bit errors be detected, but
they can also be corrected on the fly. The correct word is the "closest" good word
to the damaged word, where "closest" is measured in **Hamming distance**: the
number of bits with different values. Two-bit errors can be detected but not properly corrected. If $n$-bit errors are to be detected, legal bit patterns must not have a
Hamming distance of less than $n + 1$. In general, by adding enough redundant
bits, an **error-correcting code** can be designed to correct any desired number of
errors. The correct amount of redundancy is the amount that reduces undetected
or uncorrected errors to an acceptable level. Main store is often designed to correct
single-bit errors.

Parity and its generalizations are also used on devices like tape drives and
disk units. Here the typical error is not a random bit but rather a consecutive
string of damaged bits. A method known as the "cyclic redundancy check," or
CRC, calculates the redundant bits to be stored at the end of each chunk of data.
This set of bits is often known as a **checksum**.

Checksums and parity bits are usually below the level where the operating
system has any control. The operating system takes over when a device (including
main store) discovers an uncorrectable error. This discovery is usually converted
into an interrupt or a trap to the kernel. For devices like tape or disk, the device
driver will retry the operation that failed until either it succeeds or some retry limit
is reached. In the latter case, the device is broken (perhaps the tape or disk surface
is damaged), and whatever application was trying to use it must be cancelled. The
driver might make an entry in a log detailing the error.

For communication devices talking to other computers, retry should eventually succeed. The recipient of the damaged message could send a note to the
sender requesting retransmission. However, the request for retry might itself be
lost, and the recipient might not even know who the sender is, because that part of
the message may have been damaged. Instead, it is customary for the recipient to
acknowledge each undamaged message it gets. The sender retransmits any message
it has sent that is not acknowledged within a reasonable time, on the assumption
that the original message was damaged in transit. Of course, the acknowledgement
may be the one that was lost or damaged, so the recipient must be prepared to deal
with duplicate messages that the sender accidentally sent. Sequence numbers are
used to distinguish messages so that the recipient can discard any message with a
duplicate sequence number.

# 5 THE PROCESS INTERFACE

We started this discussion by presenting the physical structure of devices and how
they connect to the computer. Next, we dealt with the device interface and device

drivers inside the kernel. We now turn to the process interface to transput.

In keeping with the Beautification Principle, the kernel may wish to introduce devices at this level that don't actually exist at a lower level. For example, the concept of a "file," which we discuss at length in Chapter 6, is purely the invention of the operating system. Processes can pretend that each file is a separate device that can be read or written, but in fact those actions are translated by the operating system (typically by a file manager in the kernel) into actions on the underlying devices, usually disks. Very few processes, if any, deal directly with the disk device; in many operating systems, this device is completely hidden from processes.

The concept of "file" can be used as a metaphor for all devices; Unix uses this elegant idea to unify the process view of transput. Instead of presenting a different set of service calls for each kind of device, each device looks like a file and responds to service calls for files. One extra call is provided for special actions that can't be fit into the metaphor, such as setting the density of a tape drive or setting the echoing characteristics of a terminal.

Not only can devices be cast as special "device files," but also this metaphor can be extended to data structures that the kernel may want to make available to processes, such as the physical store of the computer (only available to privileged processes, of course) or a "bit bucket" into which anything may be written but which always looks empty when read. In Chapter 9, we will see that inter-process communication can also be made to look like file access.

The operating system designer has many alternatives in designing the data-transfer part of the service calls. We will discuss two issues that confront the designer: whether transput should be synchronous and how locations are specified in main store. For the sake of discussion, we will start with six basic service calls that a process may make when dealing with a device. The details of the semantics of these calls will be discussed in the following sections.

☐    Open(device name, intent). This call tells the appropriate device driver that the process plans to use the given device. The intent indicates whether reading, writing, both, or just appending are desired. At this stage, deadlock-avoidance or detection algorithms can be used, as discussed in Chapter 4, to make sure the process will not be blocked forever waiting for the device. Similarly, the device driver can check to make sure the process has the necessary privileges to open the device for the stated intent. We will discuss access control in Chapter 6 when we talk about files. The result of this call is a **device descriptor**, which the process will use to refer to the device in other service calls.

☐    Close(device descriptor). This call tells the device driver that the process is finished with the device and that it can be used now by some other process. Device-specific finalization will be performed. For a tape, this finalization might take the form of rewinding and unloading the tape and printing a message for the operator to dismount the tape.

☐    Position(device descriptor, where). This call tells the device driver to position the device to a particular location. For example, a tape may be advanced one record or one file in this way. Likewise, a disk may be set to read at a particular surface, track, and sector. In the absence of Position calls, the device might move to the "next" location after each Read and Write.

☐    Read(device descriptor, virtual address, amount). This call causes the device driver to transfer data from the device to the virtual address given in the process. If the device does not have the desired number of bytes available (for example, the user types "end of transmission" into a terminal before the requested number of bytes has been entered, or the end of a file or tape record is reached), fewer bytes may be read.

☐    Write(device descriptor, virtual address, amount). This call causes the device driver to transfer data from the process to the device.

☐    Control(device descriptor, code). This call performs other actions that do not fit into the file metaphor, such as setting the density of the tape drive or the echo characteristics of a terminal.

Figure 5.12 shows how these calls fit into our picture of an operating system.

## 5.1  To block or not to block

The most far-reaching choice is whether transfer should cause the process to block or not. A blocking transfer is called **synchronous** because when the process next executes, it can assume that the data have been transferred. The alternative is **asynchronous** transfer, in which the process knows only that the operation has started. The process may be able to discover its completion by explicit **waiting**, with a "wait" service call; by **polling**, with repeated inspection of a completion flag; or by **virtual interrupt**. A virtual interrupt affects the process much as a device-completion interrupt from a physical device affects the kernel. That is, it saves state information in a safe place (usually the stack) and sets the program counter to the address of the interrupt handler. We can devise the following service calls to help processes when transfer is asynchronous.

☐    Wait(device descriptor, timeout). The process is blocked until the action currently under way on the device (if any) has finished. The timeout tells

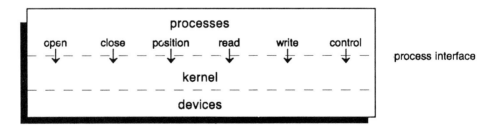

**Figure 5.12**  The process interface

how patient the process is. It can be set to infinity if the process is very patient, to zero if the process just wants to poll to see if the device has finished yet, or to some intermediate value. This service call returns information on whether the transput finished or not.

☐  Handle(device descriptor, routine). This call tells the device driver that whenever asynchronous transput completes on this device, the process should be interrupted and should start executing at the address specified by "routine." The routine will be called with arguments indicating which transput has finished.

If transput is asynchronous, the operating system designer must decide what a second Write means if the previous one has not finished or what a simultaneous Read and Write might mean. These could be treated as errors, or the second call could block (as if it had performed Wait) until the first has finished. We will see an alternative solution in the next section.

Until an asynchronous write operation has completed, the process should not modify the region in its address space that is to be written out because the transfer may be in progress. The kernel may ease this restriction by copying data to be written out first into a kernel data structure called a **buffer** before unblocking the process. Likewise, the process should not access the region into which an asynchronous read operation is in progress because it does not know when the data have arrived.

A related problem for the kernel is dealing with a process that terminates while an asynchronous transput is in progress. Those parts of its address space that are tied down must not be reallocated to other purposes until the transput has finished. It is not always possible for the kernel to halt channel programs while they are running. The kernel may note in the context block for that process that termination is pending; the main-store resources tied down for that process are reclaimed only after the transput has completed.

## 5.2 Main-store addresses

The process must somehow specify the location in main store that the data are to be read into or written from. The simplest alternative from the point of view of the process is to specify a starting place and a length in virtual space. The kernel should check, of course, that the region specified is entirely within the address space of the process. If the device is a **block device** — that is, if it requires transfers in fixed-size chunks — the kernel might provide its own buffers of the correct size as an intermediate location for the data. As we will see, the kernel can use these buffers as a cache to improve performance. If the application is time-critical and does not want to suffer the delay of copying data within main store between kernel buffers and the process address space, the appropriate part of that address space can be tied down and the device can transfer directly into or out of the process space.

A popular alternative way to specify where the data reside is by a **circular buffer pool** in the virtual space of the process. This pool is logically an array of buffers arranged in a circle, as shown in Figure 5.13. Typically, separate buffer pools are used for output and input. Buffer pools allow asynchronous transfer without the problem we saw earlier of two transputs active at the same time. Let us consider output first. Each buffer has the following declaration.

```
1 Buffer =
2    record
3       Busy : Boolean;
4       Position : DeviceAddress; { not always required }
5       Data : array 1:BlockSize of byte;
6    end;
```

The Position field (line 4) is used if every buffer to be output states explicitly where on the device the data are to be placed. For sequential output, this field can be omitted. The Busy field (line 3) indicates whether output is in progress from this buffer. Initially, all the buffers are free — that is, not busy. We have shown free buffers as open squares in Figure 5.13. As the program creates data to be written out, those data are placed in the first free buffer. As soon as the buffer is full (shown by crosshatching in the figure), a Write service call is invoked. The kernel initiates output but allows the process to continue asynchronously. The Busy flag is set true for the duration of the transfer; as soon as the kernel knows that the transfer is complete, the flag is reset to false. Meanwhile, the process may be filling other buffers. The process must pause if it needs another buffer but the next one is still busy; in this case it may use the Wait service call.

Input buffers have the same declaration as output buffers. The kernel is expected to fill these buffers ahead of the process. As soon as the process has finished using the data in a buffer, it tells the device driver by performing the

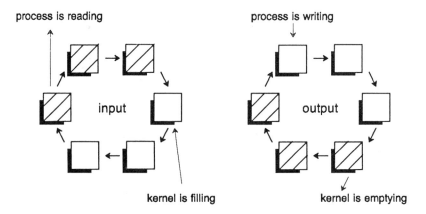

**Figure 5.13** Circular buffer pools

following service call:

☐ FreeBuffer(buffer address). This call resets the Busy flag to false and informs the device driver that the buffer is ready to be filled with new data. (Where the data come from is determined by a previous call to Read.)

Buffer pools allow the programmer to tailor the number and size of buffers to the application. The process sets up the buffer pools by a service call:

☐ CreatePool(device descriptor, buffer length, number of buffers, direction). This call creates a buffer pool for the given device. The direction specifies whether these are input or output buffers. Space may be created in a new segment or as a new region at the end of virtual store. This call might have the side effect of making transput asynchronous.

The advantage of the buffer-pool method is that programs that require more buffers for efficiency do not compete for buffers with other programs: The buffers are entirely within the address space of the process, not in a common pool in the kernel. Copying is never necessary between kernel and user buffers because the size of the data area of a buffer is exactly the correct size for the device. However, the programmer now has the responsibility to pack data into the fixed-size buffers and to handle the asynchronous nature of transput. In addition, it is often a matter of guesswork to decide how many buffers are enough.

A third alternative places even more responsibility in the hands of the programmer: The process executes channel programs instead of transput service calls. To perform a read operation, for example, the program builds a channel program of whatever complexity is desired and submits the following service call:

☐ StartTransput(address of channel program). This call starts the channel program. It returns a descriptor that can be used in the Wait or Handle calls.

The channel program could be complex enough to rewind a tape and then copy the contents of several non-consecutive disk tracks onto that tape. During the execution of the channel program, the process could be occupied in other work. This alternative is attractive because of the efficiency it permits in performing complex transput-bound operations. However, it requires programmers to be experts at channel programs or to rely on library packages that create simpler environments.

Channel programs executed by the process are a real headache for the operating-system implementor. Because typical channels do not have access to the address-mapping hardware, they expect all main-store addresses to be physical addresses. The operating system must therefore translate all the main-store addresses in the channel program. It must also tie the channel program down. Regions that are contiguous in virtual space may be scattered in physical space, so single commands in the channel program may have to be split into several subcommands.

In some cases splitting is not possible. For example, a disk block usually must be read into a physically contiguous region of main store. If the channel program specifies a virtual region that is not physically contiguous, the operating system must either declare the channel program invalid or must introduce a hidden copying of data from a kernel buffer. Device addresses must also be modified or at least checked for validity. Otherwise a process could blithely damage data on any sector of the disk. Usually the operating system provides an environment for the process that includes "virtual tracks," and references to these tracks must be mapped by the operating system to the actual tracks that are supporting them. With luck, the size of a virtual track is the same as the size of a physical track.

## 5.3 Implementing the service calls

It is not hard for the envelope (the module of the kernel that first receives service calls) to translate device service calls into requests on the upper parts of the appropriate device drivers. The context block for each process includes an array of open device descriptor records. The device descriptor given to the process can be an index into this array. The descriptor-record array might look as follows.

```
1 OpenDevices : array 0:MaxOpenDevice of
2    record { open device descriptor }
3       InUse : Boolean; { false if this array entry is free }
4       DeviceType : (Tape, Disk, File, Memory, Printer ... )
5       DeviceNumber : integer; { which tape, etc. }
6       CurrentPosition : integer; { which physical byte }
7       Mode : (ReadOnly, ReadWrite, WriteOnly, AppendOnly);
8    end { open device descriptor }
```

A free slot is characterized by a false InUse field.

When a process submits the Open call, a free descriptor record is found. The InUse field is set to true, the DeviceType and DeviceNumber fields are initialized (based on the details of the Open call), the CurrentPosition is set to zero, and the Mode field is set. The kernel then calls the "open" routine in the upper part of the appropriate device driver. The index of the open device descriptor is returned to the process so that further operations it makes on this device can be associated with the current location and checked against the Mode.

When a process requests a Read, for example, to read 10 bytes from a disk, the disk driver can calculate which sector in which track contains those bytes. A request for that entire disk block is submitted to the lower part of the disk driver. When the block has been read in, the upper part transfers the desired 10 bytes to the address space of the requesting process and then either unblocks it (if synchronous transfer was specified) or takes other appropriate action to inform the process that the transfer has completed. If the request crosses block boundaries, several requests are then made of the lower part of the device driver.

Writing bytes to a device may also require several successive calls to the lower part of the appropriate device driver. For example, to write less than a full block to a disk, the proper block or blocks must first be read in. Then their contents are modified in accordance with the details of the Write call. They are then written back out. Writing to a magnetic tape is simpler because it is assumed that such a write will destroy the previous contents. Writing to an otherwise unused disk block is also simpler because there is no need to preserve previous values.

The kernel can reduce the amount of physical transput by employing the Cache Principle. If a process has just read some bytes, the chances are good that the next bytes on the device will be read next. Instead of repeating the read operation for the entire block, the device driver can save the block that was read in last and extract the next 10 bytes, for example, when needed. In this case, many calls on the lower part of the device driver can be avoided. We can also avoid blocking the caller, in keeping with the Hysteresis Principle. Therefore, whenever a process requests input, the driver should first check to see if the desired data block is already in main store. Only if it is not must the lower part of the device driver be invoked to bring it in. The set of buffers the kernel keeps in main store in the hope they will be needed again forms a cache. A form of LRU replacement can be implemented for this cache.

Writing can also take advantage of this cache. It is not necessary to read in a fresh copy of the block about to be modified if a copy already sits in the cache. After the modification is performed on the main-store copy, that cache entry should be marked "dirty." It is not yet necessary to write it back out to the physical device, since it may be needed again soon. If any process wants to read it in the meantime, the main-store version will be used, and this version is up-to-date. Further writes may also affect the same data; it is not necessary to archive the data until all such writes have finished. The dirty buffer should be written out when its space is needed by some new buffer or when the device is idle and may as well be employed in writing it out. This method is known as **write-behind**. Write-behind is a typical form of **lazy evaluation**, in which work is delayed in the hope that it will not be needed at all. Write-behind makes sense for both synchronous and asynchronous transput; the operation is considered completed when the data block is properly modified even if it has not yet been written out.

Write-behind has some dangers. If the operating system should crash (fail unexpectedly), data that should have been written to the device may still be in main store, and it may not be feasible to recover them. For this reason, dirty buffers should periodically be archived from the cache so that the device is always relatively up-to-date. Database programs need to be able to force such archiving and to know when it is finished. Another unfortunate property of write-behind is that device errors cannot be presented to the process that wants to perform output. If, for example, the process tries to write past the end of a tape, the physical write command may be issued after the process has started doing unrelated operations or even after the process has terminated. Presenting this error to the process is then either very cumbersome or impossible.

The data-block cache can be used to reduce the amount of time processes are blocked during synchronous read, just as write-behind reduces the amount of blocking time during synchronous write. Under the **read-ahead** policy, the device driver brings in the next data block before the process has made a request that requires it.

When the process gets to that region of data, the cache will already contain it, so the process will not be forced to wait. Of course, the process may never want to read from the next block because it may be performing random accesses or reading only the initial part of the device. In these cases read-ahead wastes device bandwidth. Therefore, the kernel should avoid read-ahead if the process has recently performed a Position operation, which indicates random-access activity. (Database programs often get no benefit from read-ahead because even though they may know exactly which page of a file they need to read next, the page is often not the "next" one as far as the kernel is concerned, so no read-ahead is performed.) Read-ahead is a typical form of **eager evaluation**, in which work is performed early in the hope that it will be useful.

When the process submits a Close service call, the device driver can archive any remaining buffers in the cache. The slot in the active device array is then released by resetting InUse to false.

## 5.4 Buffer depletion

Since the kernel uses buffers to hold data that are in transit between processes and the outside world, there is a possibility that these buffers will be depleted. For example, a process may try to write to a disk faster than the disk can accept information. Eventually, all the main-store buffers will be full. The process must then be blocked when it tries another write request.

The overflow situation becomes especially interesting in the case of terminals. Let us assume that there are ten terminals attached to the computer and ten processes, each communicating with a terminal. Terminals accept information at a fairly slow rate. This rate can drop to zero if the user types a "stop terminal" character (typically <control>S), which is intended to delay further output while the user reads what is currently on the screen. Programs, in contrast, generally can accept information much faster than a user can type it in. However, the rate at which a program accepts data may drop if it must calculate some complex function before it is ready for new data. We will allow the user to type ahead in this case and store input inside the kernel until the process requests it. Finally, let us assume that characters to be written out or that are typed in are saved in 1-character buffers in the kernel and that there are only 1000 such buffers. This situation is depicted in Figure 5.14.

We will start with a straightforward policy: If a process wants to write a character out, the character is put in a buffer until it can be written. If no buffers are available, the process is blocked. A character typed by the user is placed in a buffer until the associated process requests to read it and is also echoed back to the terminal. If no buffers are available, the character is not echoed; instead, a <control>G (which sounds a beep on most terminals) is echoed.

Our first problem arises as we try to implement this policy. Let's assume that all the buffers are in use and the user types a character. How can we echo <control>G except by placing the <control>G character in a free buffer and scheduling it for output? To avoid this sort of traffic jam, we will refuse new

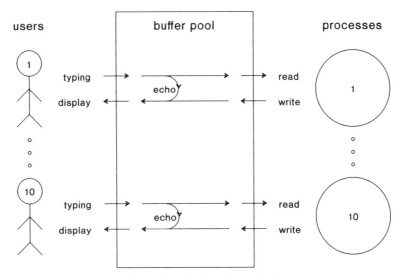

**Figure 5.14**  Buffers for terminals

characters from the users if we have fewer than ten buffers left.  Then even if every user types a character simultaneously, we will still have enough buffers to echo the <control>G.  We don't have to worry about a user typing several characters faster than we can echo <control>G's because it is not possible to type faster than the terminal can accept responses from the computer.  We also don't have to worry that the user might have stopped output and thereby prevented us from echoing characters: We release the stopped terminal whenever the user types anything other than the stop character itself.

Our next problem is that one user-process interaction can interfere with all the other users.  Let's assume that one process has tried to write more than 1000 characters while the terminal is in stop status.  All our buffers become full after 1000 characters, and then we block that process.  No other user or process can transmit information because no buffers are left.  It is not right to cause those users and processes to suffer because unrelated processes are trying to perform output to a stopped terminal.

One extreme solution is to preallocate all our buffers among the terminals, giving each terminal 100 characters.  Although this policy avoids the starvation situation we had earlier, it is an inefficient use of buffers.  To explain why, we should point out why the buffers are there in the first place.

## Buffer Principle

The purpose of a buffer pool is to smooth out short-term variations in speed between consumers and producers. This smoothing prevents needless blocking.

In particular, buffer pools allow us to obey the Hysteresis Principle and resist switching processes during transput operations. If the process is creating output, it is the producer, and the user (or the terminal) is the consumer. If the user is typing input, the user is the producer, and the process is the consumer. In the long run, the consumer and the producer must run at the same speed because the consumer cannot read more information than was produced, and the producer cannot get infinitely ahead of the consumer. However, when a process wants to print 10 characters, it would rather not be blocked after each character. To avoid this situation, the buffer pool accepts the characters and the process need not be blocked. The more buffers we have, the more smoothing we can accomplish. Therefore, restricting each process-user pair to 100 buffers prevents all of them from making temporary use of the smoothing possible with 1000 buffers.

A reasonable compromise is to give each terminal a small number of private buffers, say 20. Then 800 buffers are available for whatever application happens to need them. If only one terminal is currently very active, all 800 extra buffers will be allocated to that terminal. If all terminals are very active, each one gets at least the 20 private buffers and can continue to function, although some will have the increased benefit of the extra buffers.

We still have a problem. Suppose that all the public buffers are in use by terminal 1. Terminal 2 only has its 20 private buffers. If the user on terminal 2 has typed ahead, all the private buffers may be filled with new input that the process has not yet read. The process may be running a program that wants to print an answer to the previous query and then accept a new query. When it tries to print the answer, it blocks because there are no available buffers. It will never awaken (at least not until some public buffers are freed) because the private buffers will not be freed until the process reads them, and it can't read them because it is blocked. We see that it is necessary to preallocate at least one buffer for the process to produce into. Similarly, it is necessary to keep at least one buffer for the user to produce into; otherwise the user may not be able to type the "halt" character at a program that insists on printing at full speed to the terminal.

Here is the moral: It is necessary to preallocate at least one buffer for every producer. All the rest may be allocated by need. It is typical to preallocate at least 80 buffers to input from every terminal so that the user can always type ahead at least one complete line.

# 6 PERSPECTIVE

To live up to the Beautification Principle, the operating-system designer and implementor must deal with the most excruciating details of hardware and must turn a
bewildering tangle of complexity into a straightforward, simple, and regular view
that a process can deal with. In carrying out this responsibility, the kernel must
satisfy both masters.

Luckily, most devices can be thought of as engines that consume and/or produce data and accept other specialized requests. This abstract view of devices can
be embodied in device drivers, which hide the idiosyncrasies of particular devices
behind a mask of uniformity. Device drivers are controlled partly by interrupts and
partly by requests from the rest of the kernel. The rest of the kernel, including
such parts as the swapping manager, make use of these drivers whenever they must
deal with devices. The drivers have responsibility for three areas.

- **Efficiency**: We saw how the disk driver could employ disk-head scheduling to
  improve performance. Similarly, data compression may be used to reduce the
  amount of data that must be stored. Data compression may be applied at
  higher levels, outside the kernel.
- **Reliability**: Drivers for unreliable communication lines may employ error
  detection, positive acknowledgement, retransmission on timeout, and sequence
  numbers. The responsibility for reliability is ultimately in the hands of the
  applications program, but the responsibility for the reliable transmission of
  individual messages, which is necessary for efficiency of higher-level protocols,
  lies in the hands of the operating system.
- **Security**: Encryption may be used to provide secrecy and authentication on
  non-local communication. Encryption may be used at any level, not just by
  the device driver.

The usual point at which the kernel must deal with devices is when a process
makes a transput request. If the kernel keeps a cache of secondary-store blocks in
main store, it can sometimes bypass dealing with a device. The operating-system
designer must choose among many different styles of transput requests. The process can be given larger or smaller amounts of control over the way transput is conducted. Recent operating systems like Unix have successfully championed the policy of a very simple process interface with an efficient kernel implementation.
However, real-time operating systems tend to require more complex process control
over transput.

# 7  FURTHER READING

The Datapro handbook (Heminway, 1986) has a wealth of information about computers and devices, with both overview sections and details of particular brands. The text by Tanenbaum (1981) is a fine reference on communication devices and the protocols that are used on them. Disk-head scheduling policies have been investigated by Fuller (1974) and reviewed by Teorey and Pinkerton (1972). Public-key cryptosystems were first proposed by Diffie and Hellman (1976). One elegant extension is Gifford's notion of cryptographic sealing (1982).

# 8  EXERCISES

1.  Why is it necessary for the escape character itself to be escaped if it appears in a message?

2.  When **A** and **B** are sending messages to each other using public-key encryption, why does **A** first apply its own D and then **B**'s E? Why not perform these operations in reverse order?

3.  When **A** and **B** are sending authenticated messages to each other, how does the recipient know whose E to apply to the message? After all, the recipient doesn't know who sent the message until it can read the message, and the message is inscrutable until it is converted to cleartext.

4.  The chief of security at Marble Pillar Stocks wants to use some encryption method for communication between the main office and the branches. She likes the idea of the one-time pad because it is provably secure. She likes the idea of RSA because it has not yet been broken. But the one-time pad has a key-distribution problem, and RSA is too time-consuming to calculate. She therefore suggests that RSA be used to transmit keys for the one-time pad. What do you think of this idea? Is it secure? Is it efficient?

5.  Should a recipient of a duplicate message acknowledge it or not?

6.  How long would it take to print the contents of a floppy disk on a dot-matrix printer, assuming that blanks take as long to print as any other character?

7.  Compare the FCFS, SSF, Look, and C-Look disk-head scheduling policies by simulating the following access request list. For each policy, compute the average and the standard deviation of the time required to service requests. Assume that the disk starts at track 1; that there are 200 tracks; that a seek

takes $(20 + 0.1 \cdot T)$ milliseconds, where $T$ is the number of tracks of motion; that rotational latency is 8 milliseconds; and that servicing the request itself takes 2 milliseconds.

| Time (ms) | 0 | 23 | 25 | 29 | 35 | 45 | 57 | 83 | 88 | 95 |
|-----------|---|-----|----|----|-----|-----|-----|----|----|-----|
| Track | 45 | 132 | 20 | 23 | 198 | 170 | 180 | 78 | 73 | 150 |

8. To what extent does the theory of disk-head scheduling apply to magnetic tapes?

9. The text suggests that the main-store cache of device blocks can be managed by an LRU mechanism. Why is LRU more appropriate here but NUR more appropriate for page replacement?

10. A program needs to use a circular buffer pool, but the programmer is unsure how many buffers are needed. The program is expected to output data according to this repetitive pattern:

| Virtual time | Number of bytes |
|--------------|-----------------|
| 1 | 50 |
| 2 | 500 |
| 5 | 1000 |

The program will go through 100 iterations, each taking 5 seconds, before finishing. Assume that buffers are 100 bytes long and that the device driver responsible for the output can transfer 4 buffers per second. For a buffer pool of 1, 2, 3, 4, and 5 buffers, how long will it take for the program to finish (a) the first iteration, (b) the second iteration, and (c) the last iteration? By "finishing" we mean placing the output data in buffers; the device driver is then responsible for transferring the data to the device.

11. Suggest guidelines to programmers for choosing the number of buffers they should allocate in circular buffer pools.

12. The text suggests that a process using circular buffer pools should execute a Wait service call to acquire a buffer and submit a Write (for output buffers) or FreeBuffer (for input buffers) to release the buffer. Suggest ways in which these calls can be safely avoided and comment on the efficiency of your solution. (*Hint*: Consider tricks with virtual store.)

13. The text describes the buffer overflow problem in the case of a fixed number of producers and consumers. How does the problem change if we allow new producer-consumer pairs to be created?

14. Suggest some disk-head scheduling policies if the disk pack has two independent arms, each of which can be positioned on any track.

15. Write a simulation program that compares disk-head scheduling algorithms.

16. Would the banker's algorithm be a good substitute for the policy shown in the text for managing conflicting requests on the character-buffer pool for terminals?

17. The Position field in a circular input buffer pool can be used either by the kernel to indicate from where it got the data or by the process to indicate from where it wants the kernel to draw data. There are advantages and disadvantages of both meanings. Describe them.

18. Assume that an operating system allows processes to execute channel programs and provides virtual tracks to processes. What sort of translation is necessary if virtual tracks do not correspond one to one with physical tracks?

# File Structures

In Chapter 5, we described device control through the service calls Open, Close, Position, Read, Write, and Control. We also saw that files can serve as a unifying metaphor for devices. In this chapter, we will look more carefully at files as objects in their own right. We will refer to the operating-system module that controls file access as the **file manager**. In Figure 3.23, it would be depicted as a separate part of the kernel. When a process makes a file-related service call, the envelope task calls the file manager to deal with it. In turn, the file manager may make several requests of the disk driver in order to complete its job. For example, a request to open a file might turn into several requests to read disk blocks to find where the file is on the disk.

We define a **file** as a named collection of data. Once created, a file remains until it is destroyed, which can be seconds, days, or years later. The data in a file might be written by one process and later read by the same or different processes. We will also allow the data in files to be appended, modified, or completely overwritten. In a sense, files are an extension of the virtual store of a process. However, their continued existence after the termination of that process and their availability to other processes makes them particularly useful for long-term storage of results. Files may be stored on practically any read/write medium; disk storage is the most common, so we will concentrate on that.

Our examination of files is divided into two major parts, the virtual and the physical. Files are abstractions built according to the Beautification Principle, both hiding and enhancing the underlying physical reality. The virtual notion of a file includes how it is named, how it is protected from unwanted access, its internal structure, how it can be recovered after accidental destruction, and how it behaves when more than one process wants to use it at the same time. Files are used for a wide variety of purposes, and their virtual forms depend on their purposes. Some operating systems provide different sorts of files with different properties for different applications. Other operating systems attempt to provide one standard sort of file with properties powerful enough so that almost all applications can use it satisfactorily. For example, if a file is used only by the process that creates it, there may be no need to give that file a name. Any file that is meant to be preserved after its creator terminates must have a name so that it can be distinguished from all other files currently in storage.

The physical representation of a file, usually on disk, must efficiently satisfy the requirements imposed by the chosen virtual form. We will discuss allocation on the disk, internal file structures, directories of files, and support for simultaneous use.

# 1 NAMING STRUCTURE OF FILES

The purpose of a file name is to allow users and programs to refer to a particular file. File names can also relate to the contents or the intended use of a file. For example, a user might tell from the name of the file whether it contains a program in Fortran or Pascal. Every operating system has conventions for names. These conventions usually divide file names into parts that we will call **components**.

Some operating systems (like Exec-8 for the Univac 1100) require every file name to have exactly three components and each component to have an exact number of characters. Others (like recent versions of Unix) allow any number of components and place no restriction on the number of characters. A fairly typical arrangement (found in Tops-10 for the DEC PDP-10 and in CP/M for many microcomputers) is to allow two components. The first component has six or eight characters and the second has three. The first component may be picked at the whim of the programmer to designate the purpose for which the file has been written. The second component follows conventions that tell what sort of file it is.

For example, suppose that the programmer wishes to build a Modula program that has two modules. The program simulates an airport. The modules are Runway and Plane. The source program could be stored in files called `runway.mod` and `plane.mod`, respectively. The dot separates the components, and the `mod` component indicates that the files are Modula source files. When the compiler has created object files, they might be called `runway.obj` and `plane.obj`. Once the linker has combined these two files, the result might be an executable program called `simulate.run`. (If we are limited to six characters, we might be forced to call the file `simlat.run`. One needs many more characters to avoid feeling constrained.) The input data for the program might be stored in `simulate.dat`, and the output created by the program might be called `simulate.out`. If the program fails during execution, a copy of its address space might be saved for later debugging in a file called `simulate.spc`.

Files are retrieved by full or partial specification of their file names. A partial specification omits some of the components. It is very common to use the * character as a "wild-card" or "don't care" entry in a file name. For example,

`*.obj` refers to all files that have `obj` as their second component. The wild-card convention is usually not interpreted by the file manager. Instead, programs that deal with files, such as the command interpreter (discussed in Chapter 7), convert a name with wild cards into a list of files.

In addition to listing all files with a particular component, a user often wishes to see all files that pertain to some project or that belong to the same person. Various techniques are available for imposing selective views on the file structure. All revolve around the notion of a **directory**. A directory is a list of pairs that can be searched by the first element, called the **key**, to derive the second. In the case of files, a directory is a list of file names (the key) along with other information about the file, such as who owns it, how long it is, who is allowed to access it, or where it is stored on the physical disk. Directories are often stored as files themselves, but these files are treated specially by the file manager.

## 1.1 One-level (flat) directories

Some operating systems use one master directory for all files. Since all file names appear in a single directory, we say the directory has one **level**. Since all file names are searched by the same method, we say the directory is **flat**. Such a directory structure is shown in Figure 6.1. This figure shows file names stored in a master directory, which then points to where the files are actually stored.

A flat directory structure forbids two files to have the same name. This restriction can make it difficult for users to invent reasonable names for files. However, if there are enough components in the name, there is no difficulty. For

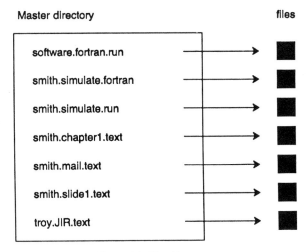

**Figure 6.1** Flat directory

example, the Univac Exec-8 operating system has a flat directory structure, but each file name has three components. The first component is, by default, the owner's personal identifying number. Most files are created with only two user-selected components, and two users may choose the same names. In fact, default selections are available for those two components as well; these defaults lead to temporary files that are deleted at the end of the day or when the session ends.

A flat directory structure has some drawbacks. The entire directory must be searched to find a file. Clever data structures to represent the directory can speed up this search. For example, a linear directory can be improved by reordering it after every search to place the searched name at the start. The directory can also be represented as a binary search tree or as a hash table. Still, generating a list of files sharing some characteristic (like owner) will require an exhaustive search. Likewise, wild-card searches must examine the entire master directory.

A flat directory structure is fine for small disks that can only hold a limited number of files. Personal computers often use flat structures for floppy disks, for example. The CP/M operating system follows this design.

## 1.2 Two-level directories

A two-level directory structure is used in the Tops-10 operating system. Every account is given a private directory, known as a user file directory. A user who wants to separate various projects can use several accounts. Now files have more complex **full names**: the name of the user file directory followed by the name of the file within that directory. The latter part of the file name is called the **local name**.

Account names may be strings of integers, but more commonly, they are strings of characters that describe the user (and perhaps the project). An account used by a student, Mary Smith, to prepare her doctoral dissertation might be called `smith.thesis`. Let's say that Mary has been writing the simulation program described earlier and has built files such as `runway.mod`, `plane.mod`, and `simulate.run`. The name for these files would be

```
/smith.thesis/runway.mod
/smith.thesis/plane.mod
/smith.thesis/simulate.run
```

and so on. We are using the slash character (`/`) to separate the account name (which we are also using as a directory name) from the file name. Of course, each operating system will have its own syntax for this separation.

The name used to refer to a file is independent of who is referring to the file. Both Mary and her adviser, Professor Helen Troy, use the same names for the same files. For this reason, we say that the names we have shown are **absolute**.

However, Mary might prefer a shorter name for her files. The name `runway.mod` is certainly easier to type than `smith.thesis/runway.mod`. We would like to assume the first part of the name by default. The rest of the name will be understood **relative** to the assumed first part. To distinguish absolute from relative file names, we will adopt a convention that absolute names begin with /, whereas relative names do not. Local names are file names relative to the directory in which the file resides.

To establish the meaning of relative names, a process might tell the file manager what the default part of the name should be. We will call this default the **working directory**. In general, we will provide service calls for all the facilities we would like to make available to the user. As we will see in Chapter 7, these service calls can be used directly by processes or indirectly by users interacting with processes.

☐    SetWorkingDirectory(new directory). This call sets the working directory for the process to the new directory (if it exists). There could be a special value for "new directory" that means the user's own directory.

When Mary logs on (interactively) or starts a job (in batch), the processes that work on her behalf will use `smith.thesis` as their working directory.

A two-level scheme is useful even if there is only one user. It is found on many computers to indicate which disk drive or which other device holds a file, even if a flat structure is used within devices. For example, a personal computer that has both a hard disk and a floppy disk might have a command like the following:

```
COPY /HardDisk/project.mod TO /Floppy/save1.mod
```

The name of the device acts as a directory. When the working directory is set to HardDisk, relative names suffice for files stored on the hard disk, but files on the floppy need absolute names.

## 1.3   Aliases and indirect files

Two different directories may need to share a file that doesn't belong naturally to either one exclusively. For example, Mary Smith may wish to access her computer-mail file whether she is using account `smith.thesis` or `smith.coursework`. She would prefer to avoid placing the mail file in one directory or the other because that would force her to use a full name on some occasions. The Multics and Unix operating systems allow the very same file to be present in several directories. We will say that the file has several **aliases**. To build an alias for a file, a process may use the following service call:

☐    Alias(old name, new name). This call builds a new directory entry that refers to the same file as the old name. Both names may be absolute or relative. Relative names are understood with respect to the working directory. The call fails if the old file does not exist or the new name cannot be used (the new name is already in use, the caller does not have necessary permissions, or the physical implementation of files cannot arrange for the alias).

Aliases for the same file are not independent copies. There is only one file, and if it is modified under any alias, the file under other aliases is likewise changed.

Figure 6.2 shows the same files as before, but now Mary Smith has two accounts, one for her coursework and another for her thesis. She has placed an alias for her mail file in both accounts to make it easy to access. Helen Troy's account is also shown, as is a software directory for such programs as the Fortran compiler. The dashed lines indicate an indirect file, which we will describe shortly. If the working directory is `smith.courses`, the following files are accessible:

| File | Also called |
|------|-------------|
| `slide1.text` | `/smith.courses/slide1.text` |
| `mail` | `/smith.courses/mail` |
|  | `/smith.thesis/mail` |
| `/smith.thesis/simulate.for` |  |
| `/smith.thesis/simulate.run` |  |
| `/smith.thesis/chapter1.text` | `/troy/smith.text` |
| `/troy/JIR.text` |  |
| `/software/fortran.run` |  |

Aliases raise several issues pertaining to naming, deletion and accounting.

- **Naming**: A file with several aliases no longer seems to have a "true" name. Is the mail file really `/smith.courses/mail` or `/smith.thesis/mail`? We can increase the confusion by giving the same file different local names in the two directories, such as `mail` and `letters`. We could even put the two aliases in the same directory, as long

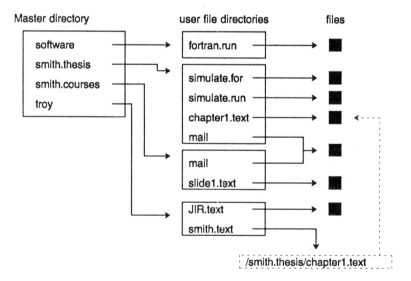

**Figure 6.2** Two-level directory

as the local names are different.

If we are willing to distinguish files from names, as our figures show, we can find this situation useful. A file may have multiple names. For example, every student in a class might be expected to build a file called `project.mod`. The teacher may wish to build an alias for each of these files in the teacher's directory. The local name for each file in the teacher's directory could refer to the student: `brown.mod`, `asaithambi.mod`, and `mogolescu.mod`.

- **Deletion**: If the file is deleted under one of its aliases, should it disappear under all aliases? If so, then it is necessary to find all the directories that contain aliases for the deleted file and remove those aliases as well. To make this search efficient, all the aliases of a file could be listed in a common place, perhaps along with the contents of the file itself.

  A nice alternative is to allow the file to remain intact until the last alias is deleted. A reference count can be stored with the file to indicate how many aliases it has. Most files have just one alias, so they have reference count 1. Files that have been placed in several directories (or several times in the same directory) have a higher reference count. Making a new alias raises the count. Deleting a file removes its entry in a directory, reduces its count, and preserves the file if the count is not yet zero. If the count is zero, the file's data can be discarded and its disk space reclaimed. A user who wants to delete a file completely must know all its aliases.

- **Accounting**: Many operating systems charge users in proportion to how much disk space (in sectors, for example) each user's files are occupying at the end of each day. Who should pay for the disk space occupied by a file that has several aliases? We might charge the "owner" of the file, that is, the user who first created it. Ownership would be stored with the file, not with the directory entry, to avoid having several owners of the same file. However, this policy can be unfair. A student, Patish Shamir, has built the file `project.mod`. The instructor has made an alias for it, called `shamir.mod`. Patish is paying for the disk space. Now Patish deletes the file at the end of the semester. Since the instructor never gets around to deleting `shamir.mod`, it remains. Patish is still paying for the file but has no way to delete it, since the instructor's files are protected from him. In fact, Patish may graduate and lose his account on the machine. There is nobody left to bill for this file.

  A different accounting policy would be to charge each user for the files in that user's directory in proportion to the percentage of the file that is in the directory. For example, a file with only one name is entirely in its directory. A file with two aliases is charged half to one directory and half to the other. Patish Shamir's project file is charged half to him and half to the instructor until Patish deletes it, after which it is charged entirely to the instructor. Even this policy is not completely fair. Before Patish deletes the file, he might (maliciously) add an enormous amount of data to it. The instructor is left paying for the whole file and has no idea that Patish was so unkind.

If the file structures allow aliasing, moving a file from one directory to another can be very inexpensive and independent of the length of the file. Instead of copying the file to a new name, the new name can be made an alias for the file, and then the file can be deleted under the old name. Since there is still at least one outstanding reference to it, the file is not deleted. If aliasing is not allowed, inexpensive file movement can still be provided by a service call.

☐ Move(old name, new name). This call has the same effect as Alias, except that it removes the old name. This call is provided only if Alias is not.

BSD4.2 Unix permits another, looser form of aliasing. An **indirect file** is a file that contains nothing but the name (either absolute or relative) of another file.

☐ Indirect(old name, new name). This call builds a new indirect file for the old file.

Figure 6.2 shows an indirect file, `/troy/smith.text`, which refers to the file `/smith.thesis/chapter1.text`. Any attempt to open the indirect file will result in opening the other one instead. (Relative names in an indirect file may be understood with respect to the working directory of the process or with respect to the directory where the indirect file is stored. Unix chooses the second alternative.) A chain of indirect files is meaningful, but to prevent getting lost in cycles, the file manager should refuse to accept a chain longer than five or so indirect files.

Indirect files raise the same issues of deletion and accounting as aliases.

● **Deletion**: Deleting an indirect file A has no effect on the file B it refers to. Deleting a file B referred to by an indirect file A makes A useless. It is then impossible to open A, but A still remains in its directory. If a file named B is later created, A is again usable.

● **Accounting**: If an indirect file A refers to B, the owner of A should pay for the (minuscule) amount of disk storage A occupies. The owner of B should pay for all of B. The owner of B can always avoid payment by deleting the file; this action renders the indirect file A worthless. If the owner of A wants to be sure that B can't be deleted, that owner should have to pay for part of B by making a regular alias.

Aliases and indirect files form interconnections by means of entries in directory structures. VMS provides **logical names** through data structures in the file manager to serve a similar purpose. Whenever a relative file name is presented to the file manager, it checks the first part of the name against several translation tables. The global table applies to all processes, the group table applies to all processes within a group, and each process has two private tables, one of which is inherited by its children. System calls are available to manipulate these tables; modifying the first two requires special privilege. Each table entry gives a logical name and its translation. The same logical name may be translated differently by different tables, and one name may have several translations in the same table. Each of these translations is tried in a standard order (recursively, since the translation may itself be a logical name) until a name that corresponds to an actual file is found. Logical names can be used to point to directories where standard software is kept. A user can then refer to `software/editor.run`, for example, without needing to know where the software directory is. People testing new versions can make a group logical name for `software` that points to a different directory.

We could have introduced aliases and indirect files when we were discussing flat directory structures, but they are much more important when full names become cumbersome, as they are with two levels. The extension from two levels to an arbitrary number of levels is the next step.

## 1.4  Hierarchical directories

It is not hard to generalize the two-level directory structure into an arbitrary number of layers. We started in that direction when we gave Mary Smith two different accounts, one for her thesis work and one for her course work. It would have been more helpful to give her one account and let her subdivide her files between the thesis and course projects. The course files might themselves be divided among the various courses she is taking. At a higher level, the files on the computer may be divided between those needed by the operating system (like source files for the kernel, documentation on the text editor, or software such as the Fortran compiler) and those needed by users (letters, programs for projects, documentation, mail).

A tree is an elegant arrangement for these divisions. We distinguish two types of nodes in the tree: directories and ordinary files. A directory can have **children** (subnodes), a non-directory cannot. Directories may be empty. Figure 6.3 shows how the files we have been discussing might be placed into a hierarchical structure. As you can see, files are not restricted to lie at a particular level in the hierarchy. The top few levels of the directory structure tend to have a lot of directories, but ordinary files can reside there, too.

In a hierarchical directory structure, absolute names are often clumsy. They are still necessary because we need a way to distinguish a mail file in Mary Smith's directory from a mail file in Helen Troy's directory. We build the absolute name of a file by starting at the root of the tree and naming all the directories on the path to that file. The last part of the full name is the local name of the file. We will separate the intermediate names by the / symbol, as before. The files in Figure 6.3 have these full names:

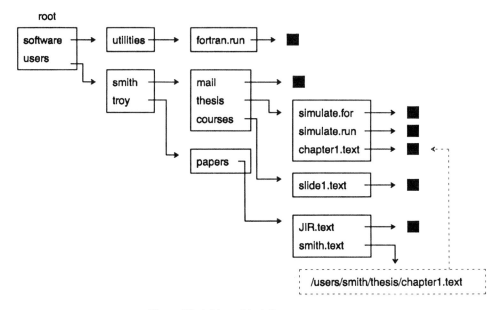

**Figure 6.3** A hierarchical directory structure

```
/ (the root directory)
/software (a directory)
/software/utilities (a directory)
/software/utilities/fortran.run (a file)
/users (a directory)
/users/smith (a directory)
/users/smith/mail (a file)
/users/smith/thesis (a directory)
/users/smith/thesis/simulate.for (a file)
/users/smith/thesis/simulate.run (a file)
/users/smith/thesis/chapter1.text (a file)
/users/smith/courses (a directory)
/users/smith/courses/slide1.text (a file)
/user/troy (a directory)
/user/troy/papers (a directory)
/user/troy/papers/JIR.text (a file)
/user/troy/papers/smith.text (an indirect file)
```

As before, we have used an initial / to indicate that these are absolute names. Names relative to a working directory can be much simpler. We assume that when Mary Smith logs onto the computer, her working directory is set to /users/smith. At this point, she can name the following files with relative names.

```
mail  (a file)
thesis  (a directory)
thesis/simulate.for  (a file)
thesis/simulate.run  (a file)
thesis/chapter1.text  (a file)
courses  (a directory)
courses/slide1.text  (a file)
```

When she wants to work on her thesis, she can change the working directory to `thesis` (using its relative name) or `/users/smith/thesis` (using its absolute name). What if she wants to copy her `slide1.text` file from her `courses` directory to her `thesis` directory? She could submit a command of the following form.

```
COPY /users/smith/courses/slide1.text
    TO /users/smith/thesis/slide1.text
```

By setting the working directory to `/users/smith`, she could reduce this command to the following.

```
COPY courses/slide1.text
    TO thesis/slide1.text
```

Aliases can also reduce the burden of long names. Files that are heavily used may have aliases in several directories, so local names usually suffice. Likewise, indirect files may specify shared files without worrying about accidentally retaining a copy after they are deleted.

Let us imagine that the command interpreter has an interactive LIST command that lists the files in any directory. By grouping related files, the file structure makes such a command both useful and efficient. Directories seldom grow to hold more than about 20 or so files. After that point, the user is likely to partition the files into several subdirectories.

How would we list the contents of the working directory? We could tell the LIST command the absolute name of the working directory, but absolute names are clumsy. We could tell LIST the relative name for the working directory, but we have no such name. We could let LIST assume that if we give it no argument at all, the working directory is implied, but the LIST program would still need to open the working directory, and it has no name for it. We will therefore adopt a convention that `%` as a relative file name refers to the working directory. Then

```
LIST %
```

will list the working directory.

Another nice feature we can add is a relative name that refers to the **parent** directory, the one right above the working directory in the tree. We will use `^` for this purpose. If the working directory is `courses`, then Mary could use the command

```
COPY slide1.text TO ^/thesis/slide1.text
```

We might as well generalize the notion of parent to include any number of levels up the tree. To move the same file into her advisor's account, Mary could submit the following command.

```
COPY slide1.text TO ^/^/troy/slide1.text
```

We see that ^ is a local file name that refers to the parent directory, and it may be used in arbitrary ways in a full file name. Likewise, we treat % as a local file name in each directory that refers to that directory. Repeated uses of % in a file name are not as useful as repeated uses of ^.

The easiest way to implement these special file names is to place these two names in every directory as aliases to that directory and to its parent. The root directory does not need a file ^.

Setting up a directory is a job for the file manager because directories must follow consistency rules to prevent the file structure from becoming confused. We provide a service call for this purpose.

☐   **MakeDirectory(new name).** This call builds a new directory with the given name. The new name may be either absolute or relative to the working directory. The new directory is initialized to contain the ^ and % files, which are aliases to its parent and itself, respectively. This call fails if the prefix of the new name (that is, all but the last part) is not a directory, if the proposed directory already exists, or if the caller does not have permission to create this directory.

# 2  ACCESS CONTROL

Files are used for long-term storage of information. Much information is either private (and should be secret) or at least important (and should be protected against modification). Therefore, the rights of users or their processes to access files must be restricted. Yet files are an indispensible means of sharing information, so, the restrictions should be selective.

Restricted access with the possibility of sharing is not a new topic for us. We encountered it in Chapter 3 when we were discussing main-store management. There were occasions when two processes would want to share a segment of information. We will now present a more formal discussion of access control in general.

## 2.1  A formal model of access control

Our formal model deals with **subjects**, which are the entities that wish to access data, and **objects**, which are the units of data that may be accessed. For our purposes, the subjects are users (or processes acting on their behalf). Subjects can be represented by **user identifiers**, which are associated with all the processes running on behalf of a particular user. The objects we will deal with are entire files. We will not deal with access control on a finer grain than entire files, although database applications often impose controls on the record or byte level of granularity. We will allow a process to access either a whole file or none of it.

The formal model of subjects and objects can be applied to other situations besides file systems. For example, one can describe the scope of identifiers in a Pascal program by considering procedures as subjects and identifiers as objects. As a second example, one can describe the interplay of a community of cooperating processes by letting processes be both subjects and objects.

In each of these subject-object worlds, individual objects may have several **access modes**. Files can be read or written. (A more complete list will be presented shortly.) Identifiers can be invoked (if they are procedures), read or written (if they are variables), only read (if they are constants), or applied to new declarations (if they are types). Cooperating processes can be asked to perform different tasks, depending on the program that the process is running.

Our formal access model will allow us to specify which access modes are allowed between each subject and each object. In the file world, for example, Mary Smith may not care who looks at her histology notes (mode = read) as long as only she can modify them (mode = write). But she doesn't want anyone else even to look at her thesis, except possibly her adviser. Her mail file should be available for people to add messages (mode = append) but not to overwrite in the middle and certainly not to inspect.

We will therefore determine whether to allow a given access by considering three factors:

- the subject
- the object
- the access mode.

To perform an access of a given mode, the subject must have the appropriate **access right**. We will use the term **privilege** as a synonym for "access right." For files, the access modes that might be provided include the following.

- Read: Derive information from the object.
- Write: Initialize or modify the information in the object.
- Append: Add new information to the object.
- Execute: Treat the object as a load image.
- Delete: Remove the object.
- Privilege: Modify the rights that subjects have to the object.
- SetOwner: Establish which subject owns the object.

Execute privilege is different from Read privilege. One way to distinguish programs from data files is by granting Execute privilege over programs. In addition, proprietary software is often licensed by the manufacturer to be used but not to be copied. In order to copy a file, a subject must be able to read it. Separating the Execute and the Read privileges lets us prohibit copying but not execution.

The Privilege privilege allows a subject to grant new privileges or revoke old privileges. It is rarely granted to any subject but the owner because it is so powerful. The SetOwner privilege is even more powerful and may be reserved for administrators.

We can represent the state of all access rights by constructing an **access matrix**, as shown in Figure 6.4. Each row in the access matrix represents one subject, and each column represents one object. The subjects are users, and the objects are files. The information stored in the entry for a given row and column is the list of privileges that subject has over that object. Figure 6.4 only uses the Read, Write, Append, Delete, and Execute privileges and abbreviates each to one letter.

All the users in Figure 6.4 may read the news file, and all may execute the editor file. Marduk is allowed to read or write any file. Fred may read, write, or delete his own mail file. Many other users may append to that mail file but not read it. Mottl isn't even allowed to append to Fred's mail file. Ramon and Cheri share `letters/love.text`. Ramon may read and write this file, and Cheri may read it and delete it. Kealoha may read, write, and delete her `prog.text` file, and she has allowed Murali to read it as well.

The access matrix is purely a logical construct that we can use to reason about the access control situation. It would be unreasonable to store the matrix in one piece, either in main store or on secondary store, because it is so large. However, we can divide it up and store it in pieces.

Whenever a process attempts to access a file, the file manager can refer to the access matrix (however it is stored) to validate the access. In keeping with the Cache Principle, the file manager might check for privileges only when the file is opened. We saw in Chapter 5 that a process indicates its intent when it opens a device. Similarly, when a process uses the Open service call to access a file, it

objects

| subjects | | fred/<br>mail | news | letters/<br>love.text | editor | prog.text |
|---|---|---|---|---|---|---|
| | fred | RWD | R | | E | |
| | murali | A | R | | E | R |
| | ramon | A | R | RW | E | |
| | cheri | A | R | RD | E | |
| | lotta | A | R | | E | |
| | mottl | | R | | E | |
| | marduk | RWD | RWD | RWD | RWED | RWD |
| | kealoha | A | R | | E | RWD |

**Figure 6.4** An access matrix

indicates the sort of access it intends. At this point the file manager checks that the access meets the restrictions in the access matrix. After the file is opened, the only check that needs to be made on every access is that the access matches the declared intent. One effect of this design is that modifications to the access matrix while files are open will not affect processes that already have the file open.

## 2.2 Capability lists

If we partition the access matrix into separate rows, we have all the information for one subject together. We might store that information in a data structure associated with the subject. This sort of data structure is called a **capability list**, because it lists all the capabilities that a subject has. Capability lists associated with the access matrix of Figure 6.4 are pictured in Figure 6.5. For our file example, we might keep a capability list of all the files that any user may access in a special "capability file" in the user's logon directory. When a process tries to open a file, the file manager can check the appropriate capability list and make sure that the file is listed with the necessary privilege.

This arrangement is awkward for several reasons:

• If each capability list has an entry for all files, many entries will indicate that no access is allowed. This waste of space can be eliminated by listing only

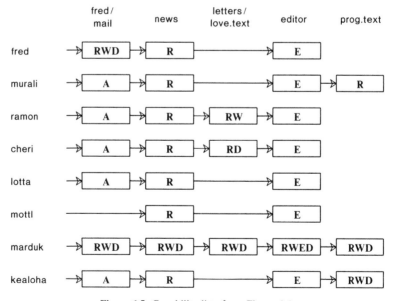

**Figure 6.5** Capability lists from Figure 6.4

files over which the subject has privileges.

- The set of files accessible by one user may be very large. It can be expensive for the file manager to check that a particular file is listed in a capability list. In particular, privileged personnel responsible for maintaining the computer installation are likely to have very long capability lists.

- When a new user is granted access to the computer, an initial capability list must be generated for that new subject. It is not at all clear which files should be on the initial list.

## 2.3  Access lists

The other obvious way to partition the access matrix is by columns. Each piece corresponds to a particular object and lists all subjects and their privileges over that object. Such a piece is called an **access list**. The access lists corresponding to our access matrix are shown in Figure 6.6. The access list for a file might as well be stored with the file, either in the directory entry for it or as part of the file itself. (We will return to this choice soon.) When a subject opens a file, the file manager checks that the subject is listed in the access list for the file and has the necessary

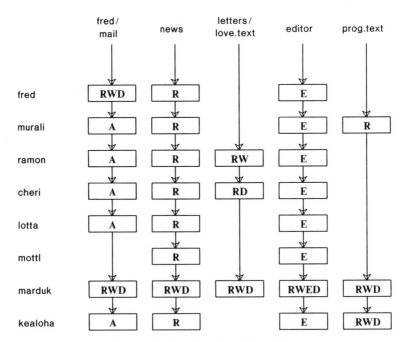

**Figure 6.6**  Access lists from Figure 6.4

privileges.

Once again, this alternative has awkward features. The set of all subjects is likely to be quite large, and many subjects will have identical privileges over the object. It is convenient to group subjects into classes. Each subject carries both a user identifier and a **group identifier**. All members of the same group can be given the same privileges for the object. The few subjects that don't fit neatly into a class can be dealt with separately. Many operating systems follow this approach. They partition subjects into four classes:

- Owner of the file
- Users in the same group as the owner
- Other users
- Utility programs that periodically back up disk storage onto tape. (We discuss file dumps later in this chapter.)

For example, Mary might set the access list for `slide1.text` to

|         |             |
|---------|-------------|
| **self**  | read, write |
| **group** | read        |
| **world** | read        |

We assume that Professor Troy, Mary's adviser, is a member of her group. The thesis chapter, `chapter1.text`, would have the following access list:

|         |             |
|---------|-------------|
| **self**  | read, write |
| **group** | read        |
| **world** | no access   |

Finally, her `mail` file would have the following access list:

|         |             |
|---------|-------------|
| **self**  | read, write |
| **group** | append      |
| **world** | append      |

Multics allows the access list to contain individual user names as well as larger groupings. If Mary belongs to the same group as all of Professor Troy's students, she may not want to grant Read privilege over `chapter1.text` to the entire group. Instead, she might set the access list like this:

| | |
|---|---|
| **self** | read, write |
| **group** | no access |
| **world** | no access |
| **HelenTroy** | read |

The file manager permits any access that is allowed by at least one entry in the object's access list. (Actually, Multics denies access if the first applicable entry on the list denies it, even if a later one allows it.)

Whenever a subject creates a new object, it is necessary to initialize the access list. The subject might be required to provide an access list at the time the object is created. Alternatively, a default access list may be supplied by the file manager in the hope that it will be adequate for most objects. For example,

| | |
|---|---|
| **self** | read, write |
| **group** | read |
| **world** | no access |

is a reasonable default setting. The default may be customized if each user indicates what privileges are *not* to be granted automatically to other subjects. For example, the default setting just shown could be represented as follows:

| | |
|---|---|
| **self** | unlimited |
| **group** | deny: write, append, execute, delete |
| **world** | deny: read, write, append, execute, delete |

If Mary is more trusting, she could change this customization as follows:

| | |
|---|---|
| **self** | unlimited |
| **group** | deny: append, execute, delete |
| **world** | deny: write, append, execute, delete |

When a process creates a file on behalf of Mary, it can specify what permissions to grant to each class of subjects. The file manager will then reduce these permissions in accordance with the customized default. It also provides a service call that allows Mary to modify the access list, possibly to add a special entry for her professor or remove Read access from the world. Such a service call may look like this:

☐   ChangePrivileges(file name, new permissions). This call establishes the permissions on the given file. The format of the "new permissions" parameter depends on the particular operating system. Typically, this parameter is a string of bits. Each bit position indicates some form of access privilege for some user class. If the bit is on, the privilege is granted. This call fails if the caller does not have the Privilege privilege for this file or if the file does not exist.

One simple form of access list is to associate one or more passwords with each file. Passwords define an access list not by explicitly naming subjects but by stipulating a criterion that subjects must meet. For example, the Exec-8 operating system uses read and write passwords to restrict read and write access to files. Files without passwords are public.

## 2.4 Directories and access control

So far we have been discussing access control on a file-by-file basis. If the operating system provides a hierarchical directory structure, directories are themselves files. Access rights for those directories can be used to control access to the files in the directories and allow greater use of the default mechanism outlined previously. We will adopt the following access rule.

---

### Access rule
A file may be accessed by a subject only if
the subject has the appropriate access rights
for all the directories in the absolute name of the file.

---

For Mary to keep outsiders from reading her thesis, she need not protect each file within the `thesis` directory separately. Instead, she can restrict that directory itself from being read.

Directories have somewhat different operations from ordinary files. We could invent a new set of permission types for directories, but for the sake of uniformity, we will use the same permissions that we use for ordinary files and give them slightly different meanings:

- Read:  Determine the names of the files in the directory.
- Write:  Modify local file names, add and delete files. However, it is *not* allowed to open the directory for writing. The only way to modify the directory is by service calls.
- Append:  Add new files.
- Execute:  Open files in this directory.
- Delete:  Remove this directory.
- Privilege:  Modify the rights that subjects have to the directory.
- SetOwner:  Establish which subject owns the directory.

Both Delete privilege for a file and Write privilege for its directory allow a subject to delete that file. The operating system can be designed without a Delete privilege, or the file manager can require that a subject hold both privileges before allowing it to delete a file. A process with Read but not Execute privilege over a directory can determine what files are in the directory but cannot open any of those files. A process with Execute but not Read privilege can open files in the directory if it knows their names, but it cannot discover their names by reading the directory. If this subtle distinction is not important, Execute privilege might be ignored for directories.

Our access rule requires that when a process opens a file, the file manager must check privileges in all the directories in the path between the root of the file structure and that file. The process must have Read (and perhaps Execute) privilege in all of them. As we mentioned earlier, this check might be performed only when the process first opens the file. If permissions are later restricted some-where in that path, the process is not prevented from continuing the access it is making.

Our access rule has some strange consequences. Consider Figure 6.7. Assume that the working directory for process X is /a/b/c/d (directory 6 in the figure). After X establishes this working directory, the owner changes the per-missions to prevent X from reading or executing /a/b (directory 3). According to the policy that was enunciated earlier, X should not be allowed to open files 11, 12, and 13, because the path from the root (directory 1) to those files is no longer free of impediment. However, X can refer to those files by giving a relative name (such as  e) from the current working directory 6. Since the relative name does not refer to directory 3, the file manager might allow access. It could still prevent access by expanding all relative names to full names. Alternatively, we can modify

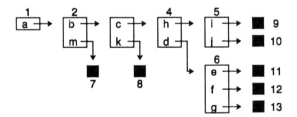

**Figure 6.7** A sample directory structure

our access rule as follows:

| **Access rule (modified)** |
| :--- |
| A file may be accessed under a given name by a subject only if the subject has the appropriate access rights for all the directories in the given name of the file. |

In particular, i (file 9) may be accessed under the name ^/h/i, since that path does not use any prohibited files, but it must not be called /a/b/c/h/i because that path goes through /a/b. Similarly, m (file 7) may be called /a/m, but it must not be called ^/^/^/m because ^/^ (directory 3) is inaccessible.

## 2.5  Aliases and indirect files

The accessibility of a file depends on what the file is called, as we have just seen. All the intermediate files between the working directory (for relative names) or the root (for absolute names) must be accessible. If a single file has several aliases, they may differ in accessibility, since the intermediate files may be different. However, after all the intermediate directories have been successfully passed, the subject must still have the necessary privileges over the file itself.

   If all directories grant Execute privilege, can a subject be granted access to some file but denied access to the same file under a different alias? The answer depends on whether privileges are associated with a file or with a name. If they are associated with the file, they are not stored in the directory (since several directory entries in several directories may all refer to the same file). In this case, the alias chosen for the file does not influence its accessibility. This is the design choice favored by Unix. If privileges are associated with a name, they might as well be stored in the directory. In this case, the alias chosen can determine accessibility.

   Indirect files are different. Consider Figure 6.8. Assume that the working directory is /a/b (directory 3). To successfully open d (file 5, through indirect file 6), the subject must have appropriate access rights for directory 3, file 6, directories 1, 2, and 4, and finally file 5. We know how to interpret access rights for ordinary files (like 5) and directories (like 1, 2, 3, and 4). How do we interpret the access rights on indirect file 6? We could ignore them completely and trust the other restrictions to create adequate security. Or we might treat file 6 as an ordinary file. To open it for reading, we would require Read privilege on both indirect file 6 and file 5 (as well as Execute privilege on directories 1, 2, 3, and 4). To open file 6 for writing, we would require Write privilege on both 6 and 5 (and Execute privilege on directories 1, 2, 3, and 4)

   This latter approach becomes awkward if we allow indirect files to point to directories, in which case we want to treat the permissions on the indirect file as directory permissions. For example, to open f/e (file 5 through indirect file 7) for writing, we would require Execute privilege on indirect file 7 and directories 1,

218    File Structures    Chapter 6

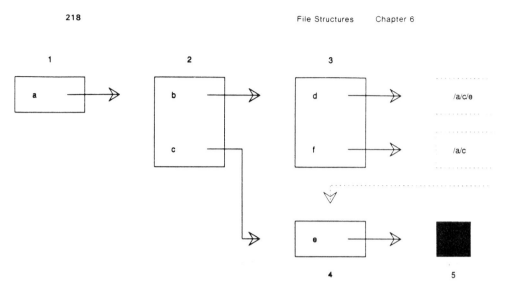

**Figure 6.8** A directory structure with indirect files

2, 3, and 4 and Write privilege on file 5. Sometimes the privileges on indirect files are taken as ordinary-file privileges, and sometimes they are taken as directory privileges. Perhaps it is simpler, after all, to ignore them. BSD4.2 Unix takes this approach. It also understands the ChangePrivileges call to apply not to the indirect file it is called on but rather to the file that the indirect file refers to.

## 3  ACCESS METHODS

Processes read and write files. Specifying which part of the file is to be read or written into depends on the **access method** for that file. The access method dictates both *which location* in the file and *how much data* at that location are to be accessed. The access method might be specified at the following times:

- When the operating system is designed. In this case, all files use the same access method.
- When the file is created. In this case, every time the file is opened, the same access method will be used.
- When the file is opened. Several processes can have the same file open and access it differently.

Let us look at some of the more popular access methods.


## 3.1 Sequential access

Many applications require only **sequential access**, in which the entire file is read or written from the beginning to the end. Each operation implicitly advances a pointer that indicates where the next operation should take place. We call this pointer the **read/write mark**. Occasionally, separate read and write marks are kept for the same open file. (An early version of the Ada programming language separated these marks, but the current design does not.) If several processes have the same file open for reading, each has its own read mark; operations undertaken by one process do not affect the behavior of the other one.

The read/write mark of an open file is therefore part of the context block of a process and is not part of the file itself. Context blocks can be designed to contain an array of open-file records. (The same array can be used for open-device descriptors.) Each record contains information describing the file that is open, the intent of the process (whether to read, write, and so on), the read/write mark, and information about where the file is stored on the physical disk. The index of a particular open-file record is a convenient number to return to the process as the result of the Open service call. The process can use this file number in its subsequent requests regarding the open file.

Sequential access might allow each operation to transfer an arbitrary number of bytes, or there might be a fixed-size increment (a block) that must be transferred on each operation. Fixed-size increments can be a characteristic of the installation, the file, or the instance of the open file. If the increment is fixed, the read/write mark may be expressed by the number of full increments from the start of the file.


## 3.2 Direct access

Some applications need to move the read/write mark to specific places without reading or writing the intervening parts of the file. They might even want to move the read/write mark backward in the file. For example, a program that traverses a large data tree stored in a file might need to move to an arbitrary place in the file to find the next node of the tree. We can use a Position service call for files just as we did in Chapter 5 for devices.

☐    **Position(file number, where).** This call tells the file manager to position the read/write mark in the file represented by the given file number. The "where" parameter might be specified by its location from the start of the file, the end of the file, or the current location of the read/write mark. The distance from that location is given as a number of fixed-size increments (perhaps bytes).

## 3.3  Mapped access

The Tenex and Multics operating systems provide a novel form of file access called **mapped access**. When a process opens a file, the entire file is mapped into the virtual space of the process. Instead of returning a file number, the Open service call returns a segment number. This number refers to a new segment that contains only the file. Similarly, the Dynix operating system for the Sequent Balance computer allows files that have already been opened to be mapped into virtual store.

Instead of submitting subsequent requests to read or write, the process treats the file as part of virtual store. To close the file, the process needs only to submit a ReleaseSegment service call.

None of the file itself needs to be brought into main store at first. Instead, as the process accesses the new segment, it will generate address-translation faults. The storage manager will convert these faults into requests on the file manager to bring in more of the file.

## 3.4  Structured files

Direct access requires the application program to compute where it wishes to seek in the file. This computation may be based on data stored elsewhere in the file, or it may be based on some secondary file that maintains indices into the main file. Database applications, which we will discuss shortly, often wish to seek to the part in the file that corresponds to some **record**, as identified by the value of some **key** field in the record.

For example, a file might contain data about all the students at a university. Each student's data could be stored in a single record, with fields for name, year in school, grade-point average, mailing address, and a list of all the courses the student has taken. An application program might wish to examine records only of second-year students. In this case, the year-in-school field is a key to the file. Another application might wish to examine records of students with straight A averages. Here, the running grade-point average field is treated as a key.

A few operating systems allow the owner of a file to declare that the file should be **structured**. Part of structuring a file is declaring what the records look like. In particular, the fields that will be used as keys must be described. Writing into the file is limited to placing new records into the file and modifying or deleting old ones. Reading the file requires specifying the keys and key values that the file manager should search for. Successive read operations yield successive records that satisfy the current search pattern. The records themselves might not have any particular order. OS/360 (and its descendants) provides structured files of several kinds. One example is ISAM (Indexed Sequential Access Method), which uses a two-level tree to access records indexed by a single key. VMS provides a record-management tool that includes a language for describing the structure of files and a set of routines that programs can use to access the structured files.

## 3.5 Databases

A **database** is a collection of structured, interrelated data, usually managed by utility programs that perform queries and updates. These programs, which are called database management systems, provide for complex searches that may involve a number of related files. For example, finding the home phone number of all students who are majoring in computer science and have a grade point average of at least 3.5 may require reference to a student file, a majors file, and a grade file. The exact details depend on the way the database is structured, which must, of course, be known to the database management system.

Large-scale database management systems often find themselves in conflict with the policies forced upon them by the underlying operating system. These conflicts include physical disk allocation strategies, kernel caching (in particular, write-behind), and main-store management.

# 4  FILE RECOVERY

Every user at some point accidentally deletes a file and thereby destroys many hours of diligent labor. It does not do much good to consider that repeating the labor will be much easier than doing it the first time and that the product will be better after this rework. The operating system can help reconstruct the lost file if necessary measures have been taken. Since recovering a lost file is a form of reliability, it is no surprise that all the techniques that the operating system might use involve redundancy of some form or another.

## 4.1  Dumps

Almost all operating systems provide for a fairly large grain of redundancy: Every so often, an archival copy (a **dump**) of files is made on magnetic tape. The unfortunate user who has lost a file to accidental deletion can recover it by finding the most recent version that is stored on tape. Since storing all the files that exist might take many reels of tape, it is not reasonable to make complete archives very often. However, infrequent archives increase the chance that an archival copy of the deleted file, even if one exists, is far out of date.

Instead, partial file dumps are commonly made every day. These tapes include only files that have been modified since the last partial backup. The user who accidentally deletes a file can recover at least yesterday's version, which is often better than nothing at all. If the file has not been modified for a few days, it can be found in a more ancient partial dump. Partial dump tapes may be reused after a few weeks; if so much time has elapsed since the file was last modified, it is likely to be on a full dump tape, which is saved for a much longer time.

Instead of two classes of dump, one-day and total, we can devise a general scheme that tries to minimize the number of tapes needed but maximize the chances that we have saved the file somewhere. Let's assume that we have eight tapes. To keep things simple, we will pretend that a single tape is always long enough to hold all the files we dump when we use that tape. (In reality, tapes 0 and 1 can be fairly short, but tapes 6 and 7 will have to be quite long.) Number all the days that the operating system runs, starting with day 1. On day $n$, dump files on tape $t$, where $2^t$ is the highest power of 2 that divides $n$. For example, on day 51, we use tape 0, but on day 52, we use tape 2. On day 64, we use tape 6. Whenever we use tape $t$, we dump all files that were modified since the last time we used tape $t$ or any tape with a higher number.

We use the lower-numbered tapes fairly frequently, so they don't have to store very many files. The higher-numbered tapes are used much more rarely, so they hold many more files. Tape 7 is written only every 128 days. If we wish to archive files longer than that, we just need to buy some more tapes.

This pattern of tape use is known as the "ruler function" because its graph looks like the pattern of marks on a ruler. Figure 6.9 shows which tape we use each day by drawing a vertical bar whose height tells the number of the tape to use. If a file is created on day $c$ and deleted on day $d$, a dump version will be saved substantially after day $d$, and the length of time it is saved depends on $d - c$ (as well as the exact values of $c$ and $d$). For example, a file created on day 5 and deleted on day 8 has existed for 3 days. During that time, it was saved on tapes 0 (day 5), 1 (day 6), and 0 (day 7). Tape 1 will not be reused until day 10, so the file is saved 2 extra days. A 3-day file created on day 6 and deleted on day 9 has been saved on tape 3 (day 8), which will not be reused until day 24.

## 4.2 Backup files and versions

Most computer installations hire operators to dump tapes according to a fixed schedule; these dumps form the last defense against lost information. There are other defenses that are worth mentioning. First, **backup files** that duplicate working

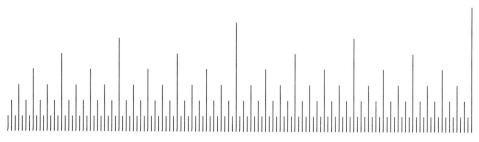

**Figure 6.9** The ruler function

files are a standard technique. If the user (or the user's program) accidentally deletes a working file, its backup can still be used. Some programs (particularly text editors) automatically save an old version of the file they are working on under a name derived from the file's name. For example, if the editor is working on file `slide1.text`, it might save the original contents under the name `slide1.text.backup`.

Backup files can be generalized to file **versions**. Whenever a file is opened for writing, a new version is created that is initialized to the data in the previous version of the file. The new version is opened, and the old version is left alone. Modifications to this version do not hurt the previous version. A wide spectrum of support is available for file versions on different operating systems.

- **Manual**: A user who is about to modify a file first copies it to a new name and modifies the file under the new name.
- **Special utility**: Some programs, particularly the text editor, copy the file they are about to modify to a new name and modify the new file.
- **General utility**: When requested, a general utility program copies the file to a new name. A variant of this is a librarian program that allows files to be checked in and out. Checking in a file creates a new version of the file. Some librarian programs save space by storing only differences between successive versions. It is possible, although perhaps time consuming, to recover any version.
- **Automatic**: When a process opens a file for writing, the storage manager opens a fresh copy of that file. The version number is part of the file name. If it is not mentioned when the file is opened, the most recent version is assumed. Tenex follows this policy. Exec-8 is similar, but only a limited number of version numbers are available. Every time a new version is started, if the maximum number of versions are already stored for the file, the oldest one is overwritten. Files under VMS can have up to about 32K versions, although the number can be restricted on a directory or file basis.

All these mechanisms provide for deleting the most recent version (usually the default deletion operation), a particular version, a set of versions, or the entire file.

## 4.3 Partial deletion

Another defense mechanism is **partial deletion** of files. The DeleteFile service call could mark the file as deleted without reclaiming its storage on the disk. If the user later decides that the file should not have been deleted, an UndeleteFile service call could change the mark and place the file back into full service. Partially deleted files might be completely deleted by a PurgeFile service call. Alternatively, they could be purged when the user's session ends or when space is needed for other files. If the operating system does not provide direct support for partially deleted files, the same effect can sometimes be implemented by letting the "delete file" interactive command move the file to a directory reserved for partially deleted files.

One variant of the partial-deletion scheme is to structure files on the disk in such a way that even though file deletion frees disk space, the file may still be reconstructed until that space is used, although possibly by a time-consuming process. A "recover file" program, which the user invokes in an emergency, tries to reconstruct the file if possible from the remnants that still reside on the disk. We will see how physical file structures can be chosen to meet this need.

At the other extreme, VMS allows the user to specify that all the disk blocks containing a file be erased when it is destroyed, to prevent others from viewing sensitive data.

# 5  TRANSACTIONS

We have been concentrating on files that are used one at a time by one user at a time. Both of these biases are inappropriate for databases, where single operations might require access to several files, and different users may undertake simultaneous operations that need to access the same file. To prevent chaos, we need to ensure that these independent operations start with all files in a consistent state and leave them in a consistent state.

The problem is similar to allocating sequentially reusable, non-preemptable resources, discussed in Chapter 4. There are differences, however. We would like to allow several processes to have the same file open for reading as long as none of the processes modifies the file. File resources are sharable up to a point, unlike the ones we saw in Chapter 4. In addition, we may need to refer to several files in order. If another process changes some of the later files after we have read the first files, we might think that the files are inconsistent.

We will use the term **transaction** to refer to a set of related file accesses, possibly to a number of files, that one process undertakes in order to perform its work. One process may be involved in several independent transactions at one time, but this situation is unusual. It is more common for a process to finish one transaction before starting the next one. Our problem is to make sure that transactions do not interfere with each other.

## 5.1  Synchronization atomicity

Our first requirement is that transactions be **serializable**:

> # Serializability
> The effect of running a number of transactions concurrently
> is the same as if they were run in some strict order
> without concurrency.

If there is no concurrency, there can be no interference between transactions. True serialization would be too conservative (in the language introduced in Chapter 4). Luckily, there are ways of enforcing serializability without requiring serialization. Another way to describe our requirement is called **synchronization atomicity**:

> # Synchronization atomicity
> Each transaction should appear to be atomic,
> that is, indivisible, without interference from other
> transactions that might be occurring at the same time.

The simplest form of synchronization atomicity applies to transactions on only one file. If process **A** is modifying a file *F* in several places, but process **B** is reading *F*, we would like **B**'s view of *F* either to omit any of **A**'s modifications or to include them all. In most operating systems, this result is achieved by preventing **A** and **B** from opening the file at the same time. This policy enforces strict serialization on accesses to the same file.

Not all simultaneous file accesses lead to failures of synchronization atomicity. There is no problem with any number of processes opening the file for reading. The problem occurs only if one process wishes to write when some other process wants to read or write. This set of constraints is commonly known as the **readers-writers problem**. We will see this problem again in Chapter 7 when we discuss process synchronization. The constraints of the readers-writers problem are shown in the following table:

|             | **Read**           | **Write**            |
|-------------|--------------------|----------------------|
| **Read**    | permissible        | Read/Write conflict  |
| **Write**   | Read/Write conflict | Write/Write conflict |

Many operating systems prevent any process from opening a file that is already open for writing (by any process). A file open for reading may not be opened for writing. This policy prevents any of the conflicts of the readers-writers problem. If the file manager does not provide this service, it can be awkward or impossible to build it out of other services that are provided.

In BSD4.2 Unix, file interlock is optional. Processes can open files requesting either exclusive or shared access to the file. Shared access is intended for processes that only want to read the file. Exclusive access is for those that want to modify the file. While a file is open with exclusive access, no process is allowed to open it with shared or exclusive access. While a file is open with shared access, no process is allowed to open it with exclusive access. However, a process may violate the rules by opening the file without specifying either shared or exclusive access. In VMS, individual records of structured files may be locked separately.

A transaction may involve several files. Most operating systems do not provide synchronization atomicity in such cases. However, we can provide this feature for database utilities that need it. Instead of forcing the file manager to undertake this task, we will speak of a **transaction manager** in the kernel that handles complex cases.

To provide synchronization atomicity in such cases, the transaction manager must know when a transaction starts and when it finishes. Every open file may be associated with some transaction. We could automatically start a transaction every time a user starts a session and associate all file actions during that session with the same transaction. However, this policy would lead to needlessly long transactions that would interfere with other users. Instead, it is better to let a process open a transaction, much as it might open a file, and to specify the transaction each time it opens a file. Here are the service calls involved:

☐   StartTransaction. This call tells the transaction manager that a transaction is starting. The call returns a transaction number for the process to use.

☐   EndTransaction(transaction number). This call tells the transaction manager that the transaction has finished. It is illegal to end a transaction for which some files are still open.

☐   Open(file name, intent, transaction number). This call opens the given file and returns a file number. The "intent" parameter indicates whether the file is to be read, written, or appended. The special transaction number OneShot means that the transaction involves only this one file. The special transaction number NoTransaction means that the process wishes to violate transaction rules for this file.

## 5.2  Failure atomicity

As we pointed out earlier, transactions are particularly useful for processes that deal with databases. During the middle of a transaction, when some file modifications have been made but others have not been made yet, the database is likely to be inconsistent. For example, transferring funds from one bank account to another might require two separate write accesses, one for each account. Synchronization atomicity ensures that no other transaction will see the two accounts in an inconsistent state, with money deducted from one but not yet added to the other or added to one without being deducted from the other. However, a hardware or software failure between the two accesses might force the transaction to terminate with the database in such an inconsistent state. Similarly, the transaction manager may need to abort a transaction that enters a deadlock as it opens a file. (We will see why later when we discuss implementing transactions.) At this time, the database may be inconsistent.

Most database management systems require that such inconsistencies be prevented. **Failure atomicity** is defined as follows:

---

### Failure atomicity

Each transaction is guaranteed either to complete or to have no effect whatsoever.

---

A failure in the middle of a transaction should either cause all modifications undertaken by the transaction so far to be undone or should preserve the state of the files so that the transaction will be completed once the failure has been repaired.

Most operating systems do not address either synchronization or failure atomicity except to forbid simultaneous multiple accesses to the same file. (Unix does not even go that far.) However, the increasing importance of database management systems is leading to more sophisticated transaction support within operating systems. Another aspect of transactions, **permanence**, is a goal of most file managers: Once a transaction completes successfully, the results of its operations will never be lost.

# 6 PHYSICAL REPRESENTATION

There are many ways to organize files on disks. A few principles seem to be universal.

- Disk blocks have numbers, and complex structures can be placed on the disk by having data in one block refer to another block by number.
- Each file is described by a **file descriptor**, which tells how the file is physically arranged on the disk.
- Each physical disk is described by a **disk descriptor**, which tells how the disk is arranged into areas and which parts are currently unused. The disk descriptor is stored at a well known location on the disk.
- Information may be stored redundantly on the disk to allow programs to try to restructure the disk if it gets confused. Confusion is the typical result of unscheduled operating-system failures, because the structure may be undergoing modification at the time of the failure. Even worse, the disk may be in the middle of writing a block when failure occurs. Restructuring a garbaged disk is called **salvaging**.
- The basic unit of allocation is the single disk block, although entire tracks or cylinders may be allocated at once to keep large regions in a file contiguous

on the disk. This attempt to keep files in local regions on the disk is called **clustering**. It is based on the Cache Principle, since it is faster to read or write on the disk at cylinders close to the current position, and the most likely request to come after one file request is another request on the same file. Clustering may also be attempted to keep files that are in the same directory positioned close together on the disk. Another form of clustering, called **skewing**, spaces consecutive blocks of a file a few sectors apart. As a result, a typical process reading the entire file will find the next file block under the disk read/write head at the time it needs it. Some disk controllers interleave sectors to place consecutively numbered ones some distance from each other on the same track. In this case, the file manager should most likely not attempt skewing.

● Searching file structures and allocating free blocks would be too time consuming if the information is stored only on the disk. In accordance with the Cache Principle, some structure and allocation information is duplicated in main store. As is typically the case with caches, the cached (main-store) data and the actual (disk) data will be out of step. Operating system failures (**crashes**) are therefore even more serious than they seem because they may lose recent changes. To mitigate the danger, all main-store caches are occasionally (perhaps every minute) archived to the disk. Perhaps the worst time for a catastrophic failure is during archiving.

● The facilities provided by the file service determine the structures that must be used. For example, direct access into arbitrary positions in a file requires different structures from sequential access. Hierarchical directories and flat directories require different structures. Different methods of access control also need different structures.

## 6.1 Allocation

We will first examine the way that free space on the disk may be allocated. If we know the size of the file and wish to maximize clustering, we may allocate entire tracks or cylinders to the file. To make this allocation efficient, **bit maps** of free cylinders and tracks may be kept for each disk. These maps are kept on the disk, but a copy is also kept in a main-store cache.

A small example of cylinder and track bit maps is shown in Figure 6.10. Each track is represented in both maps. The maps are arranged in the order of blocks on the disk so that contiguous bits refer to contiguous tracks (that is, tracks on the same or adjacent cylinders). Figure 6.10 shades tracks that are in use. In this figure, there are eight cylinders, numbered 0 to 7. (Typical disk packs have 200.) Each cylinder has four tracks.

The following table governs which cylinders and tracks are marked in use.

cylinder map

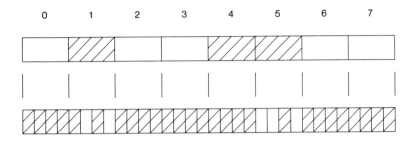

track map

**Figure 6.10**  Bit maps

| Allocation state | Cylinder bit | Track bits |
|---|---|---|
| **Whole cylinder in use** | in use | in use |
| **Some tracks in use** | in use | in use (where appropriate) |
| **Completely free** | free | in use |

Some file is using cylinder 4, so that cylinder is marked in use. All its tracks are marked in use in the track map. Two tracks of cylinder 1 and one track of cylinder 5 are also in use at the moment. For this reason the cylinder map shows these entire cylinders as in use. Cylinders 0, 2, 3, 6, and 7 are completely free, as shown by the cylinder map. The track map shows their tracks to be in use so that they are not allocated unless absolutely necessary.

When a file is to be created, if it is large enough to require at least one cylinder, it may be given a number of entire cylinders from the free-cylinder bit map. We would use cylinder 0 for a one-cylinder file. A two-cylinder file could fit either in cylinders 2 and 3 or in cylinders 6 and 7. Any larger file will have to be satisfied with non-contiguous cylinders.

If a file requires less than a cylinder, we will measure its requirements in tracks. A file that needs only one track can fit in cylinder 1, either track 1 or 3, or in cylinder 5, track 3. A two-track file can be placed in cylinder 5, tracks 0 and 1. If there are not enough contiguous tracks, cylinders may be converted to tracks. For a three-track file, we can allocate cylinder 0 and mark it in use. We could then use its tracks 0, 1, and 2, and leave 3 marked as available.

When a file is deleted and its space becomes available, the tracks it used are made available in the track map. If all the tracks in a cylinder become free, that cylinder is marked available in the cylinder map, and all the tracks are marked in use.

Allocating a file in a single contiguous region has several advantages. The directory entry (which must also be stored on the disk) needs to indicate only the starting point and the length of the file. Direct access in the file is easy because the file manager can compute the block number of any byte in the file. Clustering within files is perfect.

Unfortunately, this method produces substantial internal waste, because most files need far less than a single track, and even large files are likely to waste about half of the last track (or cylinder) allocated to them. Also, it depends on knowledge of the size of the file before the allocation is made. In many situations the size can be estimated only roughly. This deficiency leads to internal waste in some cases and inability to fit the file in other cases. If the file doesn't fit, it can be broken into individually contiguous pieces called **extents**. Within an extent, sequential and direct access are very fast, but the file manager needs to record where each extent is. That information must be read before any extent can be found, so access is slower than it would be with a single contiguous region. OS/360 allocates contiguous regions in integral numbers of cylinders or tracks and allows up to 15 extents.

External waste can also be a problem with contiguous allocation. When the disk becomes relatively full, it may be impossible to create a new file because there are not enough contiguous tracks, even though the total amount of free space is sufficient. Shuffling the files is possible but usually requires that the entire disk be copied to a staging area (another disk or magnetic tape) and then copied back.

At the other extreme, a file manager can be designed to allocate all files by single blocks. If a file needs many blocks, they may end up scattered across the disk; we will see how this dispersion can be controlled. Free-storage allocation can again make use of a bit map. The map would have a bit for each block on the disk instead of each track or each cylinder. However, this bit map might be unacceptably large. A medium-large disk has about 256M bytes. If each block contains 512 bytes, the disk has 512K blocks. The bit map occupies 64K bytes. We could cache part of the bit map in main store and keep the full map on the disk, where it would use 128 blocks.

One nice trick is to place parts of the map in the free blocks themselves. Instead of allocating a fixed region of 128 blocks for the bit map, a single block is allocated. This block does not hold a bit map but rather stores the numbers of up to 256 free blocks. (We assume that a block number occupies two bytes.) Each of these free blocks may store numbers of other free blocks. Thus free space is organized as a tree with a very large fan-out. The exercises at the end of this chapter develop this idea further.

## 6.2  File layout

Each file on the disk is associated with ancillary information stored in a **file descriptor**. It might have the following structure:

```
 1 type
 2    FileDescriptorType =
 3      record
 4        Permissions : AccessRights; { may be organized in groups }
 5        FileType : (Data, Directory, Indirect, Device)
 6        Length : integer; { in bytes or words }
 7        CreationTime : Date; { when first created }
 8        ModificationTime : Date; { when last written }
 9        AccessTime : Date; { when last opened }
10        ReferenceCount : integer; { number of aliases }
11        Layout : array of Extent; { tells which physical (disk)
12            blocks correspond to which virtual (data) blocks }
13      end;
```

The associated directory structure might look like this:

```
14 const
15    MaxFileNameSize = ... { whatever }
16 type
17    DirectoryEntry =
18      record
19        Name : array 1:MaxFileNameSize of char;
20            { For simplicity, we assume only one component }
21        Version : integer;
22        Descriptor : FileDescriptorIndex;
23      end;
24    Directory = array of DirectoryEntry;
```

The FileType field (line 5) is used to distinguish major categories of files. Directories are used in a very different way from data files. Device files are usually not files at all but a convenient way to unify transput with the file system. On some operating systems, such as Exec-8 for the Univac 1100 computer, the Data type is further categorized as "source program," "object code," or "load image." One can imagine other categories as well, such as "mail file" and "command file." In those operating systems that do not use the file descriptor to distinguish these different uses for data files, they can still be distinguished by the file name (using conventions we discussed earlier) or by the file contents.

The Layout field (line 11) is used to find the physical block that holds any given byte of the file. For the purpose of sequential access, each physical block can also contain the block number of its successor. This extra information can reduce the number of Seek operations needed to read an entire file sequentially. Of course, such redundant information must be updated when the contents of the file change (for example, when new data are written at the end). If this redundant information (which may be treated as a **hint**) is wrong, the truth (that is, the corresponding **absolute**) may be deduced from the file descriptor. At the worst, a salvage operation may be able to reconstruct the file from extra information stored in each data block identifying the file to which it belongs.

The declarations above are intended for file structures that allow aliases. Each alias for the file has its own directory entry, and all those entries point to the same file descriptor (line 22). This pointer is most likely in the form of an index into the file descriptor array. If we forbid aliasing of files, we don't need the reference count (line 10), and the directory entry for each file can include the file descriptor instead of pointing to it. That is, line 22 would read as follows.

```
22          Descriptor : FileDescriptorType;
```

The reference count (line 10) is maintained by the file manager so that it can reclaim the file descriptor, along with the data blocks in the file, when the last alias for the file is removed.

Multiple versions of a file require the Version field (line 21). Each version of a file is listed separately in the directory with its own file descriptor or pointer to a file descriptor. If two versions are almost identical, space can be saved on the disk by sharing some file blocks. Whenever the file is opened for writing, a new version can be constructed with a new directory entry.

Initially, the file descriptor for the new version is an exact copy of the one for the previous version. Both the previous and the new version have the same Layout field (line 11), so they share disk blocks. Whenever a modification is made to a block in the new version, the entire block is copied, and the descriptor of the new version is updated to show the location of the new block. That is, blocks of the file are split into separate copies only when necessary. Special care is needed to avoid splitting when unnecessary and to postpone reclaiming a disk block until all the versions that use it have been deleted. We saw a similar **copy on write** strategy earlier when we were discussing segmentation.

To save more disk space, a utility program can detect similarities by comparing versions on a block-by-block basis and discarding redundant blocks as they are found. This operation could be carried out whenever a version is closed. Since it is not critical, it can be performed **offline**, that is, whenever the opportunity arises, perhaps late at night.

Line 24 in the declarations above suggests that a directory is a linear array of directory entries. This array can be searched sequentially as long as the directory is not too long. When a file is deleted, its slot in the array can be freed (for example, by putting a special value in the Descriptor field, line 22) to be used by the next file that is created. If directories are very long, as can happen with flat directories, a hashing or tree-based technique may well be better for organizing the entries in the array.

To allow the disk to be salvaged, it is important that file descriptors be distinguishable from data blocks and from free blocks. A byte at the start of each block could be reserved to indicate the nature of the block, but that would reduce the amount of space available for data in each data block. That extra byte can get in the way if the disk driver needs to read several blocks into an extended main-store buffer. Alternatively, a region of the disk could be reserved for file descriptors. We could call this region the **descriptor area**.

To promote clustering, the entire disk can be subdivided into subdisks, each composed of a number of consecutive cylinders. Each subdisk has its descriptor area. The files described by those descriptors use data blocks preferably within the same region. A separate free-block structure would be appropriate for each subdisk.

If we want file descriptors to be recognizable, it is wise to make them all the same size no matter how large the file they represent. In that way the salvaging operation can be sure of the location of all file descriptors. Some of the information we might store in the file descriptor has a constant size: access rights (assuming that we divide the users into a fixed number of well-defined groups), creation time, time of last backup, expiration date (for automatic deletion), number of aliases (for reclamation after deletion from a directory), and file type. In contrast, pointers to the blocks that hold the file contents might require any amount of space. For the following discussion, we will assume that the file is constructed in extents, each of which comprises a number of contiguous blocks. We need to store the length and starting block for each extent.

One organization is to place length and starting-block information for the first extent in the file descriptor and to reserve space in each extent to describe the next one. This linked organization is fine for sequential access but clumsy for direct access.

Alternatively, the file descriptor could contain information about every extent. However, it would be wasteful to allocate enough overhead space in each file descriptor for the largest possible file. Instead, a fixed number of pointers may be stored and an indirect scheme used if the file is larger. Most files are very short. (A recent study at the University of Wisconsin showed that about 42 percent of all files on a Unix installation for a research community fit within one block, and 73 percent fit within five blocks. A similar study at Los Alamos Scientific Laboratory showed that half the files were smaller than 40K bytes, whereas many files reached 10M bytes or larger.)   We might therefore limit the storage in the file descriptor to describe ten extents, for example. If extents can be arbitrary in size, we are able to represent very large files this way, but if extents are typically one block long, we

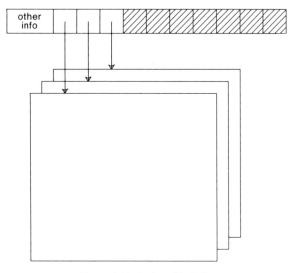

**Figure 6.11**  A three-block file

can deal only with relatively short files.

Figure 6.11 shows the format of such a file descriptor. The descriptor has room for a ten-block file. The particular file it represents uses only three blocks. For simplicity, the figure omits all the other information that might be stored in the descriptor.

If a file grows too large for the file descriptor, we could reorganize it, at some cost, to collapse some of its extents. That is, we could try to find free space on the disk large enough to hold two or more extents of the file. We would copy those extents into the free space and modify the descriptor appropriately.

If extents are required to be the same length (for example, one block), restructuring will not work. Instead, we could provide **overflow file descriptors** that contain more pointers. The file descriptor could use the first nine pointers for the file itself and, if necessary, use the tenth pointer to point not to the next extent of the file but to the first overflow descriptor. This overflow descriptor could be a full block. Assuming that we need two 2-byte integers for each extent (one for the size, one for the pointer), we could fit another 128 extents in each overflow descriptor. The last one could again be reserved for overflow.

Figure 6.12 shows a descriptor for a file that requires 13 blocks. The overflow descriptor as shown has slots for 56 extents. Only 4 are in use. The last slot, if needed, would point to yet another overflow descriptor.

The structure just described works very well for sequential access, in which the entire file is read from start to finish. When the file is opened, the file manager can read the file descriptor into main store and use its information to direct the input of the first nine extents. Then the manager can read the overflow file descriptor into main store and continue the input. In fact, most very long files are read in exactly this fashion. They are typically load images for large programs or data files created sequentially by one program to be read sequentially by another.

However, long files used as databases are often accessed in non-sequential fashion. As we saw, the Position service call might indicate the exact byte of the file that is to be accessed next. If this call is used, our use of extents and overflow file descriptors has two shortcomings.

- To find out which block holds any given byte in the file, we must first calculate which extent holds that byte. This calculation requires repeated inspection of the extent entries in the descriptor because each extent may have a different size.
- If many overflow descriptors are used, seeking a great distance in the file may require many disk operations to read all the overflow file descriptors between the current location and the desired location.

These problems can be addressed by a slight change in organization of the file descriptor. First, we can demand that all extents have the same length. Next, we can organize the file descriptor as a tree, not as a linked list. The tree has a depth determined by the size of the file; the depth is indicated in one of the fixed locations in the file descriptor. A depth-1 tree just uses the entries in the descriptor as direct pointers to extents. Figure 6.11 is a depth-1 tree. It has ten entries; therefore,

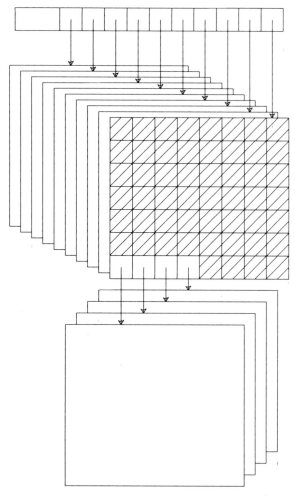

**Figure 6.12** A 13-block file

depth-1 trees may use up to ten extents.

A depth-2 tree treats *each* entry in the descriptor as a pointer to an overflow descriptor, which is full of direct pointers to extents. If overflow descriptors can hold 128 pointers, such files may use up to 1280 extents. A depth-3 tree treats those overflow descriptors as indirect pointers yet again. Such files have $10 \times 128 \times 128 = 163,840$ extents.

Let's assume that we have a depth-3 tree representing an enormous file and we wish to find the block that has byte 1,000,000. Since there are 512 bytes in a block, we want byte 64 of block 1953. (The first block is given the number 0.) Since each entry in the file descriptor is the root of a subtree of blocks that includes $128 \times 128 = 16,384$ blocks, the block we want is in the first subtree. We now read the overflow descriptor pointed to by the first entry in the file descriptor. Since each of its 128 entries governs 128 blocks, we want the 33rd block in the 16th entry. We read the overflow block pointed to by the 16th entry. Its 33d block is the one we want. We have accessed a particular byte with four disk accesses. Some of these accesses may have been avoided by cache hits because the disk driver caches recently used disk blocks in main store.

Our new organization does have its costs. If we do not know how long a file will be when it is created, we will have to assume it needs only a one-level tree. When it outgrows those limits, the organization must be changed, rearranging entries (although not recopying any data blocks). One way to avoid this rearrangement is to let the first seven entries always be direct pointers. The eighth could head a two-level tree, the ninth a three-level tree, and the tenth a four-level tree. This scheme is pictured in Figure 6.13, which only begins to suggest how huge the file can grow.

## 6.3 Disk layout

The disk is divided into different regions that serve different purposes. As we have mentioned, subdisks can be built to promote clustering. Subdisks also allow administrators to segregate files pertaining to different projects and to limit the amount of disk space each project uses. File descriptors occupy fixed locations on each subdisk. The root of a multilevel directory structure should be easy to find. One easy way to do that is to let the first descriptor in file descriptor space

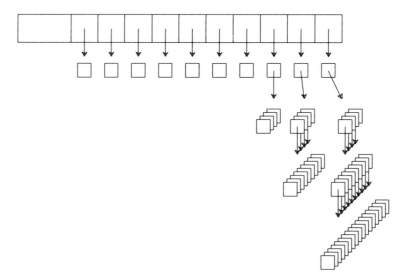

**Figure 6.13** A huge file

represent the root directory. In a flat or two-level structure, the main directory must be similarly easy to find.

When the operating system is started, it must be able to tell the structure of the disk by examining the disk itself. A **disk descriptor** could be stored at a fixed location (for example, block 0) that indicates how many subdisks there are and how many blocks of file descriptor are stored on each subdisk. It would also include the bit map of free tracks, free cylinders, or free blocks. As we have seen, free blocks might be arranged in a linked list or a tree; pointers to this structure belong in the disk descriptor. The disk descriptor might be stored in several places on the disk, because if the disk develops a flaw, some blocks may become unreadable. It is a disaster if the only copy of the disk descriptor becomes unreadable.

When a disk is formatted, bad sectors are detected by the disk controller and may be sequestered so that they are no longer addressable. Occasionally, sectors become bad after formatting. These sectors may be placed in a "bad-sector file," which is otherwise never accessed and is not placed in any directory. In this way, bad sectors are placed out of harm's way. Fancy archiving programs that read sectors directly from the disk without going through directories must be aware of the bad-sector file to avoid reading it.

## 6.4 Multiple disks

Even personal computers often have several disks. Each disk can have its own independent set of files, in which case the absolute file name can include a disk specification. For example, in MS-DOS an absolute file name starts with the name of the disk. For example, one could name a file `A:patish.mod` to indicate that it is on disk A. If the current working directory is `A:`, then there is no need to use the absolute name.

On large installations, where there may be many disks, it is an inconvenience to remember where each file resides. Instead, all the disks can be treated as a single set of files. For concreteness, we will assume that a hierarchical file structure is in use. We can imagine various ways to distribute the hierarchy across disks. These methods range from very fine grain to very course.

The finest grain method allows individual files to cross disk boundaries. Each pointer to a data block includes both the disk identifier and the block number. The list of free blocks also spans disks. This idea is depicted in Figure 6.14. This method has decided advantages: Mammoth files such as file 3 can be stored, even though no one disk can hold them, and sequential access can be extremely fast, since seeks on some disks can overlap transfers on others. However, all pointers to disk blocks are longer, and a single failed disk can make almost all files unreadable. Furthermore, disks such as floppies cannot be dismounted, since they no longer hold an independent set of files. If we were to remove disk C, not only would file 1 disappear, but also part of file 3.

At the other extreme, we can require that each disk be a self-contained subtree of the file hierarchy. Such course-grain division is used by Unix. It is shown in Figure 6.15. Each of the three disks shown has its own directory structure.

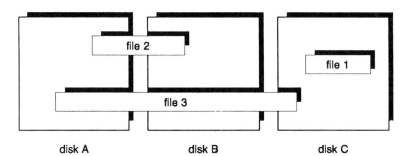

disk A                      disk B                      disk C

**Figure 6.14** Files crossing disk boundaries

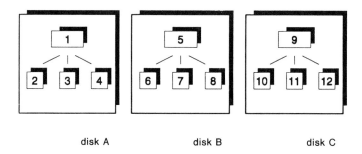

disk A                      disk B                      disk C

**Figure 6.15** Subdirectories crossing disk boundaries

When the operating system is first started, only one disk, let's say disk A, is used. Only files 1 (the root directory), 2, 3, and 4 can be accessed. However, the other disks can be **mounted** into the hierarchy by means of a service call:

☐   **Mount(device,file name).** This call updates the mount table in the file manager. Each entry in the table gives the device number (such as disk B) and the index of the file descriptor associated with the given file name (for example, file descriptor 2). Every access to a file descriptor is first checked against the table; if the file descriptor is listed there, the file descriptor for the root of the mounted device is used instead. As a result, the contents of the file mentioned in the Mount call are no longer accessible.

For example, if a process mounts disk B onto file 2 and then mounts disk C onto file 8, the virtual file structure looks like Figure 6.16. File 2 has been replaced by file 5, which is a directory leading to other files. The old contents of file 2 are hidden. Mounting disks is usually performed by a startup process during initialization. However, disks can be mounted later; this facility is especially useful for

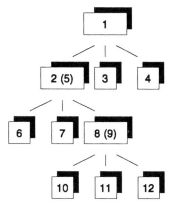

**Figure 6.16** Result of mounting disks

dismountable units like floppies. Before a dismountable disk is physically removed, the file manager must be informed by a dismount service call.

☐ **Dismount(device)**. This call writes any remaining write-behind blocks to the device and removes the appropriate entry from the mount table. The contents of the file mentioned in the Mount call are again available.

Mounting disks introduces novel security problems. Until a disk is mounted, it is just a device, which in Unix can be accessed as a single device file. While it is in that state, anyone who can access that special file can modify its data, introducing new access rights and changing ownerships of the files it contains. In Unix, the problem is particularly severe because a malicious user can set the rights on a load image for the command interpreter so that it is owned by the "superuser," an extremely privileged subject. It is also possible to set the permissions on that file so that when it runs, it acquires the rights of its owner. Then the user can mount the disk, execute that command interpreter, and be as powerful as the superuser. For this reason, Unix usually allows only the superuser to call Mount or modify unmounted disks.

## 6.5 Multiple machines

If several machines are connected by a network, files can often be accessed across machines. A network-wide file name includes its machine name. For example, in DECnet, a file /a/b on machine George would be named George::/a/b. When a process accesses a file with a remote name, messages must be sent to a server on the remote machine to open the file there and to access it on behalf of the local process. Discovering that a file name is remote and negotiating with the remote machine can be one of the functions of the file manager (as in VMS), or it could reside outside the kernel in library routines linked into programs that wish such access.

Just as mounting disks is an elegant way to simplify organizing files on several disks, **remote mounting** simplifies organizing files on several machines. One good example is the Network File Server (NFS), developed by Sun Microsystems for Unix. Instead of a local device, the Mount service call can specify a remote directory, that is, a directory in some cooperating machine's file space. Of course, the remote machine has the option of refusing to service such a request, and this decision can be based on the particular directory that is being mounted and the identity of the requesting machine. Once a remote directory has been mounted, users of the local machine see a virtual file hierarchy that includes all the files in that remote directory. Whenever the local file manager needs a block from a remote machine, it sends a request across a communication line to the remote machine.

Figure 6.17 shows a typical arrangement of files across three cooperating machines. Each machine has a disk that is used for the initial file system (here, disks A, C, and E). These disks have very similar or even identical files. Each machine also has a larger disk that holds files unique to that machine (disks B, D, F). Each machine mounts disk B onto file 2, disk D onto file 3, and disk F onto file 4. The result is that everyone on these three machines sees an identical extended file hierarchy. In fact, if accounts are the same on all three machines, users can log onto any machine that happens to be most convenient. Of course, the installation managers can decide to mount disks in a much less symmetric fashion.

Mounting disks remotely exacerbates the security problem that we touched on earlier. NFS defines the access rights of a subject making a remote access to be identical to the rights for local access. That is, a single subject can own files on various machines, and those files may be accessed as if they were local. Therefore, even if accounts are not identical on all machines, user identifiers must be unique across machines. It would be disastrous for two individuals, having accounts on machine 1 and machine 2 respectively, to have the same user identifier: They would each have rights over the other's files. Anyone who has superuser privilege on one machine automatically has it on all machines. For this reason, NFS makes an exception to its rule and treats the superuser as an ordinary subject with respect to remote files.

## 6.6 Implementing transactions

Implementing synchronization and failure atomicity is not easy. We will not give a very detailed explanation here but will present some of the fundamental mechanisms that are used. To implement syncrhonization atomicity, the transaction manager may place a shared-access lock on files as they are opened for reading and an exclusive-access lock on files as they are opened for writing. (Instead of locking files, we can lock disks, directories, file records, or file bytes.) If the new lock conflicts with an existing lock held by some other transaction, the transaction manager blocks the transaction that needs the new lock. These locks may be stored

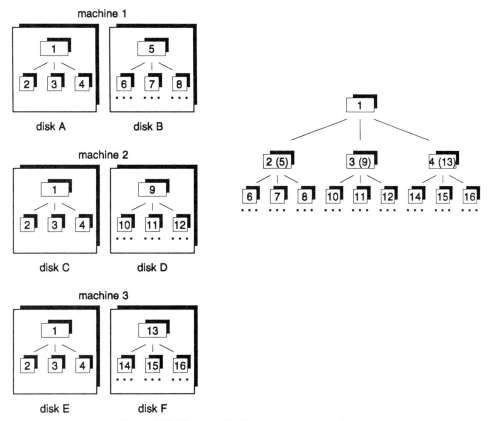

**Figure 6.17**  Network File System with three machines

in the file descriptor by recording the transaction identifiers of the holders of the lock. The **two-phase locking** policy requires that all locks created by a transaction be maintained until the transaction is finished opening and closing files. (During phase one, locks are acquired; during phase two, they are released.) This policy assures synchronization atomicity. However, the fact that Open can block leads to a possibility of deadlock, so the transaction manager must be willing to **abort** a transaction.

To implement failure atomicity, every time a change is made to a file, the state of the file before the transaction started may be saved. There are various ways to save the previous state. One is to start a new file version every time a change is made; the version is based on the time when the transaction started. If the transaction aborts, the previous version can be used. Alternatively, all changes can be recorded in a **log** that includes the old state of the file before the change.

A third alternative is to store all changes on fresh disk blocks. Those disk blocks are linked into the file descriptor only when the transaction is ready to complete. The list of operations needed to modify file descriptors is called an **intentions**

**list**. Once the transaction is ready to complete, the intentions list is written. The transaction is then marked as **committed**. After this point, no failure will prevent completion of the transaction. The intentions are then performed. If the operating system should crash, it will redo the intentions when it starts up again. The intentions must be posed in such a way that doing the same one many times has the same effect as doing it once.

Correct implementation of transactions is complicated by the possibility that the disk might fail. One way to make the disk more reliable is to build **stable storage**, which contains readable data even if the disk should fail in the middle of a write operation. Stable storage can be implemented by using two disk blocks. Writing to stable storage involves writing the same information to both blocks. Reading may use either one. If the disk fails during a write operation, only one of those blocks can be injured; the other one holds either the original data or the properly modified data. If the failure happens between the two writes, the one written first is believed. Stable storage can be used for any sensitive information. It is usually too costly to use for entire files, but it might be used for directory structures, logs, and intentions lists.

If a transaction modifies files on several disks, there is a danger that some disks will commit, but others will fail at the last minute and therefore maintain the old versions. The resulting chaos violates failure atomicity. To prevent this calamity, the **two-phase commit** (not to be confused with two-phase locking) policy first writes the intentions lists on all the disks (phase one), commits the transaction, and then starts performing the intentions (phase two). A disk failure during phase one aborts the entire transaction. A failure during phase two causes no harm; the intentions will be performed later when the disk is restored, since they are in stable storage.

# 7  PERSPECTIVE

The file manager must provide an acceptable level of service for a wide range of applications. Some file managers accomplish this goal by providing a very simple but efficient service and expect that complex applications can build on it. For example, one can make a case for the idea that a flat file space of sequential, direct-access files with minimal access restrictions is acceptable for many applications and is an adequate base for extension to other applications.

Other file managers accomplish the goal by providing many kinds of service. For example, a process might have a choice of half a dozen file types and allocation strategies at the time it creates a file. The file manager supports all these options as efficiently as it can. Such a file manager might actually implement a simple base structure and build alternative structures on top of that base.

Database management systems are the most difficult to serve well. They structure data and access it in regular ways, but few file managers are equipped to take advantage of those regularities. For example, we examined storing huge files in depth-3 trees and were pleased that a direct access required no more than four disk accesses. However, if the huge file is storing a database, the database is likely to contain internal pointers. These pointers might be expressed in terms of bytes from the start of the file. Following such a pointer requires about four read operations. If the pointers were expressed in physical block number, each would need only one read operation. The structure used by the file manager effectively decreases efficiency by a factor of 4. For this reason, database programs like to avoid the file abstraction and prefer to deal directly with physical addresses.

The internal structure of the file manager can be built in the following layers.

- **File layer**: This module creates a data structure for each open file. The data structure includes the file descriptor and the read/write mark. Procedures in this module open and close files on behalf of processes that submit the Open and Close service calls. The directory in which a file resides must be opened for a short time in order to find out where the file descriptor is. If the file is named by a path, each directory in the path must be opened for a short time.

- **Byte layer**: This module provides procedures for reading or writing any number of bytes from or to any open file. These procedures consult the open-file structure to determine which disk block is involved in each transput. They also modify the read/write mark. These procedures are called by the Read, Write, and Position service calls. They are also called by procedures in the file layer that need to read directories.

- **Block layer**: This module provides procedures to read and write entire blocks. A cache of recently used blocks may be maintained so that successive operations to the same block do not require disk actions. This layer is the upper layer of the disk driver.

Each layer smooths out chunkiness created by the lower levels and produces new structures, as suggested by the Beautification Principle. In the case of files, we can start with the atomic level, where the disk surface is composed of discrete components (iron atoms, for example). At the aggregate level, these discontinuities are evened out, and we consider each disk surface to be essentially uniform and continuous. The disk controller introduces structures by collecting together several platters and subdividing each into tracks, sectors, and bytes. The block layer flattens this hierarchy, leaving only an array of disk blocks, each composed of a fixed number of bytes. The byte layer hides disk blocks and the file-descriptor structures in order to introduce byte streams. The file layer organizes these streams of bytes into chunks called files. Finally, directories convert a linear array of files (indexed by their descriptor numbers) into a tree structure.

We can demonstrate these layers of the file manager by tracing their actions when a process executes the following program:

```
1 procedure Example;
2 var
3     MyFile : FileNumber;
4 begin
5     MyFile := Open("/a/b",ToWrite);
6     Position(MyFile,700); -- skip the first part of the file
7     Write(MyFile,"testing",7); -- seven characters
8     Close(MyFile);
9 end Example;
```

(1)     The Open call (line 5) causes a context switch to the kernel, which calls the file layer of the file manager to open this file.

(2)     The file layer needs to open / (the root directory) to find file /a, which is itself a directory. This action involves asking the block layer to bring in the file descriptor for /. By convention, we use descriptor 0 for this file. The file layer can calculate which disk block contains descriptor 0 by referring to the disk descriptor, which should be kept in main store at all times. Let us pretend that disk block 10 is needed.

(3)     The block layer checks the cache of file blocks to see if block 10 is currently in main store. If so, this layer returns immediately, passing back a pointer to where in main store it has cached block 10. In our situation, a cache hit is very likely, because block 10 is used extremely frequently. If there is a cache miss, the block layer selects some cache entry to be overwritten (based, for example, on an LRU strategy). If the entry it has chosen is dirty, it must first write out that entry. While the necessary transput is in progress, the block layer places the current process on a device-wait list and queues the appropriate read (and write) request to the lower part of the disk driver. Other processes are allowed to run until the lower part of the disk driver has finished writing, if necessary, and then reading in block 10. Then the calling process, still executing in privileged state inside the block layer, returns to the file layer. It passes back a pointer to the main store where block 10 has been read into the cache. We will ignore how the block layer performs its job from now on.

(4)     The file layer reads the descriptor for / from block 10. It determines that the caller has the necessary access privileges by checking the Permissions field of the descriptor. From here on, we will ignore all privilege checks. The file layer now creates a temporary open-file descriptor for /. Here is a possible format for an open-file descriptor.

```
10 type
11     OpenFileDescriptor =
12         record
13             Descriptor : ^FileDescriptor; { points into disk-block cache }
14             Mark : integer; { the next byte to be read or written }
15             Mode : (ToRead, ToWrite, ToReadWrite);
16         end
17 end;
```

In our case, Descriptor (line 13) points into the disk-block cache where the file descriptor has been read, Mark (line 14) starts at 0, and Mode (line 15) is set ToRead.

Let us assume that a file entry in a directory is always 20 bytes long. The file layer now calls the byte layer to read the first 20 bytes from / and store them in a 20-byte data structure (let us call it an entry descriptor) allocated for this purpose:

```
18 type
19    EntryDescriptor =
20       record
21          Name : array [0..15] of char;
22             FileDescriptorNumber : integer; { 4 bytes }
23       end;
```

(5) The byte layer, referring to the open-file descriptor for /, asks the block layer to fetch the first block (say 512 bytes) of /. It then copies the first 20 bytes to the entry descriptor, updates the file's read mark, and returns to the file layer. If it had been asked for bytes that span several blocks, it would have asked the block layer for each required block in turn and copied the relevant information. If the file is large enough so the file descriptor (line 13) is insufficient to point to all the blocks, the byte layer can ask the block layer to read in overflow file descriptors. We will ignore how the byte layer works from now on.

(6) Upon reading the entry descriptor, the file layer may discover that it does not describe /a but rather some other file, such as % or ^ . In that case, the file layer repeatedly asks the byte layer for another 20 bytes from / until it finds an entry describing /a. If it fails, the Open call was invalid, and an error return is taken to the process.

(7) Having found a directory entry for /a, the file layer releases the temporary open-file descriptor for / and opens a new one for /a in a similar fashion.

(8) The file layer follows a similar course until it has created an open-file descriptor for /a/b, set to allow writing (line 15). The write mark (line 14) is initialized to 0. All temporary open-file descriptors are released by now. The index of this open-file descriptor is passed back to the calling process to use as a file number.

(9) The process next submits a Position service call (line 6). The kernel forwards this call to the byte layer, which advances the write mark (line 14) to position 700.

(10) The process submits a Write service call (line 7). The byte layer asks the block layer to read in the second block of file /a/b, since the write mark (line 14) indicates that this is the appropriate block. This block now appears in the cache of file blocks. The byte layer then copies 7 characters from the virtual space of the calling process into the cache copy and marks the copy as "dirty." This block will eventually be cleaned by being copied back to the disk.

(11) The process submits a Close service call (line 8). The file layer releases the open-file descriptor for the file.

We have ignored a few details here, such as how we ensure that the block layer does not discard one of its cached blocks while it is still in use by a higher layer, how room is made for overflow file descriptors when the byte layer needs to bring them in, what happens if the file was only 400 bytes long at the outset, and what is different if the file is not stored on disk at all, but on a magnetic tape.

# 8 FURTHER READING

General discussions of file systems may be found in most of the textbooks cited at the end of Chapter 1. Individual file systems are discussed in a number of articles. The CAP filing system (Needham and Birrell, 1977) is designed for the Cambridge CAP computer (Needham and Walker, 1977), whose architecture supports capabilities directly. The Intel 432 computer also supports capabilities directly; its operating system, iMAX-432, takes advantage of that feature in its file structures (Pollack *et al.*, 1981). In the Demos file system for the Cray-1 computer, the file manager is a process instead of a module in the kernel (Powell, 1977). Pilot, an operating system for a personal computer (Redell *et al.*, 1980), has a flat directory structure, allows physical disks to be added and removed, provides mapped file access, and uses a label for each block that describes its use to promote salvaging.

**File servers** are machines dedicated to providing a file system for a collection of autonomous computers. Some file servers that have been described in the literature are WFS (Swinehart *et al.*, 1979), Felix (Fridrich and Older, 1981), the Xerox distributed file system (Mitchell and Dion, 1982), and the Cambridge file server (Birrell and Needham, 1980).

Several studies of file sizes have been reported, including one for the Los Alamos Scientific Laboratory (Powell, 1977) and for a Tops-10 installation in an academic environment (Satyanarayanan, 1981).

Database management is a large subject with close ties to the subject of operating systems. The special operating-system requirements of database management are discussed by Gray (1979) and Stonebraker (1981). Bernstein (1981) discusses a great number of implementations of transactions for databases.

We have shown only one way to organize the levels of a file manager. Other ways are given by Calingaert (1982), Shaw (1974), and Peterson and Silberschatz (1985).

# 9 EXERCISES

1. Implement a file system by using a normal file of length 10K bytes as a virtual disk. Your program should be built in several layers:

- **Directory control**: creates and deletes files and directories
- **File transput**: opens, closes, reads, writes, positions, and searches directories
- **Buffered transput**: Caches recently-used blocks
- **Basic transput**: Reads and writes one block.

For simplicity, you can make these assumptions: (a) There is only one user. (b) There are no aliases, either direct or indirect. (c) There is no file protection. (d) Time stamps are not needed in the file descriptor. (e) A file only has one version. To make the problem interesting, do implement hierarchical directories and direct access.

2. John makes a file called `JFile`. Deborah makes an alias for `JFile`, called `DFile`. John deletes `JFile`. Then John creates a new file, also called `JFile`. How many different files are there at the end of this scenario? Would the answer be different if Deborah had made an indirect file called `DFile` that pointed to `JFile`?

3. Distinguish between an **alias** and an **indirect file**.

4. Does it make sense to make an indirect file that points to a non-existent file?

5. What is the difference between a **local** file name and a **relative** file name?

6. Give five *different* full path names for the `slide1.text` file in the example in the text. There are no aliases in the example. (*Hint*: Use `%` and `^`.)

7. Assume that we allow introducing aliased names for directories. What problems can occur?

8. The text mentions default permissions for files and suggests both a "positive" default (permissions that all files automatically receive) and a "negative" default (permissions that all files automatically do not receive). Compare how well these two methods work for building executable files.

9. Give one good reason to prevent file owners from automatically having the SetOwner privilege over their files.

10. Suggest a reason why someone might want to build a directory over which others have Execute but not Read privilege.

11. We treat a relative file name in an indirect file as relative to the directory in which the indirect file resides. What would be wrong with treating it as relative to the working directory instead?

12. What does it mean to delete a directory that still has files in it?

13. What does it mean to delete a directory that is the working directory for some process?

14. Show a simple way to build a cycle of indirect files.

15. Why do indirect files have a problem of cycles but aliases do not? (Assume that both indirect files and aliases apply only to ordinary files, not to directories.)

16. If we use the ruler-function method of saving files, what is the average length of time a file is saved after it is deleted?

17. What criteria are important in evaluating a file-dump schedule?

18. Assume that we use the ruler-function method of saving files. A file is created on day $c$ and deleted on day $d$. It is now day $n$. Give a formula or algorithm for finding the tape that holds the most recent copy of this file.

19. In most versions of Unix, the file manager does not try to prevent simultaneous access to a shared file. Show how co-operating programs could still avoid simultaneous access. (*Hint*: Use an auxiliary empty file.) What happens if a process terminates unexpectedly?

20. The text suggests that free blocks may be arranged as a tree with a large fan-out. What advantage does this structure have over arranging free space as a singly linked list, which is a tree with a very small fan-out?

21. Why should we use cylinder and track maps for allocation of files whose length we know beforehand? Wouldn't a linked list or a tree of free blocks be better?

22. When a tree of free blocks is used, each time a free block becomes allocated, its contents must be saved, or else pointers to other free blocks are lost. The amount of saved information can grow very large. Suggest a structure intermediate between a large fan-out tree and a linked list that makes this problem disappear.

23. Should overflow file descriptors be placed in a well-known region of the disk for the scavenger to find?

24. Assume that I have a file that has 50 million bytes. How many 512-byte blocks does it take to store the data? How many blocks of file descriptor or overflow file descriptor are needed, under the following three assumptions?
(a) We use a linear chain of overflow descriptors.
(b) We use a tree of overflow descriptors of the appropriate depth.
(c) We have seven direct pointers, one indirect pointer, one doubly indirect pointer, and one triply indirect pointer in the file descriptor.

25. You are designing disk structures for files with versions. Two versions are identical except that the later version has an extra byte near the beginning. What structure is appropriate if you want to share blocks between these two versions? Comment on whether you think this structure is worth the effort.

26. Proper treatment of locks can be summed up as follows: Each file must be locked before it is accessed, and it should not be unlocked until the transaction has finished all accesses to that file. Why is the second clause important? Isn't it enough to make sure the file is locked *during* each access?

27. Why is copy on write especially appropriate for implementing file versions when the file manager supports mapped access?

28. If we implement copy on write, what extra data must be stored in the file descriptors and data blocks of files in order to avoid unnecessary splitting and to postpone reclaiming a disk block until all the versions that use it have been deleted?

# The User Interface

We have seen how operating systems satisfy the Resource and Beautification Principles and thereby provide resources and services to *processes*. We will now change our perspective to see how the operating system satisfies these principles to provide resources and services to *users*. In particular, we will look at how a user can specify what programs to run and how they should be treated. We will also mention a number of programs that are packaged with most operating systems to provide an environment in which users can get their work done.

It is not easy to draw a line separating the operating system from extraneous programs that happen to be running under that operating system. One attitude we could take is that the operating system includes only those functions that can be accessed through service calls or through interrupts. Figure 3.23 places these functions in the kernel. Most of this chapter is irrelevant to operating systems defined in this narrow way. The attitude at the other extreme is that the operating system includes every program running on the computer. In that case, a full discussion of operating systems must describe all the algorithms that might be programmed; that would certainly encompass all of computer science.

We will take an intermediate stance. The term "operating system" will include all the standard programs that are included in any distribution of the software. We can distinguish **kernel** software, which requires hardware privileges to perform its functions; **essential utilities**, which may not require privilege but which every user needs and which determine the user's view of the operating system; and **optional utilities**, which are useful programs that users may wish to use on occasion.

Different operating systems make these distinctions in different ways. For some, like Multics, kernel software is itself divided into layers. Command interpretation (discussed in this chapter), an essential utility on some operating systems, is an optional utility under Unix. The file manager (discussed at great length in

Chapter 6) can be considered either as part of the kernel or as an essential utility.

This chapter deals primarily with functions provided by the operating system either as essential or as optional utilities. Essential utilities shape the user's view of the operating system because they dictate how the user can interact with the computer. Optional utilities also loom large in the user's view, not because they are forced on the user but because the functions they provide are often not duplicated by alternative programs, so anyone who wants to use the operating system must learn the interface to many optional utilities as well.

# 1 THE COMMAND INTERPRETER

A **command language** lets the user tell the operating system what to do. It is built of a number of **commands**. The language can be interpreted by a utility process that converts commands into appropriate service calls. Instead of a utility process, a module in the kernel may interpret the commands and directly call routines to accomplish whatever the user requests. Whichever way command languages are interpreted, we will call the software that interprets commands the **command interpreter**. Operating systems may use other names for the command interpreter, such as "monitor" and "shell."

User requests to the operating system usually have two components: what programs to invoke and what their environment should be. A **program** is a set of instructions packaged in such a way that a process can be started to run them. Programs, as we have seen, are often stored in files as load images. They become processes when they are **invoked** either directly through service calls or indirectly by commands. Many invocations of a single program may exist at the same time, each in a different process. Heavily used optional utilities such as the text editor, text formatter, and compilers often have several invocations simultaneously active.

The **environment** of a process is what distinguishes it from other invocations of the same program. The environment includes where input data will come from (which file or which device), where output data are to be placed, and parameters that give extra information to programs and enable optional features.

For example, assume that the user wants to compile a Pascal program. The command or set of commands might specify the following:

- Which compiler to use
- Where the Pascal source program is stored
- Where to store the resulting load image
- Whether or not to run the resulting program
- Whether to generate a listing
- Whether to issue warnings for non-standard usages.

Only the first of these specifications describes the program to be run. The others all describe the environment for the program.

Whether the operating system is used in a batch mode or an interactive mode, commands specify exactly what the user wishes. The advantage of the interactive mode is that mistakes are easy to repair immediately. For example, a malformed command produces an error message in either mode, but in interactive mode the next command usually has not yet been entered, so a revised version of the previous command can be entered instead. In a batch mode, each command assumes that all the earlier ones were executed correctly; error contingencies must be explicitly expected and dealt with as part of the commands themselves.

Since there is such a similarity between the requirements of batch and interactive use, a number of interactive command interpreters have been developed by modifying earlier batch command interpreters. A tendency in the other direction has also occurred: Interactive command interpreters often have a batch component, which allows users to submit work now that is to be executed later or allows a number of related commands to be packaged together to be interpreted as one larger command. We will describe these **command scripts** later.

## 1.1 Invoking programs and establishing environments

The easiest way to specify a program is to name the file that contains its load image. Since it may be awkward to state the full file name, conventions may be used to make standard programs easier to invoke. For example, one or more default directories may be established for commonly used programs. The local name of a file in these directories suffices to invoke it. If more than one default directory exists, they are searched in some order. For example, each user may have a personal program directory. That one might be searched before the directory that includes optional utilities, which may in turn be searched before the directory containing software built by the local community. If a name is found in one of these directories, but for some reason the program cannot be run (the user does not have the necessary access rights, for example), either the next directory could be searched or the request could fail.

The environment can be established in a global or a local fashion. A global environment setting persists until it is changed; a local setting applies only to a single process. As an example of a global setting, we might establish that whenever a program opens a file `input`, the actual file should be `firstrun.data`. We may have several processes that are all to use the same data, so setting this global association allows each of these programs to run in the desired environment. Another global environment setting might dictate that all files created by processes are to have an initial disk allocation of three tracks, with an additional extent of one track whenever the allocation overflows. As another example, we may wish to limit all processes to use less than 15 seconds.

Global environment settings are typically made through commands that have a declarative character. A reasonable syntax would start each with the keyword `set`. The examples shown above might have this sort of appearance:

```
set association input firstrun.data
set disk allocation 3 1 { three tracks for initial extent, 1 for others }
set cpulimit 15
```

Associated with each `set` command might be a `show` command that asks the command interpreter to display the current setting of the environment.

If the command interpreter is a utility process, it might translate these declarations into service calls that modify the information in its context block. When it then asks the kernel to start a process, the new process might **inherit** these settings. Alternatively, the command interpreter might store global environment information in its own tables. When it starts a new process, it would tell the kernel not only which program to invoke but also what the global environment for that process should be.

Local environment settings might have a similar syntax. Often, local settings are used to give extra information to the process or to select an optional behavior. Such settings often take the form of **parameters**, which are optional additions to the command line that invokes the process. For example, we might have a general-purpose data-transfer facility called "Transfer." The following are some different invocations of Transfer with different parameters:

```
1.  transfer work.text work.save.text
2.  transfer #c work.text work.save.text
3.  transfer #r work.text work.save.text
4.  transfer #d work.text
5.  transfer #h #col=2 work.text /device/printer
```

The first call requests that a new file, `work.save.text`, be created with the contents copied from `work.text`. Both files are given as parameters that provide necessary information to Transfer. The second call is very similar, but an additional parameter, `#c`, is given. This parameter specifies the "careful" option, which tells Transfer not to create the new file if a file with that name already exists. Parameters that establish options are often called **flags**. The third call asks Transfer to *rename* the file instead of copying it. Perhaps the `#c` flag could be applied here, too. The fourth call does not request a transfer at all; it asks for the file `work.text` to be destroyed. The fifth call asks for the file to be copied to the printer, which is named by a full file name. The flags ask for a standard header to be printed along with the file (`#h`) and for 2-column output to be used in order to save paper (`#col=2`).

In each of these cases, the command interpreter might simply package all the parameters (flags as well as other parameters) and present them to Transfer as character strings without interpreting them at all. In that way, programs can define for themselves what a parameter should mean, and the command interpreter does not need to know anything about the multitude of flags that have meaning to different programs.

Parameters can be presented to the program by several routes.

- If the command interpreter is a process, it might send the parameters in a message to the new program. (We discuss messages in Chapter 9.)
- If the command interpreter is part of the kernel, the program can request parameters by service calls.
- The command interpreter can arrange for the new program to start with the parameters already stored in its virtual space. (We discuss starting new processes in Chapter 9.)

## 1.2 The User Principle

Command interpreters are designed to make the most common operations as easy as possible. This goal is a human-engineering equivalent of the Cache Principle.

| **User Principle** |
| --- |
| Operations that are performed frequently should be especially easy to invoke. |

The designers of the command interpreter should try to predict and simplify common patterns of invocation.

The first example of the User Principle is the use of **default settings**. Programs are often written so that in the absence of special instructions, they do what the designers assume is the most natural, most frequently desired action. For example, most compilers on interactive operating systems will not create a listing file unless asked to because most users won't want it. However, creating a listing file is an option that can be added to the environment of the compiler process (typically through a flag). Another example is that the output of many programs in an interactive operating system is to the user's terminal. A change in the environment can redirect the output to, perhaps, a file or a printer.

A second example of the User Principle is the use of a simple **built-in shorthand** for a more complex operation. Some command interpreters have a list of standard commands that invoke optional utilities that have names unrelated to the command. For example, `edit` may be used to invoke the editor utility, whose real name might be something complex like `editor.utility`. `Delete` may be used to delete a file; the actual program invoked may be the Transfer program shown earlier, which can do far more than just delete files. The command interpreter forms the correct parameters for Transfer when given the command `delete`. The `list` command might invoke the same program Transfer with different parameters. This use of built-in shorthands frees the casual user from remembering the many flags available for programs like Transfer.

A third example of the User Principle is the **initialization file**. Heavily used programs tend to acquire a host of options, most of which are irrelevant to most users. The occasional user who wants to set an option may wish to do so every time the program is invoked. For example, many users will be happy with the normal prompt given by the command interpreter. Others will want a customized prompt. Most users may not want a feature in the text editor that automatically hyphenates text at the end of a line. A few will want it every time they use the editor. Such customization may be embedded in a file as a list of initialization settings. The name of the file is related to the name of the program. For example, initialization instructions for the text editor may be stored in a file called `editor.init`. Whenever the text editor is invoked, it first looks for such a file to initialize its options.

A fourth example of the User Principle is **automatic chaining**, which invokes a frequently needed sequence of programs with a single command. In many installations, such as university computing centers, users spend much of their time preparing programs. Some command interpreters provide a shorthand that combines compilation, linking, and execution of a program in one command. For example, a traffic simulation program written in Pascal might be compiled and executed by the command `run traffic`. The command interpreter would see that there is a file in the current working directory called, for example, `traffic.pas`, decide that the file is a Pascal source program, invoke the Pascal compiler in an environment that has the compiler place the output in `traffic.obj`, link in the Pascal run-time support routines to build `traffic.load`, and then invoke this last file as a process.

Sometimes the command interpreter is sophisticated enough to look for files and to compare their creation dates in order to invoke steps in this chain only if they are needed. For example, the user might delete `traffic.load` because it uses up too much precious disk space. A later `run traffic` invocation will not invoke the Pascal compiler at all but will just repeat the final link step before executing the program. If the user modifies `traffic.pas` (to add a feature, for example), then even though `traffic.load` exists, `run traffic` will cause the command interpreter to repeat the entire compilation and linking because the date on `traffic.obj` is earlier than `traffic.pas`, so a change must have been made.

Even the cleverest designers cannot predict all the shorthands that a particular user might want. For example, some users wish to compile all their Pascal programs with a flag that disallows non-standard features in Pascal. A packaged automatic-chain facility might be unable to provide this slightly out-of-the-ordinary service. The mechanism can sometimes be stretched, for example, by letting the automatic chain itself take parameters, which are in turn converted to other parameters that affect the individual steps in the chain. This solution tends to increase the number of available options and leads to obscurity.

An alternative solution is to let the user build an individual set of shorthands that accomplish whatever is desired. **Personalized shorthands** constitute a fifth example of the User Principle. For example, a user might always want `transfer` to have the `#fake` flag set. This flag tells Transfer to delete files in a safe fashion by moving them to a different directory instead of actually destroying them. The user might invent a personalized shorthand, `delete`, for this invocation. In the future, the command interpreter will accept `delete file` to mean `transfer #d #fake file`. Personalized shorthands can be established in the initialization file for the command interpreter.

Automatic chaining can also be personalized. This act leads to a sixth example of the User Principle. A user who repeatedly needs a particular sequence of actions might build a **command script** that contains the desired invocations. The command script can be invoked instead of the individual commands. For example, to prepare a complex program that contains several modules, the user might collect the commands necessary to compile each of the modules and then link them all together. Command scripts are typically stored in files. Some command interpreters can distinguish command scripts from load images and interpret the first but invoke the second.

Introduction of command scripts has had a strange effect on command languages; they have become more like programming languages. First, they have variables. These variables are used to hold strings that can be pieced together to form commands or can be inspected to influence what is done next. Second, they have control structures. Command scripts often need to repeat a set of operations once for each file in a set or until some condition is met. If an error occurs, the entire command script might need to terminate. The command script may take one action or another depending on some condition. Therefore, loop, exit, and conditional control constructs are common in command scripts. At the least, they have a way to determine if a program ends in error and to take appropriate action (such as termination) in that case. Third, they have procedures, insofar as they can invoke other command scripts and pass them parameters.

To maintain a uniform interface, designers of command languages often allow these same constructs to appear in normal commands presented directly to the command interpreter. It is unusual, but not unheard of, for a user to submit loop control constructs as part of ordinary interactive behavior. For example, a user may wish to make backup copies of all files. The following is a loop command that might be provided by a command interpreter:

```
foreach i in * do
    transfer i i.bak
end
```

Each iteration of the loop sets the control variable *i* to the name of a different file. If the files have names `Red`, `Green`, and `Blue`, this loop command is equivalent to

```
transfer Red Red.bak
transfer Green Green.bak
transfer Blue Blue.bak
```

The culmination of this tendency is to treat process control as purely a programming-language issue. One can use the same language for job control and for programming. This approach has some problems. First, interactive and non-interactive programming are different enough so that the same constructs are unlikely to be properly tailored for both. Second, non-interactive programs are read much more often than they are written, so a considerable percentage of the characters are present to make the program readable. Such a design is cumbersome when used interactively.

An interesting programming-language approach has been taken by a few operating systems, notably ITS (Incompatible Timesharing System, for the PDP-10) at Massachusetts Institute of Technology. The command interpreter and the program debugger are the same. The debugger has the ability to invoke programs and to interrupt, examine, and modify them; all these facilities can be useful to a command interpreter.

## 1.3 Interacting with programs

Once a process has been started, the command interpreter typically retires from the scene and does not resume execution until the process that has been started is finished. At that point, it might print completion statistics, such as how long the process ran and how much that execution cost or the fact that execution failed. If execution fails, the command interpreter may provide facilities for debugging, such as a main-store dump (typically useful in batch mode) or an error message. Different error messages might indicate that the process exceeded its allotted time, made an invalid service call, or tried to access an address outside its space.

In addition to starting processes and viewing their results, interactive users also need to manipulate their programs while they are running. Remarkably often, users submit requests that start programs that are not quite what the user intended. Perhaps some flags are accidentally omitted. Perhaps the compiler is invoked, and then the user remembers another change that should be made to the program. Perhaps the request is not particularly important (for example, viewing the current load on the operating system to find out why it seems slow today), and the user decides not to wait for it to complete. Interactive operating systems provide some form of "cancel" request that can be typed while programs are running. The effect is that the running process is terminated and the command interpreter resumes execution. The mechanism involved in terminating the process is often outside the control of the command interpreter; the device driver for the terminal notices the "cancel" character and forces the running process to stop. The command interpreter notices that the process has stopped and resumes its own execution. (If the command interpreter is a utility process, it might have executed a service call "wait for this process to stop.") We discuss process control more fully in Chapter 9.

Some operating systems allow a process to stop in such a way that it can be resumed later. This feature allows the user to alternate attention among several processes. For example, during program preparation the user frequently switches between editing and compiling. One process might be a text editor manipulating a Fortran program. When a change has been made to the program, the editor might be stopped, the `run` command given to the command interpreter, and the results of execution examined. Then the user could resume the editor and try to figure out why the program behaved the way it did. It is not necessary to reinvoke the editor, an action that might take much longer than resuming it.

Another example comes from inter-user mail. A user often reads new mail as part of the ritual of starting an interactive session. If an entry in the mailbox requires immediate attention, the user might stop the program that reads mail, direct attention to that pressing matter, then resume the program and read the rest of the mail.

It is not uncommon on such operating systems for one user to have five or ten processes, all but one of which are stopped. The command language might provide commands to list the stopped processes and to resume any one of them. One way to depict a particular process is to display the command that started it in the first place.

Under many operating systems, processes can be started either by the command interpreter or by other processes. This latter kind is not directly under the control of the command interpreter. For example, the user might type `transfer #d #fake #log file.old` to tell the Transfer program to delete `file.old` in the careful manner that copies it to another directory. The `#log` flag tells Transfer to record this action in a logging file. Instead of performing these operations sequentially, let us suppose that Transfer itself invokes two processes, one to move the file and the other to create a log entry. A single command has thereby created the beginnings of a *tree* of processes, which looks like Figure 7.1. In turn, "move" and "log" might generate other processes. This particular scenario is a bit forced, but remarkably many programs use other processes to do work for them under operating systems that allow this feature. The optional "sort" utility, which is used in many applications, is often invoked as a subprocess by such disparate programs as Transfer with the `#list` flag, which is asked to list all the files in the directory (sorted alphabetically) and "checkspelling," which might first sort all the words in the file that is to be checked, removing duplicates, in order to reduce the number of words that must be searched in the dictionary.

Process manipulation gains a new dimension when processes invoked from the command interpreter can sprout trees. What does it mean to "stop" a process? Since the command interpreter might not even know that the tree exists, it is likely that the only processes that can be directly mentioned to the command interpreter are the "top-level" ones, the ones that it started. If one of those is stopped, it is reasonable for the kernel to stop its entire tree. Alternatively, commands might allow the user to direct attention to any process in the tree and to manipulate just that process.

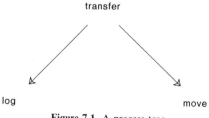

**Figure 7.1** A process tree

Interactive users often have two distinct modes of computer usage.

- Highly interactive, as is exhibited during text editing
- Batch-like, as is exhibited during compilation or while running long programs.

While a batch-like program is working, the user might well want to engage in some other, highly interactive work in order not to waste human time just because the computer is busy on the last command. To serve this need, many operating systems provide a **background** facility that allows a process to continue execution but to have the command interpreter resume without waiting for it to end. The command interpreter can now be used to start another process, perhaps a more interactive one.

Some operating systems, like RT-11 for the DEC PDP-11, allow at most one background process and one **foreground** (higher-priority, interactive) process. Other operating systems allow any number of background processes. (In VMS, the administrator may limit the number of background processes each user may have; in Unix, the limit is built into the installation.) It is even possible with some command interpreters to change the status of a process back and forth from background to foreground. (BSD4.2 Unix has this ability.) Background processes are usually not affected by the "cancel" or "stop" keys that the user might type. Instead, the command interpreter often provides explicit commands that have the same effect.

## 1.4  Advanced features

The list of command-language features supported under various operating systems is quite long; we cannot hope to cover all of them. However, a few words of introduction to some of the novel features appearing in relatively recent operating systems may be useful.

**Wild cards.**    We mentioned in the chapter on files that some programs accept a naming convention for files that allows several files to be specified with one name by having "don't care" or "wild card" entries in the name. The Transfer utility, for example, might understand  * in a file-name component to stand for anything. Thus, `transfer #list traffic.*` might generate a list of all files that have "traffic" in their first component.

The wild-card facility can be embedded in various places in the operating system.

- In the file server.
- In the command interpreter. Unix takes this approach. Processes that wish to convert wild-card names to ordinary file names start a command interpreter process that terminates after it performs the conversion.

- In particular utility processes, like Transfer. The Tops-10 operating system for the DEC PDP-10 takes this approach.

Wild cards can be generalized into file-name **patterns**, which might have ways to indicate individual-character wild cards, alternation (the "or" operator), and concatenation (the "place one pattern after the other" operator). Such patterns are applied to all the file names in a given set, typically the current working directory. For example, in the C-shell (one of several Unix command interpreters), one can build complex patterns like this:

```
[0-9A-F]{new,old}?text*
```

This pattern matches any file whose name starts with a hexadecimal digit, continues with either `new` or `old`, followed by any one character, followed by `text`, followed by anything. This pattern would match, for example, `Bold.textfile`.

## History.

A user often wants to submit the same command twice in a row, perhaps with some minor changes. For example, the user types `mail fred` to compose and send a message to Fred, decides in the middle that the message does not look right, cancels "mail," then types `mail fred` to start all over. Similarly, the user might type `mail fred` and then decide that Betsy should also get a copy of the message. In this case, the command `mail fred betsy` might have been more appropriate. It is very common for a complex command to be slightly misspelled. The user wants to fix the mistake and resubmit the command.

Under the User Principle, command interpreters should make it easy to refer to previous commands so they can be resubmitted, possibly with some changes. The device driver for the terminal might remember the previous line that was typed. When the user types the special "recall line" key, the device driver restores that line as if it were typed again. Intra-line editing might allow the user to fix any mistakes in the line before activating it with a carriage return. A very similar feature can be built into the terminals themselves to relieve the device driver of the complexity needed for this service.

The command interpreter can also store a **history** of previous commands. It can be asked to list those commands and to resubmit any of them, possibly with some modification. The BSD Unix and VMS command interpreters have a large repertoire of actions that use a history feature.

## Command completion.

It can be awkward for the user to type the entire name of a program or of a file, especially if the operating system allows long file names. The wild-card facility is a convenient way to avoid typing parts of the file name, but it can lead to ambiguities. Several files may meet the wild-card specification, but the user might intend only one of them.

A feature pioneered by Tenex and found in Tops-20 and in an alternative command interpreter for BSD Unix allows the user to specify as much of a file or program name as desired. When the user types the "please complete" key, the command interpreter finishes the command or file name. The algorithm used by the command interpreter depends on whether a command or a parameter is to be completed. In the former case, only legal commands are considered as acceptable completions. In the latter case, only file names are allowed.

If there is no legal way to complete the fragment or if there are two or more ways, the command interpreter signals an error (by ringing a bell). If the fragment can be unambiguously completed by a few more characters, but not to the very end, those few characters are added. The user can type another key to have the command interpreter list all the possible completions of the current fragment.

### Subordinate command interpreters.

If the operating system does not have a foreground/background scheme, it may still be possible for a user to start several unrelated activities. All that is needed is for one process to be able to start another and wait until it finishes. It is a common convention for interactive processes in Unix and Tenex to accept a command that starts a new command interpreter. A user interacting with process **A** who wishes to start process **B** might ask **A** to start up a new command interpreter. The new command interpreter may be asked to start **B**. Once **B** is done, a second request may be given to the new command interpreter. When the user is ready to return to **A**, the new command interpreter is told to terminate, and **A** is active again.

Figure 7.2 illustrates this situation. When the user first logs on, a command interpreter (number 1) starts. The user asks command interpreter 1 to start the mail program. The box around command interpreter 1 indicates that it is waiting for the mail program to finish. One of the messages the user reads suggests that some recently created software has a bug. To fix that bug, the user asks the mail program to start command interpreter 2. Until it finishes, the mail program is waiting, as indicated by the box around it.

The user first tells command interpreter 2 to move to the appropriate working directory. Then command interpreter 2 is asked to start a text editor so the user can inspect the program that has failed. The user finds the bug and modifies the file. It is time now to compile, link, and run the program. The user asks the editor for a new command interpreter (number 3). Command interpreter 3 is asked to run the compiler. When the compiler finishes, the linker is run. The first situation shown in Figure 7.2 holds while the linker is running.

Once the linker finishes, the user will try running the program. The bug is still there. To return to the editor, the user terminates command interpreter 3. After making more changes to the program, the user asks the editor for another command interpreter (number 4). The second situation in Figure 7.2 holds during the next compilation. If all goes well, the user will terminate command interpreter 4, the editor, and command interpreter 2, returning to the mail program. A response can be sent to the person who complained about the bug, and the user can proceed to read the rest of the mail.

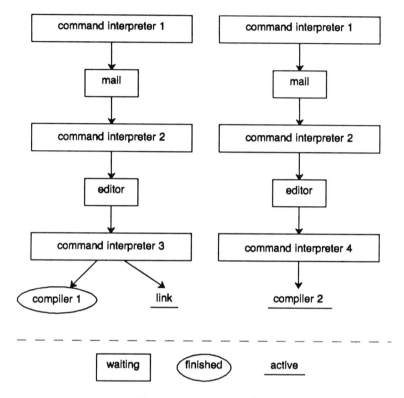

**Figure 7.2** A tree of processes

As you can see, it can be confusing to have several command interpreters at once. Each might have a different working directory. It is up to the user to remember the tree of invocations. Programs must be exited in reverse order to the order in which they are entered, and they are active only when they are at the leaf of the tree.

### Redirection of transput.

Programmers would rather not tie a program into any particular source for input or destination for output. However, these decisions must be **bound** at some point; the logical name used by the program must be associated with a physical name of a device or a file. The command interpreter can be in charge of binding these names. For example, a simulation program might call its input `simulate.in` and its output `simulate.out`. Perhaps the user wants to call this program several times with different data. Instead of rewriting the program, the command interpreter could be used. One convention is to set the environment in a global way:

```
set associate simulate.in  data.one
set associate simulate.out out.one
simulate
set associate simulate.in  data.two
set associate simulate.out out.two
simulate
set associate simulate.in  data.three
set associate simulate.out out.three
simulate
```

In this example, the simulation is run three times, each time under a different environment.

An alternative is to list the input and output files as parameters to the Simulate program:

```
simulate data.one   out.one
simulate data.two   out.two
simulate data.three out.three
```

Simulate must discover the binding by examining its parameters.

A very nice alternative is to let Simulate assume that "input" and "output" are logical names that will be bound by the command interpreter. These two logical files will be provided to every process that the command interpreter starts. If the user makes no special arrangements, the command interpreter can direct terminal input to the "input" expected by the process and direct any data placed in the "output" file back to the terminal. If data are to come from or go to a file, that stipulation can be mentioned in the command line, not as parameters passed to the process but as instructions to the command interpreter for establishing bindings; for example:

```
simulate  <  data.one    > out.one
simulate  <  data.two    > out.two
simulate  <  data.three  > out.three
```

In this example, we have followed Unix syntax, in which  < means "bind the input to the file named next in the line" and  > means "bind the output to the file named next in the line." Different symbols are used so that the command interpreter can distinguish between file names and program names. The binding for either input, output, or both could be specified in the command. Unspecified bindings remain by default bound to the terminal.

Redirection of transput can be carried one step further. The output of one process can be directed into the input of a second process. For example, the result of the simulation can be sent to a process that sorts the output before it is placed in a file. Our commands might take this form, again following Unix conventions:

```
simulate   <   data.one     |   sort   >   out.one
simulate   <   data.two     |   sort   >   out.two
simulate   <   data.three   |   sort   >   out.three
```

This ability to form "pipelines" colors the philosophy of building programs under Unix. Many programs are built to be simple elements of a longer pipeline, taking input, performing some transformation (possibly quite simple), and producing output. We discuss the inter-process communication mechanisms used in Unix to build pipelines in Chapter 9.

### Bit-mapped displays.
In the earliest days of operating systems, most transput was on punched paper tape or cards. Command interpreters understood certain combinations of characters on tape or card to distinguish data from commands. The first interactive terminals were slow (about 10 characters per second) and noisy as they produced printed output. Brevity of commands was more important than sophisticated features. Modern terminals are often quite fast (about 1000 characters per second) and quiet as they produce characters on a video screen. Many of the features mentioned so far have been developed for this sort of terminal.

A new generation of terminals is now being built. In addition to characters, they can display figures. Because they have a fairly large screen with computer control over every dot, they are called **bit-mapped displays**. They typically have about 1000 dots per line and about 1000 lines.

Bit-mapped displays are driven from reserved regions of physical store where a bit pattern is placed by the program. Since it can take a significant amount of computation to prepare figures (and sometimes even just letters) for such a device, such terminals are not yet standard on most interactive-multiprogramming machines. However, they have appeared on personal computers, where no one cares if extra computation is needed to present a better user interface.

Bit-mapped displays are often packaged with a pointing device that allows the user to specify a particular region on the display. Pointing devices have different designs. Some display screens are overlaid with a sensitive grid that can sense the touch of a finger. A separate device, usually called a "mouse," can be moved over a tablet on the desk. Its motion is conveyed to the computer, which can then display a **cursor** (a visual indicator of the current location) at the corresponding place on the display. The mouse may have a few keys that can be depressed to send signals to the computer.

Bit-mapped displays change the character of interaction. We will discuss three innovations: menus, icons, and windows. A **menu** is a list of commands that are legal in the current situation. Instead of typing commands to the command interpreter, the user requests a menu to be placed somewhere on the screen. The pointing device is used to point to the entry that is desired. Some menu entries, when selected, expand into submenus. For example, assume that the user wants to delete `one.out`. The current menu might have the following entries:

```
compile
file
status
edit
print
```

After the user selects `file`, the menu changes (or a new menu is displayed elsewhere on the screen) that looks like this:

```
rename
copy
move
link
delete
alias
view
```

The user selects `delete`. Now a third menu appears with the names of all the files. The user selects `one.out`, and the file is deleted.

Although this use of menus requires lots of computation (especially to provide the names of all the files), it takes only three keystrokes for the user. Each keystroke could involve one of the keys on the mouse. If the user wants to submit a command that is not on the menu, or requires flags that are not in the menu, there is usually a way to revert to line-oriented command language.

**Icons** are graphical representations of objects, such as files or programs, and abstractions, such as today's work or a directory. Icons can be pointed to by a mouse and moved about on the screen. Moving an icon can have an equivalent effect on the object. For example, a file can be moved from one directory to another by dragging its icon across the screen. It can even be discarded by placing its icon in the "trash can" icon!

**Windows** are regions of the display established for different purposes. Each process could have its own window. If several processes are running at once, output can be displayed for all of them. When a process fills its window, it might be blocked until the user has had a chance to see the output. Alternatively, data that disappear from the window can be saved in a file. Windows can be manipulated to change their size and position and to determine which one is on top if they overlap. Entire windows can be shrunk to icons that are stored on the screen to be re-expanded when needed. Data in one window can be selected for copying into another window. In this way the output of one program can be used as input to another.

## 2  INTERACTIVE PROGRAMS

All interactive programs should provide a good interface to the user. Some of the characteristics that improve the user interface are listed here.

- **The interface should be easy to learn.** Menus provide an especially good interface for this purpose. Single-letter commands can be very difficult to remember.

- **Facilities intended to aid the novice should not get in the way of the experienced user.** Many programs allow the user to establish the level of verbosity, for example. An experienced user may prefer terse error messages and a terser input syntax.

- **It should be possible to undo actions.** This feature decreases the anxiety felt by the novice and permits a greater range of exploration. Of course, not every application can allow undoing. It may not be possible to unsend mail, for example.

- **It should be possible to cancel actions in progress.**

- **The program should provide help on request.** Both general help and help about individual commands should be provided. Many help schemes allow the user to keep asking the same question. The first answer is very brief. Each subsequent answer is an expansion on the previous one. If individual commands invoke new programs, requests for help can be forwarded to those programs.

- **Words used for commands should be verbs, and words for arguments should be nouns.** These commands might be abbreviated (for example, reduced to a single keystroke), but if they are echoed, it is nice to echo the entire word. The echoed version may even include prepositions to make the command seem even closer to English. For example, `m foo bar` may be echoed as `Move foo to bar`.

- **Each command should have a response.** It is especially helpful if the response is different for different commands.

- **If the command cannot complete quickly, there should be some indication that work is in progress.** Otherwise, it is easy to think that the request is being serviced when the program really is waiting for some more input.

- **Humorous messages should be avoided.** The computer is *not* human, and attempts to make it appear human can be irritating. In addition, such messages can be misunderstood. For example, for very obvious syntax errors, one compiler generates the message, "The details of this error can be found in your code." The message is not very helpful, even if it *is* cute.

- **Different interactive programs should use similar commands.** It can be confusing if the termination command is `quit` for one program, `exit` for another, and `ZZ` for a third.

# 3 UTILITY PROGRAMS

The command interpreter utility is important because every user needs to deal with it. Other utility programs are also important for various classes of users. The

success of an operating system often depends on the quality of these utility programs. We will mention a number of these programs here but will not dwell on
their organization or their features.

## 3.1 Document preparation

On many computers, a very large proportion of a user's time is spent preparing
documents of all sorts. Documents range from memos to technical reports, user
guides, and books. This book itself was composed with the aid of tools provided by
the BSD Unix operating system.

At the moment this sentence was composed, 15 out of 47 user processes were
running a text-editing program. The text editor is often the first program invoked
to build a document. A text editor is an interactive program that allows the user to
create and modify text files. Some editors show only one line of the file at a time;
others use a full display. The most advanced editors use bit-mapped displays and
can show several windows into one file or several files at the same time. Such editors can sometimes embed pictures into the middle of text files.

Once a document has been entered into a file, spelling checkers and style
checkers can be useful. Spelling checkers complain if they can't find words in their
dictionary, and most understand common prefixes and suffixes. A few will suggest
a menu of respellings of disputed words and will accept new words to be added to
the dictionary. Style checkers detect potentially poor usages, such as "a number
of" or "the fact that," which might be improved by rewriting. Style checkers can
also report the percentage of nouns and verbs used.

The next step is often a text-formatting program. Text formatters can produce output acceptable to a wide variety of devices, including display screens, line
printers, high-resolution dot-matrix printers, and phototypesetters. These programs
usually take source files that contain both text and formatting commands, such as
"start new paragraph," "number every page," "don't hyphenate," and "make wide
columns." Sometimes these programs can format mathematical formulas, tables,
footnotes, bibliographic references, and even drawings. In other cases, these
features are provided by separate programs that convert higher-level descriptions
into more primitive pieces. For example, formulas can be converted into page-
location and font-selection commands. Simple drawings can be converted to short
line segments.

Some editors for bit-mapped display terminals combine the functions of text
editing and formatting. The terminal displays a reasonably accurate facsimile of
the document that will actually be produced.

## 3.2 Program preparation

University environments often have computer installations where a large proportion
of time is spent building programs. A similar situation holds in software houses
and research labs. The "life cycle" of programs involves the following steps:

(1)     Define the requirements.
(2)     Choose data structures and algorithms.
(3)     Write a program.
(4)     Verify that the requirements are met.
(5)     Compile, link, and run the program.
(6)     Test the program and diagnose the errors.
(7)     Maintain the program.

Unfortunately, these milestones are not sequential. Step 4 could discover that the requirements are not met, in which case the programmer may need to return to step 3 (or possibly step 1). Step 5 often turns up problems, both major and minor, that force the programmer to retrace some steps. Step 6 turns up harder problems, some of which may be very difficult to diagnose. As errors are corrected, the programmer may have to retreat all the way to step 1 or, more commonly, to step 3. Step 7 involves keeping the program running even though the requirements may change. It is often performed by a group of people different from the group involved in the other steps.

Tools exist to assist the programmer during various steps in the life cycle of a program. There are no particularly good tools for the first two steps. Program requirements can sometimes be written as assertions about the relationship between input and output; these assertions have a mathematical flavor.

Writing the program usually involves the text editor, which may have some features specifically designed for editing programs. These features include automatic indentation, checking for parenthesis balance, and ability to find declarations of variables quickly. Some experimental editors are tailored to particular programming languages. They can enforce syntactic correctness, prompt the programmer for declarations, correct syntax errors, and even check that types match.

If the requirements for the program are expressed in mathematical form, some experimental tools can help verify that a given program satisfies those requirements. However, these tools are still quite primitive and expensive.

Many tools have been written for the compilation phase. Modern languages are very helpful in promoting a clear program structure and in providing information (like data types) the compiler can use to check a certain amount of logical consistency. Modern compilers are very helpful in reporting syntax errors in the source program. Some can automatically switch back to the editor at the point of error to allow the programmer to fix it and then continue. Compilers often pass over the program several times, each time accomplishing a different transformation. The first pass might expand macros, the second generate assembler code, the third improve the assembler code, and the fourth create an object file. After the object files have been built for the modules that constitute a program, the linker combines them, searches libraries for missing names, and builds a load image. Tools like the Make utility of Unix accept a description of the ways compilation units depend on each other. When one unit is modified, only the necessary modules are recompiled and relinked, according to recipes supplied by the programmer.

Testing the program has two stages.

(1)    Find the obvious errors.
(2)    Try enough cases to be convinced that the program will work in every case.
       A test suite might be specified by the requirements developed in step 1.

Most debugging of this sort uses extra output statements to report the inter state of
the program. As erroneous outputs are found, more output statements are inserted
to determine where the mistake was made. Suddenly, the programmer will get a
flash of insight, determine the problem, and fix it.

Debugging tools can be helpful during this stage. Debuggers are programs
that allow the programmer to step through the program under test little by little,
examining the values in variables at any point during this execution. The debugger
might be able to display the source program associated with the current point of
execution, and it might accept source-language statements as commands. The
amount of execution before the program is stopped can be specified by number of
statements, number of executions of a particular statement, or modification of a
particular variable. Routines can be invoked out of order, and both variables and
instructions can be modified. Part of a display may be devoted to a continuous
view of the variables the programmer wishes to examine. The program might be
displayed from various points of view, including a flowchart, a picture of the run-
time stack, and the original text.

Maintaining a program is related to managing a large programming effort.
New versions of modules are created by different people at different times for
different reasons. At any time it might be useful to roll back to a previous version
to see how it worked before it was modified. If the file manager provides versions
on files, that facility can be useful in maintaining a program. Utility programs
have also been written that provide for "checking in" and "checking out" files.
When a file is checked in, these utilities prompt for a description of the most recent
change and store it in the file for future reference. They also ensure that when
several programmers are simultaneously modifying the program, the modifications
are merged instead of having one overwrite the other.

## 3.3 Data management

The computer is a convenient place to store a great variety of information. We
have seen how a directory structure assists the user in organizing files and how
structures in files can speed up searches. A typical operating system offers a large
number of utility programs for manipulating information.

The easiest form of manipulation affects entire files. The Transfer program
that we have been using as an example exists in some form on every operating system. Not all functions are necessarily provided by a single program, but the following operations are often supported on files.

```
print       (on a printing device)
display     (on an interactive terminal)
copy        (to a new file)
move        (to a new place)
rename
delete
reformat    (changing character codes, indentation, or headings)
permit      (change access rights)
```

In addition, the following operations on directories are supplied:

```
list        (tell which files are in the directory)
make        (a new directory)
delete      (an entire directory)
rename
move        (to a new place)
permit      (change access rights)
```

Various retrieval methods are often provided for information. For example, utilities are often provided to find which files satisfy some criterion. The criterion can be based on the name of the file, the date on which it was created or modified, or its type (text, load image, and so forth). Lines in text files that match some pattern can be printed.

Sorting is an important activity in many algorithms. Since the best method for sorting depends on the type and number of data, "sort packages" have been built that create the most appropriate sorting program for a particular application.

Large-scale database management systems are found in some installations. They may allow many users to inspect and modify the database simultaneously. The user interface to these programs is often a command language specially tailored for forming queries such as "find all customers in Indiana who paid their last bill within 1 week of receiving it and whose bill was at least twice as high as the average bill."

Documents are not the only objects that users wish to manipulate interactively. **Structure editors** allow users to enter and modify such varied objects as printer fonts, VLSI circuit layouts, pictures, stored speech, and file directories. Integrating these various object types into a common editing paradigm is a subject of current research.

## 3.4 Communication

The trend of the last few years is toward the use of computers as tools for allowing people to communicate with one another. Programs for mailing notes between users of the same interactive computer have been available for years. These notes are collected in files that serve as mailboxes and can be read by a program that the recipient can invoke. Notification that mail has arrived is often by a short message to the terminal of the recipient or by a note when the recipient starts a session with the operating system. The command interpreter can also check the mailbox and tell the user if new mail has arrived. Programs also allow two users to direct notes to each other's terminals without using a mailbox.

A different sort of communication involves several computers at once. Computers that are connected for transfer of data are said to belong to a **network**. Small "satellite" computers can be linked to large central computers either by permanent lines or by occasional telephone connections. The satellite computers might be used for everyday computation. The central computer might be used for archival data storage and large-scale computation that exceeds the capacity of the smaller machines. An installation might connect its several computers using a local area network to allow sharing of data and computation. Programs are often provided for data transfer and remote computation. A single operating system might control all the machines, making the existence of the network invisible to typical users. The Locus variant of Unix is a particularly successful implementation of this idea.

In the last few years, the two ideas of computer mail and computer networks have been combined. Many national and international computer networks exist. The UUCP network connects perhaps 10,000 installations, mostly in North America, but including Korea, Israel, and Europe. There is a similar network in Australia. The Arpa Internet covers thousands of installations in North America and Europe. BITNET has over 1500 computers at university computing centers, mostly in North America, Europe, Japan, and Israel. CSNET connects dozens of computers in computer science departments in universities in the United States and Canada as well as computer-industry research laboratories. Computer corporations often have internal networks connecting their sites, such as IBM's VNET and Digital Equipment Corporation's Easynet.

These networks are used mainly for computer mail, although more general data transfer and even remote computation are possible in some cases. We will return to the topic of networks in Chapter 9 when we discuss inter-process cooperation.

# 4 PERSPECTIVE

Although the range of computers and their operating systems is quite large, certain common themes apply to all of them. The User Principle leads to similar solutions on both large and small computers. For example, a personal-computer user needs a command interpreter just as much as a batch user on a central mainframe computer. Both have tasks that must be submitted to the computer. The convenience of having several processes at the same time is just as convenient for the mainframe user as for the hobbyist.

It is true that small home computers currently do not have the main or secondary storage needed to provide large-scale fancy services. Nontheless, the trend toward bit-mapped graphics, multiprogramming, and well-designed command languages is being felt even in these machines.

We have described the command interpreter as a single entity used for specifying processes to be run and their environments. As we have seen, any interactive program requires some form of command interpretation. Unfortunately, each program usually has its own command language and its own peculiarities. Even the command used to terminate a program is often different for each program in the operating system. It is not clear whether this chaotic situation is due to the unorganized way in which utility programs have been designed or whether the operations performed by each utility are unique and require unique syntax.

Several attempts to alleviate this chaos have shown some success. One direction is to provide a subroutine package that each interactive utility may use to provide a uniform structure for the command language. For example, Tenex provides a package of command-completion subroutines. Machines with bit-mapped screens can provide menu-manipulation packages. Another direction is to provide exactly one command interpreter program. Each utility specifies to the command interpreter the commands that it is willing to accept and their structure. Integrating all interactive programs by a common command interface is related to integrating all structure editors by a common interface.

# 5  FURTHER READING

Good's article (1981) presents a clear description of the desired characteristics of a command interpreter. It has an extensive bibliography that can guide you to other literature about command interpretation. Kernighan and Pike (1984) have written an extensive introduction to the Unix command interpreter and the Unix environment in general. One description of a window package can be found in the paper by Meyrowitz and Moser (1981). Another window package intended for use in a multiple-process environment has been described by Lantz and Rashid (1979). A number of integrated programming environments have been built, including the Cornell program synthesizer (Teitelbaum et al., 1981) and the Pascal-oriented editor (Fischer et al., 1984). An extremely fancy text formatting program, TeX, is described by Knuth (1984). One example of the attempt to unify all program interaction under the aegis of editing is the recent thesis by Dewan (1986).

# 6 EXERCISES

1.  Describe the features available in a command language with which you are familiar. What features described in this chapter are not available? Are these omissions due to design outside the command interpreter, or could they be added? For those that could be added, suggest a syntax. For those that cannot be added, explain why.

2.  In what way are the commands one might give an interactive file manager similar to the commands one might give a text editor? In what way are they different?

3.  If the operating system does not provide for any inter-process data transfer, how can the command interpreter establish a pipeline that directs the output of one process into the input of another?

4.  How do pipelines of processes and the ability for processes to start subordinate processes interfere with each other?

5.  Find out what computer networks are accessible to your computer. What is the form of a mail address on these networks?

6.  A message sent to someone's terminal can be a nuisance to the recipient. Design some mechanism to allow users to restrict incoming messages.

7.  It was recently discovered that the ability to send arbitrary messages to someone's terminal can introduce security problems. The problem arises because a debugging feature of the terminal allows it to enter a mode in which it echoes all data coming from the computer back to the computer. How do the two features, messages and terminal debugging, combine to create a problem?

8.  Some operating systems allow programs to load the terminal input buffer with characters as if the user had typed them in. These characters are then displayed; the user can modify them and activate the line. When would such a facility be useful? When would it be harmful?

# Concurrency

As operating systems were first built, an annoying sort of problem was discovered: Routines invoked from interrupts sometimes modify data that are in the midst of being inspected by the interrupted program. The modifications can be benign, like appending to the end of a list, or disastrous, like modifying a linked list in such a way that the interrupted program follows a dangling pointer.

Such problems crop up in various contexts within operating systems. In Chapter 5, we saw that a circular buffer pool can be simultaneously filled by a process and emptied by the kernel. It would be erroneous for the process to put new data in the buffer that is currently being emptied. In Chapter 6, we encountered read/write and write/write conflicts in file use. We invented transactions to provide synchronization atomicity to prevent such conflicts. If we allow several processes to share parts of their virtual store, similar conflicts arise. As we suggested in Figure 3.23, the kernel of the operating system may be composed of separate tasks, each of which fulfills one particular function. These tasks may communicate through shared data.

All these cases involve several activities sharing a common data area. What happens can depend on the order in which the activities access the data. Some orders give fine results; some give incorrect but not fatal results; others are disastrous. For example, in a video game, it is fine if we move the hero before the monster. It is incorrect to decide where each will go before moving the other, because they could end up in the same location on the screen. It is disastrous if such overlap leads to dangling pointers that cause the game to fail. When two cooks are working on the same soup, it is fine if one chops onions while the other measures barley. It may even be acceptable for them to add these ingredients at the same time. But if both independently decide to add salt, the result can be inedible. In this chapter we will present methods for ensuring that different activities sharing access to common data give predictable results. This general topic is known as

**concurrency control**. We use the term **activity** to avoid specifying whether our entities are processes, kernel tasks, interrupt-driven procedures, or DMA transfers.

From one point of view, shared data can be considered a resource that the operating system must manage to ensure correct use. The problem is therefore in the domain of operating systems. From another point of view, most of the solutions we will look at have a linguistic flavor; that is, we will build programming-language structures to help us enforce our policies and hide the complexity of the algorithms. To some extent, therefore, our problem is in the domain of programming languages. Concurrency control is not the only problem in which operating systems and programming languages have mutual interests. We will touch upon communication later as another example.

# 1  THE PROBLEMS

Concurrency control is a problem of resource management. When we looked at allocation of sequentially reusable resources, we characterized policies as liberal or conservative. The same characterization applies in the realm of concurrency control. A policy can be very liberal, allowing shared data to be accessed almost whenever an activity pleases. Such a strategy achieves the goal of simultaneous access and a high degree of parallelism. The danger of liberal strategies is that some execution orders lead to erroneous results. At the other extreme, a policy can be very conservative, blocking accesses until it is certain that erroneous results cannot arise. The danger of conservative strategies is that activities are unable to respond efficiently to real-time events.

Deadlock and starvation are dangers for any policy that occasionally blocks activities. As we saw in Chapter 4, **deadlock** occurs when activities are waiting for each other so that none can run, and **starvation** is a situation in which some blocked activity is consistently passed over and not allowed to run. A related danger is **livelock**, a situation in which the algorithm that decides whether to block an activity continues to run without reaching a decision. A special case of livelock is **busy waiting**, in which an activity uses computational resources without making progress as an alternative to blocking. Busy waiting is not objectionable if there is no other work worth doing during the wait.

Before we proceed with solutions, let's review the typical situation in which simultaneous access can lead to errors.

|     | process A              | process B              |
| --- | --------------------- | --------------------- |
| 1   | TmpA := x;            | TmpB := x;            |
| 2   | TmpA := TmpA + 1;     | TmpB := TmpB + 1;     |
| 3   | x := TmpA;            | x := TmpB;            |

Assume that TmpA and TmpB are variables local to processes **A** and **B** and that x is a variable shared between them. Assume that x starts with value 0. After both **A** and **B** have finished their fragments of code, x has the value 2 if we are lucky and 1 if we are not: If both processes execute statement 1 before either executes statement 3, then each will read an old x value of 0 and update it in line 3 to a 1.

Here is a simpler situation that can also lead to trouble.

|     | process A | process B |
| --- | --------- | --------- |
| 1   | x := 3;   | x := 5;   |

The resulting value of x can be either 3 or 5, depending on which process finishes second. If the constants were not small, like 3 and 5, but were so large that several words were needed to store them, these assignments might take several machine instructions. The instructions could overlap in such a way that the answer is neither what **A** intended nor what **B** intended.

We usually assume that certain operations, such as assignment into main store, are atomic and that **arbitration** takes place at some level within the computer hardware: If two requests arrive simultaneously, they are selected in some sequential order. All our methods will depend on hardware arbitration at some level. We will assume that two requests made simultaneously to main store are serviced consecutively. Such requests can arise when several computers are connected as a multiprocessor. In uniprocessors, each machine instruction is usually atomic. Traps and interrupts, which can cause a process switch, are delayed until the current machine instruction is finished. Even here, some long instructions (like block copy) may be interruptible. In addition, missing-page traps can occur in the middle of an ordinary instruction.

## 1.1 Mutual exclusion

The problem of **mutual exclusion** is to ensure that two concurrent activities do not access shared data at the same time. As we have seen, arbitration in the hardware is a form of mutual exclusion. We will see how it can be extended to provide exclusion for more complicated operations.

Instructions that must be executed while another activity is excluded are grouped into **regions**. A region often contains more than one access to the shared data. For example, the assignment

```
        x := x + 1
```

must refer to x twice. On some machines, two or more instructions are needed to accomplish this assignment. They are all part of the same region. Two regions **conflict** if execution of one requires that the other not be executed at the same time. By definition, all regions conflict with themselves. However, the region just shown would not conflict with a region that increments y instead of x.

A typical way to express mutual exclusion is to surround regions by delimiters like `BeginRegion` and `EndRegion`, as shown here.

|  | process A | process B |
|---|---|---|
| 1 | BeginRegion; | BeginRegion; |
| 2 | x := 3; | x := 5; |
| 3 | EndRegion; | EndRegion; |

The form of the delimiters, exactly what a region means, and how it is implemented distinguish the methods we will survey. In all cases we can look upon regions as a way of imposing a degree of determinism on a non-deterministic situation, since we can't predict when interrupts will happen, when activities will be scheduled, or the relative speeds of truly simultaneous activities in a multiprocessor.

## 1.2 Synchronization

Mutual exclusion prevents an activity from entering a region until other activities are out of conflicting regions. If we want to prevent an activity from continuing until some more general condition is met, we say that we wish to **synchronize** the activity with the condition. Synchronization is a generalization of mutual exclusion.

Occurrence of conditions marks the passage of time. Synchronizing with those conditions achieves a common notion of time among activities. This idea of common time gives rise to the word "synchronization."

Since synchronization is a generalization of mutual exclusion, we can expect that the techniques developed for solving the mutual-exclusion problem are also useful for achieving synchronization. We will test this expectation by presenting various synchronization problems. The first one is best described by a **synchronization graph**, which shows precedence constraints that govern when actions may begin. Figure 8.1 shows the graph we will discuss. Action **A** has no preconditions. Once it has finished, actions **B** and **D** may start. As soon as **B** has finished, **C** may start, but **E** must wait for both **B** and **D** to finish. **I** may not start until everything else has finished. Each arrow in this graph is a synchronization step. It represents the condition that the action at its tail has finished.

There are many ways to cast this graph into a program. We might code each of the nine actions separately and provide for explicit synchronization. Alternatively, we could cast each row as a separate activity. The first activity would

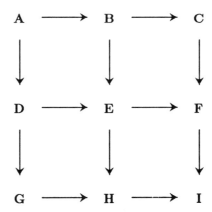

**Figure 8.1** A synchronization graph

execute **A**, then **B**, then **C**. Synchronization between these pieces would be implicit. The second activity, which executes **D**, **E**, and **F**, would synchronize with conditions created by the first activity in three places. The last activity is similar. Another alternative is to represent each column as an activity.

Choosing an alternative affects which synchronizations are implicit and which are explicit. It also affects how we perceive the flow of control. For example, this synchronization graph could represent the steps needed to complete three Fortran compilations in a simple operating system. Each compilation is represented in one row. The row represents, for example, reading the source program from disk, compiling, and writing the result to tape. If there is only one disk drive and one tape drive, and we don't allow two compilations to proceed simultaneously, the precedence constraints in the graph properly limit the amount of concurrency.

If we treat each row as a separate activity, then interactions between reading a program, compiling it, and outputting the result are implicit; interactions between this program and another are explicit. If we treat each column as a separate activity, then we have a card-reader activity, a compilation activity, and an output activity. Each signals the next when it has performed all it needs to with respect to one Fortran compilation.

Later we will introduce the producers-consumers problem and the readers-writers problem as more complex synchronization tests. We will also return to the dining philosophers problem, which we introduced in Chapter 4.

## 2 MECHANISMS

We will now turn to mechanisms that can be used to provide mutual exclusion and synchronization. We will start with simple but conservative techniques and move toward more complex, liberal ones. In each case we will show how the BeginRegion and EndRegion primitives are built.

All mechanisms for mutual exclusion and synchronization depend ultimately on the synchronous nature of hardware. Some rely on the fact that processors can be made uninterruptible. These **processor-synchronous** methods work only for individual processors. Others rely on the fact that main store can service only one access request at a time, even in a multiprocessor. These **store-synchronous** methods have a wider range of applicability.

## 2.1 Disable interrupts

Most computer architectures allow interrupts to be disabled, perhaps on a selective basis. If a device signals an interrupt while interrupts are disabled, the new interrupt will be postponed until interrupts are again allowed. If activities are preempted only when an interrupt occurs, exclusion can be enforced by disabling interrupts while any activity is in a region. Since no interrupts arrive, the current activity will be able to complete the instructions in its region before any other activity starts executing in a conflicting region.

Adjusting the interruptibility of the computer leads to a processor-synchronous technique for mutual exclusion. The BeginRegion and EndRegion procedures look like this:

```
1 procedure BeginRegion;
2 begin
3    DisableInterrupts;
4 end BeginRegion;
5
6 procedure EndRegion;
7 begin
8    EnableInterrupts;
9 end EndRegion;
```

Disabling interrupts can be quite fast. A single machine instruction often suffices to change the interrupt state of the machine. However, this method has some unfortunate properties.

- Once an activity has entered a region, real-time events, like devices that need service, cannot be treated until the activity has left the region. Therefore, lengthy processing in a region is usually unacceptable. This property is due to the fact that disabling interrupts is extremely conservative.
- It excludes not only potentially conflicting activities that might otherwise access shared data but also all activities whatsoever, no matter what their purpose.
- One reason a region might be lengthy is that the program might have to wait for some event before continuing. For example, the program might be waiting for a device to become available. The programmer should not put waits inside regions.

- The technique fails on multiprocessors because it is usually not possible for a program on one machine to block interrupts on other machines. Even if interrupts can be disabled on all machines, conflicting activities can still be executing simultaneously.

- The programmer must be careful to ensure that all paths from the region go through code to release exclusion by enabling interrupts once again. It is easy to overlook some path and introduce a deadlock.

- Another pitfall involves nested regions. If procedure **A** calls procedure **B** from inside a region and **B** also enters a region, **B** will re-enable interrupts during its EndRegion operation, relaxing exclusion before **A** was ready to do so. (See the exercises at the end of this chapter.)

## 2.2  Busy wait on MutEx

The method of disabling interrupts lets any activity into a region but prevents any other activity from running while the first one is in the region. A different approach is to wait at the entry to a region until it is safe to continue. We can introduce a Boolean variable MutEx (for Mutual Exclusion) that is set to true when an activity is in a region and false otherwise. We then code BeginRegion and EndRegion as follows:

```
1 var MutEx : Boolean := false;
2
3 procedure BeginRegion;
4 begin
5    while MutEx do
6       null; { that is, do nothing }
7    end;
8    MutEx := true;
9 end BeginRegion;
10
11 procedure EndRegion(Who : Activity);
12 begin
13    MutEx := false;
14 end EndRegion;
```

Unfortunately, this store-synchronous solution is wrong. If two activities enter BeginRegion at about the same time, they might both get past the loop in line 5 and enter the region. The problem is that an activity that decides to enter the region at line 5 does not prevent others from entering as well until line 8. By then it may be too late. We will fix this problem when we look at locks.

We introduce this "solution" to demonstrate that even though it fails for mutual exclusion, busy waiting *does* suffice to implement the synchronization graph of Figure 8.1. We will use the following convention: Every activity in the graph is associated with a shared Boolean variable "Done." For example, **A** is associated with Done[**A**]. We then build two utility procedures, Finishing and WaitFor:

```
 1 var
 2     Done : array [Activity] of Boolean := false;
 3
 4 procedure Finishing(Who : Activity);
 5 begin
 6     Done[Who] := true;
 7 end Finishing;
 8
 9 procedure WaitFor(Whom : Activity);
10 begin
11     while not Done[Whom] do
12         null;
13     end;
14 end WaitFor;
```

The code for a few selected activities could look like this:

```
 1 activity A:
 2     perform A's work;
 3     Finishing(A);
 4
 5 activity B:
 6     WaitFor(A);
 7     perform B's work;
 8     Finishing(B);
 9
10 activity E:
11     WaitFor(B);
12     WaitFor(D);
13     perform E's work;
14     Finishing(E);
```

Even though both Finishing and WaitFor use the Done array, we don't have to worry about simultaneous access, since only one activity will ever call Finishing to modify any particular value in that array. Other activities may call WaitFor, but they only inspect the array.

If we treat each row in the graph as a separate activity, some of the explicit calls to WaitFor and Finishing are no longer needed:

```
 1 activity ABC:
 2     perform A's work;
 3     Finishing(A);
 4     perform B's work;
 5     Finishing(B);
 6     perform C's work;
 7     Finishing(C);
 8
 9 activity DEF:
10     WaitFor(A);
11     perform D's work;
12     Finishing(D);
13     WaitFor(B);
14     perform E's work;
15     Finishing(E);
16     WaitFor(C);
17     perform F's work;
18     Finishing(F);
19
20 activity GHI:
21     WaitFor(D);
22     perform G's work;
23     WaitFor(E);
24     perform H's work;
25     WaitFor(F);
26     perform I's work;
```

## 2.3  Switch variable

A more liberal store-synchronous mechanism for ensuring mutual exclusion between two activities is for them to share a new variable called a **switch**. This variable lets either one or the other enter its region. We depend on the synchronization atomicity of main store to arbitrate simultaneous accesses to this variable.

In the following example, the switch variable is called Turn:

```
 1 type Activity : (A, B);
 2
 3 var Turn : Activity := A;
 4
 5 procedure BeginRegion(Who : Activity);
 6 begin
 7     while Turn <> Who do
 8         null;
 9     end;
10 end BeginRegion;
11
12 procedure EndRegion(Who : Activity);
13 begin
14     if Who = A then
15         Turn := B
16     else
17         Turn := A;
18     end;
19 end EndRegion;
```

In line 3, we initialize the switch variable to point to activity **A**. If **A** calls Begin-Region, the condition on the **while** in line 7 will be false, so BeginRegion will return. If **B** tries to enter its region, it will be blocked waiting for the switch in line 7. Turn will become **B** only after **A** has released the switch by calling EndRegion.

Switches are only slightly better than busy waiting.

- They correctly allow **A** and **B** to execute in conflicting regions, even if **A** and **B** are on different machines in a multiprocessor. If **A** and **B** call BeginRegion simultaneously, they will not conflict in their use of Turn, since BeginRegion only examines Turn without changing it. **A** and **B** will never call EndRegion simultaneously because they can't both be in their region at once.

- They may be generalized to more than two processes.

- Switches are more liberal than disabling interrupts. Unrelated conflicts are handled by different switch variables. Therefore, two activities can be executing in non-conflicting regions at the same time. For example, assume that there are two shared variables, x and y, and that activity **A** uses just x, activity **B** uses both x and y, and activity **C** uses just y. We would use one switch variable, TurnX, with values **A** and **B**, to protect variable x. A different switch variable, TurnY, with values **B** and **C**, could protect variable y. When **B** wishes to enter a region, it would specify not only its own name (**B**), but also which switch variable it wants to use.

- If several switch variables exist and a single activity might want to be in a combined region protected by several different switch variables, there is a danger of deadlock because switch variables are serially reusable resources. A hierarchy of switch variables can prevent this problem. We used the same idea in Chapter 4 when we introduced hierarchical allocation of sequentially reusable resources.

- When an activity is waiting to enter its region (line 7), it performs no useful work while it consumes computational resources. If activities are competing with each other on a single processor, these busy waits waste time because no other productive action takes place, even though there is some activity that could make use of the time (namely, the activity that is in the region). If activities are on different processors, we might not mind this waste of time so much because all activities that can make use of a processor resource might be on machines of their own. Still, a busy-waiting activity consumes main-store cycles, which are shared among all the processors. Even if other activities could run, the Hysteresis Principle tells us that busy waiting is still reasonable if the expected waiting time is less than one process-switch time. Very long busy-wait times tend to create a **convoy phenomenon**, in which many activities end up waiting for the same region. The entire convoy tends to collide at the next region, too, leading to worse contention than might have been expected.

- This solution forces **A** and **B** to alternate entry into their regions. If **A** needs to enter its region only occasionally but **B** needs to do so frequently, **B** will be blocked waiting for the region most of the time, even though **A** is not currently in the region.

## 2.4 Non-alternating switch

The principal drawback of the switch method is the strict alternation it imposes on conflicting activities. A non-alternating switch uses a switch variable and two auxiliary Boolean variables that indicate whether the two activities are currently interested in entering their regions. We will store them in an array for convenience. Here is the code that implements this store-synchronous method:

```
1 type Activity = (A,B);
2
3 var
4     Turn : Activity := A;
5     Interested : array [Activity] of Boolean := false;
6
```

```
 7 procedure BeginRegion(Who : Activity);
 8 var Other : Activity; { the other activity besides Who }
 9 begin
10    if Who = A then Other := B else Other := A end;
11    loop "outer"
12       { we exit when we may enter our region }
13       Interested[Who] := true;
14       repeat { busy wait if our turn, Other interested }
15          when not Interested[Other] exit outer;
16       until Turn = Other;
17       { we should stop objecting; it's not our turn. }
18       Interested[Who] := false;
19       while Turn = Other do { busy wait for our turn }
20          null;
21       end;
22    end loop;
23 end BeginRegion;
24
25 procedure EndRegion(Who : Activity);
26 begin
27    if Who = A then Turn := B else Turn := A end;
28    Interested[Who] := false;
29 end EndRegion;
```

The Interested variables ensure that simultaneous execution does not occur: Each activity indicates that it is interested (line 13) both before it enters its region and during the entire time it is in the region. An activity enters the region only if the other activity is not interested. The Turn variable ensures that mutual blocking does not occur. It does not change value during BeginRegion, and it is used only to determine which activity backs off (lines 17−21) if both wish to enter their region. Only activity **A** ever modifies Interested[**A**], and, likewise, only **B** modifies Interested[**B**], so there is no conflict for those variables. Only the activity currently in a region modifies Turn (line 27), so there is no conflict for that variable either.

A significant amount of effort has been directed to deriving the non-alternating switch. There are many ways in which the switch can be built incorrectly. For many years the program just shown, developed by Dekker, was the only good solution. A surprisingly simple solution was published by Peterson in 1981:

```
1 type Activity = (A,B);
2
3 var
4    Turn : Activity := A;
5    Interested : array [Activity] of Boolean := false;
6
```

```
 7 procedure BeginRegion(Who : Activity);
 8 var Other : Activity; { the other activity besides Who }
 9 begin
10    if Who = A then Other := B else Other := A end;
11    Interested[Who] := true;
12    Turn := Other;
13    while Interested[Other] and Turn = Other do
14        null;
15    end;
16 end BeginRegion;

17
18 procedure EndRegion(Who : Activity);
19 begin
20    Interested[Who] := false;
21 end EndRegion;
```

We leave the proof of this implementation as an exercise.

The non-alternating switch has the following properties:

- It is correct in the same way that the ordinary switch is correct.
- It is more liberal than the ordinary switch because it allows a faster activity to enter its region many times before the other activity has entered. However, it is still fair because priority is given to the activity that has not entered its region for the longest time.
- It is impossible for an activity to starve while waiting to enter its region, if we assume that whenever the conflicting activity enters its region, it eventually leaves that region.
- The solution can be generalized to any number of activities that conflict over the same shared variables. The generalization is called a **spin switch**.
- The solution is complex and somewhat unclear, so it is easy to make a mistake when programming it.
- The non-alternating switch uses busy waiting if a conflicting activity is in its region.

## 2.5  Locks

The switch solutions we have seen are store-synchronous; they assume that individual references to main store are atomic. Many computers offer an explicit store-synchronous instruction that makes mutual exclusion far easier and clearer. This instruction atomically reads a variable and sets it to a new value. The most common design is to set the new value to 1 no matter what the old value. In this case, the instruction is called Test and Set. It has the following behavior:

```
1 atomic function TestAndSet(var Lock : Boolean) : Boolean;
2 begin
3    TestAndSet := Lock;
4    Lock := true;
5 end TestAndSet;
```

One of the exercises explores a different atomic action that increments the old value.

Given Test and Set, we can build a simple mutual-exclusion mechanism called a **lock**:

```
 1 type Lock = Boolean;
 2
 3 procedure BeginRegion(var L : Lock);
 4 begin
 5    while TestAndSet(L) do
 6        null;
 7    end;
 8 end BeginRegion;
 9
10 procedure EndRegion(var L : Lock);
11 begin
12    L := false;
13 end;
```

Each region that an activity might enter uses a number of shared variables that must be protected. Each such group of shared variables is assigned a lock variable. Before entering a region, an activity is expected to call BeginRegion on the appropriate lock. If several locks are needed, they should be acquired in a standard hierarchical order to prevent deadlock. It makes no difference in what order they are released at the end of the region.

This solution works because the TestAndSet instruction (line 5) will return true as long as some other activity is in a conflicting region. When it returns false, it simultaneously sets the lock to true so that any other activity trying to acquire the lock will fail. If several activities are trying to get the same lock and the activity with the lock releases it (line 12), only one of the contenders will get it because TestAndSet is atomic. (Which one of the contenders gets it is arbitrary and depends on hardware arbitration.)

The lock method has the following properties:

- It works for any number of activities on any number of processors sharing main store.
- It is simple and easy to verify.
- It is liberal in that an activity that holds a lock does not prevent another activity from acquiring a different lock.
- It allows starvation because the choice of which activity to honor is arbitrary, on the assumption that the hardware is unintelligent.
- It uses busy waiting.

## 2.6 Semaphores

Each of the previous solutions employs busy waiting. The following methods all share a new property that distinguishes them from the busy-waiting methods: They depend on the ability to schedule activities. An activity that attempts to enter a region that is already occupied can be blocked, just as a process that attempts to gain a resource that is currently allocated might be blocked by the resource manager. While it waits, other activities may continue. Instead of consuming computational resources in a fruitless loop, the waiting activity only needs to suffer the cost of a context switch or two. To achieve this effect, we need to embed the BeginRegion and EndRegion operations in the scheduler instead of building them directly on the hardware. The scheduler can also maintain a list of activities waiting to enter a region so that a fair choice can be made when conditions allow.

Our first example of this approach is to protect each group of shared variables with a **semaphore**, which has the following structure:

```
1 type
2    Queue = list of Activity
3    Semaphore =
4       record
5          { all fields are initialized as shown }
6          MutEx : Lock := false;
7          Value : integer := 1;
8          Waiters : Queue := empty;
9       end;
```

The scheduler provides two operations on semaphores. We will call the first Up (sometimes people call this operation P, Wait, or Acquire). The second operation is Down (also called V, Signal, or Release). Informally, Down blocks the caller if Value (line 7) is 0. Otherwise, it decrements Value. Up increments Value and unblocks at most one waiting activity.

The correct use of semaphores to implement mutual exclusion is simple: All regions that use the same shared variables are associated with the same semaphore. An activity that wishes to enter a region calls Down on the associated semaphore (instead of BeginRegion). When the activity exits the region, it calls Up on the same semaphore (instead of EndRegion). The first activity to try to enter its region succeeds, because Value is initially 1. Another activity that tries to enter while the first is still in its region will be blocked. When the first activity leaves the region, the second activity is unblocked. The Value field is always either 0 or 1.

To give a more formal definition of Down and Up, we will implement them using locks as a more primitive mutual-exclusion tool.

```
 1 procedure Down(var S : Semaphore);
 2 begin
 3     BeginRegion(S.MutEx); { use TestAndSet }
 4     if S.Value = 0 then
 5         Block(S.Waiters); { proceed when unblocked later }
 6     else
 7         S.Value := S.Value − 1;
 8     end;
 9     EndRegion(S.MutEx);
10 end Down;
11
12 procedure Up(var S : Semaphore);
13 begin
14     BeginRegion(S.MutEx);
15     if not Empty(S.Waiters) then
16         UnBlock(S.Waiters) { Unblock one waiter.  We continue. }
17     else
18         S.Value := S.Value + 1;
19     end;
20     EndRegion(S.MutEx);
21 end Up;
```

It is important that Down and Up be mutually exclusive. In particular, any access of the Value or the Waiters field must be atomic. That is why we use the MutEx field of each semaphore to make sure that Down and Up exclude each other. We must make sure that both Down and Up retain exclusion for only a short time; otherwise our attempt to avoid busy waiting has failed.

In the simple case, Down does not find S.Value equal to 0 in line 4 and need not block in line 5. If it does block, we require that the Block routine (in the scheduler) resume some other runnable activity and that Block turn off exclusion before resumption. Block accomplishes this by calling EndRegion(S.MutEx). Block therefore needs to know which semaphore is in use; we omit this argument for clarity. UnBlock, called by Up in line 16, marks one waiting activity as runnable (for example, by placing it in a ready list). The releasing activity then continues and soon releases exclusion at line 20. When the newly runnable activity is scheduled to run, it is again given exclusion, and it finds itself running at line 5 in the Down routine. It will soon release exclusion itself in line 9.

There is some controversy over whether the scheduler should switch immediately to the waiting activity that is activated in line 16. Immediate switch guarantees that whatever condition is being awaited by that activity still holds, since the Up operation has just been called and no other activity has had a chance to run. The disadvantage of an immediate switch is that it tends to increase the total number of switches. The activity that called Up is likely to call Down for a new region soon, causing it to block in any case. The Hysteresis Principle suggests that the current process should be allowed to continue.

Semaphores are so useful that some operating systems provide service calls so that processes that share resources (particularly parts of virtual store) can synchronize their accesses. Four service calls are needed:

☐   **SemaphoreCreate(initial value).** This call returns a new semaphore descriptor (a small integer) that the calling process may use. The semaphore

structure itself is protected in the kernel and has its Value field set to the
given initial value. This semaphore may be inherited by the children of the
calling process so they can all share the same semaphore.

☐   **SemaphoreDestroy(semaphore descriptor).** This call informs the kernel
    that the given semaphore is no longer needed. This call is implicitly per-
    formed when the last process using a semaphore terminates. Any process
    waiting on a SemaphoreDown call receives an error return from that call.

☐   **SemaphoreDown(semaphore descriptor).** This call performs the Down
    operation on the given semaphore. An error is reported if the semaphore is
    not associated with this process or if the semaphore is destroyed while the
    process is blocked waiting for it.

☐   **SemaphoreUp(semaphore descriptor).** This call performs the Up operation
    on the given semaphore. An error is reported if the semaphore is not associ-
    ated with this process.

Semaphores have the following properties:

•   They correctly implement a liberal policy of mutual exclusion among any
    number of activities on any number of processors. Activities interfere with
    each other only if they refer to the same semaphore.
•   When an activity is blocked from entering its region, it does not busy wait.
•   Starvation is possible unless waiters are unblocked in first-come, first-served
    order.
•   As with all the methods we have seen so far, there is no guarantee that activi-
    ties will call Down and Up at the correct times. The wrong (or no) call may
    be made, or the wrong semaphore may be invoked.
•   A semaphore used for mutual exclusion is a serially reusable, non-
    preemptable resource. Its use is therefore subject to deadlock. A hierarchical
    order for acquiring multiple semaphores can be used to prevent deadlock.

It is easy to generalize the semaphore to allow any fixed number of activities the
right to enter their region at the same time. For example, we might have seven
tape drives and be willing to allow up to seven activities to access tape-drive code.
To enforce this policy, we would build a semaphore for tape-drive code and initialize its value to 7 instead of 1.

Semaphores allow us to implement synchronization without busy waiting. For
example, we could introduce a semaphore for each arrow in the synchronization
graph of Figure 8.1: AB, BE, and so on. Each semaphore would be initialized to 0.
A typical activity, like **E**, would have this sort of code:

```
1 activity E:
2    Down(BE);
3    Down(DE);
4    perform E's work;
5    Up(EF);
6    Up(EH);
```

We don't really need so many semaphores. Instead, we could introduce just one
semaphore per activity. Again, it would be initialized to 0. When the activity

finishes, it invokes Up on the semaphore as many times as there are activities waiting for this one to finish. Before an activity starts, it invokes Down on the semaphores of all the activities it needs to wait for. For example, **E** looks like this:

```
1 activity E:
2    Down(B);
3    Down(D);
4    perform E's work;
5    Up(E); { once for F, once for H }
6    Up(E);
```

One of the exercises at the end of the chapter explores another way to use semaphores to solve the same problem.

## 2.7 Critical regions

Semaphores provide the power we need, but they are easy to misuse. The following sections deal with ways to embed semaphores in programming-language constructs that try to minimize three problems:

(1)    Failure to protect shared variables
(2)    Failure to invoke semaphore operations in the right order and at the right time
(3)    Deadlock and starvation

We begin by a programming-language construct called the **critical region**. It is meant to be part of any language that explicitly allows several activities to share variables. Variables that are shared must be so declared; they are the only global variables that activities are allowed to access. Access to shared variables is restricted to code that lies within the **region** statement, as shown here:

```
1 var
2    v : shared integer;
3
4 . . .
5
6 region v do
7    v := 15;
8    write(v);
9 end;
```

We no longer use explicit calls to procedures BeginRegion and EndRegion; the compiler inserts those calls (most likely, calls to semaphores) for us.

There is a danger of deadlock because activity **A** might nest (that is, embed) **region** v inside **region** w, whereas activity **B** might nest them in the other order. Sometimes the compiler can check the order of nesting and disallow conflicting orders. However, if a region includes a call to a procedure that then enters another region, a nesting situation arises that the compiler cannot be expected to detect. Still, an impermissible order can be discovered when the program runs. Another way to skirt the problem is to avoid nesting. If a single region needs to use several shared variables, they may be listed in the **region** statement. In this case, the compiler may choose any order it wishes to acquire the semaphores. A consistent order is equivalent to a hierarchical allocation rule.

If several activities are waiting for the same shared variable, we can protect against starvation by making sure the underlying semaphores keep all waiting activities in a first-in, first-out queue.

Regions protect the programmer against two mistakes that are common with semaphores. First, there is no way to access a shared variable from outside a region. Variables are visible to more than one activity only if they are declared **shared**. Shared variables are invisible except within critical regions. Entry to critical regions automatically excludes conflicting activities. Second, there is no way to forget to call Up at the end of a region. Up is no longer explicitly invoked.

But several problems remain. The first is that synchronization requires busy waiting if critical regions are the only facility. The second is that accesses to shared variables may be scattered throughout the program, with the result that it is difficult to coordinate all the places that modify them. In addition, there is no way for several activities to read the same shared variables simultaneously even though simultaneous reads need not be mutually exclusive. We will address these objections in the next few sections.

## 2.8  Conditional critical regions

A slight modification to critical regions will allow us to solve the synchronization problem without busy wait. As we saw before, synchronization in general is the desire to block an action until a particular condition becomes true. For example, the "pop" operation makes sense only for a stack that is not empty. The action of popping the stack should be delayed until that condition holds. Likewise, action **B** of Figure 8.1 should continue only if **A** has terminated.

To meet these needs, we add an **await** statement that may only be used inside a critical region. **Await** names an arbitrary Boolean condition. If the condition is not met, the activity executing the **await** statement is blocked until it is met. For example, popping from a stack could be done as follows:

```
 1 type
 2    stack =
 3       record
 4          Count : integer; { How many elements in stack }
 5          Values : array 1:10 of element;
 6       end;
 7 var
 8    Trays : shared stack;
 9
10 ...
11
12 region Trays do
13    await Trays.Count > 0;
14    Result := Trays.Values[Trays.Count];
15    Trays.Count := Trays.Count - 1;
16 end;
```

To solve the synchronization problem of Figure 8.1, we can have a Boolean variable indicate when each activity finishes and test that variable in an **await** statement.

We must decide exactly what the **await** statement means. Does it relax exclusion if it blocks? If not, how can another activity ever modify the condition that is being awaited? If so, how can we be sure that no other activity has confused the data structures while we were blocked? One consistent approach is to demand that **await** statements appear only at the start of critical regions and that exclusion not start until the condition is met. (Of course, checking the condition must be atomic, a condition that can be achieved through hidden semaphores.) Another approach is to allow **await** statements anywhere in the critical region. Any **await** that blocks releases exclusion, so it is up to the programmer to make sure that data structures are consistent before encountering **await**. In this way other activities will not be confused when they enter their conflicting region, and the blocked activity will not be confused when it resumes.

We must also decide exactly when the conditions are to be tested. If each activity is on a separate processor, we may test conditions continually. However, since such busy waiting is unacceptable for most implementations, we need to limit the times when the condition may be tested. Certainly there is no need to test the condition as long as some other activity is in a conflicting region, because that other activity must maintain exclusion until it leaves its region, even though it may have made the condition true by its actions. In practice, there may be no need to test conditions when all activities are outside conflicting regions because useful conditions involve shared variables, and shared variables are changed only by activities within critical regions. One time we need to check conditions is when an activity leaves a critical region; the only conditions that must be tested are those in conflicting regions. The other time is when an activity in a conflicting region enters **await**. (This situation only arises if **await** is permitted in the middle of regions.) Checking a condition can still be very expensive because it may require switching to the environment of the blocked activity in order to access local variables involved in the condition. For efficiency, such complex conditions may be disallowed.

To show how conditional critical regions can be used to implement our synchronization graph, we present the code for activity **E**:

```
1 var
2    ADone, BDone, CDone, DDone, EDone, FDone, GDone :
3       shared Boolean := false;
4
5 activity E:
6    region BDone do await BDone end;
7    region DDone do await DDone end;
8    perform E's work;
9    region EDone do EDone := true; end;
```

Conditional critical regions are very easy to use for complex mutual-exclusion and synchronization problems. The exercises at the end of this chapter suggest some problems to try; they are based on ideas we will introduce soon.

## 2.9 Monitors

One objection to using conditional critical regions is the cost involved in checking conditions. A second objection is that code that modifies shared data may be scattered throughout a program. The language construct called a **monitor** was invented to address both these issues. It acts both as a data-abstraction device and a mutual-exclusion device. Synchronization is provided by a new data type called a **condition**.

A **data-abstraction** device is a programming construct that separates operations on data from their implementation details, thus providing new function while hiding unnecessary structure. (We have seen abstraction as a form of the Beautification Principle.) In languages that provide such devices, they usually have the form of a new name scope (a block, in the Algol sense) that may export types and procedures to the outside world but uses local variables to store state and perform necessary computations. Monitors have this structure, too, although they are principally used as a mechanism for *shared* data abstractions. They export procedures, which we will call **guard** procedures, that may be called from outside the monitor. No matter how many activities are running, only one is allowed to execute a guard procedure at a time.

The most straightforward use of monitors is to package all routines that use a set of shared data into a single monitor. All accesses to those data will be forced to use guard procedures because the data themselves are hidden from the outside world. For example, if we wish to implement a counter that records the number of times some interesting event has happened, and different activities will wish to modify and inspect the counter, we could build the following monitor. The syntax chosen here is meant to convey the ideas without introducing extraneous concepts; therefore, it differs from Modula, which also provides monitors with a different syntax.

```
 1 monitor Counter;
 2
 3 export RaiseCount, ReadCount;
 4
 5 var
 6    Count : integer;
 7
 8 guard procedure RaiseCount;
 9 begin
10    Count := Count + 1;
11 end RaiseCount;
12
13 guard procedure ReadCount : integer;
14 begin
15    ReadCount := Count;
16 end ReadCount;
17
18 begin { initialize }
19    Count := 0;
20 end Counter.
```

One way to picture the monitor is shown in Figure 8.2, which shows the monitor as a floor plan of a building. When activities wish to invoke guard procedures, they must enter through the entry queue, where they are blocked until the guard procedures are free of any activity. Entrance 2 is unlocked only if there is no activity in the main room. Door 1 is always unlocked; when it is opened to let an activity out, door 2 is unlocked.

It is not hard to implement this kind of monitor using only semaphores. A compiler could translate guard procedures into the following code:

```
Down(MonitorEmpty);
    guard procedure body
Up(MonitorEmpty);
```

The fact that the programmer does not need to remember the final Up operation makes monitors easier and safer to use than bare semaphores. The fact that all the code that can affect the shared variables is packaged in one place also makes it easier to check that the variables are properly used.

It is not hard to find situations in which the simple monitors we have shown so far are insufficient. As it stands, they have no facility for synchronization. The **producers-consumers** problem is a good example of a situation where both mutual exclusion and synchronization are needed.

### Producers-consumers problem

Any number of producer activities and consumer activities are running. At any time, a producer activity may create some data. At any time, a consumer activity may want to accept some data. The data should be saved in a buffer until they are needed. Since the buffer is finite, we want a producer to block if its new creation would overflow the buffer. We also want a consumer to block if there are no data available when it wants them. Data should be accepted in the order in which they are produced, although we relax this rule somewhat for data produced or consumed simultaneously.

We can use a monitor to implement a **bounded buffer** shared among all producers

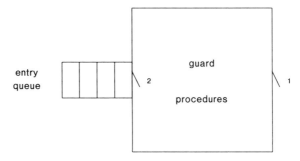

**Figure 8.2** A simple monitor

and consumers. The data-abstraction features of the monitor will collect the
BufferPut and BufferGet operations in one place, so the program is easy to debug
and maintain. The mutual-exclusion properties of the monitor will ensure that two
producers don't attempt to modify the buffer at the same time and, more generally,
that simultaneous conflicting uses are prevented. Synchronization features will be
used to block producers and consumers when the buffer is full or empty.

Here is a monitor implementation of bounded buffers:

```
 1 monitor BoundedBuffer;
 2
 3 export GetBuffer, PutBuffer;
 4
 5 const
 6    Size = 10; { number of elements in the buffer at one time }
 7 type
 8    Datum = ... { the data type of the contents of the buffer }
 9 var
10    Buffer : array 0:Size-1 of Datum;
11    Count : 0..Size; { how many elements currently in the buffer }
12    NextIn, NextOut : 0..Size-1;
13       { index of next datum to place in the buffer or remove }
14    NonEmpty, NonFull : condition;
15
16 guard procedure PutBuffer(What : Datum);
17 begin
18    if Count = Size then
19       wait NonFull;
20    end;
21    Buffer[NextIn] := What;
22    NextIn := (NextIn + 1) mod Size;
23    inc(Count);
24    signal NonEmpty;
25 end PutBuffer;
26
27 guard procedure GetBuffer(var Result : Datum);
28 begin
29    if Count = 0 then
30       wait NonEmpty;
31    end;
32    Result := Buffer[NextOut];
33    NextOut := (NextOut + 1) mod Size;
34    dec(Count);
35    signal NonFull;
36 end GetBuffer;
37
38 begin { initialization }
39    Count := 0;
40    NextIn := 0;
41    NextOut := 0;
42 end Buffer
```

This representation of bounded buffers satisfies our goals nicely. We need not
worry that some other piece of program modifies the shared variables Buffer and
Count because they are visible only within this monitor. There is no danger that
several activities will try to modify Count simultaneously, will produce into the

same cell of Buffer simultaneously, or will take data from the same cell of Buffer simultaneously, because all such behavior is restricted to guard procedures, which are mutually exclusive.

Finally, we have provided a way for activities to be blocked if necessary. The mechanism is the new (predefined) type called **condition**. Both NonEmpty and NonFull are declared as conditions in line 14. Let us concentrate on the condition NonEmpty. At line 30, a consumer that finds the buffer empty executes a **wait** on this condition. The **wait** will block this activity until some other activity signals the condition. At that time, the blocked activity may continue. When it gets to line 32, it assumes that the buffer is no longer empty. Any producer that succeeds in placing new data in the buffer executes a **signal** on the NonEmpty condition at line 24. This operation unblocks a waiting consumer.

The foregoing discussion raises some troubling questions. Exactly when does the blocked consumer continue? If immediately, then we may have two activities in the monitor at once, and our careful mutual exclusion is ruined. If later, then by the time it continues, some other consumer may already have taken the last datum, and the assumption on line 32 that the buffer is not empty is wrong. If several consumers are waiting at the same time, which one or ones are unblocked by a signal? If a producer executes a **signal** when no consumers are waiting, is this signal stored or discarded?

Not all definitions of monitors in the literature agree on the answers to these questions. We will first present a common approach and then discuss alternatives. Figure 8.3 expands the preceding figure to show the effect of conditions. For every condition we build a condition queue (shown on the bottom of the monitor). We

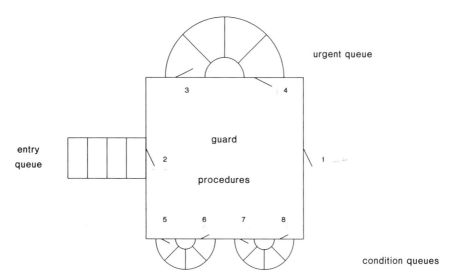

**Figure 8.3** Monitors with conditions

also introduce one urgent queue (shown at the top of the monitor). As before, we insist that at most one activity inhabit the guard procedures (the center of the monitor) at any time. Activities that are blocked will be placed in these queues. Here are the rules that govern the doors in and out of the queues and the central region:

(1)    New activities wait in the entry queue. A new activity may enter through door 2 if no activity is currently in the central region.

(2)    If an activity leaves the central region through door 1 (the exit), one activity is allowed in through door 4 (from the urgent queue) if there is one waiting there. If not, one activity is allowed through door 2 (from the entry queue) if there is one waiting there.

(3)    An activity that executes a **wait** enters the door to the appropriate condition queue (for example, 5 or 7).

(4)    When an activity executes **signal**, the signaled condition queue is inspected. If some activity is waiting in that queue, the signaler enters the urgent queue (door 3) and one waiter is allowed into the central region (door 6 or 8). If no activity is waiting in that queue, the signaler proceeds without leaving the central region. The signal is ignored.

(5)    All queues are ordered first in, first out.

These rules assure that a waiting consumer is unblocked immediately when a producer signals NonEmpty and that the producer is blocked in the urgent queue until the consumer has taken the datum. We have maintained our rule that at most one activity inhabits the central region.

People who use monitors have noticed that the signal operation is almost always the last operation performed in a guard procedure. We see this behavior in our producer-consumer solution (lines 24 and 35). Our rules will often make the signaler wait in the urgent queue and then return to the central region just to get out of the monitor altogether. This scenario violates the Hysteresis Principle. Furthermore, if the signaler does have more work to do, it can't assume that the situation of shared variables is the same when it returns from the urgent queue because the activity that was unblocked is likely to change them. For these reasons, some people require that signal must be the last operation of a guard procedure and must cause the signaling activity to leave the monitor. Then we don't need an urgent queue, and signalers never make invalid assumptions about shared data. However, this restriction makes monitors less flexible. (Such monitors are strictly less powerful in a theoretical sense.)

A related suggestion is that **broadcast** should be like **signal** but should release *all* the members of the associated condition queue. Since they can't all be allowed into the central region at once, most are placed in the urgent queue. In this way, when conditions are right, all the waiters may be released instead of the awkward alternative of having each released waiter releasing the next one in turn. However, a released activity can no longer assume that the condition it has awaited is truly met by the time it resumes. Programs written with **broadcast** usually replace the **if** statement in lines 29 through 31 above with a **while** loop:

```
29      while Count = 0 do
30          wait NonEmpty;
31      end;
```

Proper use of monitors follows the guideline that no activity should take too long in the central region. It shouldn't take too long for an activity that is waiting in the entry queue to get into the monitor and access the shared variables. Any lengthy operation should relax exclusion by entering a condition queue or by doing its work outside the monitor. A fascinating violation of this guideline arises if the activity in a guard procedure makes a call on a guard procedure in another monitor. Under our rules, this activity is still considered to be in the first monitor, preventing any other activity from entering. However, it may take a long time before it returns because it may be forced to wait in the second monitor in a condition queue. (By our guideline, it shouldn't have to wait very long in either the entry queue or the urgent queue.) This delay in returning violates our guideline with respect to the first monitor. It can even lead to deadlock if the condition it awaits in the second monitor can be signaled only by an activity that is currently waiting patiently to enter the first monitor.

A number of solutions to this problem have been proposed.

(1)    Warn the programmer but allow the bad situation to develop. That is, nested monitor calls maintain exclusion on the old monitor while in the new one.

(2)    Disallow nested monitor calls.

(3)    Release exclusion on the old monitor and enforce it only on the new one. When the activity is ready to return, it must wait in the urgent queue of the first monitor until it can once again achieve exclusive use of the central region.

(4)    Let the programmer decide whether the nested call should maintain exclusion in the old monitor or not. By default, method 1 is used. The programmer can say **duckout** to release exclusion while still in the monitor and **duckin** to acquire exclusion again. These calls can bracket a nested call to simulate method 3.

Although monitors represent a significant advance over the earlier devices we have studied, they do have some significant problems. Monitors have been criticized for not providing any control over how the queues are ordered. The policy to treat them in first-in, first-out order is not always appropriate. For example, several activities simultaneously in the urgent queue are like nested interrupts, which are usually released in first-in, last-out (stack) order. As another example, different waiters in a condition queue may have different priorities, which could be taken into account in selecting an order. Some people prefer a more general mechanism for inspecting and reordering the various queues.

Monitors also display unexpected complexity with respect to nested calls. It is not easy to describe the semantics of **wait** and **signal** without resorting to pictures like Figure 8.3. Complexity is also introduced by the artificial use of condition variables. The programmer is more likely to understand the underlying condition (like "Count $> 0$") than to represent that condition properly by judicious use of **wait** and **signal**.

Another objection to monitors comes from their data-abstraction ability. If we have several bounded buffers to implement, we would be tempted to build only one monitor and to have the PutBuffer and GetBuffer procedures take a parameter that describes which buffer is to be manipulated. This solution has two drawbacks. One is that the buffer has an existence outside the monitor and so might be inadvertently modified by a non-monitor procedure. Luckily, modern programming languages have the idea of "exported types" that exist outside a data-abstraction module but can be manipulated only from within that module. The other drawback is that using only one monitor is too conservative: Every manipulation of one buffer now excludes operations on all other buffers because mutual exclusion is governed by which monitor is to be entered, not by which data structure is being accessed. Again, modern programming languages come to the rescue. One can imagine a "monitor type" for bounded buffers. A new monitor of that type is built for each buffer needed. The program for monitors needs to be written only once, but each buffer gets its own monitor with its own exclusion.

A serious objection to monitors is related to our guideline that exclusion should not be in force for very long. However, shared data might be needed for a very long time. This is exactly the situation in the readers-writers problem, mentioned in our chapter on file structures.

### Readers-writers problem

> Any number of reader activities and writer activities are running. They share some data (for example, a file). At any time, a reader activity may wish to read data from the file. At any time, a writer activity may want to read or modify the data in the file. Reading and writing are time-consuming operations, but they always finish eventually. During the time a writer is writing, no other reader or writer may access the shared data. Any number of readers may access the data simultaneously. For fairness, we prefer that no reader or writer be **starved** (that is, forced to wait indefinitely).

If we make Read and Write guard procedures, two readers cannot execute at the same time, a restriction that violates the spirit of the problem. Therefore, Read must not be a guard procedure but rather a procedure external to the monitor. Proper use of Read would call the guard procedures StartRead and EndRead around calls to Read, but there is no assurance that a reader will follow these rules. Monitors therefore fail to protect the shared data adequately.

## 2.10  Crowd monitors

One nice extension to monitors to avoid this last problem is called **crowd monitors**. Crowd monitors distinguish guard procedures from ordinary procedures within the monitor. Only guard procedures are mutually exclusive. Ordinary procedures may be invoked only by activities that have permission to do so; this permission is granted and revoked by guard procedures. A skeleton of the crowd-monitor solution to the readers-writers problem is as follows:

```
 1 crowd monitor ReadWrite;
 2
 3 export StartRead, EndRead, Read, StartWrite, EndWrite,
 4    Write;
 5 var
 6    Readers : crowd Read;
 7    Writers : crowd Read, Write;
 8
 9 guard procedure StartRead;
10 begin
11    ... { block the caller until reading is safe }
12    enter Readers;
13    ...
14 end StartRead;
15
16 guard procedure EndRead;
17 begin
18    leave Readers;
19    ... { bookkeeping, maybe signal a waiting writer }
20 end EndRead;
21
22 guard procedure StartWrite;
23 begin
24    ... { block the caller until writing is safe }
25    enter Writers;
26    ...
27 end StartWrite;
28
29 guard procedure EndWrite;
30 begin
31    leave Writers;
32    ... { bookkeeping, maybe signal waiter }
33 end EndWrite;
34
35 procedure Read;
36 begin
37    ... { actually read from the shared data }
38 end Read;
39
40 procedure Write;
41 begin
42    ... { actually modify the shared data }
43 end Write;
44
45 end ReadWrite
```

In lines 6 and 7, we declare two **crowds** called Readers and Writers. Activities can be members of these crowds. Any member of Readers may access the Read procedure (lines 35–38), and any member of Writers may access both the Read and the Write procedure (lines 40–43). Activities initially belong to no crowds. The guard procedures, which are mutually exclusive as before, decide when it is appropriate for an activity to enter or leave a crowd. They may use conditions to wait for the right situation. When the guard procedure decides to let a reader proceed, it executes **enter** for the Readers crowd (line 12). Similarly, a guard can let a writer enter the Writers crowd (line 25). Although any activity may call Read and Write, since they are exported from the monitor, a run-time check prevents activities from calling ordinary procedures that are invisible to the crowds they are in. A member only of Readers may not call Write. However, a member of Writers may call either Read or Write, since both are specified in the definition of Writers (line 7).

It is easy to implement crowd monitors once regular monitors have been implemented. A run-time check is applied every time an activity calls a procedure like Read and Write in order to make sure that the activity is in the necessary crowd. If not, a program error has been discovered. No new blocking or unblocking rules are needed.

## 2.11 Event counts and sequencers

So far we have investigated methods that serve for both mutual exclusion and synchronization. We now turn to a technique to achieve synchronization without requiring mutual exclusion. Mutual exclusion is not always desirable because it limits concurrency. It is also difficult to enforce, as we have seen, and is not always needed on physically distributed computers. In fact, if one hasn't yet implemented mutual exclusion, the method we are about to discuss can be used to build semaphores to provide mutual exclusion, too. The semaphores we can build will even allow simultaneous Down operations on several semaphores.

The first tool we will introduce is the **event count**. An event count is represented as a non-decreasing integer variable, initially 0. It keeps a count of the number of events of interest to the program, such as the number of times a variable has been modified. As an abstract data type, event counts have three operations: Advance, Read, and Await.

- Advance(E) is used to signal the occurrence of events associated with event count E. It has the effect of incrementing E atomically.

- Read(E) returns the value of the event count E. If Read returns some number $n$, then at least $n$ Advance operations must have happened. By the time this number is returned, the event count may have been advanced again a number of times.

- Await(E **reaches** $v$) waits for the event count E to have the value $v$. It blocks the calling activity until at least $v$ Advance operations have occurred. It is acceptable if more than $v$ Advance operations have occurred when it is finally unblocked. This "overshoot" could result from very frequent Advance operations. (We adopt the syntax shown here for clarity. Await could be a procedure with two parameters, using a comma instead of **reaches**.)

These definitions allow both Await and Read to be concurrent with Advance, since we don't care if Read gives us a somewhat stale value or if Await waits a trifle too long.

We introduced the producers-consumers problem earlier to show how monitors handle synchronization. Here is a solution using event counts. For the time being, we assume that there is only one producer and one consumer.

```
 1 const
 2    Size = 10; { number of elements in the buffer. }
 3 type
 4    Datum = ... { data type for buffer contents. }
 5 var
 6    In, Out : eventcount;
 7    Buffer  : array 0:Size-1 of Datum;
 8
 9 activity Producer;
10 var
11    SequenceNumber : integer;
12    Value : Datum;
13 begin
14    for SequenceNumber := 1 to infinity do
15       ... { compute Value }
16       Await(Out reaches SequenceNumber - Size);
17       Buffer[SequenceNumber mod Size] := Value;
18       Advance(In)
19    end
20 end Producer;
21
22 activity Consumer;
23 var
24    SequenceNumber : integer;
25    Value : Datum;
26 begin
27    for SequenceNumber := 1 to infinity do
28       Await(In reaches SequenceNumber);
29       Value := Buffer[SequenceNumber mod Size];
30       Advance(Out)
31       ... { use the Value }
32    end
33 end Consumer;
```

There is no need for us to worry that the consumer and producer will simultaneously access the same cell in Buffer, since the producer will have to wait until the consumer has used that cell before its Await in line 16 will allow it to proceed. Similarly, the consumer knows that when it accesses a cell of Buffer, the producer must have placed data there, or the Await in line 28 would not have unblocked. In addition, we need not worry that both Advance operations (lines 18 and 30) will happen at the same time, because they deal with different event counts. This solution allows the bounded buffer to be used simultaneously by both activities because it guarantees that the very same datum will never be touched by both at once.

The other tool we will use is the **sequencer**, which assigns an arbitrary order to unordered events. We will use this order to decide which activity gets a resource first. A sequencer is implemented as a non-decreasing integer variable, initialized to 0. It has only one operation: Ticket.

● Ticket(S) returns the current value of the sequencer S (initially 0) and then
  increments S. This operation is atomic. We need some form of mutual
  exclusion to implement Ticket because no two calls may return the same
  value.

Now we can implement a producer-consumer situation in which there are
many producers. For simplicity, we will still have only one consumer. As before,
consumption and production need not exclude each other. However, two producers
must take turns to make sure that they don't write into the same cell in the Buffer.
Here is the new producer program.

```
 1 ...
 2 var
 3    Turn : sequencer;
 4
 5 activity Producer;
 6 var
 7    SequenceNumber : integer;
 8    Value : Datum;
 9 begin
10    loop
11       ... { compute Value }
12       SequenceNumber := Ticket(Turn); { discover turn }
13       Await(In reaches SequenceNumber); { wait for turn }
14       Await(Out reaches SequenceNumber - Size + 1);
15          { wait for Buffer }
16       Buffer[SequenceNumber mod Size] := Value;
17       Advance(In);
18    end;
19 end Producer;
```

Each producer must wait until it is its turn to produce. The call to Ticket in line
12 orders active producers. Usually there will be no wait in line 13, unless another
producer has just grabbed an earlier ticket and has not yet gotten to line 17. The
Await in line 14 is to make sure that the cell in Buffer that is about to be overwritten has been consumed. It differs from line 16 of the previous example by 1, since
here SequenceNumber starts at 0, not 1. The Advance in line 17 tells waiting consumers that this cell in Buffer may be consumed, and it tells waiting producers that
we have finished our turn.

The call to Await in line 13 might seem unnecessary. It's there to make sure
that producers write cells of Buffer in order, so that consumers may assume that
when In is advanced in line 17, the next cell of Buffer has new data. Unfortunately, one effect of this imposed sequential behavior on producers is that
separate cells of Buffer cannot be written simultaneously. If the data are large,
producers may exclude each other for a long time.

We promised earlier that a semaphore could be built with event counts and
sequencers. Here is an implementation:

```
 1 type
 2    Semaphore =
 3       record
 4          T  :  sequencer;
 5          E  :  eventcount;
 6          I  :  integer; { initial value }
 7       end;
 8
 9 procedure Down(var S  :  Semaphore);
10 begin
11    with S do
12       Await(E reaches Ticket(T)−I+1);
13    end
14 end Down;
15
16 procedure Up(S  :  Semaphore);
17 begin
18    Advance(S.E);
19 end Up;
```

The Down procedure gets a ticket (which orders all the waiters) and then waits for the event count to be advanced as many times as the ticket indicates. There is no need for Down and Up to exclude each other. However, we require that every waiter get a different ticket.

We can extend this wait procedure to wait for two semaphores at once. The dining-philosophers problem, described in Chapter 4, can be solved by such a method. Here is a procedure that waits for two semaphores. It uses a third semaphore, MutualExclusion, for its own purposes.

```
 1 var
 2    MutualExclusion : Semaphore; { initialized at I = 1 }
 3
 4 procedure DoubleDown(var S1, S2 : Semaphore);
 5 var
 6    Ticket1, Ticket2 : integer;
 7 begin
 8    Down(MutualExclusion);
 9    Ticket1 := Ticket(S1.T);
10    Ticket2 := Ticket(S2.T);
11    Up(MutualExclusion);
12    with S1 do
13       Await(E reaches Ticket1);
14    end;
15    with S2 do
16       Await(E reaches Ticket2);
17    end;
18 end DoubleDown;
```

We use the MutualExclusion semaphore in lines 8−11 to make sure that we acquire the two tickets as an atomic action. It makes no difference in what order we wait for S1 and S2 (lines 13 and 16).

## 2.12 Path expressions

A completely different way to describe synchronization is to spell out what routines may be called, and in what order, separately from the routines themselves. We will introduce a syntax known as **path expressions** that specifies all temporal relationships among invocations of procedures that control shared data. These expressions are built out of procedure names and connectors that indicate restrictions. For our examples, we will deal with the readers-writers problem and use procedures such as Read, Write, and StartRead.

The simplest expression has just one procedure name:

> **path** Read

This expression means that only one activity may call Read at a time but that when Read is finished, another activity (or the same one again) may call it again. That is, when the path expression is finished, it may be started again. If we want to specify that Read must be surrounded by StartRead and EndRead, we can say

> **path** StartRead ; Read ; EndRead

The semicolon operator indicates that after one procedure has finished, the next one may be called. Equivalently, this operator indicates that before a particular procedure may be called, the one before it must have finished. However, it does not require that the same activity that calls StartRead must call Read.

To indicate that any number of activities can simultaneously perform the same procedure, we surround that procedure in brackets, as shown here:

> **path** { Read }

This path expression says that any number of simultaneous uses of Read are permissible. If some activities are in Read, a new one may join them. When they all finish, the path expression is finished and may be started again.

The last operator is the "either-or" operator, which we will write as a vertical bar, as in the following example:

> **path** Read ¦ Write

This operator means "the left side or the right side may be active, but not both." This particular path expression specifies that one activity may read at a time and one may write at a time, and reading and writing exclude each other. After either finishes, any activity may start doing either again. We assume that activities that wish to Read or Write are served in arrival order; no activity is caused to wait forever for an either-or operator.

We can combine these operators to form more complex expressions. For example, the following begins to address the actual readers-writers problem:

> **path** { Read } ¦ Write

This expression lets any number of readers alternate with a single writer. Although this expression represents exactly the restriction we want, it is not fair to writers. If reader activities arrive fast enough so that there is always some activity in the "{ Read }" part of the path expression, writers will never be allowed to start.

This solution also has the danger that a reader will want to perform several reads in a row. A writer could be serviced between two reads, and inconsistent data would be read. To avoid this problem, we will assume that each reader wants to read only once. Similarly, we will assume that each writer wants to write only once. Otherwise, where we say Read, we could understand that to mean "perform any number of read operations in the same activity." Likewise, we can understand Write to mean "perform any number of read or write operations in the same activity."

To represent fair synchronization rules, we need some more tools. First, we will allow several path expressions to be in force at the same time, as long as they don't mention the same procedures. Next, we will want to introduce intermediate procedures. For simplicity, we will use the following notation for these procedures:

```
let procedure = sequence of procedures
```

Let's illustrate this idea with a more complex readers-writers example.

```
1 path TryRead ¦ TryWrite
2 path { StartRead; Read } ¦ Write
3 let TryRead = StartRead
4 let TryWrite = Write
5 let DoRead = TryRead ; Read
6 let DoWrite = TryWrite
```

Readers call DoRead, which expands to `TryRead ; Read` (line 5), which in turn becomes `StartRead ; Read` (line 3). Similarly, writers call DoWrite, which becomes TryWrite (line 6), which in turn becomes Write (line 4). The StartRead procedure does not need to do any work; it is called only to allow us to synchronize the rest of the operations. Line 2 expresses the constraints we want on simultaneous readers and writers. Line 1 tells us that activities must wait their turn to start TryRead and TryWrite.

This set of path expressions works, in that it properly excludes readers and writers from each other. It also enforces a policy, in that it takes readers and writers in the order in which they appear, except that readers that arrive next to each other in line are allowed to overlap their executions. It is not easy to be convinced, however, that this policy comes out of these expressions.

Implementing path expressions is not difficult; they can be converted to semaphore operations. However, we will not examine the conversion because it is complex. Luckily, a compiler can be expected to perform this work, so it can be done before the program is run, and the programmer need not deal with its intricacies.

Since path expressions have the advantage of separating the synchronization specification from the routines themselves, the procedures that accomplish work (like Read and Write) are uncluttered by extraneous considerations. Path expressions also avoid specialized guard procedures whose only purpose is to effect mutual exclusion and synchronization. However, the procedures we introduced with the **let** clause serve much the same function.

Like monitors, path expressions are not descriptive enough to describe the order in which blocked activities should be resumed. The either-or operator unblocks activities in the order in which they arrive, which may not be the order desired.

Let's step back from the complex synchronization problems we have been examining and try Figure 8.1. We can certainly impose extra constraints and require that all the activities follow a prescribed order. If we wish to implement Figure 8.1 without extra constraints, we will have to let the same procedure appear in several path expressions. We then get the following solution:

```
1 path A ; B ; C ; F ; I
2 path D ; E ; F
3 path A ; D ; G ; H ; I
4 path B ; E ; H
```

## 2.13  Invariant expressions

The method of **invariant expressions** is reminiscent of path expressions. We queue all activities that try to enter each procedure. An invariant expression associated with each queue tells when it is permissible to allow the first waiter in that queue into the crowd. If there is no invariant expression for some procedure, activities may enter it at any time.

Invariant expressions have a very limited syntax. They may use built-in counters that record the number of interesting events for any procedure P. There are only five such counters:

- RequestCount(P) counts the number of requests (since the beginning of time) for procedure P.
- StartCount(P) counts the number of times procedure P has actually been started.
- FinishCount(P) counts the number of times procedure P has been finished.
- CurrentCount(P) counts the number of current executions of P; it is equivalent to StartCount(P)−FinishCount(P).
- WaitCount(P) counts the number of waiting executions of P; it is equivalent to RequestCount(P)−StartCount(P).

An invariant expression has the form

```
expression    comparison    constant
```

Expressions are just sums and differences of counters. The comparison can be $<$, $>$, $\leqslant$, $\geqslant$, $=$ or $\neq$. For example, we might write

```
WaitCount(P) − RequestCount(Q) > 4
```

We associate such an expression with a procedure as a rule that must hold before we allow an activity to execute that procedure. (This interpretation is not the same as saying the rule must hold *while* the activity is executing the procedure.) The following is a solution to the multiple producer-consumer problem:

```
 1 module BoundedBuffer;
 2
 3 export GetBuffer, PutBuffer;
 4
 5 const
 6    Size = 10; { number of elements in the buffer at once }
 7 type
 8    Datum = ... { data type of the contents of the buffer }
 9 var
10    Buffer : array 0:Size-1 of Datum;
11    NextIn, NextOut : 0..Size-1;
12       { index of next datum to insert, delete }
13 invariant PutBuffer
14    StartCount(PutBuffer) - FinishCount(GetBuffer) < Size
15       { no overproduction }
16    CurrentCount(PutBuffer) = 0 { prevent producer conflict }
17 invariant GetBuffer
18    StartCount(GetBuffer) - FinishCount(PutBuffer) < 0
19       { no overconsumption }
20    CurrentCount(GetBuffer) = 0 { prevent consumer conflict }
21
22 procedure PutBuffer(What : Datum);
23 begin
24    Buffer[NextIn] := What;
25    NextIn := (NextIn + 1) mod Size;
26 end PutBuffer;
27
28 procedure GetBuffer(var Result : Datum);
29 begin
30    Result := Buffer[NextOut];
31    NextOut := (NextOut + 1) mod  Size;
32 end GetBuffer;
```

We have repeated the entire module to show how simple the PutBuffer and
GetBuffer procedures have become. As with path expressions, we find that moving
all the synchronization out of the procedures clarifies the entire program. Our
invariant expressions are in lines 13 through 20. Line 14 restricts calls to
PutBuffer by requiring that enough calls to GetBuffer have already happened so
that the buffer won't be overfilled. Similarly, line 18 restricts calls to GetBuffer by
requiring that enough calls to PutBuffer have already happened so that the buffer
has some data to be removed. Lines 16 and 20 restrict both PutBuffer and
GetBuffer to allow only one activity in either.

We can also use invariant expressions to represent a solution to the readers-
writers problem. We will show just the invariants and omit the rest of the module.

```
invariant Read
   CurrentCount(Write) = 0
invariant Write
   CurrentCount(Write) + CurrentCount(Read) = 0
```

We might make the same assumption we did for path expressions: that activities
forced to wait because of an invariant are unblocked, if possible, in arrival order.
Therefore, if several readers and writers arrive while a writer is active, all are
blocked. When the writer finishes, one reader or writer, whichever came first, is
allowed to start. However, while one activity is reading, any number of readers

may start; only writers are blocked.

The solution just shown may starve writers. To give writers precedence, we need to prevent new readers from starting if there are any waiting writers. The following invariant expressions serve this purpose:

```
invariant Read
    WaitCount(Write) + CurrentCount(Write) = 0
invariant Write
    CurrentCount(Write) + CurrentCount(Read) = 0
```

The only change is an extra clause in the invariant expression for Read.

Invariant expressions are easily used to represent the synchronization graph of Figure 8.1. For example, the invariant expression for procedure **E** would be as follows:

```
invariant E
    FinishCount(B) + FinishCount(D) = 2
```

Invariant expressions, like path expressions and monitors, are unable to reorder waiting queues to serve some activities out of turn. However, they are often far clearer than path expressions and can express the same sort of synchronization constraints.

# 3 PERSPECTIVE

It is necessary to distinguish carefully between simple mutual-exclusion situations, where it is dangerous for two activities both to proceed, and synchronization situations, where complex conditions might govern when an activity may proceed. To show pure forms of both situations, we considered modifying shared data (pure mutual exclusion) and Figure 8.1 (pure synchronization). Later, we turned to the producer-consumer problem and the readers-writers problem as more complex examples. These latter examples display aspects both of mutual exclusion (we don't want two producers simultaneously writing into the buffer, and we don't want two writers simultaneously active) and of synchronization (consumers must wait until data are produced; readers should wait if there are waiting writers). The situations that occur within operating systems are typically of this hybrid variety.

The methods we have seen range from simple hardware techniques to programming-language constructs that try to guarantee that the restrictions described are clear, efficiently implementable, and unlikely to be misused. The more complex solutions are invariably implemented by behind-the-scenes work using a simpler solution. For example, monitors can be implemented by semaphores. Semaphores themselves need to turn on mutual exclusion around critical parts of their implementation, and might do that with test-and-set locks. At the bottom of this ladder always stands the inherent atomicity of main store, which serves only one access at a time.

One might evaluate different proposals on the basis of three characteristics: modularity, expressive power, and ease of use. Modularity is achieved by data abstraction and by separating concurrency control from resource access. Monitors, crowd monitors, path expressions, and invariant expressions all display a high degree of modularity.

Expressive power involves ability to formulate exclusion, synchronization, and priority requirements. Each of the methods displayed is capable of formulating the first two kinds of requirement. None does well with respect to priority because queues are built into most of the methods without any mechanism for inspecting and reordering those queues.

Requirements may depend on a host of criteria. A partial list follows. For each, we show how it applies to the producers-consumers problem.

- What operation is being requested: PutBuffer and GetBuffer have different requirements.

- When the request is made: If two activities call PutBuffer, the one that called first should take precedence (in the absence of priority).

- The synchronization state of the resource: The fact that an activity is currently executing GetBuffer implies that another activity should be delayed in executing the same procedure.

- The data state of the resource: GetBuffer is blocked if the buffer is empty.

- The history of accesses: We block PutBuffer if there haven't been enough calls to GetBuffer. We could pose this same constraint as part of the data state of the resource.

- The parameters to the operation: The data that are being put in the buffer do not influence our solution, but we could imagine that some data are more crucial than others.

- The identity of the caller: We would not like a producer to call GetBuffer.

Path expressions ignore the data state of the resource, the parameters to the operation, and the identity of the caller. Invariant expressions concentrate heavily on the history of accesses, expressing other items of interest (like the synchronization state and the data state) in terms of that history.

Ease of use is a subjective criterion. Conditional critical regions are much easier to use than monitors, but they are not in as widespread use. Invariant expressions seem more usable than path expressions in the examples we have seen.

The choice of mechanisms for concurrency control depends on efficiency and on intended use. Inside the operating system kernel, it often suffices to use the simplest lock based on raising priority for short access to shared data; longer accesses that might involve synchronization considerations (like placing data in a buffer) would have to use a more expensive solution. If processes, which are outside the kernel, need to share data, the kernel might give them a semaphore facility through service calls. This facility might then be used to construct monitors or event counts.

The programming language chosen by the operating system writer has an obvious influence on the solutions chosen for the kernel. For example, an operating

system written in Modula or Concurrent Pascal is likely to use the monitor-like
concepts in those languages. Similarly, the facilities offered by the operating system have an influence on concurrency control between processes that share data
(either virtual store or files).

# 4  FURTHER READING

Most of our understanding of concurrency control is due to the early work of a few
giants: Dijkstra, Hoare, and Brinch Hansen. T. J. Dekker introduced the non-
alternating switch in the early 1960s. This concept was generalized by Dijkstra
(1965) to make the spin switch. Peterson (1981) simplified the non-alternating
switch. Monitors were already in the works when conditional critical regions were
designed. Hoare (1972) first mentioned conditional critical regions, and Brinch
Hansen (1980) later used them as the principal mechanism for concurrency control
in his language, Edison. Dijkstra (1971) introduced the notion of a "secretary,"
the forerunner of the modern monitor, at the same time conditional critical regions
were introduced by Hoare. Dijkstra's paper is worth reading for his insight into the
mutual-exclusion and synchronization problems and his foresight of problems such
as the nested monitor call. The term "monitor" was introduced by Hoare (1974).
Nested monitor calls have been discussed at length in the literature; one place to
find more discussion on this topic is in a paper by Haddon (1977). Howard (1976)
has shown that monitors with signal only at the end are strictly less powerful than
ordinary monitors. The **broadcast** version of **signal** has been used successfully in
Mesa (Lampson and Redell, 1980). Crowds are based on serializers, which were
introduced by Atkinson and Hewitt (1979) and generalized by Horn and Honda
(1977). Event counts and sequencers were introduced by Reed and Kanodia
(1979), path expressions by Campbell and Habermann (1974), and invariant
expressions by Robert and Verjus (1977).

The readers-writers problem has been discussed by many authors; Courtois
and Parnas presented an early discussion (1971). One good place to read more is
in an article by Lamport (1977). The dining philosophers problem seems to have
been introduced by Dijkstra (1971).

A discussion of criteria for evaluating concurrency control mechanisms can be
found in a paper by Bloom (1979). Scott's survey of languages for distributed
computing (1984) considers monitors and path expressions as a special case of the
more general topic of tools for distributed computation.

# 5  EXERCISES

1.  Consider the following program fragments for processes **A** and **B**.

| process A | process B |
|-----------|-----------|
| 1   **for** SeqA := 1 **to** 10 **do** | **for** SeqB := 1 **to** 10 **do** |
| 2           x := x + 1; |           x := x + 1; |

Assume that the shared variable x starts at 0, that both **A** and **B** execute once, and that SeqA and SeqB are not shared variables. The two processes may execute at any speed. What are the possible resulting values of x? Assume that x must be loaded into a register for incrementing.

2.  Consider Figure 8.1 again.
    (a) We have seen that the actions to be performed could be partitioned into three activities, {A,B,C}, {D,E,F}, and {G,H,I}, to achieve some constraints through implicit synchronization. How many ways are there to partition the actions?
    (b) Your answer to (a) most likely did not include any activities like {A,C} because even though C must wait for A, which is implicit in {A,C}, it must also wait for B, which would have to be explicit. If we allow such activities, how many partitionings can you build?
    (c) Your answer to (b) most likely did not include any activities like {C,D}. Why not?

3.  Disabling interrupts does not work correctly for nested regions. Rewrite the BeginRegion and EndRegion routines to fix this problem.

4.  Generalize the switch mechanism to three processes.

5.  Does Dekker's non-alternating switch use busy waiting if **B** is in its region, Turn = A, and **A** is trying to enter its region?

6.  Prove that Dekker's non-alternating switch makes it impossible for an activity to starve while it is waiting to enter its region, on the assumption that whenever the conflicting activity enters its region, it eventually leaves that region.

7.  Generalize Dekker's non-alternating switch to three conflicting activities. (*somewhat difficult*)

8.  Generalize Dekker's non-alternating switch to *n* conflicting activities. (*difficult*)

9.  Prove that Peterson's non-alternating switch cannot starve either activity.

10. Prove that Peterson's non-alternating switch guarantees mutual exclusion.

11. Generalize Peterson's non-alternating switch to $n$ conflicting activities.
    (*hard*)

12. Instead of test-and-set, some computers provide an atomic instruction that
    sets the new value to 1 greater than its old value, as shown here:

    ```
    1 atomic function TestAndInc(var Lock : integer) : integer;
    2 begin
    3    TestAndInc := Lock;
    4    Lock := Lock + 1;
    5 end TestAndInc;
    ```

    Show how to use this instruction to implement locks. (*Hint*: You must be
    wary of integer overflow.)

13. The Finishing and WaitFor routines in the text work fine if the entire synch-
    ronization graph is to be executed just once. Show how to modify them so
    that if we wish to run the entire graph again, the Done variables have the
    correct values.

14. What does a cycle in a synchronization graph mean?

15. Procedures Finishing and WaitFor associate with every activity a Done vari-
    able that is set when the activity finishes. An alternative is to associate a
    Start variable with every activity and have the activity check it before it
    starts. Show how the synchronization graph of Figure 8.1 could be imple-
    mented in this way.

16. Show how to use semaphores to implement the synchronization graph so that
    each semaphore is associated with an activity and the activity waits (perhaps
    a number of times) for its own semaphore before starting.

17. We claim that a compiler can check for conflicting orders of nesting in
    **region** statements. Exactly how can the compiler accomplish this task?

18. Show why critical regions cannot implement the synchronization graph of
    Figure 8.1 without busy waiting.

19. Write a solution to the readers-writers problem using conditional critical
    regions, making sure that readers and writers never starve. All you need to
    provide is StartRead, EndRead, StartWrite, and EndWrite. (*Hint*: Separate
    readers into platoons. The next one starts filling as soon as a writer arrives.
    Alternate a platoon of readers with a single writer.)

20. Write a monitor solution to the readers-writers problem. (See the discussion
    for exercise 19.)

21. Find a case where it would be desirable for an activity that executes **signal** in
    a monitor to perform more work before leaving the monitor.

22. Implement semaphores using monitors.

23. We need mutual exclusion to implement Ticket. Do we also need mutual exclusion to implement Advance?

24. Show the program for the consumers in an event count and sequencer solution to multiple producers, multiple consumers.

25. Show how to use the DoubleDown procedure to implement the dining philosophers problem. Describe what can go wrong if we don't use MutualExclusion in implementing DoubleDown. Would the same problem occur if the declaration of MutualExclusion were at line 6 instead of line 2?

26. Does the following path-expression solution to the readers-writers problem work? What policy does it enforce?

```
1 path EnterRead
2 path TryRead | { TryWrite }
3 path { StartRead; Read } | Write
4 let EnterRead = TryRead
5 let TryRead = StartRead
6 let TryWrite = Write
7 let DoRead = EnterRead ; Read
8 let DoWrite = TryWrite
```

27. Does the following path-expression solution to the readers-writers problem work? What policy does it enforce?

```
1 path EnterWrite
2 path { TryRead } | TryWrite
3 path { Read } | ( StartWrite ; Write )
4 let TryWrite = StartWrite
5 let EnterWrite = TryWrite
6 let TryRead = Read
7 let DoRead = TryRead
8 let DoWrite = EnterWrite; Write
```

28. Show how to implement path expressions with semaphores. (*difficult*)

29. Write a path-expression solution to the multiple producer-consumer problem.

30. How would you implement invariant expressions using conditional critical regions?

31. What advantage do invariant expressions have over conditional critical regions?

32. Our invariant-expression solution to the producers-consumers problem serializes concurrent producers. Rewrite the solution so that producers are serialized only long enough to reserve slots but may fill those slots in parallel. Make sure that the GetBuffer procedure never takes data from an empty slot.

33. The Sequent Balance 21000 multicomputer has a hardware test-and-set instruction. How can this instruction be used for limited busy waiting, as suggested by the Hysteresis Principle, but not cause long busy waits?

# Co-operating Processes

In Chapter 8, we concentrated on the contention issues raised by multiple activities. The opposite of contention is co-operation. In this chapter, we will see ways in which processes can co-operate and what the operating system might provide to promote such co-operation.

A simple form of co-operation is when an interactive command interpreter starts a new process in response to a command and then waits until that process completes before prompting for the next command. A more complex form, pioneered by Unix, is to solve problems by building fairly simple processes and linking them together so that their joint behavior is more complex. For example, assume that we wish to list the names of all the files in a directory in alphabetical order. We could have the directory-listing program accept a #Sorted flag. The Unix-style alternative is to connect the output of the directory-listing program to the input of the sorting program. This philosophy reduces the responsibilities of ordinary programs because they will need to provide only limited services, not fancy ones that can be placed in other programs.

The recent advent of networks of computers linked together in various ways has given great impetus to the search for mechanisms for inter-process co-operation. The challenge raised by these networks is for the operating system to provide an environment for processes so that they can do their work no matter what machine they are on and no matter what other processes they need to communicate with.

This chapter deals with process interactions. We will start by seeing how one process can create another. Then we will see how processes can communicate with each other. We will close by seeing how communicating processes can form co-operating communities.

# 1 PROCESS CREATION AND NAMING

Operating systems differ widely in how frequently they start new processes. A spooling system has only one process, which repetitively selects a job and runs it. Multiprogrammed operating systems introduced simultaneous execution of several jobs. Typical batch multiprogramming operating systems initialize themselves to have a fixed number of processes. Each process runs one job, or one job step, until completion, and then looks for another job or job step to run. Alternatively, each job step can be treated as a new process, created by the job controller at the conclusion of the previous step.

Interactive multiprogramming started with a similar philosophy. Each interactive terminal is initialized with one process, which serves any user of that terminal from logon to logoff. As the user cycles among editing, compiling, running a program, and debugging, the process that serves that user loads new programs into virtual store and executes them.

Users tend to be impatient, however, and often want to do other work while waiting for a long compilation, execution, or text formatting to finish. Some interactive operating systems retain a batch facility for this purpose, allowing the user to submit the long operation as a job to that facility and continue to use the interactive process for something else.

A fundamentally different approach is seen in Unix and related operating systems. Instead of initializing the operating system to have a fixed number of processes based on the number of terminals or the maximum allowed level of multiprogramming, we can allow processes to be created at any time. If process creation is fairly inexpensive, computation can be organized naturally into relatively small pieces, each of which is performed by a new process. If several processes are working simultaneously for a single user, they compete with each other and the other processes currently requesting service.

This **cheap-process philosophy** affects the way users view the operating system and the way individual programs work. A user who wants to execute a long compilation and also edit a file might start two processes, one for each operation. The compilation program itself might be built of several passes, each of which is implemented in a separate process. These processes can execute sequentially. Such separation of function is a form of modularity, which can make programming and maintenance easier. An extreme example of this philosophy is seen in the Thoth operating system, in which the text editor creates a new process to service every editing command.

One effect of the cheap-process philosophy is seen in the structure of the command interpreter. It is itself a process, and it creates a new process for every command. When that new process terminates, the command interpreter prompts for a new command. If the user doesn't want to wait for the previous command to finish, the command interpreter can be told to prompt immediately for the next command.

## 1.1  Service calls

Operating systems provide several process-creation service calls for the benefit of the command interpreter or any other process that might want to start a new process and wait for it to finish. A typical set of calls includes the following.

- ☐  **Load(file name)**. This call tells the operating system to take the load image stored in the named file and load it into a fresh process. The Load call returns some identification for the new process, usually represented as a number.
- ☐  **Join(process number)**. This call blocks the caller until the process with the given number has terminated.

In addition, some operating systems provide simpler forms that have a similar power.

- ☐  **Split**. This call creates a new process that is just like the old process with respect to the contents of virtual space (although they don't actually share virtual space) and with respect to what files are open. We say that the new process **inherits** the environment of the old one. The Split call returns a 0 to the child and the child's process number to the parent, but otherwise they are identical.
- ☐  **Execute(file name)**. This call tells the operating system to discard the virtual space for the calling process and to replace it with a load image stored in the named file.

The effect of Load can be achieved by Split followed by the child requesting Execute.

## 1.2  Programming language syntax

The service calls just listed also appear in some programming languages intended for use in distributed programming. For example, a process call in Modula can be seen as a shared-store Split call followed by the child jumping to the code for the desired process. Since it is so common to start a set of shared-store processes and then wait for all to finish, a number of programming languages provide a **cobegin** construct that looks like this:

```
cobegin
    statement executed by process 1
    statement executed by process 2
    ...
    statement executed by process n
coend
```

This structure is equivalent to *n* Split operations, with each child executing its own statement and then terminating. The parent executes *n* Join operations to await the children's completions. However, one must be careful to distinguish between two different implementations of the **cobegin** construct (or any other process-creation construct) in programming languages:

- When simulated by the programming language, we call the programming-language processes **threads** to distinguish them from operating-system processes. As far as the operating system is concerned, there is only one process. The run-time support routines for the language include a scheduler that switches among the threads. This approach allows threads to share data (within the scope rules of the language) without involving the operating system in data-security issues.
- When simulated by the operating system, the process-creation construct of the language is implemented by asking the operating system to start a new process. Shared data require that the operating system assist by letting the processes share part of their virtual space.

⌐

# 2 INTER-PROCESS COMMUNICATION

## 2.1 Semaphores

The fact that one process can wait for another to finish is a simple form of communication that involves only synchronization. As we saw in Chapter 8, the kernel can make semaphores available to processes through service calls for creation and use. For several processes to share the semaphore, we must have some way for them to discover the semaphore name. In Chapter 8, we suggested that semaphores be inheritable. Alternatively, semaphore identifiers could be passed in messages (described shortly) or placed in shared files.

## 2.2 Virtual interrupts

We have already seen virtual interrupts in Chapter 5 as a way for processes to be informed that asynchronous transput has completed. They can also be used as a primitive form of inter-process communication. We can introduce a service call that lets one process cause a virtual interrupt in another.

☐　**Interrupt(process number, interrupt number).** This call sends the given interrupt to the given process, if permitted.

In order to prevent processes from sending unwanted interrupts to arbitrary processes, we might want to restrict interrupts in any of the following ways:

- Interrupts may be sent only to children or other descendants.
- Interrupts may be sent only to processes owned by the same user.
- Processes create an "interrupt identifier," which is inherited by children. The Interrupt service call specifies the interrupt identifier instead of a process number, and all processes that have that identifier receive the interrupt.

When a process is the target of a virtual interrupt, it is usually forced into its interrupt handler. We might provide the following service call, which allows processes to choose alternative reactions to virtual interrupts:

☐　**Handle(interrupt number, method).** The most straightforward method is "ignore." The process is then immune to any virtual interrupts of this type. Another method is "quit," which indicates that the process considers this class of interrupt so severe that it prefers to terminate if the interrupt occurs. A related method is "abort," which terminates the process and generates a dump of its virtual space. Yet another method is "wait," which tells the operating system that the process would like to be blocked until such an interrupt occurs. Finally, the process might provide an interrupt handler that is to be invoked upon receiving the interrupt.

Some virtual interrupt numbers might be reserved by the operating system for predefined sorts of information, such as the following:

- The user typed the "attention" key.
- A child has terminated. If this event can cause a virtual interrupt, the Join service call is not needed.
- The process has performed an invalid arithmetic operation, such as dividing by zero.
- The process must terminate. We might disallow associating a handler with this virtual interrupt.
- A timer set by the process has expired.
- Some limit, such as file size or virtual time, has been exceeded.
- The process must stop, but it may be started later by its parent.
- The process has been restarted after a stop.
- A child has stopped or otherwise changed status.
- Data are available for input from a device.
- The display window to which this process is connected has changed shape.

All these interrupts have one aspect in common: They tell the process that its environment has changed in a way that it may need to know about.

## 2.3  Pipes

As mentioned earlier, Unix provides an inter-process communication mechanism that allows the output of one process to become the input of another. The heart of the mechanism is the concept of a **pipe**, which is very much like a file opened for reading or for writing. Pipes are constructed by a service call like this:

☐    CreatePipe. This call opens a new pipe and returns *two* descriptors for it. One is the read descriptor, and the other is the write descriptor.

The Read and Write operations available on files work just as well for pipes. Any information written to the pipe is later available by reading from the pipe. Of course, the kernel may wish to buffer only a limited amount of data for each pipe, so Write may block the caller if the pipe is too full. Likewise, Read will block the caller if the pipe is empty. In these cases, the Hysteresis Principle says that on a multiprocessor, it may be better to wait a while before process switching. The pipe may become nonfull or nonempty soon, and the process switch can be avoided.

Pipes are inherited by children. Figure 9.1 shows how a process **A** first creates a pipe, then calls Split, becoming process **B** and **C**. Process **B** then closes the read end of the pipe, and **C** closes the write end, leaving a simple one-way communication link between them.

If the children **B** and **C** fail to close the appropriate ends of the pipe, confusion may result. In Figure 9.2 we show a situation where first **B** writes 6 bytes on the pipe, then another 4 bytes. Next, **C** reads 5 bytes, and finally **B** reads 4 bytes. **B** will end up missing the first 5 bytes, and **C** will never be able to read the next 4 bytes. One byte remains unread. The rule is that whichever process reads the next bytes gets them.

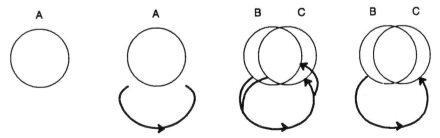

**Figure 9.1**  Building a pipe

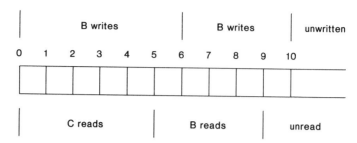

**Figure 9.2** Reads and writes on a pipe

We can enhance pipes in two ways. First, we can give them the **broadcast** property, which says that any data written to the pipe are saved until all the readers have seen them. A broadcast pipe would give **C** the first 5 bytes on the pipe, then give **B** the first 4 bytes, leaving 5 bytes unread by **C** and 6 bytes unread by **B**. This situation is shown in Figure 9.3.

As you can see, broadcast pipes require much more state information to be saved by the pipe manager (as we will call this component of the kernel) for each pipe — all the data that have not yet been read by even one of the processes having this pipe open for reading, and a pointer for each process indicating which byte it will read next. In contrast, a non-broadcast pipe has less state information — just the data that have not been read.

Second, we can define pipes with the **delimiting** property, which says that the pipe remembers boundaries between one write and the next. We provide two kinds of read:

☐ **ReadBytes(pipe number, how many).** This call returns the given number of bytes from the pipe, blocking the caller if that many bytes are not yet available.

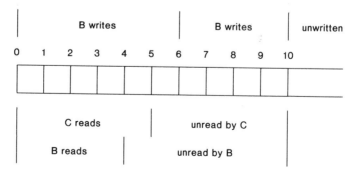

**Figure 9.3** Reads and writes on a broadcast pipe

☐     **ReadRecord(pipe number).** This call returns bytes up to the next boundary
      between two writes.

In Figure 9.4 we show **B** writing just as before. Now **C** first executes ReadRecord,
getting 6 bytes. If **C** then executes ReadByte for 2 bytes, it takes part of the next
record. Finally, **C** can get the rest of the current record by calling ReadRecord.

Ordinary Unix pipes are neither broadcast nor delimiting. They are practically never intended for multiple readers or multiple writers. Under these constraints, pipes unify terminal transput with file transput and with process transput.
Pipe descriptors behave just like file descriptors as far as reading and writing are
concerned. They also behave just like device descriptors, which are used for transput with the terminal. This unification is elegant in that the transput interface
between processes and the outside world is built entirely on a single concept.

Processes expect that they will have two descriptors when they start, one
called "standard input" and the other "standard output." Typically, the first is a
descriptor to the terminal open for input, and the second is a similar descriptor
open for output. However, the command interpreter, which starts most processes,
can arrange for these descriptors to be different. If the standard output descriptor
happens to be a file descriptor, the output of the process will go to the file, not the
terminal. The process does not know about this substitution and does not care.
Similarly, the command interpreter can arrange for the standard output of one process to be one end of a pipe and for the other end of the pipe to be standard input
for a second process. This situation is shown in Figure 9.5, where a listing program
is piped to a sorting program, which in turn directs its output to a file.

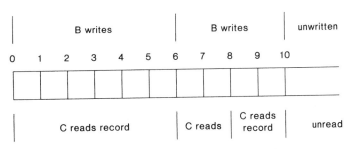

**Figure 9.4**  Reads and writes on a delimited pipe

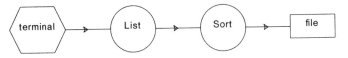

**Figure 9.5**  A pipeline of two processes

## 2.4 Ports

Unix pipes are a special case of a more general inter-process communication mechanism called **ports**. A port is a repository of data being sent from one process to another. It is like an anonymous postal address in the sense that the two processes involved in the communication do not need to know anything about each other's identities.

Ports are often used to represent services that one process can offer others. For example, many interactive operating systems have a program called Finger that will report who is logged on. It is sometimes convenient for a user on computer **A** to invoke Finger on computer **B**. Both computers can run operating systems that follow an inter-process communication convention in which a particular port, say 79, represents the Finger service. The user on machine **A** runs a program that sends a message asking for this service to port 79 on computer **B**. The Finger program spends its idle time blocked trying to read from this port. When a request arrives, Finger receives it from the port, compiles a list of the users currently logged on, and sends this list back to the program on machine **A**. This reply might be directed to a port that the program on computer **A** opened just for the purpose of hearing the reply. The original request from **A** included the identity of the return port so that Finger would know where to answer.

Not all port designs share the properties we used in this Finger example. In the following sections, we will distinguish different port philosophies.

**Data.**    Just like pipes, ports can be distinguished by whether they are delimiting and by whether they have broadcast. Some ports allow arbitrarily long messages, whereas others restrict message size, often to just a few bytes.

Another distinction involves reliability. Messages sent between computers can fail to arrive or can be garbled because of noise and contention for the communication line. As we saw in Chapter 5, there are techniques to increase the reliability of data transfer. However, these techniques cost both extra space (longer messages to increase redundancy, more code to check the messages) and time (delays and retransmissions). Some types of inter-process communication do not require a high degree of reliability. For example, the transfer may be part of a transaction (as described in Chapter 6) with its own consistency checks and the ability to abort cleanly if it fails. In such a context, reliability at the lower levels of communication (making sure that each transmission succeeds or that each message arrives) cannot itself ensure success of the overall transaction. The only reason to pay for reliability at the lower levels is to increase the overall efficiency of the transaction by decreasing the likelihood that it will have to be repeated.

A final data issue is whether messages sent to a port are received in the order in which they are sent. Differential buffering delays and routings, especially in a network environment, can place messages out of order. It takes extra effort (in the form of sequence numbers and, more generally, time stamps) to ensure order. For inter-process communication within one computer, however, order is usually easy to guarantee.

**Access.**    Pipes allow any number of writers and readers, although usually there is only one of each. Different approaches to inter-process communication have been designed that impose various restrictions on the access to ports. A **bound port** is the most restrictive: There may be only one writer and one reader. This restriction allows the operating system to implement the port with great efficiency. The state of the port can be described by considering only two processes. Unread data may be buffered by the port manager as part of the reader's process state.

At the other extreme, the **free port** allows any number of writers and readers. We have seen that free broadcast ports are complex. Even without broadcast, free ports are more complex. For example, unread data cannot be stored as part of the state of any one process but must be kept as part of the port itself. In cases of network operating systems, the port's data storage may end up on a machine distant from both readers and writers, with the result that extra inter-machine messages are needed to complete a transfer.

Between these extremes are **input ports** and **output ports**. An input port has only one reader but any number of writers. This arrangement is useful in the situation in which any number of clients may need help from the same server. Operating systems that provide input ports usually consider each port to belong to the process that can read from it. Such a concept of ownership does not apply to free or bound ports.

Output ports, in contrast, are not particularly useful: They allow any number of readers but only one writer. One application for such a port is for print servers. Assume that a process has many unrelated sets of data to print. It could send each as a message to its output port for printing. Each printer could wait for messages from that port when idle, and several data sets could be printing at once. The various kinds of ports are pictured in Figure 9.6.

**Naming and transfer.**    We have seen that Unix pipes have no names but are referred to instead by pipe descriptors that act much like file descriptors. Since descriptors can be passed between processes only by inheritance, this naming strategy limits communication to related processes.

There are many other ways to establish connections. For example, the file structures could include **port files**, which are neither directories nor data files. A process that opens a port file receives a port descriptor, which can be used for writing or reading, depending on the manner in which the port was opened. Whatever file security mechanisms are used for other files apply to port files as well.

Port files are one way to associate names with ports. Another way is to have port numbers that are globally accessible, unlike port descriptors, which have meaning only within a particular process and its descendants. Some of these numbers can have a published and fixed meaning, such as "the port for requesting the Finger service." Other numbers could be allocated and released on demand. We could use the following service calls:

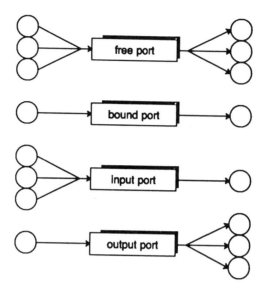

**Figure 9.6** Four kinds of ports

☐ CreatePort(port number). This call returns the number of a newly created port. If the port number given is the special value "new," the port manager allocates a currently unused number. The creating process becomes the owner of the port.

☐ DestroyPort(port number). This call deallocates the port. Any process that has the port open finds it closed and might be notified by a virtual interrupt.

A process that wishes to use the Finger service executes the following program.

```
1 const
2    FingerPortNumber = 79;
3
4 var
5    MyPortNumber : PortNumber;
6    MyPortDescriptor, FingerPortDescriptor : PortDescriptor;
7    FingerMessage : string;
8
9 begin
10    { Initialization }
11       MyPortNumber := CreatePort(new);
12       MyPortDescriptor := OpenPort(MyPortNumber,read);
13       FingerPortDescriptor := OpenPort(FingerPortNumber,write);
14    { Make request }
15       Write(FingerPortDescriptor,MyPortNumber);
16    { Get Answer }
17       Read(MyPortDescriptor,FingerMessage);
```

```
   18    { Finalization }
   19        ClosePort(FingerPortDescriptor);
   20        ClosePort(MyPortDescriptor);
   21        DestroyPort(MyPortNumber);
   22 end
```

Figure 9.7 shows the ports and the messages that are sent. The calling process, **A**, first makes a new port that it will use to get the answer (line 11). It opens this port (line 12) to listen for the answer and opens the well-known Finger port (line 13) to make its request. The request itself (line 15) includes just the "return envelope," that is, **A**'s port number. The Finger server will read this request, open **A**'s port for writing, write the answer there, and then close that port. **A** waits (line 17) for the answer to arrive and then releases both its port descriptors (lines 19–20) and its personal port (line 21). The port manager in the kernel makes sure that only owners destroy ports.

How are well-known port numbers different from port files? The main difference is that port numbers are more widely accessible. Any process that knows its number can open a well-known port, whereas only those processes that have

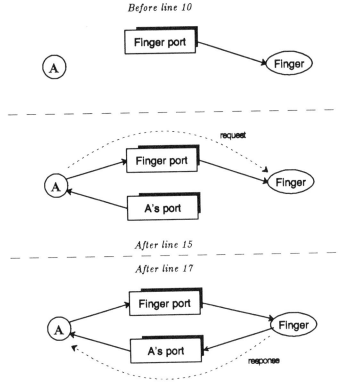

**Figure 9.7** Using well-known ports

access to the port file may open its port. The port file can be protected just as can any other file. The increased accessibility of port numbers is especially important if the computer is part of a loosely coupled network, such as Arpanet, which connects hundreds of computers across North America and Europe. The managers at an installation may not want to make the file structures accessible to outside processes, and the operating system may have no way to open a file or to search a directory on behalf of a process outside the machine. Nonetheless, many operating systems allow distant processes to open connections on well-known ports. For security, the server (like Finger in our example) could be informed whenever its port is opened and could reject the connection.

Our Finger example shows two shortcomings of well-known ports. First, the port that **A** created for the answer is public in the sense that any other process might have guessed its name, opened it, and written to it. Second, knowing a port number is not the same as having a port descriptor; the latter must be derived from the former by an OpenPort call. We can limit the dissemination of ports and unify numbers with descriptors by introducing **port capabilities**.

A process that creates a port is given a port capability by the port manager in the kernel. This number is like a port descriptor in that it has meaning only to that process and is used in the ReadPort and WritePort calls to specify which port is being used. However, we allow the process to write this capability as part of a message (sent to any port). The process that receives the message now has the transmitted capability and may use the port it refers to.

Transfer of capabilities can be used to introduce two processes to each other. For example, let us build the equivalent of a pipe between the List and Sort processes, such as was shown in Figure 9.5. We will use bound ports for this example, although other kinds could work as well. Since bound ports may have only one reader and one writer, we will stipulate that when a process writes a port capability to a port, it loses that capability. We will assume the following service calls:

☐    Load(load-image file). This call builds the new process and also builds a new bound port. It returns to the caller (the parent) the write capability for that port and initializes the new process (the child) with a read capability for the port.

☐    CreatePort. This call builds a new bound port and returns both the read and the write capability.

Here is what the command interpreter might do to connect List and Sort:

```
 1 var
 2    ToList, ToSort, MyRead, MyWrite : PortCapability;
 3
 4 begin
 5    ToList := Load(List);
 6    ToSort := Load(Sort);
 7    MyRead, MyWrite := CreatePort();
 8    Write(ToList,MyWrite);
 9    Write(ToSort,MyRead);
10    ClosePort(ToList);
11    ClosePort(ToSort);
12 end
```

This scenario is pictured in Figure 9.8.

Port capabilities allow processes like Sort and List in the previous example to be introduced to services without needing to know any name for the service. For the purpose of debugging or monitoring, the command interpreter can substitute other capabilities for the ones expected by the children.

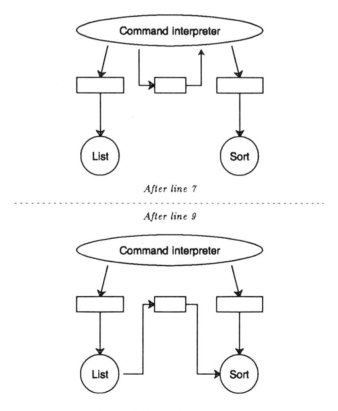

**Figure 9.8** Connecting two processes

Port capabilities are much more complex to implement than port numbers. Before we introduced port capabilities, messages were uninterpreted streams of bytes. Delimited ports required the port manager to keep track of message boundaries, but otherwise it could ignore the meaning of the bytes written to the port. The port manager must now realize when a port capability is being sent in a message so that it can remove the port capability from the writer and later install it in the reader. If port capabilities are represented to the process as small integers, like port descriptors, then a port capability that is sent in a message may have to be changed before it is received because the port-descriptor number in the writer may already be in use for something else in the reader.

The operating-system designer must also decide when to install the new port capability in the reader's capability list. It could do so as soon as the message arrives at the port, but the reading process might not try to read the message for a long time. In fact, it might terminate without reading the message, or the port might be destroyed by its owner. In this case, the designer must decide whether the capability should be returned to the writer or should be discarded.

## 2.5 Semantics of Read and Write

We have been using Read and Write as synchronous calls, and we have been assuming that ports store data that have been written but not yet read. Neither of these choices is necessary. First, we could have both calls *initiate* action but not block the calling process. The caller could discover completion by polling, by virtual interrupt, or by waiting explicitly for completion later. Such asynchronous communication introduces new situations that must be given meaning. For example, what does it mean to call ClosePort if there is a ReadPort or WritePort still active? What does it mean to send a port capability in a message if that same port capability is still in use for some ReadPort or WritePort call?

Another alternative to synchronous write is to block the caller until a reply comes from the recipient. The Hysteresis Principle implies that if the reply is expected in less time than is needed for a process switch, the caller should not be preempted in favor of another process for that expected time in the hope that no process switch will be necessary at all. The recipient would use a Reply service call to indicate that its message is a response to the previous one it received. Reply itself does not block. This approach requires that the port allow messages in both directions.

Second, we could relieve the port manager of the responsibility for buffering unread data by keeping such data in the virtual space of the writer until they are read. This decision is independent of whether Read and Write are synchronous. An unbuffered write does not complete until its data have been read from the port. Until the unbuffered write completes, it is an error for the writer to modify the data being written because the port manager has not made a copy. It can be more efficient to implement unbuffered communication, since data don't have to be copied as often.

A process with several open ports may wish to read next from whichever one has data. Alternatively, it may wish to read from a particular port but ignore data on other ports for the time being. An even greater level of selectivity is to accept only messages that have a particular form but to ignore others for the time being. Operating systems with ports provide varying degrees of selectivity for ReadPort. For example, the Demos operating system, which uses capabilities that allow the holder to write to input ports, lets the ReadPort call specify any subset of input ports. In contrast, the Charlotte distributed operating system, which uses capabilities to bound ports, allows ReadPort to specify either all ports or just one, but not an arbitrary subset. The Soda inter-process communication mechanism allows the recipient to look at a small amount of the message before deciding whether it wants the message.

# 3 DISTRIBUTED OPERATING SYSTEMS

Once an operating system provides inter-process communication, it lends itself to implementation on a distributed computer. Before we discuss how to generalize uniprocessor operating systems to more general machines, we will need to define the sorts of machines we will discuss.

Computer installations often experience crises in which the available resources no longer satisfy the demand that users are making. The first action a manager might take is to determine the **bottleneck** — that is, the limiting resource. It may be that adding an additional disk unit or replacing a device controller with a faster one will remove the bottleneck. Often installing more main store will increase throughput to an acceptable level. Or the limiting resource may be computation: More work is being presented to the computer than can be completed. In this case, it is necessary either to replace the current computer with a faster one or to introduce new computers.

Both these approaches are common. Manufacturers make several models of their computers that differ in cost, performance, and modernity. The newer and the faster models usually support the same instruction set as the older and the slower models. An operating system that runs on one computer will often run without modification on another model of the same machine.

## 3.1 Multiprocessors

A related approach offered by some manufacturers is to add a second or third central processing unit to the machine. When several cpu's share a common main store, we call the resulting machine a **multiprocessor**. Main store is often subdivided into independent modules, each of which can service one access request (from a cpu or a channel) at a time. The purpose of this division is to allow separate cpu's to access modules simultaneously if the requests do not conflict. If there are several cpu's, a switching network is used to direct requests from cpu's to the correct main store module. This switching network introduces new delays and contention points because two requests directed to different main store modules might still have to traverse the same switch.

Converting a uniprocessor operating system to a multiprocessor requires careful attention to concurrency issues, as discussed in Chapter 8. One successful approach is to let one machine handle all the devices and to let the other execute processes. Another approach is to treat the machines equally and let devices interrupt whichever machine will currently allow interrupts. Under this approach, an idle machine waits until there is a process on the ready list, and then it executes that process. All data structures that are shared by several machines, such as the ready list and device-request lists, must be guarded in regions of mutual exclusion.

Instead of modifying an existing operating system, one may design a new operating system with inter-process communication as the primary structuring tool. We will discuss this approach later when we deal with multicomputers.

## 3.2 Local-area networks

Instead of upgrading the current machine to a faster model or to a multiprocessor, many installations choose to buy an independent new computer. If the new computer is of the same type as the old one, the same operating system can be run on the new one, and software developed for the old one will run on the new. If the new computer is different, it will usually have a different operating system. Users will have to learn the peculiarities of the new system and may have to modify their software extensively.

The agony of transporting programs to the new computer can be mitigated by connecting the computers by a communication device. A user who has an investment in software on the old machine might still be able to submit jobs to that machine across the communication device from the new machine. The results of the jobs can be shipped back to the new machine and stored in its file system. This style of computing is called **remote job entry**.

As the installation purchases more computers, they are added onto the network of machines either by direct connection to some of the machines already there or by a connection to a shared communication device, like an Ethernet. Historically, each installation that built such a **local-area network** would develop its own protocols for inter-machine communication. Later, manufacturers developed their own protocols. For example, Digital Equipment Corporation has a protocol known as DECnet for interconnecting its machines. More recently, international standards have been designed for inter-machine protocols. These standards describe a number of distinct levels in order to promote modularity. In particular, the following levels can be distinguished:

- **Host-to-line level**: Defines the meaning of various wires and what voltages they should have.

- **Host-to-switch level**: Defines how acknowledgements are generated and what parts of a message contain routing and sequencing information.
- **Host-to-host level**: Defines how connections are built, used, and destroyed between two computers.
- **Process-to-process level**: Defines how individual processes request and provide services. Certain standard services (like the Finger server) have protocols defined at this level.

These particular divisions are not necessarily standard. The CCITT/ISO model, for example, distinguishes seven levels of protocol. Each network tends to build its own protocols, and the levels at which services are defined tend to fit only roughly into any standard description.

Each protocol level builds an abstraction, according to the Beautification Principle, both to hide details of the lower levels and to introduce new structures. In the language introduced by the ISO model, each level provides "service data units" to the next level up. In order to perform its function, it uses "protocol data units" built on the service data units of next lower level. This structure is shown in Figure 9.9, which shows the names of some of the ISO levels. The protocol data units and service data units for the ISO model change at each layer. At the atomic level, electrons are discrete. (We will not concern ourselves with quantum-mechanical details.) At the aggregate level, physics becomes continuous, with measures such as voltage and current. The physical level (the lowest ISO level) is

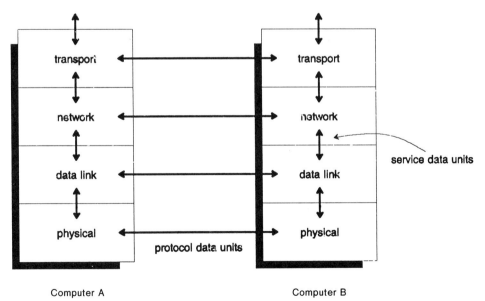

**Figure 9.9** Protocol levels

discrete, providing bits. The data-link level groups bits into frames, which it transports reliably. This level uses acknowledgements and sequence numbers as part of its protocol data units. The network layer converts frames into packets, which provide routing, congestion control, and accounting services. The transport layer provides arbitrarily long data segments, transmitting them as numbered packets and reassembling them at the other end. The division into packets is hidden from view, but segment boundaries are still made visible. (The U. S. Department of Defense TCP protocol, in contrast, also hides the sender's segment boundaries from the receiver.) Higher levels also provide new services built on lower ones, such as checkpointing and converting between different floating-point formats.

## 3.3 Long-haul networks

These protocols were initially designed for **long-haul networks**, although they have been used since in local-area networks as well. A long-haul network is a collection of widely scattered computers connected by a common communication network following a set of protocols. The Arpanet, mentioned earlier, is a good example of such a network. It is part of the Arpa Internet, which also includes MilNet (military sites), SatNet (satellite links), and many local networks. There are at least 2000 computers in the Internet. Routing of messages is automatic, based on a hierarchical addressing scheme and a backbone of relay computers. Messages are divided into packets, each of which is routed separately.

The computer on which this text was created is a member of a local-area network, part of the Arpa Internet, that connects it to other local research and instructional machines. The machine is thereby connected as well to CSNET, BITNET, and the UUCP network. CSNET is an organization connecting academic computer science departments. It uses both Arpanet and PhoneNet, which has a central computer that phones member sites on a regular basis to collect and deliver messages. BITNET connects over 1500 computers worldwide using dedicated leased lines. Routing of messages is performed automatically, using manually maintained files distributed from a central site. The UUCP network is is a community of perhaps 10,000 computers that use the UUCP (Unix-to-Unix copy) protocol, usually over telephone connections. It is by no means restricted to Unix sites. Routing of messages is often explicitly specified by the source computer.

Networks can be connected together my means of **gateway** computers that reside on two or more networks. They relay packets from one network to the other, modifying the format when necessary to accommodate the different protocols. They must sometimes divide packets in order to obey packet-length requirements. A single message may go through several gateways as it makes its way from a local area network through several long-haul networks until it reaches its final destination.

Long-haul networks often provide a number of services, most important of which is the ability for users to mail messages to each other across the country. Naming conventions for mail addresses are not standardized across networks, but recent attempts to unify addresses have been helpful. A more general way to transfer information is by transferring files from one machine to another across the network.

Another service is **remote logon**, which allows a user to log on to a machine across the network. Every character typed by such a user is typically transmitted through the network to the distant machine, echoed there, and sent back to the local machine. Of course, most installations require that users who want to log on to their machines must have accounts (and passwords) for those machines.

Long-haul networks also provide information services that allow one to obtain information about users of any machine on the network. For example, the Finger server we have been discussing is available on many machines and allows remote requests about the local user community. Some machines maintain databases of information about the entire user community of the network. These databases may be queried from any machine in the network. Information often includes mail addresses (both computer and normal postal service), telephone numbers, and current projects.

A new facility supported by software on many machines is a **bulletin board**, which accepts notices posted by individuals and makes them available to all interested users. Typically, notices are cataloged by subject, and users may subscribe to particular subjects that interest them. Distributed bulletin boards on long-haul networks allow people with common interests across the country to participate in continuing discussions.

These facilities of long-haul networks have recently become standard within local-area networks as well. For example, BSD4.2 and BSD4.3 Unix are available on a number of different machines, including computers made by Digital Equipment Corporation, Gould Corporation, Sun Microsystems, and Pyramid Technology. This operating system includes drivers for a number of communication devices. A local-area network of machines running this operating system automatically enjoys remote job entry, remote logon, mail, remote file transfer, and user-information services.

## 3.4 Multicomputers

The uses mentioned for local-area and long-haul networks omitted one important possibility — complex algorithms that require several machines in order to achieve acceptable performance. Distributed algorithms have not been commonly run on such networks, mostly because the area of distributed algorithms is still quite young. Recently, however, several operating systems have been designed with the goal of unifying a local-area network into a single operating system.

**Multicomputers** are different from the multiprocessors we saw earlier in that multicomputers do not share main store but send messages to each other in order to co-operate. We distinguish multicomputers from networks in that multicomputers have a single operating system that governs all the individual machines, whereas a computer network is built of autonomous machines often under separate management.

These distinctions are not always simple. A recent trend toward less expensive computers has led to the emergence of the **workstation**, a powerful one-user computer, usually with a small local disk and a high-quality display. The workstations at an installation are usually linked by a network so that they can share expensive devices like printers and large secondary store. All the workstations use the same operating system, but each has its own copy and is mostly autonomous. However, each might provide services to the others on request, and processes on separate machines can communicate with one another through the network. Except for that facility, the operating systems on the workstations are fairly conventional. Workstation networks occupy a role somewhere between computer networks and true multicomputers.

Operating systems designed especially for multicomputers often resemble those designed especially for multiprocessors. Certain characteristics are fairly common in these operating systems:

- Each machine has a copy of the code necessary for communication and primitive service to processes (such as setting up mapping registers and preempting at the end of a quantum). This code is the kernel of the operating system.
- The environment of a process is defined by the communication ports it has access to and the processes that serve those ports.
- It makes no difference to a process what machine it runs on, except for its speed of execution and communication. Processes that deal directly with devices are an exception to this rule.
- Policy decisions, such as on which machine to run a new process, are made outside the kernel by utility processes.
- Utility processes are also used for accessing files and performing transput. Services are therefore represented by open ports to these utility processes.
- When one machine fails, the performance of the entire operating system is degraded, but only work that was under way on the failed machine is actually lost. Suitable redundancy can ensure that nothing at all is lost.

One feature that is only beginning to be seen in distributed operating systems is **migration** of processes from one machine to another to improve the balance of load and to shorten communication paths. Migration requires a mechanism to gather load information, a distributed policy that decides that a process should be moved, and a mechanism to effect the transfer. Migration has been demonstrated in a few Unix-based distributed operating systems, such as Locus and MOS, and in communication-based distributed operating systems, like Demos/MP.

# 4 THE COMMUNICATION-KERNEL APPROACH

An increasingly popular style of operating system follows a style that we will call the **communication-kernel approach**. This approach is intended to apply to a fairly wide variety of machines, including traditional mainframes, multiprocessors, multi-computers, microcomputers, and even loosely coupled remotely connected machines. It is also intended to apply to a wide variety of applications, including interactive multiprogramming, databases, and distributed computation. Finally, it is intended to apply to a wide variety of environments, including university research (which places a premium on easy sharing and efficient text processing), the military (which emphasizes security considerations), and embedded applications (computers inside other devices, like microwave ovens).

The communication-kernel approach agrees with conventional operating system design in that it constructs an operating system out of two pieces, the **kernel** and **processes**. It differs in the division of labor between these components. In particular, the kernel contains only those parts of the operating system that are both indispensible and time-critical.

- Every application is assumed to need these services, so providing them once allows for correct and consistent implementation. Basic communication is in this category.
- Services that need to respond quickly to external events (represented by interrupts) might be provided by the kernel for speed. The speed comes from the fact that context switches from process to kernel and back are less expensive than a process switch from one process to another.

A decision to embed a service in the kernel carries a price of inflexibility (there is no alternative to using the provided service) and potential inadequacy (the provided service may not fit the needs of all its customers). For this reason, shared resources are usually managed not by the kernel but by separate processes. This design holds even for hardware resources like magnetic disk.

Part of the goal of the communication-kernel approach is to keep the kernel as small as possible. Therefore, it is restricted to provide mechanisms (and not policies) for three purposes:

- Processes
- Main-store management
- Inter-process communication.

All matters of policy are relegated to processes.

Processes can be classified as **servers** or **clients**. A typical application program is a client that makes calls on servers for file access and other forms of transput. A client with regard to one conversation might well be a server with regard to another.

Whether a particular process is on one machine or another of a multicomputer is usually immaterial, except for servers that need to access physical devices. Special processes decide on which machine to place each new process and whether to migrate the process during its execution. That is, the resources of time and space are managed by servers written for that purpose.

## 4.1 Processes and threads

A **process** is an entity that corresponds to a virtual space. Creating a process involves allocating the necessary amount of space and loading it with a program. Creating and destroying processes is relatively expensive. The kernel needs to be involved only in the establishment of mapping tables and process control blocks. The loader can be an ordinary process that determines how much virtual space is needed and initializes it by reading the appropriate load image.

The active entities that inhabit a process are called **threads**. When a process is first created, a single thread begins to execute. New threads within a process can be created either by internal events (an existing thread spawns a new one) or by external events (a message arrives at the process that causes a new thread to be formed). Creating and destroying threads is relatively inexpensive.

All threads within a process potentially share the entire virtual store of that process. Sharing may be controlled, however, either by programming language support or, more expensively, by kernel efforts.

The threads that inhabit a process may execute simultaneously, particularly on a multiprocessor. In this case, the kernel might provide simple synchronization mechanisms (like semaphores) to allow the threads to protect shared data. However, experience with the Lynx programming language has shown the benefits of preventing a thread from executing simultaneously with any other thread of the same process, that is, letting a thread execute until it terminates, blocks for communication, or explicitly waits for a condition. This restriction simplifies the construction of correct programs.

## 4.2 Communication

The principal points of differences among proponents of the communication-kernel approach involve communication. All agree that the facility supported by the kernel must be extremely efficient, because inter-process communication (including process switching, not just context switching) is needed to accomplish all operating system functions. It appears that the more facilities the kernel provides for communication, the less efficient they become.

Communication is accomplished by messages sent from one process (actually, from an active thread within the process) to another. Destinations for messages can be specified by port names or port capabilities. For efficiency, input or bound ports are typically used. It is up to the kernel to take a port name or capability and discover where the destination actually is. One technique is to keep a cache of recently used port names and to broadcast searches when there is a cache miss. If processes can migrate, cache entries can become obsolete. They are then treated as **hints**, not **absolutes**; the kernel can always resort to broadcast if the hint turns out to be wrong. As an alternative to broadcasting when a process must be located, each process can have an original home machine whose kernel maintains accurate information about its current location. The location of the home can be embedded in the process identifier.

The space of port names may be sparse to prevent one process from guessing a name used by another. Many different names may refer to the same process; the process may provide different levels of service to requests made on different identifiers.

A sending process directs its messages to **entries** within the program of the destination process. The sender of the message specifies which entry is meant either implicitly (by which port it sends the message to) or explicitly (as part of the message). Entries may be invoked as remote procedures, in which case **in** parameters (in the Ada sense) are passed by value in the first message, and **out** parameters are carried back to the caller in a reply message. Remote procedure call has been championed by many as an elegant way to structure distributed computation. However, some conversations do not fit the procedure-call model. Examples are found in data retrieval, where one query returns many responses, one at a time, and in graph algorithms, where more complex activity takes place. For such cases, a simple message transfer, initiated either by the sender or the receiver, is appropriate. Language-level support can be used to enforce type security of messages without incurring significant run-time cost.

A thread can **bind** one of its input or bound ports to an entry, which causes incoming messages to create new threads executing that entry. Alternatively, the thread can explicitly receive messages. This decision is made dynamically by the destination thread. For large messages, a facility to inspect a small request before deciding to engage in an expensive transfer (in either direction) is useful.

## 4.3 Space management

The kernel provides support for the address-translation tables and allows privileged processes (such as the storage manager) to modify those tables. One way to keep the cost low is to map the translation tables themselves into the address space of the storage managers. Address-translation faults are converted by the kernel into some form of call on the appropriate storage manager. (Each machine might have its own.) This invocation can take the form of a return from a kernel call or a message that appears to come from the faulting process.

Storage managers on different machines in a multicomputer may exchange information about their allocation state to help make reasonable decisions about where to start new processes. A single storage manager can control more than one machine, but if so, it may be unacceptably slow in responding to faults. If the kernel is unable to grant the necessary support to a remote storage manager, an intermediary process may reside on the target machine and relay requests from a remote storage manager to the local kernel.

Storage managers can prevent overcommitment of main store by swapping processes to backing store. A port bound to a swapped-out process is still usable, but communication with such a process will be delayed until the process is swapped back in. Such a communication event causes the relevant storage manager to be informed of the problem.

## 4.4  Other services

Catalogs are used to find the port identifiers of servers. These catalogs are themselves implemented as server processes. Newly created processes can establish their environment by knowing the process identifier of at least one catalog process.

File services may be provided by a hierarchy of processes. Many arrangements are possible. One arrangement is to have three levels for file access:

(1) **Directory server**: Given the name of a file, this server returns the process identifier of a file server that manages this file.

(2) **File server**: This server supports file open, read, write, and close.

(3) **Disk server**: This server supports seek, read block, write block.

Some applications, like database programs, will want to deal with the lowest level of the hierarchy. There may be more than one server at each level, particularly if the tree of files is distributed across many machines.

It is not easy to fit devices into the communication-kernel approach. Ideally, we would like each device to be controlled by a server process. Unfortunately, the server process might be too slow or too powerful.

- The kernel must transform each device-completion interrupt that arrives into a virtual interrupt to the associated server process. This action requires a context switch to the kernel, followed by a process switch to the server. The time required may be excessive.

- Either the server process must pass its device commands to the kernel to pass on to the device, which is expensive, or it must have a means of submitting such requests directly. If device registers are used, the server must have access to those registers, but not to any others that do not belong to this device. If channel programs are used, the server must be given the privilege to start channel commands. Most current hardware is incapable of main-store mapping that has a fine enough grain to allow access only to the registers of a single device. Similarly, it is impossible to allow some channel commands and not others purely by hardware support. Therefore, the server process will have privileges beyond what it needs, and a malicious or erroneous server can do damage.

One challenge under the communication-kernel approach is to write managers that can survive hardware failures. In a multicomputer, a single manager may be distributed over several servers, which can replicate data about the state of the resource. A client might make requests of any of the servers. The others need to be informed about changes to shared data so that if a server should fail in the middle of a request, the surviving members of the team agree about the state of the resource. Such agreement requires sophisticated communication protocols. A weaker form of reliability partitions the resource into disjoint chunks and assigns a separate server to each chunk. For example, a file hierarchy can be partitioned into subtrees, each of which is managed by a different server. Failure of a disk (or its controlling computer) will affect only files stored there. Unaffected files can still be accessed during the failure. A still weaker form of reliability can be provided by a **checkpoint** operation, which copies the state of a process (including its virtual space) either onto disk or to another process. If there is a failure, the operations of the failed process can be restarted from the checkpoint.

# 5 PERSPECTIVE

In this chapter, we have touched on a number of issues that are the subject of active research. This research is the result of several sources of pressure.

- Computers always become saturated eventually.
- New technologies, particularly the Ethernet, have made it inexpensive to connect computers together.
- Workstations that have extensive computing power are becoming relatively inexpensive.
- Communication is necessary for networks of computers to co-operate with each other.
- Standards make it easier to expand facilities without requiring retraining of users and reimplementation of programs.
- Some problems are too expensive to solve on standard machines. As computers become faster, users' expectations become greater, with the result that there will always be a demand for increased computational power. The only hope is to build a multicomputer and distribute the problem.

One result of these pressures has been a trend toward operating systems whose processes communicate with each other by standard protocols. Local-area networks of machines with such operating systems allow sharing of services. A version of this trend is for fairly small and inexpensive individual machines, possibly even lacking backing store, to be used as high-performance workstations. File and backing-store transfers are conducted through the communication medium to file-server machines.

Personal computers are already showing the results of this trend. They have only a few standard operating systems, such as CP/M, and most can connect to other computers either by direct connections that obey a universal protocol at the host-to-line level (called RS-232) or by phone connections that translate to RS-232. Workstation-class computers are more expensive (as of 1987, they cost about $10,000), but they still cost much less than the mainframe computers of the previous generation.

A second trend has been to connect local-area networks into continental networks of computers to link researchers with common interests. These networks are used mostly for correspondence between people, but also to support remote file transfer, remote logon, user-information services, and distributed bulletin boards.

The gateway between the local-area network and the long-haul networks is any one machine in the local-area network.

A third trend has been to design operating systems especially for multicomputers. These operating systems provide only communication and scheduling services to their processes. Files, other devices, and other services are provided through utility processes. Policy decisions are also made by utility processes. These multicomputers are particularly appropriate for large computations that will not fit on single machines because of either space or time limitations. Multicomputer operating systems are the subject of major research efforts both in industry and at universities. The communication-kernel approach seems to be viable not only for multicomputers but also for a wide range of other computer organizations.

# 6  FURTHER READING

There are several good introductions to inter-process communication methods. An excellent survey of the facilities proposed in high-level languages for distributed computing has been written by Scott (1984). The distinction among input, output, and free ports was invented by Cashin (1980), who also surveyed various kinds of communication. Another survey, by Andrews and Schneider (1983), discusses mechanisms for concurrency control as well as inter-process communication.

Tanenbaum's excellent text (1981) is a standard reference for details on communication devices and protocols at various levels. A shorter form of the same treatment can be found in his survey article (1981).

A number of distributed operating systems have been designed and built for a variety of multiprocessors and multicomputers. Hydra was designed for C.mmp, a multiprocessor with 16 cpu's with shared access to 16 main store modules (Wulf *et al.*, 1974). StarOs (Jones, 1979) and Medusa (Ousterhout, 1980) were both designed for Cm*, a more advanced multiprocessor in which each cpu has its own main store but can access the main store of other cpu's with some delay. Locus (Popek *et al.*, 1981) and MOS (Barak and Litman, 1982) are distributed versions of Unix that unify the file system into one hierarchy, identically visible to all machines. Both have demonstrated process migration.

Many research-oriented operating systems display the communication-kernel approach in some form, including Accent (Rashid and Robertson, 1981), Amoeba (Tanenbaum and Mullender, 1981), Arachne (Solomon and Finkel, 1978), Charlotte (Finkel *et al.*, 1983), Clouds (Allchin *et al.*, 1982), Demos/MP (Powell, 1977), Eden (Lazowska *et al.*, 1981), Micros (Wittie and van Tilborg, 1980), SODS/OS (Sincoskie and Farber, 1980), Thoth (Cheriton *et al.*, 1979), and V kernel (Cheriton and Zwaenepoel, 1983). A number of programming language efforts are also related to the communication-kernel approach, particularly Argus (Liskov and Scheifler, 1983) and Lynx (Scott, 1985). Lynx, for example, imposes Algol-like scope rules on the virtual space shared by threads to help limit the chaos of shared space. It also provides inexpensive type checking of all messages. Birrell has reported on efficient implementation of remote procedure calls (Birrell, 1984).

Other operating systems have novel features. Soda (Kepecs84a) proposes an unusual communication mechanism that uses a global set of port numbers and allows the initiator of communication to be either the reader or the writer. The responder to the communication is allowed to see a small amount of data before deciding whether to accept the communication. NonStop (Bartlett81a) is a multi-computer operating system marketed by Tandem. It provides redundancy at a number of levels to allow for graceful degradation when parts fail. A discussion of distributed operating systems in general can be found in the article by Tanenbaum and Van Renesse (Tanenbaum85a).

# 7 EXERCISES

1. The **cobegin** construct is a synchronization tool in the sense discussed in Chapter 8. Can it build the synchronization graph of Figure 8.1?

2. Show how to build the synchronization graph of Figure 8.1 using only Split and Join.

3. In the scenario of Figure 9.7, why did **A** have to make its own port? Assuming that the Finger port is a free port, why couldn't **A** have received its answer on that port?

4. Demos/MP uses write capabilities to input ports for communication. The reader for an input port (called the *owner*) is fixed for the life of the port, but writers can give their capabilities away.
   (a) What information should be stored by the port manager for the holder of a write capability?
   (b) What information should be stored by the port manager for the owner of that port?
   (c) In Figure 9.8, we used bound ports to show how the command interpreter can introduce the List and the Sort processes. How does this situation look in Demos/MP?
   (d) What information passes between the port managers for the three processes when the command interpreter introduces List to Sort? (Assume that each of these processes is on a different machine.)

5. What information would be useful in deciding if a process should be migrated in a multicomputer operating system?

6. WorkEasy Computers is designing a new product in which individual machines are used for predefined functions. For example, one machine is used as a file server, another runs the text editor, and a third runs the compiler. A fourth machine is the user's interface into the network. Is this organization reasonable?

7. **Bandwidth** is the number of bits that can be sent from one machine to another every second. **Delay** is the amount of time between when the writer submits the WritePort call and the reader's ReadPort call finishes. High bandwidth and low delay are important for efficient communication. Suggest a multicomputer application in which high bandwidth is more important than low delay. Suggest an application where low delay is more important.

8. Instead of piping List and Sort, as in Figure 9.5, the standard output of List could be directed to a file. After List is finished, Sort could be invoked with standard input coming from the file. Which method is likely to execute faster?

9. Ports that buffer unread data require some policy for deciding when to block a writer. For simplicity, assume a uniprocessor operating system. Assume that there are currently ten ports and buffer space to hold 10,000 bytes. Suggest a blocking strategy.

10. On multiprocessors, some buffer space may be used for messages that are in transit — that is, messages written by a process on a second machine to be read by a process on a third machine. The current machine happens to be in the communication path and must therefore buffer messages. How does this situation change your answer to exercise 9?

11. Charlotte uses capabilities to bound ports, for both reading and writing. A **link** is a pair of bound ports such that the reader of one is the writer of the other, and vice versa. Capabilities are always transmitted as a pair and are never separated.
(a) What should the CreatePort call return?
(b) A client process has a link to a file server process. Suggest a protocol for opening a file for sequential read or sequential write. Try to make file read and file write use as few port read and port write operations as possible.

12. The Locus operating system has only one file hierarchy, which spans all the machines in the multicomputer. Assuming that each file actually exists on the secondary storage of only one machine and that each machine has secondary storage, suggest an allocation design for associating files with machines.

13. Your answer to exercise 12 may suffer from a situation in which more files cannot fit on one machine, but other machines still have plenty of file space. Suggest an allocation design that lessens this problem. Do not allow individual files to cross machine boundaries.

14. We suggested that unread data might be kept in the virtual space of the writer until they are read. For output ports and bound ports, this design makes sense. This strategy is more difficult to implement in a multicomputer for input ports or free ports. Discuss what the semantics of Read should be in those cases and what messages must be sent from one kernel to another to implement this design.

15.  The text suggests that intermediary processes are useful for allowing a server on one machine to interact with the kernel on another. A second use for intermediary processes is to transmit messages between machines in a multi-computer. The alternative is to let the kernel transmit such messages. What are the advantages of each alternative?

16.  The text suggests that if synchronous write on a port blocks the caller until a reply comes, the caller should not be preempted for another process for a while. When is this suggestion inapplicable?

# References

J. E. ALLCHIN, M. S. MCKENDRY, AND W. C. THIBAULT, *Clouds: A Testbed for Experimentation in Distributed Systems*, Working Paper 3: Status Report, Georgia Institute of Technology, Atlanta (June 1982).

G. R. ANDREWS AND F. B. SCHNEIDER, "Concepts and Notations for Concurrent Programming," *ACM Computing Surveys* **15**(1) pp. 3-44 (March 1983).

R. ATKINSON AND C. HEWITT, "Synchronization and Proof Techniques for Serializers," *IEEE Transactions on Software Engineering* **5**(1) pp. 10-23 (January 1979).

O. BABAOGLU AND W. JOY, "Converting a Swap-based System to do Paging in an Architecture Lacking Page-referenced Bits," *Proceedings of the 8th Symposium on Operating Systems Principles*, pp. 78-86 (December 1981).

A. B. BARAK AND A. LITMAN, *MOSES: An Integrated Multicomputer Distributed Operating System*, DCL TR 82-05, Department of Computer Science, Hebrew University of Jerusalem (September 1982).

J. BARTLETT, "A NonStop Kernel," *Proceedings of the 8th Symposium on Operating Systems Principles*, pp. 22-29 (December 1981).

L. L. BECK, *System Software: An Introduction to Systems Programming,* Reading, Mass.: Addison-Wesley (1985).

L. A. BELADY, "A Study of Replacement Algorithms for a Virtual-storage Computer," *IBM System Journal* **5**(2) pp. 78-101 (1966).

L. A. BELADY, R. A. NELSON, AND G. S. SHEDLER, "An Anomaly in Space-time Characteristics of Certain Programs Running in a Paging Machine," *CACM* **12**(6) pp. 349-353 (June 1969).

P. BERNSTEIN AND N. GOODMAN, "Concurrency Control in Distributed Database Systems," *ACM Computing Surveys* **13**(2) pp. 185-221 (June 1981).

A. D. BIRRELL AND R. M. NEEDHAM, "A Universal File Server," *IEEE Transactions on Software Engineering* **SE-6**(5) pp. 450-453 (September 1980).

A. D. BIRRELL AND B. J. NELSON, "Implementing Remote Procedure Calls," *ACM Transactions on Computer Systems* **2**(1) pp. 39-59 (February 1984).

T. BLOOM, "Evaluating Synchronization Mechanisms," *Proceedings of the 7th Symposium on Operating Systems Principles*, pp. 24-32 (December 1979).

P. BRINCH HANSEN, *Operating System Principles,* Englewood Cliffs, N.J.: Prentice-Hall (1973).

P. BRINCH HANSEN, *The Design of Edison,* Computer Science Department, University of Southern California, Los Angeles (1980).

P. CALINGAERT, *Operating System Elements: A User Perspective,* Englewood Cliffs, N.J.: Prentice-Hall (1982).

R. H. CAMPBELL AND A. N. HABERMANN, "The Specification of Process Synchronization by Path Expressions," pp. 89-102 in *Operating Systems,* ed. E. Gelenbe and C. Kaiser, Berlin: Springer-Verlag (1974).

R. W. CARR AND J. L. HENNESSY, "WSCLOCK: A Simple and Effective Algorithm for Virtual Memory Management," *Proceedings of the 8th Symposium on Operating Systems Principles*, pp. 87-95 (December 1981).

P. M. CASHIN, *Inter-process Communication,* Technical Report 8005014, Bell-Northern Research (June 1980).

D. R. CHERITON, M. A. MALCOLM, L. S. MELEN, AND G. R. SAGER, "Thoth: A Portable Real-time Operating System," *CACM* **22**(2) pp. 105-115 (February 1979).

D. R. CHERITON AND W. Z. ZWAENEPOEL, "The Distributed V Kernel and its Performance for Diskless Workstations," *Proceedings of the 9th Symposium on Operating Systems Principles*, pp. 129-140 (October 1983).

E. G. COFFMAN AND L. KLEINROCK, "Computer Scheduling Methods and their Countermeasures," *Proceedings of the AFIPS Spring Joint Computer Conference*, pp. 11-21 (1968).

E. G. COFFMAN, M. J. ELPHICK, AND A. SHOSHANI, "System Deadlocks," *Computing Surveys* **3**(2) pp. 67-78 (June 1971).

D. E. COMER, *Operating System Design: The Xinu Approach,* Englewood Cliffs, N.J.: Prentice-Hall (1984).

D. E. COMER, *Operating system design: Internetworking with Xinu,* Englewood Cliffs, N.J.: Prentice-Hall (1987).

F. J. CORBATO ET AL., "An Experimental Time-sharing System," *Proceedings of the AFIPS Fall Joint Computer Conference*, pp. 335-344 (May 1962).

P. COURTOIS AND D. PARNAS, "Concurrent Control with Readers and Writers," *CACM* **14**(10) pp. 667-668 (October 1971).

H. M. DEITEL, *An Introduction to Operating Systems,* Reading, Mass.: Addison-Wesley (1983).

P. J. DENNING, "Virtual Memory," *Computing Surveys* **2**(3) pp. 153-188 (September 1970).

P. J. DENNING AND H. S. STONE, "An Exchange of Views on Operating Systems Courses," *Operating Systems Review* **14**(4) pp. 71-82 (October 1980).

P. DEWAN, *Automatic Generation of User Interfaces,* Ph.D. thesis, Technical Report 666, University of Wisconsin—Madison (August 1986).

W. DIFFIE AND M. E. HELLMAN, "New Directions in Cryptography," *IEEE Transactions on Information Theory* **IT-22**(6) pp. 644-654 (November 1976).

E. W. DIJKSTRA, "Solution of a Problem in Concurrent Programming Control," *CACM* **8**(9) p. 569 (September 1965).

E. W. DIJKSTRA, "Cooperating Sequential Processes," pp. 103-110 in *Programming Languages*, ed. F. Genuys, Orlando, Fla.: Academic Press (1968).

E. W. DIJKSTRA, "Hierarchical Ordering of Sequential Processes," *Acta Informatica* **2**(1) pp. 115-138 (1971).

C. M. ELLISON, "The Utah TENEX Scheduler," *Proceedings of the IEEE* **63**(6) pp. 940-945 (June 1975).

R. FINKEL, M. SOLOMON, D. DEWITT, AND L. LANDWEBER, *The Charlotte Distributed Operating System: Part IV of the First Report on the Crystal Project*, Computer Sciences Technical Report 502, University of Wisconsin—Madison (July 1983).

C. N. FISCHER ET AL., "The POE Language-Based Editor Project," *ACM Sigsoft/Sigplan Symposium on Practical Software Development Environments*, (April 1984).

M. FRIDRICH AND W. OLDER, "The Felix File Server," *Proceedings of the 8th Symposium on Operating Systems Principles*, pp. 37-44 (December 1981).

S. H. FULLER, "Minimal Total Processing Time Drum and Disk Scheduling Disciplines," *CACM* **17**(7) pp. 376-381 (July 1974).

D. K. GIFFORD, "Cryptographic Sealing for Information Secrecy and Authentication," *CACM* **25**(4) pp. 274-286 (April 1982).

R. P. GOLDBERG,, "Survey of Virtual Machine Research," *Computer*, (June 1974).

M. GOOD, "Etude and the Folklore of User Interface Design," *Proceedings of the ACM SIGPLAN SIGOA Symposium on Text Manipulation, SIGPLAN Notices* **16**(6) pp. 34-43 (June 1981).

J. GRAY, "Notes on Database Operating Systems," in *Operating systems: An advanced course*, Berlin: Springer-Verlag (1979).

A. N. HABERMANN, *Introduction to Operating System Design*, Chicago: Science Research Associates, Inc. (1976).

B. HADDON, "Nested Monitor Calls," *Operating systems review* **11**(10) pp. 18-23 (October 1977).

P. G. HEBALKAR, "Coordinated Sharing of Resources in Asynchronous Systems," *Record of the Project MAC Conference on Concurrent Systems and Parallel Computation*, pp. 151-168 (June 1970).

M. C. HEMINWAY AND ED., *Datapro 70: The EDP Buyer's Bible*, Delvan, N.J.: Datapro Research Corp. (1986).

C. A. R. HOARE, "Towards a Theory of Parallel Programming," pp. 61-71 in *Operating Systems Techniques*, ed. C. A. R. Hoare and R. H. Perrott, , London: Academic Press (1972).

C. A. R. HOARE, "Monitors: An Operating System Structuring Concept," *CACM* **17**(10) pp. 549-557 (October 1974).

R. C. HOLT, "Comments on Prevention of System Deadlocks," *CACM* **14**(1) pp. 36-38 (January 1971).

R. C. HOLT, "Some Deadlock Properties of Computer Systems," *Computing Surveys* **4**(3) pp. 179-196 (September 1972).

F. HORN AND M. HONDA, Personal Communication (1977).

J. H. HOWARD, "Signaling in Monitors," *Proceedings of the 2nd International Conference on Software Engineering*, pp. 47-52 (October 1976).

K. JENSEN AND N. WIRTH, "Pascal: User Manual and Report," *Lecture Notes in Computer Science* **18** Berlin: Springer-Verlag, (1974).

A. K. JONES ET AL., "StarOS: A Multiprocessor Operating System for the Support of Task Forces," *Proceedings of the 7th Symposium on Operating Systems Principles*, pp. 117-127 (December 1979).

L. J. KENAH AND S. F. BATE, *VAX/VMS Internals and Data Structures*, Digital Press (1984).

J. H. KEPECS AND M. H. SOLOMON, "SODA: A Simplified Operating System for Distributed Applications," *Proceedings of the Third Annual ACM SIGACT-SIGOPS Symposium on Principles of Distributed Computing*, (August 1984).

B. W. KERNIGHAN AND R. PIKE, *The Unix Programming Environment*, Englewood Cliffs, N.J.: Prentice-Hall (1984).

L. KLEINROCK, *Queueing Systems, Vol. 2: Computer Applications*, New York: Wiley (1976).

D. E. KNUTH, *The Art of Computer Programming, Vol. 1: Fundamental Algorithms*, Reading, Mass.: Addison-Wesley (2nd ed.) (1973).

D. E. KNUTH, *The TeXBook*, Reading, Mass.: Addison-Wesley (1984).

L. LAMPORT, "Concurrent Reading and Writing," *CACM* **20**(11) pp. 806-811 (November 1977).

B. W. LAMPSON AND D. D. REDELL, "Experience with Processes and Monitors in Mesa," *CACM* **23**(2) pp. 105-117 (February 1980).

K. A. LANTZ AND R. F. RASHID, "Virtual Terminal Management in a Multiple Process Environment," *Proceedings of the 7th Symposium on Operating Systems Principles*, pp. 86-97 (December 1979).

S. LAUESEN, "Job Scheduling Guaranteeing Reasonable Turn-around Times," *Acta Informatica* **2**(1) pp. 1-11 (1973).

E. D. LAZOWSKA ET AL., "The Architecture of the Eden System," *Proceedings of the 8th Symposium on Operating Systems Principles*, pp. 148-159 (December 1981).

E. D. LAZOWSKA ET AL., *Quantitative System Performance*, (et al.), Englewood Cliffs, N.J.: Prentice-Hall (1984).

R. LEVIN ET AL., "Policy/mechanism Separation in Hydra," *Proceedings of the 6th Symposium on Operating Systems Principles*, pp. 132-140 (1977).

B. LISKOV AND R. SCHEIFLER, "Guardians and Actions: Linguistic Support for Robust, Distributed Programs," *ACM TOPLAS* **5**(3) pp. 381-404 (July 1983).

D. C. LITTLE, "A Proof of the Queueing Formula: $L = \lambda W$," *Operations Research* **9** pp. 383-387 (May 1961).

H. MADDURI AND R. FINKEL, "Extension of the Banker's Algorithm for Resource Allocation in a Distributed Operating System," *Information Processing Letters* **19**(1) pp. 1-8 (July 1984).

H. MADDURI AND R. FINKEL, *A Note on Starvation Control Policies*, Computer Sciences Technical Report 564, University of Wisconsin—Madison (November 1984).

S. E. MADNICK AND J. J. DONOVAN, *Operating Systems*, New York: McGraw-Hill (1972).

M. MAEKAWA, A. E. OLDEHOEFT, AND R. R. OLDEHOEFT, *Operating Systems: Advanced concepts*, Benjamin-Cummings (1987).

B. H. MARGOLIN, R. P. PARMELEE, AND M. SCHATZOFF, "Analysis of Free-storage Algorithms," *IBM System Journal* **10**(4) p. 283 (1971).

T. MASUDA, "Effect of Program Localities on Memory management strategies," *Proceedings of the 6th Symposium on Operating Systems Principles*, pp. 117-124 (November 1977).

N. MEYROWITZ AND M. MOSER, "Bruwin: An Adaptable Design Strategy for Window Manger/Virtual Terminal Systems," *Proceedings of the 8th Symposium on Operating System Principles*, pp. 180-189 (December 1981).

T. MINOURA, "Deadlock Avoidance Revisited," *Journal of the ACM* **29**(4) pp. 1023-1048 (October 1982).

J. G. MITCHELL AND J. DION, "A Comparison of Two Network-based File Servers," *CACM* **25**(4) pp. 233-245 (April 1982).

R. M. NEEDHAM AND A. D. BIRRELL, "The CAP Filing System," *Proceedings of the 6th Symposium on Operating Systems Principles*, pp. 11-16 (November 1977).

R. M. NEEDHAM AND R. D. H. WALKER, "The Cambridge CAP Computer and its Protection System," *Proceedings of the 6th Symposium on Operating Systems Principles*, pp. 1-10 (November 1977).

J. K. OUSTERHOUT, D. A. SCELZA, AND S. S. PRADEEP, "Medusa: An Experiment in Distributed Operating System Structure," *CACM* **23**(2) pp. 92-105 (February 1980).

D. L. PARNAS AND A. N. HABERMANN, "Comment on Deadlock Prevention (with reply by R.C. Holt)," *CACM* **15**(9) pp. 840-841 (September 1972).

G. L. PETERSON, "Myths about the Mutual Exclusion Problem," *Information Processing Letters* **12**(3) pp. 115-116 (June 1981).

J. L. PETERSON AND A. SILBERSCHATZ, *Operating System Concepts,* Reading, Mass.: Addison-Wesley (2nd ed.) (1985).

F. POLLACK, K. KAHN, AND R. WILKINSON, "The iMAX-432 Object Filing System," *Proceedings of the 8th Symposium on Operating Systems Principles*, pp. 137-147 (December 1981).

G. J. POPEK AND C. S. KLINE, "The PDP-11 Virtual Machine Architecture, A Case Study," *Proceedings of the 5th Symposium on Operating Systems Principles*, (November 1975).

G. J. POPEK ET AL., "LOCUS: A Network Transparent, High Reliability Distributed Sytem," *Proceedings of the 8th Symposium on Operating Systems Principles*, pp. 169-177 (December 1981).

M. L. POWELL, "The Demos File System," *Proceedings of the 6th Symposium on Operating Systems Principles*, pp. 33-42 (December 1977).

R. RASHID AND G. ROBERTSON, "Accent: A Communication Oriented Network Operating System Kernel," *Proceedings of the 8th Symposium on Operating Systems Principles*, pp. 64-75 (December 1981).

D. D. REDELL ET AL., "Pilot: An Operating System for a Personal Computer," *CACM* **23**(2) pp. 81-92 (February 1980).

D. P. REED AND R. K. KANODIA, "Synchronization with Eventcounts and Sequencers," *CACM* **22**(2) pp. 115-123 (February 1979).

P. ROBERT AND J. P. VERJUS, "Toward Autonomous Descriptions of Synchronization Modules," pp. 981-986 in *Information Processing 77*, ed. B. Gilchrist, (proceedings of the 1977 IFIP congress, Toronto, August 1977) New York: Elsevier—North Holland (1977).

D. E. ROSSI AND R. O. FONTAO, "A Parallel Algorithm for Deadlock-free Resource Allocation," *Revista Telegrafica Electronica (Argentina).*, (824) pp. 1062-1068 (November 1981).

M. Satyanarayanan, "A Study of File Sizes and Functional Lifetimes," *Proceedings of the 8th Symposium on Operating Systems Principles*, pp. 96-108 (December 1981).

C. H. Sauer and K. M. Chandy, *Computer Systems Performance Modeling,* Englewood Cliffs, N.J.: Prentice-Hall (1981).

M. L. Scott, *A Framework for the Evaluation of High-Level Languages for Distributed Computing*, Computer Sciences Technical Report 563, University of Wisconsin—Madison (October 1984).

M. L. Scott, *Design and Implementation of a Distributed Systems Language*, Ph. D. Thesis, Technical Report 596, University of Wisconsin—Madison (May 1985).

A. C. Shaw, *The Logical Design of Operating Systems,* Englewood Cliffs, N.J.: Prentice-Hall (1974).

B. Shneiderman, "Response Time and Display Rate in Human Performance with Computers," *ACM Computing Surveys* **16**(3) pp. 265-285 (September 1984).

J. E. Shore, "On the External Storage Fragmentation Produced by First Fit and Best Fit Allocation Policies," *CACM* **18**(8) p. 433 (1975).

A. Shoshani and E. G. Coffman, "Sequencing Tasks in Multiprocess Systems to Avoid Deadlocks," *IEEE Conference record of the 11th Annual Symposium on Switching and Automata Theory*, pp. 225-235 (October 1970).

W. D. Sincoskie and D. J. Farber, "SODS/OS: A Distributed Operating System for the IBM Series/1," *Operating Systems Review* **14**(3) pp. 46-54 (July 1980).

A. J. Smith, "Bibliography on Paging and Related Topics," *Operating Systems Review* **12**(4) pp. 39-56 (October 1978).

M. H. Solomon and R. A. Finkel, "ROSCOE: A Multi-Microcomputer Operating System," *Proceedings of the 2na Rocky Mountain Symposium on Microcomputers*, pp. 291-310 (August 1978).

M. Stonebraker, "Operating System Support for Database Management," *CACM* **24**(7) pp. 412-418 (July 1981).

D. Swinehart, G. McDaniel, and D. Boggs, "WFS: A Simple Shared File System for a Distributed Environment," *Proceedings of the 7th Symposium on Operating Systems Principles*, pp. 9-17 (December 1979).

A. S. Tanenbaum and S. J. Mullender, "An Overview of the Amoeba Distributed Operating System," *ACM Operating Systems Review* **15**(3) pp. 51-64 (July 1981).

A. S. Tanenbaum, *Computer Networks,* Englewood Cliffs, N.J.: Prentice-Hall (1981).

A. S. Tanenbaum, "Network Protocols," *ACM Computing Surveys* **13**(4) pp. 453-489 (December 1981).

A. S. Tanenbaum and R. Van Renesse, "Distributed Operating Systems," *Computing Surveys* **17**(4) pp. 419-470 (December 1985).

A. S. Tanenbaum, *Operating Systems: Design and Implementation,* Englewood Cliffs, N.J.: Prentice-Hall (1987).

T. Teitelbaum, T. Reps, and S. Horwitz, "The Why and Wherefore of the Cornell Program Synthesizer," *Sigplan Notices* **16**(6) pp. 8-16 (June 1981).

T. J. Teorey and T. B. Pinkerton, "A Comparative Analysis of Disk-Scheduling Policies," *CACM* **15**(3) pp. 177-184 (March 1972).

R. W. Turner, *Operating systems: Design and implementations,* Macmillan (1986).

N. Wirth, "Modula: a Language for Modular Multiprogramming," *Software—Practice and Experience* **7** pp. 3-35 (1977).

L. D. WITTIE AND A. M. VAN TILBORG, "MICROS, a Distributed Operating System For MICRONET, a Reconfigurable Network Computer," *IEEE Transactions on Computers* **C-29**(12) pp. 1133-44 (December 1980).

W. WULF ET AL., "HYDRA: The Kernel of a Multiprocessor Operating System," *CACM* **17**(6) pp. 337-345 (June 1974).

# Glossary

Many standard English words are used in a technical sense in this book. Careful and consistent use of these terms is a worthwhile habit to cultivate. Alternative expressions that you might find in the literature are also given here. This glossary should be taken as a guide to the sense in which I have used these terms rather than as a prescription for their proper use. Since there are many different kinds of operating systems, not all of these terms have meaning in all implementations.

**Abort**. To announce that a transaction has failed.

**Absolute file name**. A file name that indicates where a file lies with respect to the root of the file structure.

**Absolute**. (1) With respect to a standard reference point. For example, an *absolute file name* is given as a path from the root of the file tree. (See *Relative*.) (2) Certain to be true and up to date. For example, each disk block can include absolute information identifying the file to which it belongs. (See **Hint**.)

**Abstraction**. Higher-level resources created out of lower-level ones. Details of the lower-level structures are hidden, and higher-level structures are introduced. (See *Physical* and *Virtual*.)

**Access control**. A policy that determines the forms of access that subjects may make over objects.

**Access list**. A list of all the subjects that can access a given object and the privileges of each one.

**Access matrix**. A matrix with one row for each subject and one column for each object that shows the privileges each subject has over each object.

**Access mode**. The manner in which a subject accesses an object, such as reading as opposed to writing.

**Access right**. Permission for a subject to access an object via a particular access mode.

**Activate**. A line of text interactively entered into the computer is buffered by the operating system until the line has been activated. A typical line activator is the carriage return.

**Activity**. An executing entity, whether a process, a kernel task, an interrupt-driven procedure, or a DMA transfer.

**Address translation**. Converting a virtual address into a physical address. This operation is performed by hardware for the sake of efficiency.

**Advised paging**. A situation in which processes inform the storage manager that a page should be swapped in or out.

**Alias**. An alternative file name. Also called a *link*. *use the same inode*

**Aligned**. Starting on a particular boundary.

**Allocation state**. The number of resources held and claimed by each process and the number of resources not allocated to any process.

**Analysis**. Mathematical formulation of a set of interrelated objects and derivation of their collective behavior.

**Anomaly**. A situation in page replacement where increasing the number of page frames increases the number of faults.

**Arbitration**. Selection between simultaneous requests to decide which to honor first.

**Archive**. (1) A place where data may be stored, typically slow to access but large in capacity. (2) Long-term storage of large data files, typically on magnetic tape. (3) To transfer data from a cache to an archive. (See *Cache*.)

**Arrival**. When a process appears in the view of the short-term scheduler, either because it is a new process, because it has finished waiting for transput or some other resource, or because the medium-term scheduler has favored it. (Opposite of *Departure*.)

**Arrival rate**. The rate at which new processes arrive in the ready queue, usually represented by $\alpha$. The expected time between arrivals is $1 / \alpha$.

**Asynchronous communication**. The requesting process is not blocked while a send or receive operation undertaken on its request is completed. Instead, it discovers completion by waiting, polling, or virtual interrupt. (Opposite of *Synchronous communication*.)

**Asynchronous transput**. The requesting process is not blocked while transput undertaken on its request is completed. Instead, it discovers completion by waiting, polling, or virtual interrupt. (Opposite of *Synchronous transput*.)

**Atomic transaction**. A set of operations on files that behave as if they all happened at the same time or, in case of failure, as if none of them has happened at all.

**Authentication**. Discovering the identity of a subject, either to find out whether that subject has access rights over some object or to discover which subject created a particular object.

**Automatic chaining**. Invoking a frequently needed sequence of programs with one command.

**Backing store**. The large storage area used for swapping space. Backing store is typically disk or drum.

**Background**. A non-interactive process that executes at the same time as other processes owned by the same user but is not waited for by the command interpreter. (Opposite of *Foreground*.)

**Backup file**. A file that duplicates the contents of another file to protect against accidental deletion of information.

**Bandwidth**. The amount of data a communication line can carry every second.

**Base**. (1) A hardware register that indicates the physical address where a segment starts. (2) A program-accessible register that is used as part of effective address calculation for instructions.

**Batch**. A style of computer use in which programs are invoked and input is presented to them in a non-interactive way.

**Baud**. The bandwidth of a communication line, measured in the number of transitions per second.

**Beautification Principle**. An operating system is a set of algorithms that hide the details of the hardware and provide a more pleasant environment.

**Best fit**. A space-allocation policy that accepts the region of space that comes closest to meeting the space requirements. (See *First fit*.)

**Binding**. (1) Converting an abstract representation into a concrete one. (2) Associating a logical name with a physical name. (3) Associating an input or bound port with an entry.

**Bit map**. A mechanism for representing chunks of free and used space by associating one bit with each chunk.

**Bit mapped display**. A kind of display device where each dot on the display is controlled by a bit in main store.

**Bit-oriented**. A protocol that sends any number of bits, even if the number does not fit exactly into bytes. (Opposite of *Character-oriented*.)

**Bit stuffing**. Insertion of extra bits in a message to prevent the header bit pattern from being sent accidentally.

**Block**. (1) The fundamental chunk size for data stored on a disk. (2) To place a process in a wait list. Such a process is said to be *blocked*.

**Block device**. A device such as the disk that transfers data in fixed-size blocks.

**Bottleneck**. The limiting resource.

**Boundary tag**. A mechanism for delimiting blocks of free and used space that allows freed blocks to be coalesced with neighbors and allows free space to be linked together.

**Bounded**. A resource class is bounded if the number of elements in the class is limited.

**Bounded buffer**. A data object shared between producers and consumers of data. (See *Producer-consumer*.)

**Bound port**. A communication port with one writer and one reader.

**Bounds**. A hardware register indicating the length of a segment.

**Broadcast**. A situation in which many recipients can see the same message.

**Buffer**. A region in main store used to hold data that are about to be output to a device or that have recently come in from a device.

**Buffer Principle**. The purpose of a buffer pool is to smooth out short-term variations in speeds between consumers and producers. This smoothing prevents needless blocking.

**Bulletin board**. A program that accepts notices and distributes them to interested users.

**Busy waiting**. Polling in a tight loop.

**Byte stuffing**. Use of an escape convention to avoid transmitting a header byte by accident.

**Cache**. (1) A place where data can be accessed quickly. (2) To transfer data from an archive to a cache. (See *Archive*.)

**Cache hit**. The situation in which a cache is accessed and is found to contain the desired information.

**Cache miss**. The situation in which a cache is accessed but does not contain the desired information.

**Cache Principle**. The more frequently data are accessed, the faster the access should be.

**Capability**. An entity owned by a process that gives the process certain rights to access a particular object.

**Capability list**. A list of all the capabilities owned by a process.

**Central processing unit (cpu).** The part of the hardware of a computer that executes machine instructions. It communicates with main store and with devices.

**Chaining.** See *Automatic chaining* and *Command chaining*.

**Channel.** A subsidiary computer whose programs, called *channel programs*, are kept in main store. Channels govern transput for a set of devices.

**Characteristic number.** The area under a curve in a fault-rate graph.

**Character-oriented.** A protocol that sends messages 1 character (typically 8 bits) at a time. (Opposite of *Bit-oriented*.)

**Cheap-process philosophy.** Using a new process for each stage in a computation.

**Checkpoint.** A copy made of a process so that it can be restarted later from that same point if there is a hardware failure that prevents it from completing normally.

**Checksum.** A bit pattern derived from a chunk of data, usually by exclusive-or operations, appended to that chunk so that errors in storing or transmitting that chunk of data can be detected.

**Child.** A subnode in a tree, whether the tree is composed of files, processes, or other entities. (Opposite of *Parent*.)

**Ciphertext.** The result of encrypting data.

**Circular buffer pool.** A set of data buffers used for transput. As soon as one is finished, the next one in circular order may be used.

**Claim.** In the banker's algorithm of resource allocation, a limit specified by each process that restricts the number of resources it can request.

**Cleartext.** Data that have not been encrypted or that have been restored from encrypted form.

**Clock.** A device that interrupts at the end of an interval. Also called a *timer*.

**Close.** To finalize data structures or hardware when a data object or device is no longer to be used.

**Clustering.** (1) In paging, bringing in a set of pages adjacent in virtual space when any one of them needs to be swapped in. (2) In physical file layout, placing the blocks that represent a file on the same cylinder or within a small contiguous group of cylinders.

**Cold start.** (1) In simulations, beginning measurements from a bare initial state. For example, cold-start page-replacement analysis counts page faults required to start up a process. (2) In initializing operating systems, a cold start means that file storage is not formatted or may be corrupted and must be checked.

**Command.** (1) An instruction in a channel program, typically specifying the transput of a single block of information between main store and some particular device. (2) An interactive request given by a user to a program, particularly to the command interpreter of the operating system.

**Command chaining**. Allowing a channel program to contain more than one command.

**Command interpreter**. The software (part of either the kernel or a utility process) that interprets requests from the user. Also called *monitor* or *shell*.

**Command language**. A language the user employs to describe what programs are to be run and what their environment should be. Also called *job-control language*.

**Command script**. A command-language program given as a single interactive command to a command interpreter.

**Commit**. The point in a transaction after which the transaction is guaranteed to terminate without failing.

**Communication-kernel approach**. A design of operating system in which a small kernel provides mechanisms for processes to communicate with each other, but most policy decisions are outside the kernel.

**Communication line**. A device used for transferring information between computers or between a computer and a user.

**Component**. A file name is divided into components, each of which may follow a convention that indicates what the file contains.

**Composite address-translation table**. An address-translation table that composes the mappings specified by two or more address-translation tables at adjacent levels of a virtual-machine hierarchy.

**Compute-bound**. A process is compute bound if its running time depends mostly on the speed of the central processing unit, not on the speed of the transput devices. (Opposite of *Transput-bound*.)

**Concurrency control**. Synchronization and mutual exclusion to assure that activities that share data have predictable behavior.

**Conditional critical region**. A programming language construct used to enforce synchronization and mutual exclusion. (See *Synchronization*, 2, and *Mutual exclusion*.)

**Conflict**. Two regions conflict if execution of one must exclude execution of the other.

**Conservative**. A resource allocation policy is conservative if it avoids allocating resources unless stringent requirements are met. These requirements are intended to prevent deadlock and starvation. (Opposite of *Liberal*.)

**Context block**. The data used by the operating system to describe each process. The context block typically includes information about current use of main and backing store, the relationship between this process and others, the status of the process, and accounting information.

**Context switch**. The events involved in switching the hardware between execution of a process and execution of the kernel or in switching in the other direction. Switching from the kernel to the process is also called *dispatching*. (See *Process switch*.)

**Controller**. Hardware that connects a device either to the cpu or to a channel. The controller keeps track of the status of its devices and governs their actions.

**Convoy phenomenon**. A situation caused by long busy waiting in which many activities end up waiting for the same region and then proceed as a group through subsequent regions.

**Copy on write**. A form of lazy evaluation in which a segment is shared by two processes until either one tries to modify its data, at which point a separate copy is made.

**Crash**. (1) A calamity in which a disk head touches the disk surface and destroys it. (2) An unplanned halt in the operating system.

**Critical region**. A programming language construct used to enforce mutual exclusion. (See *Mutual exclusion*.)

**Crowd monitor**. An extension to a monitor that distinguishes guard procedures from ordinary procedures within the monitor and imposes run-time restrictions on when ordinary procedures may be invoked. (See *Monitor*.)

**Cursor**. A visual indicator of the current location of interest on a display.

**Customization**. Modifying the interface between the operating system and the user according to the personal desires of the user. Line-editing characters, command syntax, and default settings for programs are useful to customize.

**Cylinder**. A collection of tracks on a disk pack that can be simultaneously accessed by the read/write heads on the different disk surfaces.

**Data abstraction**. A programming-language tool that separates operations on data from their implementation, thus hiding details of lower-level structures and introducing new facilities. (See *Abstraction*.)

**Database**. A collection of structured, interrelated data, usually managed by utility programs that perform queries and updates.

**Data chaining**. A channel's ability to gather data from different places in main store or to scatter data to different places in main store.

**Debugging**. Discovering the sources of errors in a program and fixing them.

**Decryption**. A transformation used to convert ciphertext back to the original cleartext.

**Deadlock**. A situation in which each process in a cycle is waiting for resources held by the next process in the cycle. Also called *deadly embrace*. (See *Livelock* and *Starvation*.)

**Deadlock detection**. Noticing deadlock situations when they arise instead of applying deadlock prevention.

**Deadlock-free**. A resource allocation state is deadlock-free if the processes form a sequence, each element of which might finish if all the previous ones do.

**Deadlock-free sequence**. A sequence of processes used to show that a resource allocation state is deadlock-free.

**Deadlock prevention**. Avoiding a deadlock situation by using an appropriate resource allocation policy.

**Deadlock recovery**. Terminating one or more members of a deadlock for the good of the community.

**Default setting**. An assumption that may be overridden if necessary.

**Delay**. The amount of time between the moment a writer sends information on a communication line and the moment a reader gets that information.

**Delete**. To remove a file from secondary store. Also called *remove* or *destroy*. (See *Partial deletion*.)

**Delimiting**. A property of a communication link that data written to the link are separated into discrete messages.

**Demand paging**. A page is brought in when a page fault requires it.

**Departure**. When a process disappears from the view of the short-term scheduler, either because it has terminated, because it must wait for transput or some other resource, or because the medium-term scheduler is discriminating against it. (Opposite of *Arrival*.)

**Descriptor**. A small number given by the kernel to a process to allow it to refer to an opened resource.

**Device**. A piece of hardware connected to the computer. Devices are principally used for transput.

**Device descriptor**. A small integer returned by the kernel when a device is opened by a process. The process then uses the descriptor to refer to the device in other service calls.

**Device driver**. A device-specific program in the kernel to control a particular type of device.

**Device interface**. The interface between the kernel and devices, consisting of control requests and interrupts.

**Device register**. A means of communication between devices and the cpu used to carry data, instructions from the cpu to the device, and the status of the device.

**Difference encoding**. A data compression technique that converts values into differences between one value and the next.

**Direct access**. A file access method in which the read/write mark can be positioned explicitly. Also called *random access*.

**Direct memory access (DMA)**. A hardware technique that allows a device to transfer large quantities of data to or from main store.

**Directory**. A list of pairs that can be searched by the first element, called the *key*, to derive the second.

**Dirty field**. A field in the translation table set by the hardware when a page or segment is written into.

**Discrete**. A resource is discrete if it can be granted entirely or not at all but not partially.

**Disk**. A device used for secondary and backing store.

**Disk descriptor**. Information recorded in a well-known place on a disk that describes the layout of data on the disk.

**Disk-head scheduling**. Ordering the outstanding disk-access requests to minimize seek latency.

**Disk pack**. The part of the disk on which information is stored.

**Distributed computation**. Co-ordinated work on several computers simultaneously. (See *Multicomputer* and *Multiprocessor*.)

**Driver**. See *Device driver*.

**Dump**. (1) A file dump is a backup copy of one or more files to protect against accidental loss. (2) A main-store dump is a file copy of the address space of a process that has encountered a run-time error.

**Dynamic**. Something that changes over time. For example, the number of processes competing for service is a dynamic property of an operating system.

**Eager evaluation**. Doing work that may prove useful to save time later if the work is required. (Example: *Read-ahead*. Opposite of *Lazy evaluation*.)

**Echo**. Repeating information that has been heard back to the sender is called echoing. In particular, the terminal driver of an operating system may echo all characters typed into keyboards back out to the associated display.

**Editing**. Entry or modification of textual information, usually interactive. Files are edited with the assistance of programs called *text editors*. Command lines and other lines input to programs may be edited with the direct assistance of a *line editor*, which is part of the terminal driver in the operating system.

**Encryption**. A data transformation intended to provide secrecy (and possibly authentication).

**Entry**. In the communication-kernel approach, the recipient of a message, much like a procedure.

**Error-correcting code**. A data encoding method that is capable of detecting and correcting some recording or transmission errors.

**Escape convention**. A character that means that the next character is to be treated as data, not as a control character.

**Essential utility**. A part of the operating system that every user must use but which does not need special privileges. (See *Optional utility* and *Kernel*.)

**Event count**. A counter that is used for synchronization without mutual exclusion. Its operations are Read, Advance, and Await.

**Execution**. When a process is running, we say it is in the execution phase, as distinct from the loading phase.

**Explicit**. Explicit process information is provided by the user before the process is first scheduled.

**Exponential average**. An averaging technique that updates a statistic by this formula:

$$NewValue := w \cdot OldValue + (1 - w) \cdot NewMeasurement$$

**Extent**. A group of contiguous disk blocks that constitute part of a file.

**External waste**. See *Waste*.

**Extrinsic**. Extrinsic properties of a process are characteristics associated with the user who owns the process, such as how urgent the process is.

**Failure atomicity**. A property of transactions that either all or none of the operations in the transaction take effect. (See *Synchronization atomicity*.)

**Fault**. A trap generated by the hardware when address translation cannot continue because of an absent page or segment. These situations are known as *page faults* and *segment faults*, respectively.

**Fault-rate graph**. A graph showing the behavior of a page-replacement policy for a given page-reference string across a range of main-store sizes.

**File**. A named collection of data. Files may be written by a process and later read by the same or another process. Files are usually represented by a logically connected set of bytes on a disk or magnetic tape.

**File descriptor**. A structure on a disk that stores data associated with a file, such as its access rights, physical arrangement, and usage statistics.

**File descriptor area**. A region on disk dedicated to file descriptors.

**File manager**. The portion of the operating system that deals with file structures.

**File server**. A computer dedicated to providing files to a collection of computers.

**Finalization**. Action taken when a resource is released to put it in the proper state.

**First fit**. (1) A space-allocation policy that accepts the first region of space that has adequate contents. (2) A resource-allocation policy aimed at reducing starvation by granting resources, if safe, to processes that have been waiting longer. (See *Best fit*.)

**Flag**. A parameter in a command that specifies an optional behavior of the process that the command invokes.

**Flat**. A file structure is flat if all file names are in the same directory. Also called *one-level*.

**Foreground**. An interactive process, usually given higher priority than the non-interactive background processes. (Opposite of *Background*.)

**Format**. (1) To establish the structure of a disk pack, laying out sector boundaries. (2) To establish the disk structures for a file system.

**Frame**. (1) A region on magnetic tape that is 1 bit long and (usually) 9 bits wide. (2) A unit of transmission that is short enough so that the sender and receiver clocks remain synchronized during the transmission.

**Free port**. A communication port with many writers and many readers.

**Full duplex**. A kind of communication line where data may travel in both directions simultaneously. (See *Half duplex* and *Simplex*.)

**Full name**. The name of a file that includes its path name and its local name.

**Gateway**. A computer on two networks that can transfer messages from one to the other.

**Global**. A global page replacement policy selects pages to discard from any process. (See *Local* and *Pool*.)

**Group identifier**. A number associated with all the processes and files created for a particular group of users. This number is used for accounting and protection purposes. (See *User identifier*.)

**Guard**. A procedure exported from a monitor. Guards are mutually exclusive.

**Half duplex**. A kind of communication line where data travels in either direction, but only in one direction at a time. (See *Full duplex* and *Simplex*.)

**Hamming distance**. The number of bit positions at which two strings differ.

**Handler**. A program that responds to interrupts.

**Hardware**. The bare computer, including its main store, the devices attached to it, and its central processing unit.

**Header**. (1) The prefix on a transmission frame, used to synchronize the sender and the receiver. (2) More generally, extra information placed in a message by a level of transmission protocol.

**Hierarchical allocation**. A policy for resource allocation under which a process may only request resources that have a higher level than any resource it currently holds.

**Hint**. Usually but not necessary true and up to date. For example, the name of the machine where a process resides may be cached as a hint on other machines but not updated if the process moves. (See **Absolute**.)

**History**. (1) A log of past commands recorded so that they can be modified and resubmitted. (2) A log of past events recorded for debugging or accounting purposes.

**Hit ratio**. The percentage of time that accesses to a cache result in a cache hit.

**Hysteresis Principle**. Resist change. In particular, when data are brought into a cache, leave them there for a while before archiving them again.

**Idle time**. Time during which no process is ready to run.

**Icon**. A graphical representation of an object or abstraction on a bit-mapped display.

**Implicit**. Implicit process information is gathered by the operating system while it is servicing the process.

**Indirect file**. A file that contains the full name of another file. Opening the indirect file has the effect of opening the file it names. Also called a *symbolic link*.

**Inheriting**. When a process splits into two or creates a new process, we say that the new processes inherit from the old one if they start with the same contents of virtual space, open files, or other resources.

**Initialization file**. A file that contains customized settings for a program. The program reads this file during initialization.

**Input port**. A communication port with one reader and many writers.

**Intentions list**. A list of operations that must be executed to finish a transaction. Intentions lists are usually written in stable storage.

**Inter-file gap**. An empty region on a magnetic tape that separates one file from another.

**Inter-record gap**. An empty region on a magnetic tape that separates one record from another.

**Interactive**. A style for using a computer in which users type in commands and see responses on a display. New commands can therefore be based on the results of previous commands. Interactive computing is often found in conjunction with monoprogramming on single-user microcomputers and multiprogramming on larger machines.

**Internal waste**. See *Waste*.

**Interrupt**. A hardware event that signals some external condition, such as completion of transput. Interrupts cause a context switch to the kernel.

**Intrinsic**. Intrinsic properties of a process are characteristics that distinguish one process from another, such as service-time requirements, storage needs, and amount of transput required.

**Invariant expression**. A syntax for specifying synchronization information.

**Invocation**. Turning a program that is stored in a load image into a running process.

**I/O**. Either input or output. (See *Transput*.)

**IOP**. Input-output processor. Also called *channel*.

**Kernel**. The core of the operating system; a permanently resident control program using special hardware privileges to react to interrupts from external devices and to requests for service from processes. (See *Essential utility* and *Optional utility*.)

**Kernel space**. The virtual space of the kernel.

**Kernel time**. Time spent by the kernel making policy decisions and carrying them out.

**Key**. (1) A security mechanism used with locks. (See *Lock*.) (2) The first element in a pair that is used for searching for that pair in a directory. (3) A field of a file record used for searching for that record.

**Knot**. A set of vertices in a generalized resource graph such that starting at any vertex of the knot, paths lead to all the vertices in the knot and to no vertices outside the knot.

**Label**. An initial file on a magnetic tape that describes the tape.

**Latency**. Delay between a request and its completion. (See *Seek latency*, *Winding latency*, and *Rotational latency*.)

**Law of Diminishing Returns**. The first policy you think of is very poor. The next one works fine. With enormous effort, you can do even a little better.

**Lazy evaluation**. Avoiding doing work when it is first discovered in the hope that it might never be needed. (Example: *Copy on write*. Opposite of *Eager evaluation*.)

**Level Principle**. What appears as an active entity from one point of view often appears as a data structure from a lower level.

**Liberal**. A resource allocation policy is liberal if it grants resources whenever asked. Liberality is intended to maximize the level of multiprogramming. (Opposite of *Conservative*.)

**Line editor**. An interactive program used to enter and modify the contents of a single line. This program is often part of the terminal driver. (See *Editing*.)

**Line clock**. A device that generates an interrupt every 60th (or 50th) of a second.

**Linker**. The program that combines the output of compilers or assemblers with library routines and prepares a load image.

**Livelock**. A situation in which the algorithm that decides whether to block an activity fails to reach a decision and continues to use computational resources. (See *Deadlock* and *Starvation*.)

**Load**. To construct a new process, initializing its virtual store, including its instructions and data, from a load image. (See *Split*.)

**Loader**. A program that brings a load image into main store. Also called *Image activator*.

**Load image**. A representation of the virtual space for a process, usually kept in a file. This file is constructed by a linker and brought into main store by a loader.

**Local**. (1) A local page replacement method is one that selects pages to swap out from the virtual space of the process whose page needs the space. (See *Global* and *Pool*.) (2) A local file name is the name the file has in its directory.

**Local-area network**. A set of computers at a single installation connected by communication devices.

**Locality**. The phenomenon that programs actively use only a limited set of pages during any particular time period of execution. This set of pages is called the locality of the program during that time.

**Lock**. (1) A security device, used with keys. (See *Key*.) (2) A note on an object (like a file or a page) indicating that it is in use by some transaction for reading or writing. (3) A device for mutual exclusion that uses an atomic test-and-set or test-and-add instruction.

**Log**. A record of changes made to files during a transaction so that the changes can be reversed or reapplied.

**Logical names**. Names expanded by the file manager according to tables.

**Logoff**. The end of an interactive session.

**Logon**. The start of an interactive session.

**Long-haul network**. A network of computers that spans a large geographic region.

**Long-term scheduling**. A policy that decides when to let new processes enter the ready list.

**Main store**. The fast random-access memory of a computer, typically between 64K and 16M bytes. Also called *primary memory* or *core*.

**Mapped access**. A file access method in which the entire file is mapped into the virtual space of the process.

**Mechanism**. A technique by which an activity is performed. (See *Policy*.)

**Medium-term scheduling**. A policy that removes processes from the ready list in order to reduce contention for resources, particularly space and time.

**Memoryless**. The exponential distribution is called memoryless because the expected time to the next event does not depend on how long it has been since the previous event.

**Menu**. A list of commands that are legal in the current situation, typically presented on a bit-mapped display.

**Migration**. Moving a process from one machine to another to improve throughput and to balance load.

**Mirrored tables**. The kernel duplicates information that is also stored in a hardware table. The kernel table represents the truth, possibly with fields that the hardware table does not possess. This technique is used especially for address translation tables. Also called *shadow tables*.

**Miss**. When a cache does not have the information needed to complete an operation.

**Missed time**. The elapsed time between the instant a process arrives in the ready queue and the time it leaves that queue minus the required time for the process.

**Mode**. See *Access mode*.

**Model**. A mathematical description of a physical situation, used for deriving analytic or simulation results.

**Monitor**. A programming-language construct for mutual exclusion and synchronization.

**Mounting**. Placing the contents of one disk as a virtual subdirectory in another disk.

**Multicomputer**. A computer built of several processors that do not share main store. The processors communicate by sending messages through a communication device.

**Multiprocessor**. A computer built with more than one processor sharing the same main store. Also called *attached processor*.

**Multiprogramming**. The situation in which many processes may be in the ready list at one time and share the computational resource through some policy of short-term scheduling.

**Mutual exclusion**. Ensuring that two activities that use the same data may not occur at the same time. (See *Region*.)

**Name space**. The set of identifiers in a program, representing variables and procedures.

**Network**. A number of computers connected by communication lines for the purpose of transmitting data.

**Nickname**. A simple way to invoke a complex operation.

**Non-alternating switch**. A device used to determine which of two conflicting activities may enter a region.

**Non-preemptive**. A policy that never preempts a resource from a process.

**Non-privileged state**. See *Processor state*.

**Object**. A unit of information that a subject wishes to access. (See *Access control*.)

**Offline**. (1) A device is offline if it is disconnected from the computer and no transfers can be made. (2) A set of operations is performed offline if they may be done at any convenient time instead of at the time they are requested.

**Offset**. An address given as the distance from the beginning of some object, often a segment or page.

**One-level structure**. A one-level file structure has one directory for all file names. Also called *flat*.

**One-shot allocation**. A resource allocation policy that requires each process to acquire all the resources it needs at one time. Also called *preclaiming*.

**Operating system**. Software for a computer, including the kernel, essential utilities, and optional utilities.

**Operator**. An employee of a computer installation in charge of loading jobs and collecting output.

**Open**. (1) To initialize data structures or hardware when a data object or device starts to be used. (2) A process that wishes to use a resource (like a file) might open the resource before it starts. (See *Descriptor*.)

**Open shop**. A style for using a computer in which users sign up for a block of time, typically 15 or 30 minutes. During that time, the user has complete control of the machine.

**Optional utility**. A program that is distributed as part of the operating system software but is not needed by every user. (See *Essential utility* and *Kernel*.)

**Output port**. A communication port with one writer and many readers.

**Overflow file descriptor**. A block on the disk that holds disk-block pointers that did not fit in the file descriptor.

**Overhead space**. See *Waste*.

**Overhead time**. Time needed to perform the computations needed for a policy.

**Overlay**. A technique whereby the same region of virtual store is used for different purposes at different times.

**Overloading**. Use of one object for two purposes. The object could be a field of a record, the name of a subroutine, an error message, or anything else. Which purpose is intended depends on the context in which the object is used.

**Overrun**. An error that occurs in direct-memory-access transfers if main store cannot supply the next byte to write to the device when it is needed, or if it cannot store the next byte from the device before that byte has been discarded to make room for more data.

**Page**. A region of virtual store. The page size is determined by the hardware (and occasionally by the operating system) and is a constant over all pages.

**Page fault**. A trap generated by the hardware when a page absent from main store is accessed by a program.

**Page frame**. A region of physical store exactly long enough to hold one page.

**Page reference string**. A list of the pages referenced by a process during the course of execution.

**Page-replacement policy**. A policy that decides which page to swap out to make room for a page that must be swapped in.

**Page table**. The name of the address translation table when paging is used.

**Parameter**. (1) An adjustable quantity that tunes a distribution to fit the data or to describe the situation of interest. (2) An argument to a procedure. (3) An argument to a command in command language. (See *Flag*.)

**Parent**. A direct ancestor in a tree, whether the tree is composed of files, processes, or other entities. The parent of a process is the one that submitted a service call leading to the creation of that process. (Opposite of *Child*.)

**Parity**. The count of some event, modulo 2. A parity bit is an extra bit on a word that is set or cleared to make the number of one bits in the word 0 or 1 mod 2 (that is, even or odd).

**Partial deletion**. A file is partially deleted if it is no longer directly accessible but can be recovered without much effort. (See *Delete*.)

**Partition**. A fixed region of main store used as a virtual space. The partition method was supported by the IBM 360 and used in the OS/360 operating system.

**Password**. A secret combination of symbols. Subjects that know a password have access to the objects it protects.

**Path expression**. A syntax for specifying synchronization information.

**Path name**. Part of a full file name that specifies the directory in which the file is found.

**Pattern**. A string that represents a set of file names.

**Penalty ratio**. The ratio of response time to required time for a given process, represented by *P*. *P* is always greater than or equal to 1. Also called *Execution time multiplication factor*. (See *Response ratio*.)

**Permanence**. A property of transactions that once one completes successfully, the results of its operations will never be lost.

**Personalized shorthand**. A phrase acceptable to the command interpreter that is expanded to a different phrase as established by the user.

**Phase change**. When a program leaves one region of locality and enters another.

**Physical**. The raw materials of an abstraction, typically actual hardware, as opposed to a virtual view of it. (Opposite of *Virtual*.)

**Pipe**. An inter-process communication device that appears like a file opened for reading by one process and writing by another.

**Platter**. A part of a disk pack, divided into tracks.

**Policy**. A way to choose which activities to perform. (See *Mechanism*.)

**Polling**. Periodically checking the status of a physical or virtual device, usually to detect completion of a transput operation.

**Pool**. A pool page replacement method chooses a page to swap out from a pool of available page frames. (See *Local* and *Global*.)

**Port**. A virtual device through which processes communicate.

**Port capability**. Permission to read or write to a particular port. This permission can be transmitted in messages.

**Port file**. A file that allows processes that open it to communicate with each other.

**Preemption**. Reclaiming a resource from a process before the process has finished using it.

**Prefetching**. Bringing pages into main store before they are needed by a process in order to avoid wasting time servicing page faults or file transput requests. (See *Locality*.)

**Present field**. A field in the translation table set by the software when a page or segment is swapped in.

**Privilege**. Access right.

**Privileged state**. See *Processor state*.

**Process**. The execution of a program. The kernel causes the process to run by switching context to it. The process submits service calls to request resources from the kernel. Also called *task* or *job*.

**Process interface**. The interface between a process and the kernel, consisting of service calls and their responses.

**Processor**. A device able to execute computer instructions. Most computers have just one processor; those with more are called multiprocessors. Also called *central processing unit*.

**Processor sharing**. A theoretical scheduling policy in which every process gets an identical fraction of the computing resources. Equivalently, each process has its own virtual processor that runs at a varying fraction of the speed of the physical processor.

**Processor state**. A hardware state that determines which instructions are currently legal and which address-translation tables are currently in use. Some machines have only two states, privileged and non-privileged; others have more.

**Processor-synchronous**. A class of mutual-exclusion and synchronization methods that work by making a processor uninterruptible. (Opposite of *Store-synchronous*.)

**Process switch**. The actions taken by the kernel to cause a different process to run the next time the context switches from kernel to process. (See *Context switch*.)

**Producer-consumer**. A situation in which one set of activities creates data and another set of activities uses those data. (See *Bounded buffer*.)

**Program**. A set of instructions packaged into a form that can be run by a process.

**Program counter**. A hardware register that indicates the address of the currently executing instruction.

**Programmable clock**. A device that can be set to generate an interrupt after an arbitrary interval.

**Progress diagram**. An *n*-dimensional picture where dimension *i* refers to virtual time in process *i*. A path through that diagram starting at the origin shows how those processes are scheduled. Some regions of the diagram may be forbidden because of resource conflicts between processes.

**Protection**. Preventing a subject from modifying objects it should not modify. For example, preventing a process from modifying the virtual store of another process or preventing a user from writing into another user's file. (See *Security*.)

**Protocol**. A set of conventions that governs the co-operation between two activities. It includes a specification of the kinds of data that are transmitted between them and what those data mean.

**Queueing network**. A mathematical description of a set of queues, servers, and processes that can be used to derive quantities such as expected penalty ratio.

**Read-ahead**. An eager-evaluation policy that prefetches data blocks from serial devices into a main-store cache before any process requests them. Also called *prefetching* and *anticipatory buffering*.

**Readers-writers problem**. A situation in which any writer conflicts with all other readers and writers.

**Read/write mark**. A logical position in a file that indicates where the next data transfer will occur.

**Realizable**. An allocation state is realizable if it makes sense. For example, the number of resources currently in use cannot exceed the total number of resources.

**Record**. (1) A chunk of data stored on magnetic tape, delimited by inter-record gaps. (2) A chunk of data stored in a file and structured by fields.

**Reduction**. A technique to manipulate a waits-for graph to detect deadlock.

**Redundancy**. Using more bits than necessary to store or transmit data in order to provide reliability.

**Reflecting**. A virtualizing kernel receives traps when its clients perform privileged instructions and interrupts when devices need service. If the kernel causes one of its virtual machines to see this trap or interrupt, we say the trap or interrupt has been reflected.

**Region**. A set of instructions that must be executed excluding some other activity. (See *Mutual exclusion*.)

**Register**. A hardware-supplied fast region of store. Many computers have addressing modes that use registers. Not to be confused with *Device register*.

**Relative**. With respect to a standard reference point. For example, a *relative file name* indicates where a file lies with respect to the current working directory. (See *Absolute*.)

**Remote job entry**. Submitting a job from one computer to another, with the results transmitted back to the first computer.

**Remote logon**. Logging on to a computer over a network. (See *Logon*.)

**Remote mounting**. Placing the contents of a directory as a virtual subdirectory on another machine. (See *Mounting*.)

**Resident monitor**. A simple operating system that starts the next process when the previous one finishes.

**Resource class**. A kind of resource (like a tape drive) for which the individual resources are indistinguishable, or at least the differences are immaterial to the requesting process.

**Resource graph**. A graph of processes and resources with arcs from processes to resources they are waiting for and from resources to processes that are using them.

**Resource Principle**. An operating system is a collection of algorithms that allocate resources to processes.

**Response ratio.** The ratio of required time to response time for a given process, represented by R. R is always less than or equal to 1. (See *Penalty ratio.*)

**Response time.** The elapsed time between the instant a process arrives in the ready queue and the time it leaves that queue. Also called *turnaround time*, especially in a batch environment.

**Rotational latency.** The delay in accessing a disk block while the disk rotates into the correct position.

**Run-length encoding.** A data compression technique that replaces a run of similar characters with a run-length indication.

**Safe.** A resource allocation state is safe if the processes form a sequence, each element of which can acquire its resources and terminate if all the previous ones do.

**Safe sequence.** A sequence of processes used to show that a resource allocation state is safe.

**Salvage.** To examine the data on a garbaged disk and recover the original structure.

**Saturation.** The ratio of arrival rate to service rate, usually denoted by $\rho$. Also called *Traffic intensity*.

**Scatter-gather.** See *Data chaining.*

**Scheduling.** (1) Managing the time resource by deciding when each process should be allowed to run. (2) Orchestrating the starting times for any set of operations, such as disk reads or transaction operations.

**Secondary store.** Long-term storage used for files, typically disk.

**Secrecy.** Preventing unauthorized inspection of data. (See *Security.*)

**Sector.** A region of a track on a disk pack that holds one block of information.

**Security.** Preventing unwanted accesses to objects. (See *Protection, Secrecy*, and *Authentication.*)

**Seek.** (1) Motion of the disk read/write head from one track to another. (2) File operation that moves to a given point in the file.

**Seek latency.** The delay in accessing a disk block necessitated by a disk seek operation.

**Segment.** A region of virtual space whose addresses all specify that segment and which is allocated as a single unit.

**Segment fault.** A trap generated by the hardware when a segment absent from main store is accessed by a program.

**Segment table.** The name of the translation table when segmentation is used.

**Semaphore**. A mutual-exclusion and synchronization device that contains a lock, a count of concurrent activities, and a queue of waiting activities.

**Sequencer**. A counter used to assign an arbitrary order to unordered events.

**Sequential access**. A file access method in which the read/write mark is incremented after each data transfer by the amount of data transferred.

**Serializability**. A property of the simultaneous execution of a number of transactions that has those transactions produce the same result they would have had they been run sequentially in some order.

**Serialization**. Running one process or transaction at a time, or only allowing one at a time to acquire resources.

**Serially reusable**. A resource that may be granted to a process after it has been used by another.

**Service**. (1) To service an interrupt is to give the next data to or accept the last set of data from a device that has interrupted because it has finished the previous transput. (2) To service a device is to service the completion interrupt for that device.

**Service call**. A request that a running process makes of the kernel to acquire or release a resource or to perform transput. Service calls always switch context to the kernel.

**Service rate**. The rate at which processes can be executed, usually represented by $\beta$. The expected time to service a single process is $1 / \beta$.

**Session**. A period of interactive use lasting from logon to logoff.

**Short-term scheduling**. Any policy that determines the order in which ready processes are executed. The short-term scheduler is also called a *dispatcher*.

**Shuffling**. Moving segments within physical store to coalesce free space into one piece. Also called *compaction*.

**Simplex**. A kind of communication line where data travels in only one direction. (See *Full duplex* and *Half duplex*.)

**Simulation**. Deriving the behavior of a collection of interrelated objects by using random-number generators to make probabilistic decisions and measuring a large number of samples.

**Skewing**. Spacing consecutive blocks of a file a few sectors apart on a disk.

**Space**. A resource that the operating system allocates among the various processes that compete for it. Space is the ability to store information, whether in main or backing store.

**Spin switch**. A generalization of the non-alternating switch to $n$ conflicting activities. Also called *Spin lock*.

**Split**. To create the virtual space of a new process by copying an existing process. (See *Load*.)

**Spooling system**. A simple operating system that collects jobs on a disk until it can run them and stores output on a disk until it can print it, but runs only one job at a time.

**Stable storage**. Storing data redundantly on the disk so that any single failure results in a readable version of the data.

**Stack property**. A property of a page-replacement algorithm that prevents anomalies. At each point in any page-reference string, the set of pages that would be in an $n$-page-frame main store is a subset of those that would be in an $(n + 1)$-page-frame main store.

**Startup phase**. The time after a process enters the ready list from the main-store wait list until it has acquired its working set.

**Startup phase conflict**. The situation in which several processes are simultaneously in startup phase.

**Starvation**. The situation in which a process continues to be denied a resource that it needs, even though the resource is being granted to other processes.

**Starvation detection**. Noticing starvation situations when they arise and treating them by preventing new processes from acquiring resources.

**State vector**. Part of the context block that the operating system keeps available at all times. It stores the contents of registers while the process is not running.

**Steady state**. The situation that holds after the load has been constant for a long enough time that average behavior has begun to occur.

**Storage module**. The part of the operating system kernel that makes and implements main-store allocation policy.

**Store-synchronous**. A class of mutual-exclusion and synchronization methods that rely on the fact that main store services only one request at a time, even on a multiprocessor. (Opposite of *Processor-synchronous*.)

**Structured file**. A file built of records, some of whose fields are treated as keys.

**Structure editor**. An interactive program used to enter and modify the contents of an object such as a printer font or a VLSI layout. (See *Editing*.)

**Subdisk**. A region of the disk introduced to promote clustering. An attempt is made to keep files entirely within subdisks.

**Subject**. An entity such as a process or a user that wishes to access an object. (See *Access control*.)

**Swapping**. Moving part of or all the virtual store of a process between main and backing store. The area on backing store reserved for this purpose is called *swapping space*. A process (or page or segment) on backing store is *swapped out*. A process (or page or segment) in main store is *swapped in*.

**Switch**. (1) See *Process switch* and *Context switch*. (2) A variable used to determine which of two conflicting activities may next enter a region. (See *Non-alternating switch* and *Spin lock*.)

**Synchronization**. (1) Achieving a common notion of time, either by sharing clocks or by passing information. Synchronous transmission uses a header to achieve common clocks. (2) Causing an activity to wait for a condition.

**Synchronization atomicity**. A property of transactions that each one is atomic, that is, indivisible, immune to interference from other transactions that might be occurring at the same time. (See *Failure atomicity*.)

**Synchronization graph**. A graph whose nodes are activities and whose arrows are precedence constraints. Also called *precedence graph*.

**Synchronous communication**. The situation where a process that has requested a send or receive is blocked until the request completes. (Opposite of *Asynchronous communication*.)

**Synchronous transput**. The situation where a process that has requested transput is blocked until the transput completes. (Opposite of *Asynchronous transput*.)

**Task**. A thread of control within the kernel.

**Text**. The contents of a file intended to be read by humans.

**Text editor**. An interactive program used to enter and modify the contents of a text file. (See *Editing*.)

**Thrashing**. The situation in which computation is blocked most of the time waiting for data to be transferred between two levels of the storage hierarchy. The usual case is thrashing due to page traffic between main and backing store.

**Thread**. An active entity that inhabits a process. Programming-language "processes" are often implemented as threads.

**Tie down**. Mark a segment or page as not susceptible to swapping out or shuffling, usually because DMA is in progress. Also called *lock*, *pin down*, or *fix*.

**Time**. The resource of instruction execution, which the operating system shares among the various processes that are competing for it.

**Timeout**. A parameter that indicates how long an activity is willing to wait for a particular event.

**Timesharing**. Usually refers to interactive multiprogramming. We do not use this term.

**Timestamp**. A field that records the time at which some event happened.

**Track**. A band on the platter of a disk pack.

**Transaction**. A group of file accesses (or other transput operations) that together accomplish a goal. (See *Synchronization atomicity*, *Failure atomicity*, and *Permanence*.)

**Transaction manager**. The module of the kernel that provides transaction services.

**Transfer latency**. The amount of time needed for a sector to pass under the read/write head of a disk.

**Translation look-aside buffer**. A cache used by the hardware to hold the most frequently used parts of the translation table.

**Translation table**. A table used by the hardware to assist in performing address translation. (See *Page table* and *Segment table*.)

**Transparent**. Invisible or indistinguishable to a process. Transput is transparent with respect to a device if the process need not know which device is being used. Address translation is transparent to processes under paging.

**Transput**. Either input or output. Transput is often called *I/O*, which stands for *input/output*.

**Transput-bound**. A process is transput-bound if it spends most of its time waiting for transput to complete. An operating system is transput-bound if the ready list is usually empty and the transput wait lists have members. (Opposite of *Compute-bound*.)

**Trap**. A hardware event that signals a program error such as division by zero or accessing an invalid virtual address. The service-call instruction also causes a trap. Traps cause a context switch to the kernel.

**Trap-door encryption**. An encryption algorithm that has no associated decryption algorithm, or whose decryption algorithm is very difficult to discover.

**Used field**. A field in the translation table set by the hardware when a page or segment is accessed.

**User**. The human being who interacts with a computer and who has personal interest that the computer interpret instructions properly.

**User identifier**. A number associated with all the processes and files created for a particular user. This number is used for accounting and protection purposes. (See *Group identifier*.)

**User interface**. The interface between the user and the operating system, especially the command language.

**User Principle**. Operations that are performed frequently should be especially easy to invoke.

**Utilization**. The fraction of time the computer spends performing computation, as opposed to transput, resource management, and other kernel work.

**Version**. A file version holds the contents of a file at one point when it was written. Later modifications to the file create new versions.

**Virtual**. The result of an abstraction, typically as seen by a process. (Opposite of *Physical*.)

**Virtual device**. A device that is provided not by hardware but by the kernel, often with physical devices used for actual data storage.

**Virtual interrupt**. The kernel interrupts a process by modifying its program counter to the address of its virtual-interrupt handler.

**Virtualizing kernel**. The kernel of a virtual-machine operating system. Also called a *virtual-machine monitor*.

**Virtual machine**. A process interface that looks just like the bare hardware.

**Virtual space**. The address space of the computer as seen from a process.

**Virtual store**. The memory associated with the virtual space.

**Virtual time**. The amount of time used by a process, advanced only when the process is running.

**Wait**. A service call used to block the calling·process until a previously requested asynchronous transput operation has completed.

**Wait list**. A list of processes that are not currently runnable because of a scheduling decision or because they require resources that have not yet been granted.

**Warm start**. (1) In simulations, waiting until measurements have reached a steady state. For example, warm start page replacement analysis does not start counting page faults required to start up a process. (2) In initializing operating systems, assuming that file storage is uncorrupted (or at least present).

**Waste**. Unused space. External waste is outside of any virtual space. Internal waste is inside a virtual space but not needed. Overhead space is space occupied by tables needed for translation. Also called *fragmentation*.

**Wild card**. A convention that allows a number of files to be specified with one pattern.

**Winding latency**. The time needed to wind a magnetic tape to the desired place.

**Window size**. A parameter used in defining the working set of a process.

**Working directory**. A directory that constitutes the environment for a process so that the process may refer to files in that directory by their local name.

**Working set**. Pages belonging to a process that have been accessed by the process during the most recent $w$ units of virtual time, where $w$ is the window-size parameter.

**Working-set policy**. A page replacement policy that restricts the number of processes on the ready queue so that physical store can accommodate all the working sets of ready processes.

**Workstation**. A powerful single-user computer with a high-quality display, usually with some local disk and a network connection.

**Write-behind**. A policy that caches data blocks intended to be written out to devices in main store and writes them when the device is available or when the cache entry is needed for another purpose.

**Write-through**. A policy that caches data blocks but writes them to the device whenever they are changed.

# Index

**380**